A Path to (Re)Interpreting the International Drug Conventions

Francisco E. Thoumi

First published in November 2021

A Path To (Re)Interpreting the International Drug Conventions
Thoumi, Francisco E.

Includes bibliographical references and index

Copyright © Francisco E. Thoumi
ISBN 9798766403951

All rights reserved. This book or any portion thereof may not be reproduced or used in any manner whatsoever without the express written permission of the publisher/author except for the use of brief quotations.

1.International Drug Control System. 2. International Narcotics Control Board. 3. United Nations Drug Conventions. 4. History of international drug policy development

CONTENT

ACKNOWLEDGEMENTS ix

A CAVEAT xi

LIST OF ACRONYMS 1

INTRODUCTION 3

PART ONE. THE BUILDING OF THE INTERNATIONAL DRUG CONTROL SYSTEM 25

CHAPTER ONE. A SHORT HISTORICAL BACKGROUND ON PSYCHOACTIVE DRUG ISSUES, THE ORIGIN AND CONSTRUCTION OF THE INTERNATIONAL DRUG CONTROL SYSTEM 27

    1.1 DRUG USES AND POLICY ISSUES ARE NOT NEW 27

    1.2 THE OPIUM ISSUE IN CHINA 33

    1.3 GLOBALIZATION, COLONIALISM AND THE AMERICAN INTERESTS IN THE CHINESE OPIUM TRADE 38

CHAPTER TWO. THE QUEST TO RESTRICT CONTROLLED DRUGS' USES TO MEDICAL AND SCIENTIFIC PURPOSES 41

    2.1 THE ORIGIN OF THE MEDICAL AND SCIENTIFIC USE RESTRICTION 41

    2.2 THE 1909 SHANGHAI COMMISSION 43

    2.3 THE HAGUE 1912 INTERNATIONAL OPIUM CONVENTION 45

    2.4 THE HARRISON ACT AND HEROIN ADDICTION MAINTENANCE IN THE UNITED STATES 47

    2.5 DRUGS IN THE LEAGUE OF NATIONS 50

    2.5.1 The Period before the 1925 Treaties 50

    2.5.2 The 1925 Treaties 52

2.5.3 The 1931 Convention for Limiting the Manufacture and Regulating the Distribution of Narcotic Drugs 56

2.5.4 The 1936 Convention for the Suppression of the Illicit Traffic in Dangerous Drugs 58

2.6. COCA CHEWING AS AN INTERNATIONAL POLICY ISSUE 60

2.6.1 Social and Political Background 60

2.6.2 The Report of The 1950 UN Commission of Enquire on The Coca Leaf 69

2.6.3 Some Characteristics of the Report 75

2.7 THE END OF THE LEAGUE OF NATIONS AND THE 1948 AND 1953 PROTOCOLS 77

2.8 THE SINGLE CONVENTION ON NARCOTIC DRUGS OF 1961 85

2.8.1 The Road to the Drafting and Enactment of the Convention 85

2.8.2 The Main Achievements of the Single Convention According to UNODC 88

CHAPTER THREE: THE CONVENTIONS THAT ROUNDED UP THE IDCS AND THE IDCS ORGANS 93

3.1 THE CONVENTION ON PSYCHOTROPIC SUBSTANCES OF 1971 93

3.2 THE 1988 CONVENTION AGAINST ILLICIT TRAFFIC IN NARCOTIC DRUGS AND PSYCHOTROPIC SUBSTANCES 97

3.3 IDCS ORGANS 99

3.3.1 The Economic and Social Council (ECOSOC) 99

3.3.2 The Commission on Narcotic Drugs (CND) 99

3.3.3 The United Nations Office on Drugs and Crime (UNODC) 100

3.3.4 The International Narcotics Control Board (INCB) 101

CHAPTER FOUR. CHARACTERISTICS OF THE DRUG CONVENTIONS 103

4.1 SOME OBVIOUS ONES 103

4.2.INCONSISTENCIES, IMPORTANT UNDEFINED TERMS, LEGAL VOIDS AND GAPS IN THE DRUG CONVENTIONS 109

PART TWO: A COMPLEX PROBLEM, A SIMPLE POLICY IN PURSUIT OF AN UNACHIEVABLE GOAL 119

CHAPTER FIVE. THE ROLE OF INCB AS INTERPRETER OF THE CONVENTIONS 121

5.1 THE INCB 121

5.2 THE INCB AS THE INTERPRETER OF THE UNDEFINED CONVENTION TERMS 122

5.3 THE LEGALIZATION OF NON-MEDICAL DRUG USES 128

5.4 CONSEQUENCES 137

CHAPTER SIX. THE IDCS POLICY CHARACTERISTICS AND THE EVOLUTION OF ITS NARRATIVE 141

6.1 OVERVIEW 141

6.2 THE UNGASS 1998 POLITICAL DECLARATION AND THE CND 2009 ACTION PLAN 142

6.3 THE INCB POLICY RESPONSES TO THE 2009 POLITICAL DECLARATION 157

6.4 THE UNGASS 2016 164

6.5 THE POST UNGASS 2016 167

6.6 THE 2019 CND: A THIRD TRY WITH THE SAME RECIPE 169

CHAPTER SEVEN. THE INCB AND HUMAN RIGHTS: OLD AND NEW POSITIONS 177

CHAPTER EIGHT. THE HARM REDUCTION CHALLENGE 189

8.1 OVERVIEW 189

8.2 NEEDLE AND SYRINGE EXCHANGE AND DISTRIBUTION PROGRAMS (NSEDP) 192

8.3 DRUG CONSUMPTION ROOMS 194

8.4 OPIOID ADDICTION MAINTENANCE 198

8.5 HEROIN ADDICTION MAINTENANCE 199

CHAPTER NINE. COFFEE SHOPS IN THE NETHERLANDS VS MARIJUANA LEGALIZATION IN URUGUAY 205

9.1 OVERVIEW 205

9.2 THE INCB AND THE COFFEE SHOP POLICY IN THE NETHERLANDS 205

9.3 THE INCB AND MARIJUANA LEGALIZATION IN URUGUAY 217

CHAPTER TEN. BOLIVIA AND THE COCA CHEWING CONUNDRUM 225

10.1 OVERVIEW 225

10.2 THE EARLY INCB POSITION ON COCA CHEWING 226

10.3 THE PERSISTENT IMPORTANCE OF COCA 230

10.3.1 Relevant Changes in Bolivian Society 230

10.3.2 The 1988 Convention and the Bolivian Reservation 233

10.3.3 Traditional Coca Uses and the Bolivian Rebellion 238

PART THREE. THE CHALLENGES FOR DRUG PUBLIC POLICIES 249

CHAPTER ELEVEN: COMPLEXITY, PUBLIC POLICY, SOCIAL VULNERABILITY AND POLICY EFFECTIVENESS 251

11.1 OVERVIEW 251

11.2 LAWS, SOCIAL NORMS AND SELF CONTROL 254

11.3 THE CHALLENGE OF COMPLEXITY 258

11.3.1 The Cynefin Framework 258

11.3.2 Drug Markets as a Complex System 262

11.3.3 The IDCS Agencies accept Complexity, but only when it does not challenge IDCS Policies 264

11.4 DIVERSE SOCIETIES, DIFFERENT GOVERNMENTS, DIFFERENT POLICIES 269

11.5 SOCIAL HARMS, SOCIAL VULNERABILITY AND CRIMINAL POLICY EFFECTIVENESS 274

CHAPTER TWELVE: PROPOSALS TO TACKLE DRUG POLICY REFORM 283

12.1 OVERVIEW 283

12.2 MEDICAL AND SCIENTIFIC PURPOSES AND THE LACK OF DEFINITIONS 283

12.2.1 Lack of Definitions and the Need for Consensus 283

12.2.2 A Policy Discussion among Activists 286

12.2.3 A Good Example of a Paradigm Conflict about Drug Policies 292

12.3 POLICY REFORM VIA "INTER SE" TREATY MODIFICATION 299

12.4 SHOULD DIFFERENT DRUGS BE TREATED DIFFERENTLY? 303

CHAPTER THIRTEEN. OTHER INESCAPABLE DRUG POLICY ISSUES 307

13.1 SUSTAINABLE DEVELOPMENT GOALS (SDG): THEIR CONFLICTS WITH AND CHALLENGES TO IDCS POLICIES 307

13.2 THE WHO'S DEFINITION OF HEALTH AND ITS CONSISTENCY WITH THE IDCS 313

13.2.1 WHO and the Definitions of Health 313

13.2.2 WHO's Principles, Constitution, and Policies 315

13.2.3 The Reality of Scarcity and the Mathematical Conditions for Total Health Maximization 319

13.2.4 Is There a Conflict Between the IDCS Policies and WHO's Principles? 322

13.3 HEALTH SECTOR SERVICES AND LEGAL PSYCHOACTIVE DRUGS 325

13.4 THE NEED TO CONTROL THE INTERNATIONAL TRADE OF PSYCHOACTIVE DRUGS AND CHEMICAL PRECURSORS 330

13.5 THE IDCS PROBLEMS IN FEDERAL GOVERNMENTS WHERE STATES ARE AUTONOMOUS REGARDING DRUG POLICY 335

13.6 FACING NATIONAL POLICY POSITIONS THAT DEPEND ON STRONG AND BLINDING FEELINGS AND EMOTIONS: THE UNITED STATES AND COLOMBIA AS AN EXAMPLE 340

13.7 IS THE ADMINISTRATIVE STRUCTURE OF THE INCB FIT FOR PURPOSE? 344

13.7.1 Administrative Characteristics of the INCB 344

13.7.2 Vulnerabilities and Conflicts 348

13.7.3 The Expanded Tasks of the INCB 351

13.7.4 Consequences of the Administrative Structure of the INCB and a Need for Change 354

CHAPTER FOURTEEN. FINDINGS AND THE DRUG POLICY CHALLENGE 357

14.1 A SUMMARY OF THE INTERNATIONAL DRUG CONVENTIONS' POLICY APPROACH 357

14.2 POLICY CHALLENGES OF A COMPLEX "WORLD DRUG PROBLEM" 362

14.3 ARE THERE ANY STEPS THAT MAY BE TAKEN TO IMPROVE THE IDCS? 365

EPILOGUE 371

REFERENCES 373

ANALYTICAL INDEX 401

ACKNOWLEDGEMENTS

I have researched illegal drug markets for over thirty years. When I started looking at those markets, I did not have a policy agenda. Since then, I have interacted with innumerable academics, government policy makers and law enforcers, journalists, NGO activists, United Nations staff, and others interested in drug issues in many countries. Some have been supporters and others, critics of the current International Drug Control System (IDCS) and its policies. I owe a lot to many of them who helped me understand the system's complexity and develop a new way to look at it.

Concerning this book, I must give special thanks to my colleagues at the International Narcotics Control Board (INCB), a group of people from diverse cultures, life experiences, political, religious, and professional backgrounds, who recognized the complexity of current drug issues and are committed to a fair implementation of the international drug conventions. I also must thank former Colombian President Juan Manuel Santos, who in 2012 responded quickly and effectively to my request to be nominated to the INCB, and former Mexican President Ernesto Zedillo for listening to and supporting some of my ideas about drug policies. I am grateful for the extensive talks about different parts of this book with Professor John Collins, of the London School of Economics; Sandeep Chawla, former World Drug Report coordinator, United Nations Office of Drugs and Crime (UNODC); Professor Vicknasingam B. Kasinather, Director, Centre for Drug Research, Universiti Sains Malaysia; Professor Juan G. Tokatlian, Vice-president, Torcuato Di Tella University, Buenos Aires; Moisés Wasserman, former President of The National University of Colombia; and Professor Wolfgang J. Munar, Department of Public Health, The George Washington University. They all helped me develop the central thrust of this book. Some of them have commented on various parts of the book and made important suggestions. Sir Keith Morris, former British Ambassador to Colombia, has also commented and expressed support and encouragement to my work on this book. Nabil Katkhouda, INCB and, Thomas Pietschmann, UNODC staffers, have provided good data and some institutional memory and insights on the IDCS. Former INCB staff Paulsen Bailey made extensive editorial comments to earlier drafts. He also contributed some institutional memory from the earlier years of the INCB. I am aware that I have not incorporated all the suggestions I received in the book. Not all those who have helped me agree with all the arguments and conclusions of this volume, for which I assume all responsibility. Finally, I thank Marcela Anzola, my wife, colleague, and accomplice who has provided immense intellectual and moral support to my efforts to question many beliefs about psychoactive drug policies.

A CAVEAT

This book is about the United Nations and its drug agencies. On several occasions, I participated in United Nations programs and research projects related to illegal drugs. In 1992-1994 I was part of a research project of the UN Research Institute for Social Development and the United Nations University on the Impact of the Illegal Drug Trade. In 1994 and 1995, I coordinated three extensive United Nations Development Program (UNDP) research projects on the coca and cocaine industry in Bolivia, Colombia, and Peru. From July 1999 to September 2000, I was the research coordinator of the Global Program Against Money Laundering of UNODCCP (now UNODC) in Vienna. From May 2012 to August 2020, I was a Member of the International Narcotics Control Board (INCB). Since its establishment in 2016, I have been a member of the UNODC's Scientific Advisory Committee for the World Development Report. However, none of the arguments developed in this volume expresses the positions or policies of any United Nations Agencies. I have fully funded the research and writing of this book.

LIST OF ACRONYMS

APRA	Alianza Popular Revolucionaria Americana
BEIC	British East India Company
CBD	Cannabidiol
CICP	Centre for International Crime Prevention
CND	Commission on Narcotic Drugs
DND	Division of Narcotic Drugs
DSB	Drug Supervisory Body
ECOSOC	United Nations Economic and Social Council
ENACO	Estanco Nacional de la Coca
EMCDDA	European Monitoring Center on Drugs and Drug Addiction
FBN	Federal Bureau of Narcotics
IDCS	International Drug Control System
ILC	International Law Commission
INCB	International Narcotics Control Board
MDMA	3,4-methylenedioxymethamphetamine (Ecstasy)
MMT	Methadone maintenance treatment
NGO	Non-Governmental Organization
NPS	New Psychoactive Substances
NSEDP	Needle and Syringe Exchange and Distribution Programs
OAC	Opium Advisory Committee
PCOB	Permanent Central Opium Board
PWID	People who inject drugs
RCT	Randomized Control Trials
S-DDD	Statistically Defined Daily Doses
SDG	Sustainable Development Goals
SDH	Social Determinants of Health
SIH	Supervised injectable heroin
SPY	Sociedad de Propietarios de Yungas
THC	Tetrahydrocannabinol

UN	United Nations
UNDCP	United Nations International Drug Control Program
UNDP	United Nations Development Program
UNFDAC	United Nations Fund for Drug Abuse Control
UNGASS	United Nations General Assembly Special Session
UNODC	United Nations Office on Drugs and Crime
UNODCCP	United Nations Office for Drug Control and Crime Prevention
VCLT	Vienna Convention on the Law of Treaties
WFAD	World Federation Against Drugs
WHO	World Health Organization
WWII	Second World War

INTRODUCTION

1. THE UNITED NATIONS DRUG POLICY: THE SEARCH OR AND SUPPORT OF A SIMPLE GLOBAL DRUG POLICY

The International Drug Control System (IDCS) is based on three international conventions: The Single Convention on Narcotic Drugs of 1961 as amended by the 1972 Protocol, the Convention on Psychotropic Substances of 1971, and the United Nations Convention against Illicit Traffic in Narcotic Drugs and Psychotropic Substances of 1988. Three United Nations organs implement these conventions: The Economic and Social Council (ECOSOC), The Commission on Narcotic Drugs (CND), and the United Nations Office on Drugs and Crime (UNODC), and a subsidiary organ, The International Narcotics Control Board (INCB).

The IDCS provides a framework to deal with the social problems generated by addiction to psychoactive drugs (those that alter people's perception, mood, consciousness, or behavior) and with the international control of their production, trade, and human bodily consumption. Some of these drugs can be used freely and be self-prescribed by those who choose to do so, others can be used legally only under medical prescription and supervision, and others cannot be lawfully consumed. This framework also controls the production and trade of some key chemicals used to manufacture the controlled drugs.

In the second half of the 19th century, psychoactive drugs' production, marketing, and use raised policy concerns in a few countries. By the turn of the 20th century, some governments were alarmed with the growth of opium use in some Asian countries, and the international trade of that substance led to a pioneer effort to develop an international control system for opium and convened the 1909 Shanghai Opium Commission. This effort did not produce a binding agreement, a goal that was achieved for the first time in the 1912 The Hague International Opium Convention.

Since its origins, the United States promoted the IDCS and looked for a simple solution to what it perceived to be a pressing drug problem. Supported by China, they sought to limit psychoactive drug-human consumption to medical uses. Some European countries with strong pharmaceutical industries, Peru and Bolivia where traditional non-medical uses of coca were common, and India where *quasi-medical*[1] opium use was common, lobbied for regulated drug uses. After a long quest that took 52 years and that included several international treaties, the policy to limit the uses of controlled psychoactive drugs to *medical and scientific purposes* was achieved in the 1961 Single Convention on Narcotic Drugs, whose Preamble states:

> The Parties,
>
> Concerned with the health and welfare of mankind, (or with the physical and moral health of humankind, as it reads in the official French and Spanish versions of the Convention)
> Recognizing that the medical use of narcotic drugs continues to be indispensable for the relief of pain and suffering and that adequate provision must be made to ensure the availability of narcotic drugs for such purposes,
>
> Recognizing that addiction to narcotic drugs constitutes a serious evil for the individual and is fraught with social and economic danger to mankind,
>
> Conscious of their duty to prevent and combat this evil,
>
> Considering that effective measures against abuse of narcotic drugs require coordinated and universal action,

---

[1] Used in non-Western medicine.

Understanding that such universal action calls for international co-operation guided by the same principles and aimed at common objectives.

Acknowledging the competence of the United Nations in the field of narcotics control and desirous that the international organs concerned should be within the framework of that Organization,

Desiring to conclude a generally acceptable international convention replacing existing treaties on narcotic drugs, limiting such drugs to medical and scientific use, and providing for continuous international co-operation and control for the achievement of such aims and objectives [...] (UNODC, 2013, 5)[2].

This restriction of psychoactive drug uses has determined international drug policies since the Single Convention on Narcotic Drugs was enacted in 1961. However, the 1961 Convention fails to provide specific policy details and only requires a commitment to eliminate all non-medical and non-scientific drug uses. Article four of the Convention states:

The parties shall take such legislative and administrative measures as may be necessary:
[...] (c) Subject to the provisions of this Convention to limit exclusively to medical and scientific purposes the production, manufacture, export, import, distribution of, trade in, use and possession of drugs. (Ibid, 12).

The IDCS policies are based on the simple premise that psychoactive drugs must only be used for medical or scientific purposes. All other uses are prohibited. In article four of the 1961

---

[2] The three international drug conventions are available in a free eBook (UNODC, 2013) at the UNODC web page.

Single Convention on Narcotic Drugs, the Parties commit themselves to "take such legislative and administrative measures as may be necessary" to enforce this drug use limitation. The IDCS requires countries to prevent some individual behaviors and change them if they exist or appear in their societies. This policy has been a unique experiment that attempts to change and regulate individual human behavior globally.

The 1971 Convention on Psychotropic Substances[3] reasserted this policy and expanded it to include psychotropic drugs. Articles 5 and 7 of this convention also limit the uses of controlled drugs to medical and scientific purposes. Both conventions established four lists (schedules) of controlled psychoactive drugs and some of their chemical precursors (inputs). Each schedule establishes different drug uses and trade restrictions.

From the perspective of contemporary public policy in non-authoritarian, liberal, or open societies, this is a vague, open-ended policy prescription that does not provide guidelines or specify policy constraints. This fact raises many interesting issues that should be clarified for drug policies to be effective. The following are a few of them:

- What forces played a role in the process of achieving this broad policy agreement?
- Was the restriction of any non-medical or scientific uses founded on scientific evidence, or was it based on ideology, traditional social beliefs, sentiments, and emotions?
- Were the signing governments aware of the possible consequences of this policy?

---

[3] The Single Convention on Narcotic Drugs of 1961 focusses on plant-based drugs, mainly opium/morphine/heroin, coca/cocaine, and marijuana. The importance of opioids at the time led to the word "narcotics" in the title of the 1961 Convention, although some of the drugs controlled by the Convention were not narcotics. For example, cocaine is a strong stimulant.

- Were all stakeholders considered, or was the policy imposed top town by the centers of power?
- Given such a broad aim, why were no exceptions considered?

The Commentary on the 1961 Single Convention,[4] which is not binding but carries weight for its interpretation, confirms that limiting the production, uses, and trade of controlled drugs exclusively to medical and scientific purposes was the fundamental purpose and the most important achievement of the IDCS.

The object of the international narcotics system is to limit exclusively to medical and scientific purposes the trade in and use of controlled drugs. From the beginning, this has been a fundamental principle of the multilateral narcotics system, although all the treaties providing for it authorize some exceptions. The 1912 and 1925 Conventions and the 1953 Protocol contained provisions incorporating this principle. The gradual extension of the scope in its application is a characteristic feature of progress in this branch of treaty law. It is one of the most important achievements of the Single Convention that it ended the exceptions permitted in earlier treaties, subject only to transitional provisions of limited local application and duration (United Nations, 1973, 110).

This approach prohibits all non-medical uses as decided by Western medicine professionals and organizations. It excludes most medical uses in traditional medicine, the uses for relaxation, work, recreation, making and enjoying music and art to experience new feelings, communicate with ancestors and with the divinity, socialize,

---

[4] The Commentaries to the conventions are documents written by experts and witnesses of the debates and discussions that took place along the process of the convention writing. They are not binding but help understanding and interpreting the conventions.

seduce, go to battle, etc. All these uses have existed throughout history.

This restriction has determined all IDCS policies and has received overwhelming support from governments across the world. The three United Nations international drug conventions that are the core of the IDCS are among the most ratified United Nations treaties. Indeed, the 1961 Single Convention, the 1971 Convention on Psychotropic Substances, and the 1988 United Nations Convention against Illicit Traffic in Narcotic Drugs and Psychotropic Substances as of February 2021 had been ratified respectively by 187, 184, and 190 countries and territories that are home to more than 99.5% of the world's population.[5]

2. THE MAIN CHALLENGES TO THE INTERNATIONAL DRUG CONTROL SYSTEM

Psychoactive drugs have had many uses throughout history. This creates tension between the governments' commitment to eliminate those drug uses and people's desires to use drugs. This tension has been a constant since the origins of the IDCS. It has varied across time and space depending on cultural, political, and social factors. It results in different opinions about dealing with peasants that grow plants used in drug production, other drug producers, traffickers, and drug users.

During the early 20th century, when the "world drug problem" was politically limited to a few addictive substances in a few countries, the prohibition of non-medical uses was a simple solution to what appeared to be a simple policy problem. Since then, drug policy issues have become increasingly complex. Today they include an ever-larger number of psychoactive substances and their chemical precursors.

---

[5] The only countries that in 2021 were non-Parties of the 1961 Single Convention were Timor-Leste, Equatorial Guinea, Kiribati, Nauru, Samoa, South Sudan, Tuvalu, Vanuatu, Cook Islands and Niue.

The technologies to produce, traffic, and use drugs have also become complex and spread worldwide. The exponential growth in education, information, and access to communications have globalized many illegal drug markets. Current actors - producers, traffickers, and drug users - are extraordinarily varied. They include financial advisers, lawyers, chemists, experts in transportation, marketing, and high tech. The illegal drug industry also purchases services from police officers, other law enforcement personnel, corrupt politicians, physicians, and public health experts, pilots, etc. Illegal drug-producing and trafficking organizations have taken many shapes, from individual minor drug seller-users to complex international organizations whose members come from many countries. Governments involved with drug issues have evolved. Their number increased from about 34 when The Hague International Opium Convention was signed in 1912 to over two hundred countries and territories today.

Despite widespread and solid political support across countries, the policies implemented to limit the use of controlled drugs *for medical and scientific purposes* have had criticisms and challenges that have increased in recent years. These have come from governments and civil society organizations. They argue that some flexibility to allow regulated and well-controlled non-medical drug uses may increase the social costs of addiction. Still, it would produce a larger decline in the social costs of drug trafficking, corruption, weakened governability, and other social ills.

The following have been some of the most important developments that have challenged the IDCS policies:

- In the 1960s, marijuana use became a symbol and an instrument of social protest in the developed Western countries, and in 1976 the Netherlands became a pioneer in the process of "domestication" of marijuana. Since that year, it has tolerated selling small quantities of marijuana in designated "coffee shops."[6] This measure aimed to separate the markets of marijuana and "hard" drugs to lower the risks of harms to marijuana users.

- During the early 1980s, a hepatitis B epidemic followed by the HIV/AIDS crisis led some European countries to promote *harm reduction* policies such as needle and syringe exchange and distribution. Also, injection rooms provided clean needles and syringes to people who inject drugs (PWID) and tested their drugs to prevent fatal overdoses and intoxication.[7] These policies were justified on human rights and social welfare grounds, but until recently, some were rejected by the United Nations drug organs because, in their view, they breached the drug conventions

- Bolivia and some native communities in the Andean Region have argued that traditional uses of the coca leaf should be allowed because they are an integral part of the human rights of traditional communities and their culture. After Evo Morales, the head of the coca growers' confederation, was elected President of Bolivia in 2006, his government started a movement to amend the IDCS conventions to allow traditional coca uses. In 2009 the Bolivian government proposed an amendment to the 1961 Single Convention on Narcotic Drugs to allow coca chewing without altering other coca plantings and cocaine production controls. This request was made following the Single Convention's amendment process (article 47). It was justified by the country's new

---

[6] As of May 2021, coffee shops were still technically illegal, but tolerated.

[7] This *harm reduction* approach to psychoactive drug use was opposed by the INCB, that became a target of strong criticism from some NGOs, journalists and academics that argued that harm reduction policies were legitimate ways to promote and protect the citizens' welfare, that drug users and addicts did not forfeited their human rights, and that the INCB was acting beyond its mandate and conflicting with the UN human rights conventions (Bewley-Taylor (2012b), Small and Drucker (2007), Csete and Wolfe (2007), Barrett (2008) among others). In recent years, the INCB has softened its position. See chapter eight.

constitution that declared that the coca leaf was part of the national cultural heritage. The amendment was rejected by the UN Economic and Social Council (ECOSOC), and Bolivia denounced the Convention. Following the Convention's procedure, Bolivia applied to access again to the Convention with reservations. It re-accessed to the Convention on February 10, 2013.[8]
- The growth of the illegal drug industry in Latin America triggered very high levels of corruption across the region and violence in some countries and localities. In 2008 seventeen of the most prominent Latin Americans, including three former presidents of Brazil, Colombia, and Mexico, convened the Latin American Commission on Drugs and Democracy to reject the war on drugs policy approach and promote drug policy reforms. In March 2009, they issued a report that asserted that the war on drugs had failed and argued for a drug policy paradigm shift. In November 2011, Colombian President Juan Manuel Santos publicly asserted that it was time to rethink drug policies. That year Otto Pérez Molina was elected president of Guatemala with a policy platform that included drug legalization. In Mexico, after ending his presidential term in late 2012, Felipe Calderón joined the choir of former Latin American presidents claiming significant drug policy changes.
- The Latin American Commission on Drugs and Democracy 2009 Report acted as a catalyst. It led to the establishment of a broader Global Commission on Drug Policy that, as of January 2021, had twenty-six members, including 16 former presidents and prime ministers from around the world, four Nobel Prize winners, and other influential policymakers and writers. Since 2011 the Commission has produced annual reports. The last five reports have been on *Advancing Drug*

---

[8] This process is detailed in chapter ten.

Policy Reform: a new approach to decriminalization (2016), *The World Drug PERCEPTION Problem - Countering Prejudices About People Who Use Drugs* (2017), *Regulation: The Responsible Control of Drugs* (2018), *Classification of Psychoactive Substances: When Science was Left Behind* 2019), and *Enforcement of Drug Laws: Refocusing on Organized Crime Elite* (2020). These documents analyze the complexity and human rights issues associated with drug policies. The Global Commission on Drug Policy has continued challenging the IDCS policy consensus.

- In the United States, marijuana for medical uses was approved in California in 1996. Since then, other States have followed liberalizing marijuana uses, and by August 2021, marijuana was fully illegal in only six states. In twenty-one others, its use had been decriminalized. In the rest, medical marihuana was allowed. And 17 of them plus the District of Columbia and the territories of Guam, and Northern Mariana and the reservations of the Flandreau Santee Sioux Tribe, and the Oglala Lakota Sioux Tribe (South Dakota), Squaxin Island Tribe, and Suquamish Tribe (Washington state), Eastern Band of Cherokee Indians (North Carolina) St. Regis Mohawk Tribe (New York) approved various forms of non-medical (recreational) marijuana. Five states where medical marijuana is illegal allow the sale of Cannabidiol Oil, which is not psychoactive.[9]

---

[9] Marijuana contains over 300 substances of which over 60 are "cannabinoids", unique to the marijuana plant. "The major psychoactive constituent in cannabis is Δ-9 tetrahydrocannabinol (THC). Compounds which are structurally like THC are referred to as cannabinoids" (http://www.who.int/substance_abuse/facts/cannabis/en/). Many of the substances in marijuana are not psychoactive. Cannabidiol (CBD), the substance with most medical uses, is one of them. Medicinal marijuana has mostly been smoked without separating its substances. In many locations prescribing medicinal marijuana has been very lax and de facto became a pretext to legalize its recreational use.

- In December 2013, Uruguay was the first country to legalize non-medical marijuana. The government has proceeded with caution establishing a system of strict controls. Retail marijuana became available only in sixteen pharmacies in July 2017. Uruguay has not challenged the IDCS and argues that its marijuana policy complies with the conventions because it is designed to promote the health and welfare of its population.
- On June 21, 2018, Canada enacted the Cannabis Act that legalizes non-medical marijuana uses. This Act is a complex law that seeks to regulate all aspects of the marijuana market. It disregards the IDCS, but the government of Canada has not openly stated that it does not comply with the international norms. However, those close to the legislative process assert that "the Government of Canada takes its international obligations very seriously. Throughout the legislative process, we will continue to communicate our overall objectives for strictly regulating and restricting access to cannabis to the international community, which include protecting our society from the adverse consequences of illegal drug use and combating international drug trafficking. The Government of Canada will also continue to engage in constructive dialogue with our international partners."[10] The Canadian argument is that its policies seek to protect the health and welfare of the country, and thus, they comply with the purposes of the IDCS.
- On January 17, 2019 (acts II 2018/19, No. 42, items 5 and 8), the States-General of the Netherlands (bicameral legislature) approved the *Closed Coffee Shop Chain Experiment*, involving the cultivation of cannabis for recreational use. The purpose of the experiment is to determine whether and how

---

[10] Personal communication of the author with Canadian delegates to the INCB, on May 14, 2019.

controlled cannabis can be legally supplied to coffee shops and its effects. The experiment also seeks to investigate the effects on crime, safety, and public health, and it is limited to some coffee shops in a few municipalities.

These developments are indicative of a growing de facto questioning of the worldwide IDCS policy consensus. Although the number of dissenters is small today, some have enough power to proceed without fearing consequences. There is no doubt that psychoactive drug addiction can be devastating to addicts and their families and cause high social and economic costs. But illegal drug industries and markets, generated by the prohibition of the production, marketing, and consumption of those drugs have also been associated with exceedingly high social and economic costs, including increased corruption, violence, and weakened governability. The IDCS fails to confront one fundamental problem: the global prohibition and any legalization of non-medical psychoactive drug uses generate social and economic costs and benefits, but their distributions vary significantly across societies. Thus, the consequences of any global drug policy are unevenly distributed across countries.

As mentioned, the IDCS policies are based on a set of treaties that require government policies to pursue the elimination of all human bodily consumption of the controlled drugs except for medical or scientific purposes. However, questions arise

- When governments that are Parties to those treaties consider that the costs of that policy exceed its benefits.
- When those governments have ideological differences regarding the right of people to use drugs that alter their perception, mood, consciousness, cognition, or behavior.
- When they also differ in their approaches to formulate and implement public policies.

These are the real sources of the challenges faced by the IDCS. To answer these challenges, it is necessary to recognize the need for a consequential dialogue and analyze the relevance of the United Nations system in contemporary policymaking.

3. THE NEED FOR A CONSEQUENTIAL DIALOGUE

Drug policy debates tend to be dialogues of the deft in which reasons for or against any drug policy are presented as truths. However, reasons alone do not prove anything, they could explain why people make decisions, but they hide the causes of such decisions. For example, the profitability of coca, poppy, or marijuana plantings is used to explain why peasants grow those crops. But that argument does not explain why most peasants in the world do not grow them. Others argue that the prohibition of non-medical psychoactive drug uses generates violence. However, most illegal markets, including drugs, are not particularly violent. The point is that the correlation between illegal drug markets and violence is very weak. These facts indicate that illegal drug markets are complex and are not only driven by profits. Social mores, sentiments, and emotions are important determinants of their development.

To formulate and implement effective drug policies, it is necessary to understand why when discussing drug policies, intelligent, educated, and well-meaning people frequently arrive at opposite positions that they defend with polarized zeal? The question of how humans form their opinions and beliefs about issues they care has been a perennial challenge for philosophers, social scientists, politicians, and all others interested in explaining how humans understand their lives and the world. The academic literature about these issues has been growing at a fast pace in recent decades, as many academic disciplines have adopted empirical methods to establish how and why people develop their world view and how they evaluate the evidence about social issues. One common conclusion of many of these studies is that people use their reason to explain life and decide what to believe. But this process is not only rational. It is also influenced by their innate inclinations (implicit biases), feelings, and sentiments shaped by the environment in which they grow and live. Socialization and education experiences are important determinants of any person's beliefs.

This book does not pretend to review and evaluate the literature about the humans' decision-making process that has exploded and continues to grow fast, which would take more than a lifetime to do. However, it uses some of the basic conclusions of those works that contribute some lights to understand why humans produce, market, and consume psychoactive drugs.

4. THE UNITED NATIONS IMPLICIT POLICY MODEL AND CONTEMPORARY PUBLIC POLICY

The United Nations and international law are a product of modernity and the concept of state set out in the Peace of Westphalia of 1648. They are both designed to provide frameworks for solving international conflicts and prevent confrontations among sovereign states and new world wars. This "implicitly assumes that all governments have full control of their territories, where they have the monopoly of power, force, and the law. This implies that current international norms are designed for nations, that is, for groups of humans that have a common purpose, and form a cohesive society" (Thoumi, 2017b: 74).[11] The current system of international law that has evolved from it has been functional to solve issues arising from relations among countries that frequently led to wars in the past. The system was developed to solve conflicts among countries, respecting each one's sovereignty. It has been instrumental in solving issues related to country borders, international migrations, international debt payments, regulating international travel, control of non-State

---

[11] That is why we have the "United Nations" rather than the "United Countries".

areas, and the like. However, the system was not intended to regulate the individual behaviors of people within a country.

The international drug conventions require their parties to control legal domestic and international trade in the controlled substances and take measures to prevent and attack their illegal production, trade, and use, including their chemical precursors. These controls were put in place to help enforce the prohibition of non-medical and non-scientific uses. To comply with the drug conventions, the parties are committed to enforcing some individual behaviors through their domestic legislation. The restriction of drug use to *medical and scientific purposes* enacted in 1961 and first proposed and promoted in 1909 fitted the historical context in which the IDCS and its policies arose. Within that context, the terms *medical and scientific* were left to be defined by the health sector professionals and their organizations. The drug conventions policies were to be applied equally in all countries independently of the capacity of their governments to enforce them. Since then, the world has evolved drastically, and the context in which drug policies are formulated and implemented has changed similarly. The question is whether the IDCS cornerstone policy may be applied successfully across all countries under all circumstances in today's world.

As noted, when the IDCS was first promoted in 1909, the perceived drug addiction problems were limited to a few drugs in a few countries. The main policy issue was the addiction to opium in China and other South-East Asian countries. In 1884 Merk & Co., in Germany, and Park & Davis Co. in the United States made cocaine commercially available in small quantities. By the first decade of the XX century, its medical and non-medical uses had expanded. Still, addiction to it had not grown to be an international problem comparable to opium's addiction. The use of hashish was also confined to a few places. The addiction problem was very much limited to drugs based on three plants: opium poppy, coca, and marijuana. The international conventions and protocols of the following fifty-two years, including the 1961 Single Convention on

Narcotic Drugs, were focused on those drugs. Since then, the use of other plant-based drugs has increased, but the growth in the production and use of synthetic drugs has been enormous. The 1971 Convention on Psychotropic Substances was a response to that development. Today Amphetamine Type Stimulants are the most widely used illegal drugs except for marijuana. A significant number (around 50) of new psychoactive substances (NPS) appear every year, and a few get established in the illegal market. The chemical inputs required to produce all those drugs (precursors in the jargon of the drug field) are also controlled by the IDCS, but when one is controlled, chemists develop new precursors or pre-precursors which require new controls.

Since 1961 illegal drug markets have increased a lot. Drug-producing and trafficking organizations have used their illicit profits to control some country regions and sometimes even some national states that end up being referred to as "narco-states." The 1988 United Nations Convention against Illicit Traffic in Narcotic Drugs and Psychotropic Substances responded to the growth of international drug trafficking. Illegal markets have a risk of violence since conflicts about prices, quality, and payments cannot be solved by appealing to legal conflict resolution systems. At times, some drug markets have become extraordinarily violent. Corruption has also been endemic to illicit drug markets. The response of the IDCS to a changing world has been to strengthen the system within their traditional/modernity framework. Criminal organizations have evolved, and drug trafficking ones have diversified and developed other activities such as extortion, kidnappings, human trafficking, illegal sex services, killing services, investment networks, illegal mining, cybercrime, etc. Drugs are today just one branch of international criminal organizations.

The developments of the illegal drug markets since 1961 raise questions about the current fitness of that policy model. The modern state has evolved as technology and globalization have advanced. But these developments have also allowed the growth of non-state actors that weaken the State's monopoly of power and the law. These actors exert their power to formulate and enforce their own rules, influence public opinion, and alter political processes. Some of these actors are domestic, but some powerful ones are either foreign or trans-national. Some of those emerged as a reaction from civil society and multilateral organizations. Some NGOs and even some of the United Nations System's agencies exert pressure on many governments. In today's globalized world, these developments have changed most states from modern to postmodern.

Many countries today have diverse communities and are multicultural, multiracial, multireligious, multiethnic, and multiregional. Diverse groups within countries frequently have different world views and attitudes. In some countries, the coexistence of two or more legal systems seeks to guarantee the rights of other groups. Many sociologists and anthropologists have adopted the term *legal pluralism* to describe this phenomenon (Anzola, 2014: 54). *Legal pluralism* may arise from sociological, anthropological, and legal factors. It, however, could pose a problem for the implementation of the IDCS in several country contexts. For example, the federal government prohibits non-medical marijuana use in the United States, but many of its states approve it. In Colombia, where coca plantings are illicit, the courts protect them for traditional uses in Amerindian communities subject to their legal jurisdictions. The IDCS policies frequently conflict with consuetudinary practices among natives across Latin America.

Contemporary public policy theories and models recognize the complexity of policy issues, the interdependence among many of them, and the institutional, cultural, technological, economic, legal, strategic, geopolitical, etc., factors that must be considered for public policy success. Within this framework, a simple global policy requirement that instructs governments to do whatever they decide necessary to eliminate all non-medical or non-scientific drug uses is vague, naïve, and ineffective.

The IDCS was an interesting experiment fit for the moment in which it was created. The issue, however, is whether a global public policy system developed in the early and mid-20th century that has a simple policy prescription -to eliminate all nonmedical psychoactive drug human bodily consumption- is fit for the 21st century. The formulation of the IDCS policy was informed by what policymakers in some powerful countries believed was correct for humankind, rather than on an evidence-based approach that would evolve according to society's changing needs.

These developments have produced challenges to the IDCS that question the suitability of a simple policy solution to solve an increasingly complex problem. This issue was the primary motivation to write this book.

5. PURPOSE AND CONTENT OF THE BOOK

The purpose of this book is to explore the formation, evolution, and limitations of the IDCS, focusing on its internal logic and the consequences of a one-fits-all public policy in a fast-changing world that is increasingly more diverse and complex. This book does not pretend to be a handbook on illegal psychoactive drug policy issues, and many relevant ones are not studied. The book focuses on the problems that have been particularly important and conflictive for the IDCS agencies. The analytical examples provided in the book reflect my thirty-five-year experience working on illegal drug issues and frequent participation in the activities of the United Nations' drug agencies. This also responds to many of my concerns during the eight years (May 2012-August 2020) as an INCB board member and the issues in countries where I have had significant drug policy research experience.

The book's approach is consistent with the "deconstruction" concept developed by Derrida. The book offers a critical analysis of the international drug conventions' texts and of the basic narrative used to write the conventions and justify its policies (the INCB annual reports, the CND policy declarations, the United Nations General Assembly Special Sessions (UNGASS) on drug issues outcome documents, the volumes on the Commentaries of the three United Nations drug conventions, and other relevant UN publications. It also emphasizes the internal structure of the language and conceptual systems used and the qualitative relationships of the meaning of words and assumptions implicit in its forms of expression. Therefore, the book provides long quotations of those documents to support the arguments developed in this book.

The book also follows Albert O. Hirschman's approach. His work on economic development was inspired, to a degree, by his experience in Colombia during the 1950s. It exhorted economists to trespass the limits of the prevailing paradigms in their profession and take advantage of the contributions of other social sciences to improve their understanding of government policies.[12]

The main conclusion is that the IDCS, formulated when psychoactive drug issues were relatively simple, cannot effectively tackle the current complex drug problems. A second main conclusion is that there are no silver bullets and a unique solution applicable worldwide. However, the book does not pretend to provide specific policy solutions to the current complex drug problems. It only hopes to improve the understanding of these problems and suggest ways to formulate and implement better drug policies that fit the context of the society in which they are applied.

The book has three parts. The first one reviews the building of the IDCS. It analyzes the conditions that led to the international opium trade becoming an international issue and the origin of the core international policy limiting worldwide drug use to *medical and scientific purposes*. It follows four international conventions and several international protocols that failed to limit controlled drug uses

---

[12] Adelman (2013) is an excellent work about the live, work and the contributions of Albert O. Hirschman. Its Chapter Ten focusses on Hirschman's experience in Colombia.

to medical and scientific purposes. It took 52 years before this process succeeded in the 1961 Single Convention on Narcotic Drugs.

This part continues with a chapter on the development of the two conventions that rounded up the IDCS, the 1971 Convention on Psychotropic Drugs and the 1988 Convention Against Illicit Traffic in Narcotic Drugs and Psychotropic Substances. It also explains the structure of the United Nations' drug agencies that are engaged in drug issues. The part ends with a chapter on the characteristics of the IDCS, highlighting a bias towards law enforcement and authoritarian policies and the interpretation problems that arise from the lack of definition of essential terms of the conventions, legal voids and gaps, and differences in their texts in the United Nations' official languages. All these factors create ambiguities that present significant interpretation difficulties.

The second part studies how the unachievable "drug-free world" goal was sought and how the IDCS agencies, mainly the INCB, interpreted the drug conventions and the consequences of their decisions. This part shows how the INCB position concerning human rights, needle and syringe exchange and distribution programs, drug consumption rooms, opioid and heroin addiction maintenance, non-medical marijuana, and traditional coca uses have varied across time and place depending on the composition of the INCB. It also shows that the United Nations General Assemblies devoted to drug issues and the annual CND session have reasserted their support of the "drug-free world" goal.

The third part of the book focuses on the challenges faced by psychoactive drug policies in a complex world in which societies internally have pluralistic legal systems, diverse social norms, and individuals with various levels of self-control. These societies have varied structures and policies are vulnerable to different forms of social weaknesses. Because of these factors, countries present significant differences in their vulnerability and risks to developing criminal organizations and illegal drug industries. These vulnerabilities limit policy effectiveness and require drugs policies that respond to different situations.

Despite the prevailing inflexible interpretations of the drug conventions, some drug policy options advanced by a few analysts are reviewed. It is shown that the lack of definitions of essential terms and the ambiguity in the conventions, as argued in this book, open the possibility to expand the interpretation of the terms *medical and scientific* to recognize the scientifically obtained knowledge in the social sciences and reinterpret the drug conventions accordingly. Another policy reform option is to make an *inter se* treaty agreements allowed by the 1969 Vienna Convention on the Law of Treaties.[13] Finally, the possibility of treating different drugs differently depending on their effects on the human body and their risks of addiction is explored.

This part also discusses some "unescapable" policy issues for the IDCS: the possible conflicts between the 2030 United Nations' Sustainable Development Goals (SDG) and the current IDCS policies; the logical conflicts between the essential principles of the World Health Organization (WHO) and the IDCS focus on its "drug-free world" goal; the need for control of international trade of psychoactive drugs and their chemical precursors; the IDCS problems in some federal governments where their States are sovereign and do not apply the IDCS policies; the challenges posed to drug policies by how the health sector services and the legal psychoactive drugs markets operate. This section ends with an evaluation of the internal organization of the INCB. It questions its fitness for its purpose in the current postmodern world.

The final, short chapter summarizes the main findings, draws a few lessons, and highlights the policy challenges presented by the complex "world drug problem."

---

[13] This allows a group of Parties to a convention to join and make a change to the convention that is valid only within their countries.

PART ONE. THE BUILDING OF THE INTERNATIONAL DRUG CONTROL SYSTEM

CHAPTER ONE. A SHORT HISTORICAL BACKGROUND ON PSYCHOACTIVE DRUG ISSUES, THE ORIGIN AND CONSTRUCTION OF THE INTERNATIONAL DRUG CONTROL SYSTEM

1.1 DRUG USES AND POLICY ISSUES ARE NOT NEW

Psychoactive drugs have been used continuously in diverse ways in all societies where they have been available.[14] However, societies have perceived the dangers of addiction and other effects of psychoactive drug use in many ways that have changed through time. Psychoactive drugs have had multiple uses: "for relaxation, for recreation, for healing and easing pain, for making and enjoying music, for seduction, for work, for battle and for worship" (Kleiman, Caulkins and Hawken, 2011, xviii-xix). These uses have varied significantly across time and place.[15] The following paragraphs point out some common uses.

For many drugs, particularly opiates, medical uses prevailed. Until not long ago, medicine did not cure many illnesses, and psychoactive drugs, mainly sedatives, and narcotics, killed the pain and allowed sick people to sleep and feel better. Most psychoactive drugs do not eliminate the root causes of health problems but play a

---

[14] Buxton (2006, 4) found that only four cultures out of 237 surveyed across the world have not used toxic psychoactive drugs. These exceptions have been isolated societies that were unable to cultivate plants from where to extract psychoactive drugs. Some like the Eskimos did not know psychoactive drugs, but when they got in contact with Western civilization and alcohol, developed a terrible alcoholic addiction epidemic.

[15] Musto (1999) is the pioneer study of the history of drugs and the evolution of the attitudes toward drugs and drug policy in the United States. Lerner and Ferrando (1989) detail the history of coca and drug use in Peru, Carter and Mamani (1986), Henman (1992), Del Olmo (1992), and Vidart (1991) studied the role of coca and other drugs in the native societies of Bolivia, Colombia, and Amazonia, and show how those societies developed norms and social controls aiming to minimize the harms of drug use.

role in allowing people to control anguish and anxiety, facilitate other medical treatments and make more tolerable the end-of-life period (De Rementería, 1995).

For centuries, hemp seeds (low tetrahydrocannabinol -THC- marijuana) were a source of food in China, Southeast and Central Asia, and the Balkans (Buxton, 2010). Fermented beverages had been reliable sources of sugar, carbohydrates, and some vitamins. In many areas, alcoholic beverages have been a lot safer to drink than water. For example, apple cider was the main liquid ingested in many rural regions of the United States for several centuries. Many Latin American native and peasant communities have used fermented corn, pineapple, and sugar cane drinks instead of plain water.

Alcohol, opium, coca, khat, caffeine, and nicotine, drugs that relax or disinhibit, are used in cultural rituals and facilitate social interaction in ceremonies and important social events such as births, funerals, and weddings to close contracts and show friendship. Drugs have also been used as status symbols. In many societies, specific drug uses were associated with bohemian, artistic, and intellectual groups. In others, like in the United States in the 1960s, drug use was a social protest symbol and a way to show identity with a counterculture.

Psychoactive drugs have strategic uses in crime and wars (hot and cold). They are used to motivate fighters and increase their battle aggressiveness.[16] Some drugs make people lose their will and follow

---

[16] Alcohol has been used for these purposes for a long time. In the recent conflicts in Syria and Iraq "captagon" use has been common. The INCB (2003, 36) documents some such uses during World War II: "The use of narcotic drugs and psychotropic substances in military warfare and for law enforcement purposes has a long history. During the Second World War, for example, while the use of cocaine or opiates by German soldiers would result in imprisonment, Pervitin (methamphetamine), together with alcohol, was distributed to soldiers in the armed forces. During the same period, amphetamines were widely used in the Japanese armed forces to increase soldiers' performance. Such specific use of drugs in a military context can be considered in some countries to be the origin of later drug abuse problems, as those drugs subsequently gained popularity in other segments of the population".

orders. Government security agencies use them to obtain information from enemies and thieves to steal without using violence.[17]

Stimulant drugs have been used in many ways. Coca chewing allows the user to be more alert and work longer hours, and it also tames hunger. In the Andean countries, it has also been used in place of food during famines (Gagliano, 1994). Caffeine, nicotine, amphetamines, and cocaine are also used as stimulants.[18]

Plant-based psychoactive drugs have some characteristics of money and have been used as such. In some Bolivian, Colombian, and Peruvian haciendas, until the mid-20th century, part of the peasants' salary was paid in coca leaves. In Afghanistan, loans to poppy growing peasants frequently must be paid only with opium. Many psychoactive drugs have high prices relative to their weight and volume, making them good stores of value, at least for a few months or years, before they deteriorate. These drugs also have characteristics analogous to commodities, and their continuous demand based on addiction makes them very liquid assets.

Alcoholic beverages and other drugs have been used to increase productivity in traditional farming societies, where many jobs have been repetitive, lonely, and boring. In the Andean countries, fermented corn and sugar cane drinks are commonly used this way. Bolivian truck drivers have been known to chew coca to keep alert and drive continuously for about -24 hours to deliver Bolivian products to Buenos Aires. Coca chewing in the Andean countries was used for several centuries to improve the productivity in the silver and quicksilver mines and the haciendas (Carter and Mamani, 1986; Henman, 1992; Vidart, 1991).

Because of this broad diversity in uses, some argue that many of the problems associated with alcohol and other psychoactive drug consumption are just social constructs (Heath, 1992, 279). Others like Del Olmo (1992) argue that societies have "domesticated" some

---

[17] Scopolamine is an example of this kind of drug.
[18] Cocaine allows Wall-Streeters and others financial sector workers to perform better under great stress.

drugs to allow consumption, neutralizing its most damaging effects. These effects have been considered negative, neutral, or positive, depending on the society, drug, and epoch.

The "domestication" of psychoactive drugs was altered by the last couple of centuries' urbanization, modernization, and industrialization. These developments changed working and other social relations, and for the first time in human history, non-aristocrats had some leisure time and income to spend at their will. When that happened, in urban societies, the social costs of drug addiction grew and became evident. While in some traditional settings, drug use increased productivity, in modern urban environments, drugs became an obstacle to productive activities that require coordination and collaboration among workers (Husch, 1992). That was one reason manufacturing entrepreneurs supported alcohol prohibition in the United States in the early 20th century.

Illnesses have always been associated with religion and magic.[19] They have frequently been considered punishments or tests given by God to humans, caused by witches' curses and spells, or to the actions of evil spirits. Not surprisingly, humans pray to Gods, saints, and other spirits requesting healings. Recent research also indicates that drug effectiveness depends on the interaction between mind and body in some cases.[20] The human search for altered state of mind experiences has not been limited to psychoactive drugs. Humans have achieved comparable results using hyperventilation, Yoga, and meditation. They induce the body to produce serotonin and dopamine.

Furthermore, that search has not been limited to humans. Animal use of psychoactive drugs has been well documented. Siegel (2005, 106-123) provides significant examples of diverse animals that

---

[19] Escohotado (1997) provides many examples of these links.
[20] Recently Harvard University has developed an interesting "Initiative on Health, Religion and Spirituality" (https://projects.iq.harvard.edu/rshm/home).

use drugs and even "produce" them. Elephants, for example, collect fruits and do not consume them until they are fermented.

Many plants from which psychoactive drugs are derived also have industrial uses. Until the development of synthetics, hemp was an important source of fiber used in many industrial activities. Hemp, coca, and poppy can be inputs in paper, cloth, rope, and other products. After extracting the cocaine from the coca leaves, they are used as a flavoring agent for Coca-Cola.

The list of psychoactive drug uses can be extended. Still, the ones shown are enough to illustrate the complex challenges faced by any successful psychoactive drug control policy and show that humans have always had a propensity to use substances that may provide them with new experiences.

The scientific and technological advances that began in the XIX century started an exponential expansion of the menu of possible *experience-inducing drugs* that persists today. This process, of course, has also happened with all goods and services that can be used by humans, not only with psychoactive drugs. Innovations today considered simple and low tech, like the invention of the hypodermic syringe in 1853, were revolutionary and enormously expanded the medical uses of many drugs. It also provided extraordinarily new non-medical uses by injecting the drugs directly into the bloodstream and allowing them to arrive much faster and with greater strength to the brain.

Even though the great diversity of psychoactive drug uses in many social settings, their human use always has had restrictions. They have been the social response to how each society deals with the tension between the attraction felt by humans to use those drugs and their perceived and genuine personal and social risks and harms. Thus, every society has developed its social mores and government norms to cope with psychoactive drug use. These legal and social behavior controls have varied substantially across time and space.[21]

The laws and norms that regulate the production, trade, and consumption of psychoactive drugs have been generated by many social organizations: governments, families, religious organizations, schools, peer groups, social clubs, professional associations, neighborhood groups, etc.

Until the 18th-century psychoactive drugs were generally legal, and their use was mainly regulated by social mores and legal norms that reflected those mores.[22] For example, religion-inspired laws prohibited alcohol in some countries, but most drugs were legal. Drug markets were mainly local, and drug marketing and consumption were primarily limited to areas close to where they were produced. The geographical expansion of plant-based psychoactive drugs was done through seeds brought from other regions. The *domesticated drugs* varied across societies mainly because the high costs of transportation limited drug availability to those substances originating in areas close to the consumers. Many plant-based drugs were used for a long time without grave addiction problems in societies that learned how to manage their use. Alcohol has been used worldwide, and its use restrictions have also varied in time and space.

Drug use was an important government issue when there were conflicts between government laws and social mores or interest groups. For example, Buxton (2010, 67) found that before the 19th century: "successive Chinese emperors had sought to restrict the use of opium, which was seen as offensive to Confucian morality. However, prohibition decrees issued by Emperors Young Cheng in 1729 and Kia King in 1799 met with resistance from British merchant smugglers". Also, traditional coca chewing in the Andean region was

---

[21] The literature about the history of drug use is large. Siegel (2005), Escohotado (1997 and 1999) and Inglis (1975) are good references.
[22] Bicchieri (2006) analyses the development of social mores in the current social context. Coleman (1990) is a detailed and analytical study of the ways in which a society generates a demand for norms and rules. See also North (1990).

opposed by the Spanish conquerors:[23] "[t]he early Catholic missionaries realized the ceremonial value of coca in the religious practices of the Indians and considered it an obstacle to converting them to Catholicism" (Thoumi, 2003, 30).

The transportation revolution of the 19th century lowered transportation costs and expanded the ability of drug producers to reach distant markets. International drug commerce became a significant factor in spanning Western capitalism and European empire-building (Courtwright, 2002, Part I).

Technological change has accelerated rapidly and continues to force governments to adapt their policies. That is why effective psychoactive drug policies must adjust to a changing world.

1.2 THE OPIUM ISSUE IN CHINA

Opium was used in China from time immemorial, but interpretations of the evolution of opium production, trafficking, and consumption are contradictory. The main point of debate is the role played by European colonialist powers in the growth of opium consumption. A commonly accepted version presents opium as an instrument of colonialist market exploitation implemented through the British East India Company (BEIC): "The Governor-General of India, Marquis Warren Hastings, was the main promoter of opium in the Celestial Empire after he took over control of BEIC's opium monopoly in 1757 and ten years later obtained a permit to sell it in China" (Arango and Child, 1986: 142)[24]. The Chinese Communist Party has a similar position: "The opium war was deliberately provoked by the British invaders. It was the first of a series of aggressive wars launched by capitalist powers that aimed to make

---

[23] Unsuccessfully, except in Ecuador where coca chewing has not been a common habit since then. The success of the anticoca Spanish campaign in Ecuador is still a historical mystery.

[24] This position prevails among many Latin American academics.

China their semi-colony or their colony" (Redacción de la Colección de Libros sobre la Historia Moderna de China, 1980, 3).

A less popular version based on a combination of historical and economic analyses shows a more complex phenomenon. There is no doubt that the United Kingdom's policies in India, where opium poppy was a significant crop, sought to open the Chinese markets to international trade. But the Qing dynasty that ruled China from1644 to 1911 was reluctant to trade and isolated China from the rest of the world. That reluctance was reinforced by its great distance from many growing economies, which increased trading costs. Its government was willing to trade only from one port, Canton, although the Portuguese enclave in Macao facilitated smuggling. But the government was not willing to import manufactured British products like textiles. Furthermore, Chinese exports such as silk, spices, and fine china, highly demanded in the West, had to be paid only with hard currency: gold or silver.

The nature of the monetary system of the time was a critical factor in the genesis of the opium wars. Gold and silver were the national currencies, and when a country had an international trade deficit, it had to pay with those metals. This payment arrangement lowered the amount of money circulating in the importing country, which generated price deflation and economic recessions. To be sustained, the system required international trade flows without large unbalances that would hurt the importing countries, and "Europeans emptied their coffers to buy the goods they craved. Attempts to redress this unbalance provided a principal impetus for western expansion" (McAllister, 2000, 10). This impetus was not limited to seeking legal exports to China. It was also an incentive to use contraband to pay for Chinese exports.

During its over two-thousand-year history, China experienced periods of substantial social and economic progress, followed by periods of conflicts and decline. By the 18th century, it had declined substantially. It was a vast, diverse, and fragmented society that included many peoples. The Manchu-led Qing dynasty was considered foreign by most. Furthermore, the Manchu population was a very small minority.[25] Throughout the 19th century, several rebellions and separatist movements highlighted the law enforcement difficulties of the empire and the weak loyalty that many subjects had to the Manchu emperor. This politically unstable environment encouraged illegal economic activities and made contraband attractive. The Boxer Rebellion (1898-1901), an anti-foreign, anti-Christian, and anti-colonial movement, raised fears of political chaos in China, with widespread consequences for East and Southeast Asia.

Besides, Chinese culture was deeply Sino-centered and rejected contact with the "Western Barbarians" (Escohotado, 1997, Vol 2, 24). This characteristic is common in societies that have remained isolated for a long time. They develop a self-centered view of the world and look at international relations through that prism. In China, the lack of knowledge about the external world was widespread, and its prevailing Confucianism reinforced its Sino-centric approach to the world. This fact promoted a feeling of superiority and a rejection of contact with the rest of the world. The Chinese marine forces' weakness, which allowed a British contingent to win the opium wars, was a consequence of its isolation (Walker III, 1991, 6-8).

Escohotado (1997, vol. 2, 30), evaluating the standard interpretations of the opium wars, concludes: "There are three common and inexact clichés. One is that Europeans brought opium to a country where it was unknown and demanded its legalization. But on the contrary, smugglers satisfied a persistent ancient demand and [...] tried to prevent opium from becoming legal because prohibition was a lot more profitable for them. The second cliché concerns the intentions of the Manchu court that are presented as therapeutic and

---

[25] Manchuria had a different history and traditions from the rest of China. The Manchu were considered invaders by the majority Han population (Escohotado, 1997, Vol. 2, 27). Even today the Manchu population is a small minority of less than one percent of the population of China. In 2001 there were 1,230 million Han (91.6% of the total) and 10,6 million Manchu (0,86% of the population) http://es.wikipedia.org/wiki/Etnias_chinas.

moral initiatives when their initial reason was purely economic. The third cliché is based on the failure to consider the catastrophic situation of China during all the XVIII century,[26] which allows perceiving opium issues as the cause of social ills rather than their symptom. These three falsehoods combined led people to think of a government ready to make any sacrifice to have a healthier and modern country but frustrated by a Western conspiracy that exported something considered as a poison in their own countries."

The estimates of the volume of opium consumed, the number of addicts and users in China, and the changes in those variables are contradictory. This is not surprising given their high uncertainty because of the enormous size of the country, its many isolated areas, and the difficulties to measure those variables accurately in a low-tech environment.

Estimates of Chinese users and addicts reflect those measurement difficulties. Walker III (1991, 12) asserts that in 1900 "perhaps as many as one-fourth of all Chinese smoked prepared opium. Imports of Indian opium had peaked some years earlier, but domestic growth showed no signs of abating." Paoli, Greenfield, and Reuter (2009, 18) conclude that "[o]pium filled many roles in China. It served as a medical product, a recreational item, an addiction soother, a badge of social distinction, and a symbol of elite culture (Dikötter, Laamann, and Xun, 2004, 46; see also Zheng, 2005). A remarkably high percentage of China's population consumed opium, but only infrequently. For example, Newman (1995, 786-788) claims 'that, as of 1906, about 60% of the adult men in China and 40% of adult women smoked approximately fifteen grams of opium a year for festive purposes. Even the number of 'light users' (smoking about 1.5 grams every three days) was about 37.8 million (about 20% of adult men and 8% of adult women)' [...] Newman (1995) concludes that about sixteen million Chinese (6% of the adult population) were drug dependent."

---

[26] And in the 19th century (author's note)

The INCB (2008b, 9) argued that at the beginning of the XX century, "in China alone at least 25 percent of the male population were smoking opium, and there were around 10 million opium addicts in a total estimated population of approximately 450 million". But "Newman (1995) and a new generation of new historians believe that most users, including many regular users, were still able to have normal lives and suffered no negative consequences from their opium use" (Paoli, Greenfield, and Reuter, 2009, 18), which raises doubts about the gravity of the *opium use problem* in China.

A detailed study of Chinese opium imports, using estimates of the opium demanded by addicts in the rest of the world, shows that in 1880 opium imports could not supply more than two million addicts, or 0.5% of the country's population at that time (Escohotado,1997, 165-171). This study concludes that if there was a big opium epidemic, domestic opium supplied most of it. Paoli, Greenfield, and Reuter (2009, 17) concur: "Responding to a budding internal demand, China became a major opiate producer during the second half of the 19th century. According to Newman (1995), in 1879 (the peak year of China's imports from India), China already produced two-thirds of its domestic consumption, by the turn of the 20th century, the share was even larger".

It is not surprising that analysts and scholars arrive at conflicting positions about the opium problem in China at the end of the 19th century, after all, "Just as opium was portrayed in China as a poison used by foreigners to destroy the 'race,' in western countries its demonization was used for the racist discrimination against the Chinese [...] It was portrayed as a means through which the Chinese would undermine Western, and especially American society" (Paoli, Greenfield, and Reuter, 2009, 22).

Despite these different opinions, there is no doubt that the perception of a large growth in opium addiction drastically changed the world's imaginary and beliefs about China's situation. The UNODC highlights the importance of the consequences of that event: "Today's international drug control system is rooted in efforts made a century ago to address the largest substance abuse problem the world has ever faced: the Chinese opium epidemic" (UNODC, 2008,173). Thus, the growth of opium addiction in China, independent of its size, was the trigger that encouraged the creation of the IDCS. Still, other factors also played roles in shaping that development.

Unprecedented scientific developments produced new drugs like morphine, cocaine, heroin, and codeine, and inventions like the hypodermic needle enhanced the uses of these drugs that became the main part of medicine's pharmacopeia and the basis of an important pharmaceutical industry in some countries. As their use expanded, their addiction problems became apparent, as did the need for control.

1.3 GLOBALIZATION, COLONIALISM AND THE AMERICAN INTERESTS IN THE CHINESE OPIUM TRADE

Before the mid-19th century, psychoactive drug policies were generally not an international relations issue. This changed when opium exports from India to China became a critical factor in the Opium Wars of 1839-1842 and 1856-1860 between the British and Chinese empires. After these wars and the growth of internal political problems and uprisings in China, many associated them with a significant increase in opium addiction in that country. Opium was perceived by European colonial powers and the United States as a threat to the country's stability.[27]

At the same time, several factors contributed to developing the United States' interest in the opium trade in Southeast Asia. As international trade expanded substantially across the globe, American and other religious missionaries, who opposed opium use on moral

---

[27] See for example Musto (1999, 28-30).

grounds, developed substantial social and political networks to promote opium prohibition in China.

The Spanish American War (1898) gave the United States control of The Philippines and interests in Southeast Asia. American business leaders, mainly from the country's Northwest, became interested in opening trading relations with China. The United States had welcomed Chinese immigrants to help build the transcontinental railroad after discovering gold in California in 1849. However, after it was finished, these immigrants were discriminated. The Page Act of 1875 de facto prohibited the immigration of Chinese women, and the 1882 Chinese Exclusion Act prohibited all Chinese immigration. These policies generated strong anti-American feelings in China. They were an obstacle to the growth of international trade with China. The perceived expansion of the opium problem in China offered an opportunity for the United States to befriend China, promoting an international effort to control opium use in that country.

Besides, a civic movement against opium exports appeared in Great Britain, and the overwhelming Liberal Party's electoral victory in 1906, led to its recommendation to eliminate Indian opium exports to China (Musto, 1999, 29).

Other developments like the scientific advances that encouraged the development of schools of medicine and pharmacy promoted the establishment of formal requirements to practice those professions and the development of their professional organizations, which led to the establishment of regulations for the legal use of drugs.

The innovations in transportation that lowered international trade costs during the second half of the 19th century contributed to making psychoactive drug regulations a critical policy issue for the main countries involved in its production, consumption, and international trade.[28] It also motivated the United States, China, and the United Kingdom to convene the 1909 Shanghai Opium

---

[28] Like Persia (Iran), Turkey, India, China, Mexico, Portugal, Great Britain, Germany, Switzerland, Bolivia, Peru, and others.

Commission to discuss how to regulate the international market of opium.

This Commission was a pioneer and revolutionary institutional development. As shown below, by then, the United States had set the goal to have an international treaty to restrict the use of psychoactive drugs to medical purposes globally. Other countries concurred with the need to control the international trade of those substances, but they supported less restrictive positions. Although there was no binding resolution from the Shanghai Opium Commission, it opened an international process that produced several protocols and four conventions before the Second World War. The United States promoted the international restriction of drug use to medical purposes through this process, but it did not achieve that goal despite some advances in that direction.

CHAPTER TWO. THE QUEST TO RESTRICT CONTROLLED DRUGS' USES TO MEDICAL AND SCIENTIFIC PURPOSES

2.1 THE ORIGIN OF THE MEDICAL AND SCIENTIFIC USE RESTRICTION

A complex set of political and economic factors and interests played a role in promoting an international opium control system. Still, the restriction to "medical and scientific purposes" could not have become the primary purpose of the IDCS without the generalized prevalence in the involved societies of strong moral and religious feelings against the use of drugs that alter a person's perception of reality. That is why several analysts and historians refer to the process that generated the IDCS as a crusade that used moral panics to achieve results (Escohotado, 1997, Section IV, Dhywood, 2011, chapter 2; Falco, 1994, chapter 2).

Thus, "British and American Protestant and Catholic missionaries, who occupied the leading positions among those proselytizing in China, became stalwart opponents of the international opium trade. Despite valiant efforts and substantial funding, decades of labor had produced few converts in China. While on home leave, missionaries regularly addressed congregations about their work, noting the need for further contributions. By the late 1800s, however, the lack of 'successes' led many to question whether the effort should continue. Missionaries cited opium as a key impediment. Addiction ruined lives and deadened morals" (McAllister, 2000, 21).

Missionaries then sought to establish a system that prohibited non-medical uses: "[a]s early as 1899 an American missionary, the Reverend Hampden C. Du Bose of Soochow, China, called the Attention of the American government to the opium situation in the islands.[29] Declaring that the United States had a great responsibility in

---

[29] The Philippines (author's note).

the matter, he set forth the principle which was to become the basic tenet of American policy throughout the international movement, that 'there can be no judicious use of opium save as administered by a physician......" (Taylor, 1969, 32).

Bishop Charles Henry Brent, a Canadian-born Anglican minister who had served as Episcopal Bishop of The Philippines since 1901 became the leader of the promotion of the international non-medical drug use restriction: "Brent took an extreme prohibitionist position on the opium question. He viewed any non-medical use as immoral and opposed state-sponsored opium distribution monopolies because he believed they corrupted both government and populace" (McAllister, 2000, 27-28).[30] Not surprisingly, in The Philippines, "Washington imposed a policy of suppression, excepting medical needs" (ibid, 28).

The moral arguments importance in the formation of the IDCS is linked to the beliefs of Western European and American superiority prevailing at the turn of the 20th century. Racism and cultural superiority beliefs were common in countries that had experienced the industrial revolution and had colonized a large part of the rest of the world. The advances in medicine in the 19th century, and the belief in eugenics, supported a dutiful intervention of the "superior" cultures on the "primitive" ones.

The link between Colonialism and the leadership of the United States in the search for a global restriction of psychoactive drug uses was strong. Before the Industrial Revolution, the American Colonies and the United States had been very inward-looking. However, in the 19th century, the country experienced great social and economic transformations that established the basis for becoming a global power in the 20th century. The internal western expansion, the displacement of the Native Americans, and the Mexican American war victory encouraged the idea of a *Manifest Destiny* for the country.

---

[30] See also Musto (1999, 11), and Buxton (2006, 29-33),

After its easy victory in the Spanish American War of 1898, in the United States, the expansion of the American influence and power in East Asia appeared a natural consequence of the shared world vision of the "white man's burden" prevailing at the time among white Europeans and Americans. In 1899 Rudyard Kipling wrote the famous "poem 'The White Man's Burden.' Originally subtitled The United States and The Philippines' that was published in a popular U.S. magazine. Kipling's poem urged Americans to take up the burden of joining Europe in what the poem represents as the thankless task of colonial administration" (Murphy, 2010, 1).

These developments gave Americans "indisputable proof of their new status as a world power and an opportunity to accept the eagerly sought burden of uplifting inferior peoples" (Faulkner, 1958, 239).[31]

Therefore, the origins of the limitation of psychoactive drug uses must be traced back to high solid moral ground and superiority feelings of western religious and colonialist actors. These are at the roots of the prevailing top-down, paternalistic, and authoritarian approach to drug policymaking.

2.2 THE 1909 SHANGHAI COMMISSION

As bishop in The Philippines, Brent developed a close relationship with William Howard Taft, the Chief Civil Administrator in that country. He supported Brent's efforts to convene a Conference to establish an international agreement to control the opium trade. Several countries involved in the opium trade were reluctant to participate in a conference that could have the capacity to produce a binding document.

After some negotiations, it was agreed to convene the Shanghai Opium Commission of 1909, in which "Bishop Brent, the US Chief Delegate, was elected president. The delegates to the

---

[31] See Musto (1999, Chapter 2)

Commission, which was expressly differentiated from a 'conference,' had no power to sign a diplomatic Act - indeed, they did not even sign the final resolutions (even though these were all carefully qualified recommendations): instead, they voted that the president should sign for all" (UNODC, 1959, 45).

However, the purpose of the Commission was clear.[32] In the opening speech, His Excellency Tuang Fang, Viceroy of Liangkiang, stated: "On the whole, since the main object of this Conference will be to consider the question of putting a stop to the consumption of opium [...]" (International Opium Commission, 1909, 10)

A review of the proceedings of the Commission (International Opium Commission, 1909) confirms that it focused on a series of opium issues and how to deal with them. Still, no agreement was achieved because "the US delegation, supported by China, proposed to limit the use of opium and other psychoactive drugs to 'medical and scientific purposes.' Other countries opposed efforts to restrict their burgeoning pharmaceutical industries via international regulation. Meanwhile, colonial powers which produced or exported opium and allowed domestic consumption argued that some traditional 'quasi-medical' uses were legitimate. That regulation was a better policy than complete prohibitions on non-medical and scientific uses" (Collins, 2015).[33]

The American position in Shanghai was simple and based on beliefs or "common sense" norms that did not have to be proved and were not based on science or evidence. Musto (1999, 315) quotes Dr. Hamilton Wright, who seconded Bishop Brent in the American Delegation in Shanghai: "We believed in prohibition for ourselves in the use of opium – except for medicinal purposes, and for the principle of prohibition for all other nations as soon as it could be accomplished" (Wright, 1909). Musto also highlights the declarations

---

[32] An administrative division in China (author's note).
[33] The difference between these two positions has been extensively documented. See UNODC (1959, 45-46) McAllister (2000, 28-29), Buxton (2006, 33-36), Sinha (2001, 9).

of the American representatives regarding the other nations: "there is no non-medical use of opium and its derivatives that is not fraught with grave dangers if it is not actually vicious." They were expressed in the Report to the Department of State by the American Delegation to the International Opium Commission in Shanghai (Musto, 315).

The Commission produced a list of non-binding resolutions, "urging gradual suppression of opium smoking and measures intended to stop the smuggling of narcotics, including opium, especially by prohibiting their exports to territories which did not legally admit them. An appeal was also made to the governments controlling foreign concessions and settlements in China to take various measures to co-operate with the efforts of the Government in China, including the closing of opium divans and the application of domestic pharmacy laws in the concessions and settlements" (UNODC, 1959, 45).

After the Shanghai Commission, the United States delegations have always advocated the prohibition of *non-medical and scientific uses* of controlled psychoactive drugs in every conference that negotiated international drug-related treaties

2.3 THE HAGUE 1912 INTERNATIONAL OPIUM CONVENTION

The Shanghai Commission did not satisfy the United States delegation, but it left open to convening a Conference to produce a binding treaty. Dr. Wright returned to the U.S. and took the position of official adviser on International Narcotics Matters at the Department of State. Wright and Brent, supported by then-President William H. Taft (1909-1913), worked to call for an international conference to produce a binding agreement. European countries reluctantly accepted this call. They were wary of the moralistic American positions and implications for European powers that wanted to protect their pharmaceutical industries (Bruum et al., 1975, 12; Sinha, 2001). The Conference met in The Hague, without the participation of Switzerland and Turkey, two of the main stakeholders. The Convention's purpose expressed in its preface was quite vague: "[d]esirous of advancing a step further on the road opened by the International Commission of Shanghai in 1909".[34]

As in Shanghai, Bishop Brent presided over the Conference, and Dr. Wright headed the American Delegation. The United States proposed controls on production, trade, and use of opiates. But some European delegations preferred to regulate. The main American achievement was the prohibition of opium exports to countries where it was prohibited. The Parties to the Convention agreed to gradually lower opium smoking, although there was no specific schedule. They also concurred that heroin and cocaine were the primary drugs subject to control, but codeine produced by the German pharmaceutical industry was exempted. Germany and other European countries conditioned the Convention's entry into force to its ratification by all thirty-four producing and consuming countries, independent of their size (McAllister, 2000, 30-34).

Even though the Convention did not produce the results sought by the United States, it allowed it to set the agenda with the issues to be discussed and to promote the two criteria that have influenced international drug policies since then: limiting controlled drug uses to medical purposes, and the need to emphasize drug supply control (Buxton, 2006, 35). These criteria required the producing countries of plant-based drugs to assume greater responsibility in drug policy implementation (Sinha, 2001, 9).

Few countries ratified the Convention before the start of the First World War in late July 1914, but the war significantly influenced the Convention's entry into force. First, the war increased the fear of addictions because soldiers tended to use opiates to calm themselves in situations of danger, and the injured were treated with morphine. Second, Germany and Turkey, the war's main losers, were two of the

---

[34] The text of the Convention is available online at the UN Depository, United Nations Treaty Collection.

most vigorous opponents of the drug control promoted by the United States. Then, through "a complicated series of overtures, both the British and American delegations to the Paris conference concluded that a clause requiring ratification of The Hague Opium Convention should be included in the peace treaties. The Chinese insisted on German and Austrian adherence as a condition for concluding peace" (McAllister, 2000, 36).[35] This way, the Convention was *de facto* ratified as a condition to signing the Treaty of Versailles. However, since Turkey did not sign the Treaty, the Convention entered into force with less than the thirty-four ratifications initially required. The League of Nations, whose Covenant was attached to the Treaty of Versailles in 1919, received the mandate to oversee the implementation of The Hague 1912 Convention.

2.4 THE HARRISON ACT AND HEROIN ADDICTION MAINTENANCE IN THE UNITED STATES

The United States promoted The Hague Opium Convention of 1912, but the country did not have domestic legislation regulating the opiates market. Dr. Hamilton Wright, who had presided over the American delegation at The Hague Conference, worked from the Department of State to enact such legislation. The Harrison Narcotics Tax Act was enacted in December 1914 to fill that gap. This act regulated the production, imports, and distribution of opiates and coca products. The Act, however, did not directly prohibit the use of opiates and coca-based products, but it required psychoactive drug products to pay a stamp attached to them.

The United States Constitution imposes many restrictions on the Federal Government. They prevented the federal government from prohibiting drugs, but the *Constitution's Commerce Clause* has allowed Congress to regulate the psychoactive drugs markets.[36]

---

[35] See also Bruum et al., 1975, 13.
[36] The Constitution limits the federal government's powers to the *enumerated powers*. They are those that the sovereign states transfer to the federal government.

Besides, it required prescribing doctors to keep a registry of all patients and their prescribed doses of opiates and coca products.

Even though none of the Act's provisions allow doctors in their professional practice to prescribe opiates to their patients, it was unclear whether prescribing opiates to an addict as part of the treatment of addiction was a legitimate medical activity. Many Americans did not see addiction as a disease, and the addict was not seen as a patient but as someone with a frail character whose behavior had to be corrected. According to them, doctors should not have been allowed to prescribe or supply opiates for addiction maintenance because that was not "in the course of his professional practice" (Strang, Groshkova and Metrebian, 2012, 26).

This belief was consistent with the denial that addiction was a disease and thus implied that there were no incurable addicts, only drug users whose behavior had to be changed. But "[t]he Harrison act made no mention of addicts and, although the wording seemed clear to reformers, it did not define for indifferent or hostile interpreters 'legitimate practice of medicine' and 'good faith' in prescribing. The manifest lack of federal power to regulate medical practice as well as the need to unify professional support of the Harrison Act may have required these vague phrases [...] The chief problem the Justice Department encountered in the attempt to prohibit maintenance of addiction was that the federal courts thought any federal regulation of medical practice unconstitutional" (Musto, 1999, 124-125).

This Act led the Justice Department to seek a case in which it accused a doctor of conspiracy "to place the drugs unlawfully in possession of the addict by prescribing and dispensing, the prescription not having been made in good faith" (ibid, 125). Such

---

These are mainly defense and security, the regulation of interstate and foreign trade, and the monetary issues related to the central bank (the Federal Reserve) and the federal budget. The limitations of the federal government to formulate national drug policies, including its constraints to force states to prohibit drug uses, are analyzed in Thoumi (2014).

case was decided in the 1916 Supreme Court's decision *U.S. v. Jin Fuey Moy* "[b]y seven to two the Court rejected the government's arguments" (ibid, 129). This decision allowed drug use for addiction maintenance.

In the American legal system, the decisions of the juries and the courts tend to reflect "public opinion" and vary through time as "public opinion" changes. They are political decisions that science may inform, but they are not scientific or necessarily evidence-based.

But the mood of the public opinion in the United States rapidly changed as the prohibitionist movement strengthened and the fear of the Bolshevik Revolution induced a "red scare" that heightened a moral panic against drugs.[37] In 1919 in *U.S. v. Doremus* a divided Supreme Court "confirmed the constitutionality of the Harrison Act's tax[38] on physicians and the concomitant control over the way the drugs could be dispensed" (ibid, 132).[39] In the same year, the Supreme Court followed with another divided decision (*Webb et al. v. U.S.*) that rejected any legitimate medical practice that could include prescribing medicines to support an addiction (ibid, 132).[40] This decision was consistent with the prevailing attitude during the late 1910s and early 1920s that considered the "use of narcotics as morally wrong, physically and morally debilitating to the human body and personality, contagious in its growth, and a menace, both physically and morally to society" (Taylor, 1969, 131).

The *Webb et al. v. U.S.* Supreme Court decision of over a century ago is still today the law of the land in the United States, and

---

[37] Alcohol prohibitionists took advantage of the fear of an expanding communist revolution and argued that it was the United States responsibility to support a war weakened Western Europe that was confronting the Soviet Union. Thus, the country's grain crops should have been exported to Europe rather than used to produce liquor.

[38] This was not technically a tax and refers to the value of the stamp that had to be attached to drug products (author's note).

[39] The Supreme Court vote was 5 to 4, the dissenters included Chief Justice Edward D. White (author's note).

[40] The vote in the Supreme Court was 5 to 4
(https://www.law.cornell.edu/supremecourt/text/249/96).

heroin cannot be prescribed as an addiction maintenance drug. However, doctors can prescribe some substitutes like methadone or buprenorphine, synthetic opioids used to counter the addiction to heroin and other opiates.

The United States played a key role in developing the IDCS, and the rejection of addiction maintenance was implicitly accepted as a sensible policy by most countries. As shown below (Chapter Eight), today, very few countries accept heroin maintenance as a medical procedure. In those where it is legal, health professionals are extremely cautious in its use, and very few heroin addicts are treated with it.

2.5 DRUGS IN THE LEAGUE OF NATIONS

2.5.1 The Period before the 1925 Treaties

As noted, the League of Nations assumed the implementation of The Hague 1912 Convention. Its implementation became an important function of the League of Nations. In a resolution (December 15, 1920), it established the "'Advisory Committee on the Traffic in Opium and Other Dangerous Drugs,' usually referred to as the 'Opium Advisory Committee' (OAC) authorized to take over the functions laid down in The Hague Opium Convention of 1912" (UNODC, 2008, 192).

The OAC is the predecessor of today's Commission on Narcotic Drugs (CND). Besides, "the League created an 'Opium and Social Questions Section' (often referred to as the 'Opium Section') within its secretariat for administrative and executive support. The League's Health Committee (forerunner of the World Health Organization) took responsibility for advising on medical matters" (ibid, 192).

The main task of the OAC and the Opium Section was to estimate the requirements to satisfy "legitimate" medical needs. Other tasks were to determine the effects of those drugs on users, the magnitude of the drug problem, the definition of addiction, treatment methods, and the *quasi-medical* uses of opium (McAllister, 2000, 47-49).

The Opium Section could not agree about the estimates of opium, coca, and the drugs derived from these plants because of differences in country interests and perceptions about dealing with addictive drugs. However, "[t]hey generally supported the emerging control paradigm that emphasized regulation of substances, marginalization of users, and exploration in search of better drugs. As a result of such factors, the international drug control regime came to be defined primarily as outside the social and medical spheres. While social and medical questions never disappeared entirely, the system focused on economic calculations, regulatory statutes, and enforcement measures. Medical expertise played an essential role in defining which drugs possessed addiction potential, but those determinations focused on narrow physiological manifestations and eschewed addiction's more significant social implications. Supply control emerged as the regime's *raison d'être"* (McAllister, 2000, 49-50).

To strengthen the supply control, the League of Nations convened two drug treaties in 1925. Even though President Woodrow Wilson was the leading promoter of the League of Nations, the United States failed to join the League because of opposition from Congress. The U.S. membership was important to the League, and its members thought that making the United States party to international drug treaties was an instrument to get it to join the League. The U.S.'s importance to the League gave it leverage in setting the agenda for drug policy negotiations, and "[i]n May 1924 the United States set in stone the uncompromising attitude that animated the international drug control strategy for the remainder of the decade. Indeed, for the rest of the century, the elusive quest – control of agricultural production in the field – remained a central tenet of US drug policy. Such strategy required little sacrifice from

Americans while demanding fundamental social and institutional changes from others" (McAllister, 2000, 66).

2.5.2 The 1925 Treaties

After a series of diplomatic contacts, the U.S. agreed to participate in the Conference. But differences in the interests of various countries led to convening two conferences that produced:

1. The Agreement Concerning the Manufacture of, Internal Trade in, and Use of Prepared Opium, also known as the Agreement concerning the Suppression of the Manufacture of, Internal Trade in, and Use of, Prepared Opium signed in Geneva in February 1925. This treaty was motivated by a significant increase in opium production and consumption in Southeast Asia, mainly in China, and exhorted the governments to discourage opium smoking, and established the goal to eliminate this practice in 15 years (Buxton, 2006, 40). Also, its "Article I required that, with the exception of retail sale, the importation, sale, and distribution of opium be a government monopoly, which would have the exclusive right to import, sell, or distribute opium. Leasing, according, or delegating this right was specifically prohibited. Article II prohibited the sale of opium to minors, and Article III prohibited minors from entering smoking divans. Article IV required governments to limit the number of opium retail shops and smoking divans as much as possible. Articles V and VI regulated the export and transport of opium and dross. Article VII required governments to discourage the use of opium through instruction in schools, literature, and other methods" (UNODC, 2008, 193).
2. The 1925 International Opium Convention whose purpose was to control international drug trafficking and drug abuse: "[t]aking note of the fact that the application of the provisions

of the Hague Convention of January 23rd, 1912, by the Contracting Parties has produced results of great value, but that the contraband trade in and abuse of the substances to which the Convention applies, still continues on a great scale".[41]

The Convention created a system of import certificates and export authorizations designed to assure that every international transaction in controlled substances had to be known and approved by the competent authorities of the importing and exporting countries. This system was overseen by the newly created Permanent Central Opium Board (PCOB). It was "set up as an impartial body whose members should not be Government representatives but should serve in a personal capacity, not holding any offices which would put them in a position of direct dependence on their governments. The Board could not sanction any country, but it could recommend an embargo of drug exports and imports to any country that exported or imported in excess of stated production levels or medical need. This extended to countries that were not a party to the convention, universalizing the control system" (Buxton, 2006, 41).

Since the PCOB could not sanction any country, it had to rely on its moral authority and shaming capacity. This situation has remained in the current INCB, the heir of the PCOB. Following "a passionate speech by the head of the delegation from Egypt" (UNODC, 2008, 194), the Convention included marijuana for the first time among the controlled drugs. However, its regulation was limited to the international trade of marijuana and hashish.

The United States delegation was presided by Stephen G. Porter. Since 1919 he had led the Foreign Affairs Committee of the House of Representatives, from where he guided American foreign drug policy. He was intransigent and belligerent and had disagreed strongly with the legitimacy of *quasi-medical* drug uses. Porter's

---

[41] Preface of the Convention. The text of the Convention is available online at the UN Depository, United Nations Treaty Collection.

position "in essence was that the use of opiates for other than medical and scientific purposes was an abuse, and that control of production was necessary in order to curb it" (Musto, 1999, 199). He had opposed opium imports to produce heroin and believed that banning heroin production across the entire world would solve the American heroin addiction problem (ibid, 200).

The Americans appeared to have advanced toward that goal as "[i]n Chapter III, dealing with the internal control of manufactured drugs, as opposed to the cultivation of plant-based drugs, the drafters were able to go a step further. Article 5 declares: 'The Contracting Parties shall enact effective law or regulation to limit exclusively to medical and scientific purposes the manufacture, import, sale, distribution, export, and use of the substances to which this Chapter applies....'" (UNODC, 2008, 193). However, this wording did not commit countries enough to satisfy the Americans because it did not require any enforcement and did not make illegal non-medical and scientific drug uses. The American delegation left the Conference in disgust and did not sign the Convention.[42] China and Peru did not sign it either. China was immersed in a civil war, and it was inconvenient for the country to make any international commitment. Peru because of concerns about hurting the prospects of its incipient cocaine manufacturing industry.

The American attitude generated widespread press coverage and strong reactions across the world. Canada, Japan, India, Great Britain, France, and Holland quickly ratified the convention to support the League of Nations. The American behavior induced rapid ratification by fifty-six countries and the Convention entered into force in 1928.

One consequence of the Convention was a decline in opium production in India that had ratified it. However, opium production increased in Persia, providing an early example of what was later known as the *balloon effect*: when the production of illegal drugs or

---

[42] See also Musto (1999, 197-200) and McAllister (2000, 76-78).

their trafficking is eliminated in one place, those activities are displaced somewhere else.

The League of Nations proceeded to obtain information about opium, looking for cases of diversion. It also organized the OAC and the PCOB, separated their roles, and sought ways to allow the participation of the United States in the activities of these drug organs.

In 1930 Stephen G. Porter, shortly before his death, promoted the creation of the Federal Bureau of Narcotics (FBN) by Congress and the appointment of Harry J. Anslinger as its director, a convinced hard-liner who headed the FBN from 1930 to 1962 and who played a legendary role in shaping the IDCS.[43]

The 1925 Convention did not issue guidelines to regulate the international markets of morphine, codeine, cocaine, and heroin.[44] Another issue was the impossibility of controlling the vegetable sources of those drugs, particularly opium production, which was growing fast due to domestic political conflicts in China. Coca and cocaine, on the other hand, were a relatively minor issue.

The great depression and the balance of payments crises of many countries made illegal exports attractive as a source of scarce foreign exchange. It was suspected that countries that had not signed the 1925 Convention took advantage of the market and reexported drugs for non-medical uses. Also, that Persia and other countries were

---

[43] Every history of the IDCS coincides in giving Anslinger credit as a key figure in the development of the IDCS that "would dominate American (and international) drug control efforts for the next four decades. A young and extremely capable bureaucrat, he had a shrewd political instinct, a willingness to massage and fabricate data, and an ability to cultivate the media and loyal domestic constituencies ('Anslinger's Army') and leverage them to forward his control agenda. More pragmatic than his legion of domestic detractors gave him credit for, his overarching priority remained to build and maintain the FBN as the US' lead drug agency. His single-mindedness on the drug issue betrayed a certain moral zealotry, but this was usually outweighed by a desire to protect the FBN and his suzerainty over it. He was in this sense more of a bureaucratic entrepreneur than a moral entrepreneur" (Collins, 2015, 34-35).

[44] The Convention rejected a proposal by British delegate Sir Malcolm Delevingne to establish production quotas, an issue left open to be decided in the future.

replacing India as suppliers of opium for quasi-medical uses. Besides, colonialist countries kept opium state monopolies in their colonies, which were important government revenue sources. These factors induced the League of Nations to seek ways to strengthen drug market controls (UNODD, 2008, 192-198).

2.5.3 *The 1931 Convention for Limiting the Manufacture and Regulating the Distribution of Narcotic Drugs*

Those developments led to a call for a new Convention that had an excellent response. Fifty-seven countries attended the 1931 Conference, although many participants were members of their countries' delegations to the League of Nations in Geneva and did not have any expertise in drug issues.

The justifications for the Convention were expressed in its preface: "[d]esiring to supplement the provisions of the International Opium Conventions, signed at The Hague on January 23rd, 1912, and at Geneva on February 19th, 1925, by rendering effective by international agreement the limitation of the manufacture of narcotic drugs to the world's legitimate requirements for medical and scientific purposes and by regulating their distribution".[45]

The Conference sought to regulate the production and trade of manufactured drugs, but countries could not agree on a quota system to distribute the world market. The Convention, however, promoted a drug market system aiming to maintain a healthy level of competition, avoiding monopolies. The Convention was signed in July 1931 and entered into force in July 1933. It was ratified by 67 countries and was the only one of the three League of Nations drug conventions signed and ratified by the United States (UNODC, 2000, 195).

---

[45] The text of the Convention is available online at the UN Depository, United Nations Treaty Collection.

The Convention established a compulsory system that required countries to estimate the volume of their drug needs, which could be modified in emergencies. Every importing country could seek the cheapest provider but could not import more than the amount reported as required to satisfy its needs. A Drug Supervisory Body (DSB) was created to estimate global drug needs. Governments were required to report import and export drug quantities to the DSB, but only after the selling order had been executed. The Convention also introduced the *drug scheduling system.* Two lists of drugs subjected to different treatments depending on the danger of use and medical usefulness: "[d]rugs such as codeine and dionine were subjected to the least stringent measures due to their medical utility and lower abuse potential. Heroin, in contrast, was banned for export, except under special conditions. Under the Convention, any heroin seized should either be destroyed or converted,[46] rather than diverted to medical or scientific use, as was permitted for seizures of some other drugs" (UNODC, 2008: 195).[47] The Convention also required countries to establish an especial government agency to implement the convention (McAllister, 2000, 108).

The United States did not achieve its goal to establish the principle to limit legitimate drug uses to *medical and scientific purposes* for all scheduled drugs. Still, the system of estimates based on medical needs was a progress in that direction. This development, and the desire to avoid another international reaction like the one after the 1925 Convention, led the United States to sign the 1931 Convention.

The 1931 Convention strengthened the international drug control system and encouraged the League of Nations' drug organs and the FBN to press forward. In the United States, Anslinger, a republican, used the Convention's requirement to strengthen the

---

[46] Heroin can be converted back into morphine (author's note).
[47] McAllister (2000, 96-97) argues that the flexible treatment of codeine and the requirement to inform about drug exports only after the selling order had been fulfilled were concessions to drug producing countries, especially Germany.

FBN. He also convinced New York, Representative Fiorello La Guardia, to introduce a bill to require searching for drugs in all imports from producing countries that had not ratified The Hague 1912 Opium Convention. Turkey, whose exports were threatened, complied, and ratified the Convention (McAllister, 2000, 107-108).

The main goal of the League of Nations was to regulate weapons production and markets and prevent a Second World War. Many hope that the drug treaties would become an international cooperation model to be followed in the weapons field. This fact increased the endeavor to overcome the obstacles faced in formulating and ratifying the drug conventions.

2.5.4 The 1936 Convention for the Suppression of the Illicit Traffic in Dangerous Drugs

The experience of the 1920s and early 1930s convinced the OAC and the DSB that there was a need to extend the regulatory efforts to control the drug trafficking organizations, particularly those in East and Southeast Asia, where opium trafficking was growing at a fast rate. However, by 1933 the League of Nations had been significantly weakened by the departure of Germany and Japan that had induced an exodus of other countries like Brazil, Costa Rica, Guatemala, Honduras, Nicaragua, and Paraguay. Despite these signs of weakness and crisis, the League convened the 1936 Convention for the Suppression of the Illicit Traffic in Dangerous Drugs, signed on July 22. The preface of the preamble of the Convention expresses its purpose: "[h]aving resolved, on the one hand, to strengthen the measures intended to penalise offences contrary to the provisions of the International Opium Convention signed at The Hague on January 23rd, 1912, the Geneva Convention of February 19th, 1925, and the Convention for Limiting the Manufacture and Regulating the Distribution of Narcotic Drugs signed at Geneva on July 13th, 1931, and, on the other hand, to combat by the methods most effective in the present circumstances the illicit traffic in the drugs and substances covered by the above Conventions".[48]

The United States was invited to the conference but agreed to join only after receiving written assurances that specific issues were included. The American delegation was headed by Anslinger and Stuart Fuller, Chief of the Far Eastern Bureau of the Department of State. They proposed to "criminalize all non-medical, production and distribution, and perhaps individual use as well. When several delegations offered the standard objection that such an alteration lay outside the competence of the Conference, Fuller produced the letter from the secretariat stating otherwise. Delegates opposed to the American proposals then pounced on Ekstrand,[49] complaining that the secretariat had no right to make such a promise. Having nevertheless to abide by the ruling, the Conference gave the American proposal a superficial hearing before rejecting it" (McAllister, 2000, 123).

The American delegation wanted to leave the Conference, but the State Department did not approve such a move to avoid similar consequences to those generated by their leaving the 1925 Conference. In any case, the United States did not sign this Convention (Buxton, 2006, 42-46).

It was the first treaty to focus explicitly on drug trafficking and make certain drug offenses international crimes. Article 2 of the 1931 Convention states:[50]

> Each of the High Contracting Parties agrees to make the necessary legislative provisions for severely punishing, particularly by imprisonment or other penalties of deprivation of liberty, the following acts – namely:

---

[48] The text of the Convention is available online at the UN Depository, United Nations Treaty Collection.
[49] Eric Einar Ekstrand was the head of the Opium Section and the author of the letter (author's note).
[50] The text of the Convention is available online at the UN Depository, United Nations Treaty Collection.

(a) The manufacture, conversion, extraction, preparation, possession, offering, offering for sale, distribution, purchase, sale, delivery on any terms whatsoever, brokerage, dispatch, dispatch in transit, transport, importation, and exportation of narcotic drugs, contrary to the provisions of the said Conventions;

(b) Intentional participation in the offenses specified in this Article;

(c) Conspiracy to commit any of the above-mentioned offenses;

(d) Attempts and, subject to the conditions prescribed by national law, preparatory acts.

Also, for the first time, the Convention dealt explicitly with the issues related to international drug trafficking and the extradition of drug criminals. Only thirteen countries ratified the convention that entered into force in October 1939, about a month before WWII started.

International drug trafficking declined sharply because of the war. It was not an important subject of international legislation until the United Nations 1988 Convention against Illicit Traffic in Narcotic Drugs and Psychotropic Substances.

2.6. COCA CHEWING AS AN INTERNATIONAL POLICY ISSUE

2.6.1 Social and Political Background

Native communities in the Andean countries have had multiple uses of coca since time immemorial. These have included many social rituals used to support social cohesion and to facilitate social interaction. Coca has been used:
- As a work stimulant,
- In religious functions,

- As an instrument of divination,
- As medicine (i.e., to cope with high altitude syndrome and in uses that could be classified as *quasi-medical* by Western medicine)
- As food because of its vitaminic content and as a post-meal digestive,
- For recreation and as an input in some industries.[51]

Coca chewing is ubiquitous in Bolivia and Peru and limited in Colombia, where native organized communities are small in the country's population. It is also present among a few non-native communities in the North of Argentina and Chile.

Coca chewing was rejected by the Spanish conquistadors that sought to spread the Catholic religion across the world: "[t]he early Catholic missionaries realized the ceremonial value of coca, linked it to the religious practices of the Amerindians, and considered it as an obstacle to their conversion to Catholicism. This led to the condemnation of coca by a Catholic Council that met in Lima in 1567 as 'something useless and pernicious that lead to superstition because it is a talisman of the devil'" (Vidart, 1991, 88).[52]

However, despite attempts to prohibit it, Spaniards' interests were conflicted. Coca chewing is a hunger and exhaustion palliative. It is an anorectic and stimulant that was conveniently used by hacienda and mine owners to allow workers to have long shifts without a food supply. In the conflict between religion and money, money won, and coca chewing was accepted as an Amerindian custom of an inferior race and culture that few "whites" adopted. At

---

[51] Carter and Mamani (1986) is a classic work that has a documented in detail those uses.

[52] References to the demonization of coca by the Spaniards have been frequent in the Latin American literature about coca. It should be noted that coca chewing was not the only demonized native practice. In 16th century Latin America, the Spaniards demonized many aspects of the Indian culture to the point that it became anathema to study the history, values, mores, and culture of the Indians (See González, 1997, 51-55).

the 1567 Catholic Council in Lima, many testified against supplying coca to workers because it created malnutrition and addiction. Today it would be called an Amerindian genocide. But the coca planters and merchants argued that the negative consequences of coca chewing were exaggerated and pointed out several of its benefits, including the economic ones that also benefited some of the clergymen that derived income from coca. In the end, the Council adopted "a more moderate, albeit reformist, position regarding the coca question. Submitted to the Crown in 1569, the council's coca declaration requested the enactment of comprehensive legislation that would discourage the use of the leaf in 'superstitious practices,' limit its cultivation, and reduce camayo[53] deaths by preventing forced labor in Andes Province" (Gagliano, 1994, 56).

The conflict about coca use that started in the XVI century persists today: "the social role of coca transcended its use as a hunger and exhaustion palliative and became a symbol of Indian identity. The use of coca in Indian religious ceremonies led to a debate about whether the coca leaf was sacred in Indian culture. According to Indian mythology, coca was a gift from *Pachamama*, Mother Earth, and 'The Andean Indians chew coca because in that way they affirm their identity as heirs and owners of the land that yesterday the Spaniard took away and today the landowner keeps away from them. Chewing coca is to be Indian and to quietly and obstinately challenge the contemporary lords that descend from the old *encomenderos*[54] and the older conquistadors.'" (Vidart, 1991, 61).

---

[53] Highland peasants that were forced to work in coca plantations in the very unhealthy lower altitude jungle (author's note).

[54] Encomienda was a legal system by which the Spanish crown attempted to define the status the indigenous population in Spain's American and Philippine colonies. It was based upon the practice of exacting tribute from Muslims and Jews during the Reconquista ("Reconquest") of Muslim Spain. Although the original intent of the encomienda was to reduce the abuses of forced labour (repartimiento) employed shortly after Europeans' 15th-century discovery of the New World, in practice it became a form of enslavement (https://www.britannica.com/topic/encomienda).

Until cocaine was extracted from coca in 1860, coca chewing and other uses were a local phenomenon with deep social and cultural roots that distinguish it from cocaine: "[c]ocaine culture, which practically anyone with the urge and cash can join, is famously hedonistic, risky, and individualistic, whereas coca is usually savored by Andean Indians to reinforce their shared traditional and community mores. Coca is bought and sold but historically integrated in a bounded regional circuit reproducing a cultural belt of highland 'Andeanness;' cocaine in its far briefer history has become a rootless and ruthlessly global commodity" (Gootenberg, 2008, 18).[55]

The difference between coca and cocaine uses in the Andean countries reflects "[t]he confrontation between Spanish and Indian cultures in the Andes [that] has gone on for five centuries. At times it has been overt, but most of the time, it has simmered covertly. This confrontation underlies many of the values and cultural characteristics of Bolivia, Peru, Ecuador, and Colombia, and it has not been resolved yet. Indeed, in the Andes, the process of 'the conquest of the other' has not finished (De Roux, 1990, 11), and the Indians' abuse has been a constant in the region's history.[56] As a symbol of Indian identity, coca use and policies became an integral part of the confrontation between the two cultures" (Thoumi, 2003, 33).

In 1884 French-born pharmacist Alfredo Bignon started publishing scientific papers on the benefits of coca and cocaine. At the turn of the XX century, coca chewing began to be debated in Peru. Psychiatrist Hermilio Valdizán began to advocate controls to coca cultivation and the elimination of coca chewing, convinced that it, rather than alcohol, was the main reason for the "degeneration of

---

[55] Gootenberg's book is a comprehensive modern history of cocaine based on deep archival research. It is a must reading for anyone interested in understanding the history of legal and illegal cocaine markets.

[56] This has been the case not only in high Indian-population density countries like Bolivia, Peru, and Ecuador, but also in Colombia. As an example, De Roux (1990, 11-12) recounts an incident in 1967 in which seven Colombian settlers killed sixteen Indians and were exonerated because "they did not know that killing Indians was a crime."

the Indian race." His positions were supported by evidence that American Seventh-Day Adventist missionaries had dissuaded coca chewing Amerindians and showed that they did not need coca to live well at high altitudes (Gagliano, 1994, 122). An anti-coca *Indigenist* movement led by Carlos Paz-Soldán argued the need to assimilate the Indians into Western society. He claimed that they were victims of a toxic "indigenous cocainism" and concurred that coca chewing was "degenerating the Indian race" (Gootenberg, 1999, 56-57, see also 2008, 168-169). After Dr. Valdizán became incapacitated in 1929, another physician, Carlos Ricketts, introduced a bill in the Chamber of Deputies to establish a national coca monopoly to eliminate the Indians' coca chewing habit and their immoderate use of alcohol. This bill was supported by strong-arm conservative Peruvian president Augusto Leguía (1919-1930), who argued that coca leaf production had to be limited to supply only medical and scientific requirements. Despite this support, the opposition of *hacendados* won, and the Bill was not enacted (Gagliano, 1994, 126-131). This failed bill was the first proposal to create a government coca monopoly to control coca uses in Peru.

By the late 1920s, Peru produced and exported coca leaves and *crude cocaine*.[57] Paz-Soldán started to advocate the industrialization of coca and the production of cocaine for exports. "An admiration for scientific and pure cocaine, combined with disgust for backward Indian coca (now a pathology) was a medicalized form of Peru's intensifying national schizophrenia around coca" (Gootenberg, 1999, 58). The Paz-Soldán efforts to start cocaine production generated an "astonishing covert international activity [...] Maywood Chemical [...] would try to get the Peruvians talking to the League again,[58] over the next few years 'to protect their legitimate sale of coca'" (ibid, 59). During the depressed 1930s, public opinion in

---

[57] What today would be called cocaine base.
[58] As shown above, Peru had not signed the 1925 Opium Convention, its relationship with the League of Nations had not been smooth and the dialogue had been interrupted (author's note).

Peru supported the industrialization of the coca project and the claim to bigger "export cocaine quotas" from the League of Nations, under the erroneous belief that the League assigned such quotas. "Strangely, few Peruvians doubted this campaign's larger promise: that a substantial licit cocaine market was somewhere out there beckoning for Peruvian action" (ibid, 61).

Coca-Cola was interested in maintaining a cheap, stable, and secure coca leaf supply and worked jointly with Maywood lab, the producers of its coca-based flavoring agent. And, for "[o]ver four decades from the 1920s to the 1960s, a political pact reigned between Coca-Cola and the FBN on coca and related cocaine issues, a relationship richly documented in FBN files. In this area, the personnel and practices of Maywood and Coca-Cola became indistinguishable. [...] Maywood officials frequently spied and informed on errant coca sellers and buyers. Coca-Cola and Maywood tapped their overseas clients to gather data about coca crops or policy changes coveted by Anslinger, who became highly knowledgeable about Peruvian cocaine. Maywood worked to persuade the Peruvian state of the wisdom of U.S.-style drug policies, while Coca-Cola lawyers participated in world drug conferences and Andean missions, offering technical advice and political intelligence on evolving coca issues. [...] In return, the Anslinger-era FBN paid rapt, consistent attention to Coca-Cola needs at home and abroad" (Gootenberg, 2008, 202). For example, the FBN opposed the Peruvian attempts to establish a state coca monopoly and "facilitated a good strategic status for Maywood and allocated it scarce shipping during World War II, a dramatic era for Coca-Cola's global expansion" (ibid, 204). Coca-Cola's interest was guaranteed by article 27 ¶1 of the 1961 Single Convention: "The Parties may permit the use of coca leaves for the preparation of a flavouring agent, which shall not contain any alkaloids, and, to the extent necessary for such use, may permit the production, import, export, trade in and possession of such leaves."

In the meantime, Bolivia followed a different path. It did not produce *crude cocaine,* and its exports of coca were primarily to the border areas of Argentina and Chile that had coca chewing communities (ibid, 117). The lack of significant coca exports outside the region made coca chewing less controversial internationally than in Peru. Bolivian governments acknowledged that coca chewing was a way in which coca had been *domesticated* in the Amerindian communities and advocated tolerance of traditional cultural coca uses: "Bolivia's bold but unknown pro coca stance during the League's fleeting raw material debates of the mid-1920s stemmed from lobbying by its elite coca growers' association, the Sociedad de Propietarios de Yungas" (SPY) (ibid, 214).

The Bolivian Congress ratified the 1925 International Opium Convention with reserves that rejected limits on coca output and the use of coca among the indigenous population.[59] Coca's human ingestion was so crucial to the peasant and mining communities that in 1940 it was included in the list of staples that the government required to be available in all mining and railroad station locations (Quiroga, 1990, 12). "The social place of coca leaf in Bolivian culture, then as now, defied drug control syllogisms" (ibid, 216).

The Second World War increased the demand for cocaine. In the late 1930s, countries expecting a new world war increased their demand for medical cocaine. The Japanese bombing of Pearl Harbor on December 7, 1941 ended any possible Peruvian legal cocaine exports to Germany and Japan. However, during the early 1940s, Peru experienced a resurgence of cocaine exports that reached 3,000 kilos in 1943. To assure cocaine supply in case of war, Anslinger also promoted Maywood's pilot coca projects in Puerto Rico and Hawaii

---

[59] The Bolivian reservation had three points: 1. Bolivia does not undertake to restrict the home cultivation or production of coca, or to prohibit the use of coca leaves by the native population. 2. The exportation of coca leaves shall be subject to control by the Bolivian Government, by means of export certificates. 3. The Bolivian Government designates the following as places from which coca may be exported: Villazon, Yacuiba, Antofagasta, Arica and Mollendo
 (https://treaties.un.org/pages/ViewDetails.aspx?src=TREATY&mtdsg_no=VI-6-a&chapter=6&clang=_en).

(Gootenberg, 1999, 64; McAllister, 2000, 130-131), which never materialized.[60]

European visitors to Peru in the late XIX and early XX centuries had a favorable opinion on the coca chewing habit. Some considered it "an indispensable stimulant for the *sierra* Indians" (Gagliano, 1994, 117). Dr. Carlos Monge followed this idea. He began to study high-altitude biology in the 1920s and "gained an international reputation for his theory that dwellers in the high Andes represented a new biological type" (ibid,136). Monge identified the clinical syndrome of chronic mountain sickness or altitude sickness, also known as *Monge's disease*.[61] "While doubting that the use of coca would produce a form of addiction for most chewers, he suggested that it more than likely contributed to successful acclimatization in extreme Andean altitudes" (Gagliano, 1994, 137).

However, in 1938 Dr. Luis Sáenz's landmark studies about Peruvian toxicomania "reduced coca uses in all forms to an alkaloid poisoning of the Indian nation" (Gootenberg, 1999, 66). Dr. Carlos Gutiérrez-Noriega followed this work with a series of anti-coca publications. They emphasized the harmful effects of coca and cocaine that drew American praise (ibid, 66).

Both Monge and Gutiérrez-Noriega were part of the Indigenist movement that started in the 1910s in Peru and Bolivia, whose leaders revalued the native culture and promoted the Amerindians' wellbeing. However, they had opposite positions toward coca. They became the main actors in a very intense national debate about the consequences of coca chewing on the population. The Indigenist movement produced some of the best-known Peruvian literary figures of the first half of the 20th century, like Ciro Alegría, who highlighted the role of coca as an instrument of

---

[60] However, those visiting Puerto Rico's El Yunque National Forest can hike the coca trail (Thoumi, 2015, 488).
[61] https://en.wikipedia.org/wiki/Carlos_Monge_Medrano

exploitation of the Amerindians.[62] The movement was formed almost exclusively by educated non-natives concerned with the Amerindians' terrible social and economic living conditions.

The election of left-leaning president José L. Bustamante in 1945, with the support of the leftist APRA party,[63] opened the door for Monge to follow his agenda and in 1947 got the president to request a United Nations mission to do a study on the consequences of coca leaf uses. Another reform of the Bustamante government was a decree that granted the Peruvian State a government monopoly to manufacture, export, and sell cocaine, its salts, and derivatives.

However, things changed quickly when on October 27, 1948, right-wing anti-APRA, and pro-American General Manuel Arturo Odría led a successful military coup against the Bustamante government. In 1949 an Estanco Nacional de la Coca (ENACO) was established with the exclusive rights to export coca. After the requested United Nations Mission (the UN Commission of Enquiry on the Coca Leaf) was programmed to arrive in Lima in September 1949, the government established a Peruvian Commission for the Study of the Coca Problem to collaborate with the UN Commission (ibid, 68-70), and appointed Dr. Monge to head it. The government followed attempts to modernize the cocaine industry, and "by late 1950 the State monopoly was finally online, endorsed by the UN and Article IV of the 1931 Geneva Manufacturing Convention. Peru was finally making genuine crystal hydrochloride, in a run-down government shop, [...] which could legally export around the globe" (ibid, 71). By 1955, ENACO reported exports between 500-600 kilos, about 1/5 of its exports in 1943 and only 5% of its exports at the turn

---

[62] In his novel "*la serpiente de oro* characterized the Indian use of the leaf as representing a euphoric escape from the miseries of oppressive sierra life. This same anti-coca position was more precisely and emphatically articulated in his subsequent novel *El mundo es ancho y ajeno*" (Gagliano, 1994, 138).

[63] American Popular Revolutionary Alliance.

of the century. ENACO was a money-losing proposition, and it closed soon after (ibid, 71).[64]

2.6.2 The Report of The 1950 UN Commission of Enquire on The Coca Leaf

The purpose of the mission requested by President Bustamante apparently was misunderstood by the United Nations, "[t]he Peruvian request sent to the United Nations called for an *'estudio científico en el terreno'*" (Monge Medrano, 1950),[65] which means a scientific in situ study. Still, the interpreters at the United Nations translated into a "field survey."[66] This misunderstanding led to a mission that disappointed the leading group that sold the mission's idea to President Bustamante (Motta-Ochoa, 2018, 3). However, "the new hard-line president Odría soon found a vociferous ally in Anslinger" (Gootenberg, 2008, 233). Odría would not have objected to a "field survey" over Carlos Monge's vision "of a set of rigorous laboratory experiments carried out by a team of international scientists in laboratories located in the Andean highlands" as Warren (2018, 9) asserts that was the original purpose of the study. Besides, "further hidden was Anslinger spying and prying to push the upcoming coca mission in a prohibitionist direction. It was not difficult, for his old friend Howard B. Fonda [...] headed the group, mailing 'dear Harry' letters replete with tip-offs for locating illegal factories of cocaine" (Gootenberg, 2008, 237).

The commission was made of two experts in administrative questions and international narcotics control and two experts on

---

[64] ENACO was reopened as Empresa Nacional de la Coca in 1978 during the military government of general Francisco Morales Bermudez. It oversees the legal coca market for traditional uses in the country (author's note).
[65] Cited by Warren (2018, 9).
[66] Until the works of Motta-Ochoa (2018) and Warren (2018), "field survey" was accepted in the English literature as the purpose of the Bustamante request.

medical questions.[67] The Bolivian government also supported the Commission, and it visited Peru and Bolivia from September 11 to December 3, 1949. The Commission was headed by Mr. Fonda, that as noted, was close to Mr. Anslinger

The Mission appeared to have underestimated the importance of the coca debate going on among Peruvian scientists, politicians, and intellectuals: "[o]ne camp saw coca as a cause of poor health, limited mental capacity, and widespread degeneration among indigenous people, while another saw it as a relatively benign, unique, and healthy form of adaptation to the demands of life at high altitude for a population associated closely with nature. Ironically, despite the forms of implicit racism evident in both positions, each camp saw itself as a defender of Indigenous people, interested in their uplift through scientific research and government intervention" (Warren, 2018, 3).

The mission landed on the wrong foot. The day of his arrival, Mr. Fonda gave an interview to the leading newspaper of the country, and "when asked whether he believed that coca chewing was harmful to the health of highland Indigenous people, Fonda emphatically responded that chewing the leaves on a daily basis not only harmed their health 'but is also the cause of racial degeneration in many population nuclei, and of the decline that many indigenous and even mestizo inhabitants visibly exhibit in certain zones of Peru and Bolivia' (El Comercio de Lima, 1949)".[68] Even though the Mission's

---

[67] Mr. Howard B. Fonda (United States of America), president of the commission. Senior vice-president and director of Burroughs Wellcome and Co; vice-president and director of the American Pharmaceutical Manufacturers' Association; Mr. Jean-Philippe Razet (France). Chief Inspector of the Ministry of Agriculture of France; director of the Narcotics Bureau of France for twenty years; Professor Frederic Verzar (Hungary), MD, Professor of Physiology, former Rector and Dean of the Medical Faculty of Debreczen University. Dr. Marcel Alfred Graxier-Doyeaux. Professor of Pharmacology, Central University of Venezuela; permanent member and rapporteur of the Board for the Revision of Pharmaceutical Specialties, Ministry of Health and Social Assistance.

[68] "Llegada de la Comisión de las Naciones Unidas que estudiará el problema de la coca", *El Comercio* (Lima, Perú), September 12, 1949. Cited by Warren (2018, 3).

final position was quite different, it gave the impression that it had arrived with strong preconceptions about the problem at hand. Perhaps unintendedly, the Mission ended being an active actor in the national coca debate in Peru.

The Mission's schedule was very intense. It had contacts with the central authorities in both countries, the liaison officials appointed by those governments, local, civic, and military authorities, the medical profession, pharmacists and academics, coca leaf producers and in Bolivia with the SPY, religious authorities and missionaries, representatives of groups interested in the coca-leaf problem, and their counterpart Peruvian Commission. It also participated in conferences and in an international symposium on high-altitude biology. The Mission traveled extensively, mainly to coca growing and coca using regions of both countries.

The Mission's report was very comprehensive. This explains the characteristics of the Quichua and Aymara -the main Amerindian ethnic groups of both countries-, their hygienic conditions, housing, education, access to medical care and nutrition, the state of nutrition research in both countries, and the role of foreign assistance. It did extensive work on coca and coca chewing issues: consumption methods, quantities of coca chewed and cocaine absorbed daily and during chewing, and alkalis use to increase the cocaine extraction. It studied the effects of chewing, including cocaine concentration in the blood, the detoxification and excretion of cocaine; the action of cocaine, coca leaf, and fatigue; hunger and sensitivity; physical alterations on blood circulation, respiratory alterations of mucous membranes, skin, and teeth, physical alterations, especially in chronic abuse of coca-leaf chewing; race degeneration, cretinism, growth, epilepsy, liver diseases, alcoholism. It also discussed whether coca-leaf chewing was a habit or an addiction.

Attempting to deal with the Peruvian policy debates, the Mission devoted a chapter to the connection between coca-leaf chewing and life at high altitudes that covered medico-biological research and the general physiological conditions of the high Andean natives compared with the acclimatized white man. The topics studied were fertility, changed pharmacological excitability, the adaptation of the Andean man to high altitude, and coca's role in that adaptation.

The Mission explored the relationship between coca chewing and the living conditions of miners and agriculture workers. It explored the labor conditions, some prevailing beliefs like workers' refusal to work unless given coca, the Amerindians' customs regarding holiday celebrations, deaths, agricultural tasks, illnesses, and magical practices.

The Mission also sought to analyze the social and economic aspects of coca-leaf chewing and was shocked by the appalling living conditions of the Amerindians, identified harmful social effects of coca chewing, and highlighted some economic ones such as a short-term increase in the capacity to work, but significantly lower long-term productivity generated by lack of concentration and increases in work accidents.

The Mission enquired about the systems used to cultivate coca, the relevant labor laws, the value of the coca output, the possibility to find substitution crops, and set some principles on which the limitation of coca-leaf production and the control of its distribution might be based. It had several important conclusions:

- It acknowledged the complexity of the coca chewing issue that must be considered not as an isolated phenomenon but because of the social and economic conditions under which large sections of Peru and Bolivia's population were living.
- It recognized that cocaine makes coca chewing risky, but "it does not at present appear that the chewing of the coca leaf can be regarded as a drug addiction in the medical sense." (United Nations, 1950, 93)

This conclusion was based on the definition of addiction of WHO's Expert Committee on Drugs Liable to Produce Addiction (WHO, 1950, 6-7):

> *Definition of drug addiction.*
> Having considered the request of the Commission on Narcotic Drugs, the committee drafted the following definition of 'drug addiction':
> Drug addiction is a state of periodic or chronic intoxication that is detrimental to the individual and society, produced by the repeated consumption of a drug (natural or synthetic). Its characteristics include:
> (1) An overpowering desire or need (compulsion) to continue taking the drug and to obtain it by any means;
> (2) A tendency to increase the dose;
> (3) A psychic (psychological) and sometimes a physical dependence on the effects of the drug.

Following the definition, the Commission observed that "coca-leaf chewing is not an addiction (toxicomania) but a habit. It may, however, in some individuals, become an addiction, but generally it can be given up like other habits" (United Nations, 1950, 93). The Commission found many harmful effects of coca chewing:

> (1) It inhibits the sensation of hunger and thus maintains, by a vicious circle, a constant state of malnutrition.
> (2) It induces in the individual undesirable changes of an intellectual and moral character. This is especially clear in exceptional cases, and it is much discussed how far this is general. It certainly hinders the chewer's chances of obtaining a higher social standard.

(3) It reduces the economic yield of productive work, and therefore maintains a low economic standard of life (ibid, 93).

The Commission recognized that coca has many vitamins, but "it would by no means be advisable to supply these vitamins in the form of coca-leaf chewing, i.e., together with the toxic substance, cocaine. In no way can the chewing of coca leaves, therefore, be regarded as a substitute for an adequate diet" (United Nations, 1950, 94). It dismissed the need for coca chewing at high altitudes for both natives and non-natives because they could not find evidence that the natives had developed a different human phenotype. It argued that "the solution of the problem involves two fundamental and parallel aspects: first, the need for improving the living conditions of the population amongst which chewing is a general habit, and secondly, the need for initiating simultaneously a governmental policy to limit the production of coca leaf, to control its distribution and eradicate the practice of chewing it" (ibid, 94). It found that coca chewing can be eradicated if the conditions under which it originated are suitably modified, but "in view of the social and economic nature of the factors determining coca-leaf chewing, an immediate and radical suppression of the habit is not possible. Instead of solving the problem, such a suppression would only aggravate the existing situation. Consequently, the Commission envisages only a gradual suppression of the habit, that is, a process which, while taking into account the complexity of the problem, should not be so long as to permit the harmful continuation of the habit nor so short as to damage the economic interests involved" (ibid, 94).

Interestingly, it was optimistic about eliminating coca chewing and quickly finding viable substitute crops that would yield equal or better income to the peasants (United Nations, 1950, 88). Indeed, the vast future profits of the international cocaine markets were something that nobody imagined.

2.6.3 Some Characteristics of the Report

The report did not satisfy many important stakeholders. Dr. Monge was highly disappointed and produced a controversial rebuttal (Comisión Peruana para el Estudio del Problema de la Coca, 1951). He argued that most of the evidence used by the United Nations report was impressionistic and did not meet the required scientific criteria to derive solid conclusions. He also defended his positions about high altitude medicine and medical coca uses. It should be noted that the report failed to consider the issue of non-Western medicine or *quasi-medical* coca uses, which implicitly were considered illegitimate.

The confronting sides interpreted the consequences of the anorectic effects of coca chewing in the Peruvian coca debate in two contradictory ways. Some argued that the extreme poverty of many Amerindians that did not have enough to eat and coca chewing helped them feel less hungry. Others argued that the hunger inhibiting effect led people to avoid food and generated malnutrition. Of course, both positions may have reflected different situations that required different solutions.

Although the report was ambivalent, it tried to support both sides. The Mission agreed that there was a need to eliminate coca chewing because it contributed to malnutrition upset the former group. But the Mission recognized the importance of social issues as determinants of the coca chewing habit. It concluded that coca chewing was not a typical addiction, emphasized the poor living conditions of the Amerindians as the main reason they chewed coca, and proposed a gradual decline in that habit. These findings and recommendations upset both Anslinger, who wanted a quick elimination of coca, and those Peruvians that considered coca a principal obstacle to the country's economic development. The conclusion that increases in nutrition would eliminate coca chewing and that coca itself was not responsible for the "degeneration" of the Amerindian race was also unsatisfactory to that group of Peruvians.

The goal to eliminate coca chewing, even if it was a gradual process, disappointed the main powerful Bolivian coca lobby: "In 1949, Bolivia lent its cooperation to the UN tour, adopting an official stance to 'concur' with any Peruvian objections, presumably because of Peru's established coca science. Yet behind the scenes, the coca-growing SPY renewed its decades-long protest 'that Coca is Not a Narcotic.' This time, however, Bolivia's Foreign Ministry did not relay the SPY's vital message to the UN itself" (Gootenberg, 2008, 239).

The mission met with the SPY and peasant groups that grew coca. Still, the report did not consider the traditional uses in religious and social rituals and festivities in ways analogous to alcohol and tobacco in the Western world. As Gootenberg (2008, 238) points out, "the UN had yet to discover 'culture' (indigenous or otherwise) as an obstacle to or an ally in its vision." Most coca users were illiterate and not organized. Therefore, the Mission could not interact effectively with them, and its report did not recognize the role that coca chewing had in the Indian communities as a symbol of identity and as an instrument of social cohesion. This gap left out an important stakeholder group.

The report was written right after the end of WWII, when policymakers were confident in implementing policies. The goal to eliminate coca chewing as part of a development goal to incorporate Amerindians into the modern age and find agricultural products to substitute coca plantings seemed reasonable to policymakers, experts, and academics. Besides, illegal cocaine markets were small, existed in a few countries, and nobody could have predicted the growth of cocaine demand that started around 1970. Thus, the report's optimistic conclusions can be considered normal or expected in the early postwar.

2.7 THE END OF THE LEAGUE OF NATIONS AND THE 1948 AND 1953 PROTOCOLS

During the years leading to WWII, international tensions were remarkably high, and drug issues lost importance in the countries' political agenda that had promoted the IDCS. Drugs became significant only when they were related to national security. Governments that foresaw a new war sought to stock enough morphine, heroin, and cocaine for medical uses and hemp to supply mainly their need for marine ropes. The United States promoted production for those purposes, including experiments with coca plantings in Puerto Rico (McAllister, 2000, 130-131).

The war strengthened Anslinger's hand, who continued promoting a firm supply control policy. He decided where to purchase morphine and cocaine and pressured countries to comply with the conventions.

> During 1940, he banned exports[69] to Mexico until authorities suspended an experimental ambulatory treatment program that involved the free distribution of morphine to registered addicts. When Chile commenced domestic opium production in 1942, the Commissioner embargoed drug exports and cajoled Britain into similar action. Anslinger pressured pharmaceutical giant Hoffmann-LaRoche to ensure that its Argentinian subsidiary did not sell medicines to Axis powers or their intermediaries (McAllister, 2000, 145).

During the war, the availability of opium and its derived pain killers were the main psychoactive drug issue for the involved countries. The non-medical use of marijuana and cocaine was not a

---

[69] Of controlled drugs (author's note).

relevant problem in North America, Europe, or China and did not attract the attention of policymakers.

The United States had always been the leading supporter of the drug organs of the League of Nations, even though it was not a League member, and during WWII financed the move of those organs to New York, Princeton, and Washington D.C. to protect the IDCS. The end of the war de facto ended the League, but the United States continued funding the operation of its drug organs. A few countries continued submitting estimates, and at least formally, the IDCS remained in operation.[70]

The war weakened Germany and other European countries with significant pharmaceutical interests who opposed the American drive for more restrictive policies. At the same time, Anslinger developed a staff of professionals who were convinced of the benefits of strongly prohibitionist policies and were ready to promote that policy agenda. The first task was to reorganize and strengthen the IDCS, a goal quickly achieved by the Lake Success Protocol, signed on December 16, 1946, that entered into force in October 1947. This Protocol placed the IDCS under the Economic and Social Council (ECOSOC) and established the Commission of Narcotic Drugs (CND) as the drug policy-making organism, substituting the OAC. The DSB and PCOB, now under the United Nations, continued overseeing the conventions' compliance, and the Opium Section functions of collecting estimates of crops and drug production were taken over by a new Division of Narcotic Drugs (DND) (Sinha, 2001, 17; UNODC, 2008, 137).

It was the first UN protocol after establishing the organizational structure and finances of the UN, and it also preceded the Universal Declaration of Human Rights. At the beginning of the Cold War, it was easier to arrive at an international agreement about drugs than about other international issues (Thoumi, 2015, 243).

---

[70] These organs were all legally created by the international conventions that did not disappear when the League of Nations did. The conventions were treaties among countries that continued to be legally binding.

Despite the quick success in creating a drug control structure in the United Nations, there were frictions among individual countries and groups of them regarding the controls' goals, means, and other characteristics. These frictions "derived from a triangulation of three international drug control blocs: control advocate states, led by the US; producing states and their noninterventionist allies, led by Turkey and the Soviet Union; and moderate manufacturing and consuming countries, led by the UK. In this triangulation process, the UK and US remained the lead international actors and represented the two core policy strands within the system: regulation and prohibition respectively" (Collins, 2015, 3).

The development of pain killers during the 1930s and 1940s produced new substances that required international control. These synthetic drugs caused fears of a "drug revolution" generated by substances not covered by the drug conventions, which would be used as substitutes for the existing drugs (ibid, 178-179).

These changes moved the 1948 CND to draft "a separate agreement ('protocol') that required states to submit the new substances to the same estimates-of-need and statistical reporting provisions that applied to existing opium-based narcotics. The DSB and PCOB could then oversee the synthetic narcotics trade in the established manner. The 1948 Synthetic Narcotics Protocol quickly gained wide acceptance, coming into force only a year later. [...] The application of the 1948 Protocol meant the placing of 14 new substances under international control by 1951 and a further six by 1954" (UNODC, 2008, 197).

In the view of many UN staff and CND members, the IDCS was very cumbersome and difficult to manage. It was made up of eight international treaties that were subscribed by different nations, and not all the important stakeholder countries had signed and ratified all the treaties. Besides, the functions of the different control organs were not always precise.

The United States, under Anslinger's leadership, considered that the existing conventions and protocols were not restrictive enough. During the war, the US had continued seeking its goal to limit drug production, trade, and use to *medical and scientific purposes*: "in 1943, the US administration issued a resolution to end all opium smoking in the areas liberated from Japan, which also included previous colonies and territories controlled by various European countries. Further, the US undertook, as of the late 1940s, new initiatives to finally prohibit the production and use of opium for other than medical and scientific needs" (UNODC, 2008, 197).

The US also opposed *quasi-medical uses* of opium. It wanted to limit opium production to very few countries to facilitate controls, a measure opposed by those that feared being excluded from a profitable industry. Right after the war, "[t]he US saw Japan[71] as the perfect opportunity to implement its strict prohibitionist model. Further, the US prosecuted Japan's violations of the narcotics conventions as war crimes and thereby as a precedent to dissuade other countries from flouting international narcotics laws. US control advocates also found an important ally in Japan with General MacArthur" (Collins, 2015, 144).[72]

However, the United Kingdom doubted that more restrictive policies could be implemented successfully, advocated less restrictive policy alternatives, and "maintained an essentially pragmatic attitude to its colonies underpinned by a willingness to compromise with local needs" (ibid, 144).

Following its plan, the US started to draft a "Single Convention" and presented the idea at the 1948 CND meeting. The goal was to consolidate all previous norms into one treaty and limit controlled drug use to *medical and scientific purposes*. The CND recommended this measure, and in 1948 ECOSOC moved to start a process to draft a new convention based on that principle (McAllister,

---

[71] Under American occupation (author's note).
[72] See also McAllister, 2000, chapter 6.

2000, 204, UNODC, 2008, 197, Collins, 2015, 180). China feared a challenging and lengthy process to elaborate a draft of the convention. During the CND, the "Chinese representative suggested, as an intermediate measure, negotiating an interim agreement limiting opium production" (McAllister, 2000, 172). The CND approved a feasibility study for that project by one vote "over the objections of the British, Canadians, and Americans, who wished to concentrate in the long-term project" (ibid, 172).

As usual, before the 1960s, the main drug issues were related to opium and its derivatives and included:[73]

- The legal distribution of opium and its derivatives markets among the several producing countries. It was a prime issue for poppy-growing and drug manufacturing countries.[74]
- The allowed uses of those substances.
- The definition of any legitimate quasi-medical uses.
- Controls of production, trade, and use in the established legitimate markets.
- The controls to be applied to the markets that supply the demand for illegitimate uses of opium and opium-based products.

Leon Steinig, the director of the CND (1946-1952), followed the Chinese suggestion and proposed in 1949 an *international opium monopoly* under the UN as a solution to control the opium market. This proposal went beyond establishing a monopoly. It was a monopsony-monopoly that would buy all opium from producing countries and create a single distribution network. This idea reflected the confidence in economic planning prevalent in many political circles during the mid-20th century. Steinig underestimated the complexity of such an endeavor. After conflicting studies and debates

---

[73] Indeed, at that time the directorship of the CND was jokingly referred to as the Poppy Throne (McAllister, 2000, 176).
[74] At the time, the pharmaceutical boom of the second half of the 20th century was just beginning, and opiates were a main revenue source for the drug industry.

and several meetings to discuss prices and production quotas, reality set in, and the proposal was rejected at the 1951 CND session (McAllister, 2000, 172-179, Collins, 2015, 206).

Other countries had different interests. At the end of WWII, the US, the USSR, France, and the UK agreed about Germany's controlled drugs supply and use. After the 1950 U.N. Commission of Enquire on the Coca Leaf, reviewed above, recommended eliminating the traditional coca chewing practice in Bolivia and Peru, they had to confront pressures to control coca supply and its possible cocaine manufacture. The USSR was wary of any policy considered as foreign intervention or restriction in their domestic affairs. Turkey and Iran wanted to protect their opium crops that were important revenue sources for the government. Opium production in China grew in an environment where the weak government control of significant parts of the territory had induced an official tolerance of opium production in areas where the government needed the warlords' support to confront the Communist challenge. Tolerance was so accepted that when the Communist Party took over, it confiscated 500 kilograms of opium that a British citizen had obtained during the previous regime and tried to sell them in the international market. At the same time, Great Britain had to cope with opium production in its colonies and decolonization's consequences on opium markets (Walker III, 1991, chapters 7 and 8; Collins, 2015, chapter 6).

Different interests and goals led to a sharp confrontation between the United States and China in the 1950 CND. Anslinger argued that there was an international conspiracy to flood the opium market. Based heavily and uncritically on Nationalist Chinese propaganda, claimed that: "Opium production and trade have formed an essential part of the Chinese Communists economic program. Thus, during the early 30's poppy cultivation and opium smoking were encouraged. On the other hand, the Chinese

Nationalist Government made strenuous efforts to suppress opium traffic and smoking[75]" (Collins, 2015, 198).

These negotiations took place in a context of high international tensions as the Korean War (25 June 1950 – 27 July 1953) continued. The United States and United Nations troops supported the South. The USSR and China the North.

Not surprisingly, drug issues were difficult to discuss among country delegations that distrusted each other and represented countries engaged in violent confrontations on other fronts. In this environment, "Anslinger used the 1952 CND Session to castigate the PRC,[76] prompting a furious response from the Soviet Delegate, who described Anslinger's statement as 'a planned slander and completely unfounded'. The Soviet Delegate then raised US 'aggression' in Korea. Anslinger threatened to call a 'point of order,' and the session descended into bickering.[77] Afterwards the USSR delegate circulated a PRC statement refuting Anslinger's claims and arguing the PRC had pursued strict prohibition. Infuriated, Anslinger spent the next ten months planning a detailed rebuttal for the 1953 CND Session" (ibid, 198-199).

In the following CND, "Anslinger labeled the PRC statement of the previous year 'a diatribe of abuse' and claimed: 'The United States is a target of Communist China to be regularly supplied with dollar-earning, health, and morale-devastating heroin. According to reliable information, the financial and economic organs of Red China's Central Regime met behind closed doors in Peiping in early December and decided to expand sales activities abroad this year,

---

[75] Report: 'Informational on Opium Production and Traffic by the Chinese Communists', 18 November 1950, FBNA/ACC170-74-5/Box121/File1230-1, UN 5th Session #4 (1950-1).

[76] Peoples Republic of China (author's note).

[77] Remarks of Soviet Representative on CND, 5 May 1952, FBNA/ACC170-74-5/Box122/File1230-1, UN 7th Session #1 (1952).

primarily in Japan, Southeast Asian countries, and the United States[78]"" (ibid, 240).

This political climate was not conducive to a successful conference that would consolidate the IDCS and produce a Single Convention and induced Anslinger to advance his agenda, convening a new Opium Protocol in response to the Chinese and Southeast Asian opium problems.

The Protocol for Limiting and Regulating the Cultivation of the Poppy Plant, the Production of, International and Wholesale Trade in and Use of Opium, generally known as the 1953 Opium Protocol,[79] "contained the most stringent drug-control provisions yet embodied in international law. The agreement extended to raw opium the reporting requirements placed on manufactured drugs under the 1931 treaty. Aimed primarily at producing states, signatories would submit to the DSB estimates concerning the amount of opium planted, harvested, consumed domestically, exported, and stockpiled. Year-end statistics would be reported to the PCOB. The treaty also gave the Board responsibility for making inquiries into discrepancies, conducting inspections, and imposing embargoes. As with earlier treaties, the Board was empowered to fix estimates and could take investigatory and punitive action even concerning states that were not a party to the Protocol. In a victory for Anslinger, symbolic of a general trend, the Protocol also stipulated that opium use should be restricted to medical and scientific needs. Although signatories were allowed a fifteen-year grace period before the provision had to be enforced, the treaty nevertheless shattered the 'quasi-medical use barrier' for the first time" (McAllister, 2000, 181).[80]

The 1953 Opium Protocol also required countries to establish a government agency to regulate the opium market and

---

[78] Anslinger Remarks, 8th Session CND, April 1953, FBNA/ACC170-74-5/Box122/File1230-1, UN 8th Session (1953).
[79] Available at https://www.unodc.org/unodc/en/data-and-analysis/bulletin/bulletin_1953-01-01_3_page015.html
[80] This paragraph was also published almost verbatim in UNDCP (2008, 198).

ensure compliance. Other measures gave Bulgaria, Greece, India, Iran, Turkey, the USSR, and Yugoslavia a monopoly on the licit sale of opium and established some production limits to each of these countries (UNODC, 2008, 198). However, the 1953 Opium Protocol was ratified very slowly by the signing countries and entered into force only in July 1963, one and a half years before the entering into force of the Single Convention that superseded it.

The 1953 Opium Protocol's article 2 about the use of opium reads: "The Parties shall limit the use of opium exclusively to medical and scientific needs." It is the only mention about drug use made in the protocol that is silent about how to deal with opium use and opium addicts and did not include a requirement to treat addicts in "closed institutional" quarters and eliminate ambulatory treatment, another of Anslinger's project. The rest of the Protocol deals with the production and markets of opium. The Protocol supports a drug control strategy based on supply control at the source. Article 14 compels the Parties to "adopt all legislative and administrative measures necessary for the purpose of making fully effective the provisions of this Protocol."

2.8 THE SINGLE CONVENTION ON NARCOTIC DRUGS OF 1961

2.8.1 The Road to the Drafting and Enactment of the Convention

The 1953 Opium Protocol did not satisfy some of the main stakeholders, for whom it was a temporary measure before the Single Convention could be enacted, and a "protracted battle ensued between shifting coalitions of governments and non-state actors" (McAllister, 2000, 186).

A significant conflict arose between the United States and British positions: "[t]he US had clear goals for the Single Convention: incorporate the 1953 Protocol provisions around opium; extend strong production controls to coca and cannabis; expand the mandate of the proposed INCB and to advocate for a strict 'closed institutional' model for treating drug addiction.[81] The UK wanted none of those things and doubted the feasibility of the entire Single Convention project. However, faced with the 1953 Opium Protocol as their alternative, the UK threw its weight behind driving the Single Convention forward in a manner commensurate with their interests and goals" (Collins, 2015, 224).

As noted above, the drug discussions were not independent of the international tensions of the cold war. The United States had several more critical international issues, leading to conflicts between Anslinger and the State Department that weakened the American position at the CND. China was a charter member of the United Nations. Still, after the Communist revolution of 1949, the Nationalist government, led by Chiang Kai-Shek, remained representing China in the UN until October 25, 1971. This was a problem for the implementation of the Opium Protocol because "unwilling to risk the ire of Anslinger, the PCOB acquiesced in an absurd situation by accepting statistics submitted by Taiwan for the whole country" (McAllister, 2000, 188).

The growth of synthetic drugs also generated conflicts. Manufacturing countries argued that those drugs did not require international controls, while other countries, like Turkey, insisted on them. "Only the weight of evidence presented by the WHO and others eventually forced western industrialized states to concede that psychotropics might indeed present a hazard. Nevertheless, their representatives watered-down CND resolutions to the point of impotence" (McAllister, 2000, 201-202).[82]

The 1953 Opium Protocol divided the legal production of opium among seven countries: Bulgaria, Greece, India, Iran, Turkey,

---

[81] 713 US Del Position Paper, 9th Session CND, undated, FBNA/ACC170-74-5/Box122/File1230-1, UN 9th Session #1 (1953).

[82] France, however, supported strong controls for psychotropics because at the time there was no such industry in the country (McAllister, 2000, 308).

the USSR, and Yugoslavia. However, Afghanistan insisted on a quota in the Single Convention, which required diminishing those of other countries.

These issues illustrate some of the difficulties encountered in arriving at an acceptable draft of the Single Convention at the CND. Indeed, before convening a Plenipotentiary Conference to produce a Convention, it was necessary to spend several years discussing three successive convention drafts. The result was a compromise that did not meet the hopes of many actors. This is not surprising for an international agreement about an issue that raises strong emotions, influenced by religious and cultural beliefs and important economic interests.

In the end, despite limiting all controlled psychoactive drug uses to *medical and scientific purposes*, most of the rest of Anslinger's agenda was not adopted by the treaty. For example, the strictest controls over agricultural production introduced in the 1953 Opium Protocol not only were not extended to other crops but were eliminated. Despite support from the USSR, the proposal to require the "closed institutional" treatment of addicts was rejected (ibid, 209-210).

The preamble of the 1961 Single Convention on Narcotic Drugs states that the Convention was enacted because the Parties were "Concerned with the health and welfare of mankind, (or with the physical and moral health of humankind" as it reads in the official French and Spanish versions of the Convention). However, in the earlier treaties (except the 1931 Convention for the Suppression of the Illicit Traffic in Dangerous Drugs), the purpose was always to limit drug use to medical and scientific purposes as asserted in the Commentary to the 1961 Single Convention on Narcotic Drugs mentioned above: "The object of the international narcotics system is to limit exclusively to medical and scientific purposes the trade in and use of controlled drugs" (United Nations, 1973, 110). None of the earlier treaties needed to justify this object.

The ratification of the Single Convention was quick and entered into force on December 13, 1964, after 61 countries had ratified it. The United States, frustrated with the outcome, did not ratify it until three and a half years later, on May 25, 1967.[83]

2.8.2 The Main Achievements of the Single Convention According to UNODC

The 2008 World Drug Report, celebrating the 100th anniversary of the Shanghai Commission, devotes fifty pages to the history and development of the IDCS. The following paragraphs summarize the major advances and accomplishments of the 1961 Convention according to UNODC (2008, 198-200):

It consolidated and simplified the IDCS into a Single Convention and provided definitions of the substances under control. It also established the organizational infrastructure for the operations of the international drug control bodies, the reporting obligations of the State Members regarding the production, manufacture, trade, and consumption of controlled substances, and the actions to be taken against illicit traffic and penal provisions.

Most importantly, the primary objective of the convention, limiting the uses of controlled substances to "*medical and scientific purposes,*" was achieved.

The estimates, statistics, and import and export authorizations systems remained and the provisions for controlling the manufacture of narcotic drugs.

The PCOB and the DSB were joined and became the International Narcotics Control Board (INCB). Some administrative duties were consolidated and simplified, but there was no consensus

---

[83]https://treaties.un.org/pages/ViewDetails.aspx?src=TREATY&mtdsg_no=VI-15&chapter=6&clang=_en. The Civil Rights Act enacted on July 2, 1964, contributed to change the American position about involuntary hospitalization and/or treatment. However, it was only in 1975 when the U.S. Supreme court ruled in O'Connor v. Donaldson that those practices violated an individual's human rights.

about merging the CND with the secretariat of the INCB that remained separate.

The existing controls to opium production were extended to the production of poppy straw,[84] the coca leaf, and cannabis. These controls included the obligation to create national agencies for opium, coca, and, if applicable, for cannabis for countries deciding to produce these crops to cover their medical and scientific needs. Such agencies were required to:
- designate the areas in which the cultivation could take place.
- allow only licensed cultivators to engage in such cultivation.
- take charge of importing, exporting, wholesale trading, and maintaining stocks.

The Single Convention requires that production, of whatever scheduled substance, could only take place under certain conditions and only for as long as there was a legitimate medical or scientific use for such drugs.

The Convention prohibited the nonmedicinal recreational practices of opium smoking, opium eating, coca-leaf chewing, and the smoking and other human bodily consumption of cannabis resin and cannabis herb. At the same time, it enabled countries to opt for a transition period to abolish these practices. For instance, under the Convention, only persons officially registered as addicts by the competent authorities in 1964 were permitted to continue smoking opium. Countries also committed themselves to abolishing the quasi-medical use of opium within 15 years after the Conventions' ratification (by 12 December 1979) and the practices of coca leaf chewing and the use of cannabis within 25 years (by 12 December 1989).

The *Penal Provisions* were laid down in Article 36, paragraph 1 (a) that states: "Subject to its constitutional limitations, each Party

---

[84] Poppy straw is a mechanical process that bypasses the extraction of opium from poppy plants in the process to produce morphine and other opioids.

shall adopt such measures as will ensure that cultivation, production, manufacture, extraction, preparation, possession, offering, offering for sale, distribution, purchase, sale, delivery on any terms whatsoever, brokerage, dispatch, dispatch in transit, transport, importation and exportation of drugs contrary to the provisions of this Convention, and any other action which in the opinion of such Party may be contrary to the provisions of this Convention, shall be punishable offences when committed intentionally and that serious offences shall be liable to adequate punishment particularly by imprisonment or other penalties of deprivation of liberty."[85]

It is notable that Article 36 mentions *possession* but does not say anything about sanctions for possession for personal use. However, the Commentary to the Convention (United Nations, 1973, 428) asserts that: "the term 'possession' [...] does not include possession for personal consumption, and that in any event Parties which do not share that view need not consider possession for personal consumption [...] to be a 'serious' offence punishable by imprisonment or other penalties of deprivation of liberty".

Since the Commentary is not binding, this should be interpreted only as a guideline that the CND and the INCB have accepted. Thus, the Single Convention is tough on illegal production and trafficking. Still, it gives governments a high degree of flexibility in dealing with their local drug consumption problems, as long as the Parties remain committed to the general obligation spelled out in Article 4: "to take such legislative and administrative measures as may be necessary: [...] Subject to the provisions of this Convention, to limit exclusively to medical and scientific purposes [...] (the) use and possession of drugs" (UNODC, 2008, 199).

The Single Convention required State Members to assist their drug addicts with medical treatment and rehabilitation. However, the 1972 amendment to the Single Convention weakened this

---

[85] The Convention also establishes criteria for extraditions of those accused of drug crimes (author's note)

requirement. The original wording of Article 38, paragraph 1 was: "The Parties shall give special attention to the provision of facilities for the medical treatment, care, and rehabilitation of drug addicts." But the amended one reads: "The Parties shall give special attention to and take all practicable measures for the prevention of abuse of drugs and for the early identification, treatment, education, after-care, rehabilitation and social reintegration of the persons involved and shall co-ordinate their efforts to these ends." Today the requirement only applies when it is practical to do so.

To summarize, UNODC considered that the 1961 Single Convention achieved most goals proposed by those promoting the IDCS. This supports the assertion that the Convention's purpose was to limit human drug uses to "*medical and scientific purposes.*"

CHAPTER THREE: THE CONVENTIONS THAT ROUNDED UP THE IDCS AND THE IDCS ORGANS

3.1 THE CONVENTION ON PSYCHOTROPIC SUBSTANCES OF 1971

During the 1960s, there were many changes in psychoactive drug use. In the United States, the Vietnam war promoted a substantial increase in the use of opium, its derivatives, and other drugs among soldiers. Drug use prevalence within this group may have reached 25% (UNODC, 2008, 200). This increase was due to the need to calm pain from combat injuries, but more importantly, from growing opposition to a war that many Americans considered unjustified. Frustrated soldiers demanded drugs to escape the war reality. In the United States, many started to question the American way of life. Many young people reacted by challenging the traditional American values toward sex, racial segregation, and consumerism as a symbol of success.

Psychoactive drug use grew as a protest and an expression of rebellion against the establishment. Marijuana use became generalized among the youth, and many experimented with hallucinogenic drugs like LSD and other synthetic drugs: "a national survey in 1971 revealed that 24 million Americans used cannabis at some point in their lifetimes.[86] The number of heroin addicts was estimated to have risen from about 50,000 in 1960 to roughly half a million by 1970. In addition to ongoing diversions of opium from licit producers, illegal opiate production also increased strongly in South-East Asia, notably in Myanmar. Starting in the early 1970s, Myanmar became the world's largest supplier of illicit opiates for two decades. Much of the transformation of Myanmar's opium into heroin took place in neighbouring Thailand, although clandestine heroin laboratories also appeared in Myanmar and Laos" (ibid, 200).

---

[86] That was 11.6% of the country's total population (author's note).

Other countries also experienced significant growth in drug use: "after World War II, Japan suffered a major epidemic of methamphetamine abuse, due to the distribution of wartime stocks. This problem was addressed by a major market crack-down in 1954 and the passage of very strict legislation. In Europe, amphetamine use had become particularly widespread in Sweden and other Scandinavian countries, as well as in the UK, in the post-war years. A growing methamphetamine problem was also reported from the USA in the 1960s. Many of these drug problems initially appeared to have been regionally isolated phenomena, but a general upward trend in the use of synthetic drugs was seen globally" (ibid, 201).

On July 14, 1969, President Nixon sent a written message to Congress. He declared: "Within the last decade, the abuse of drugs has grown from essentially a local police problem into a serious national threat to the personal health and safety of millions of people Americans." Two years later, on June 17, 1971, President Nixon, with his newly appointed drug authority at his side, declared drug abuse "public enemy number one." He continued, "it is necessary to wage a new, all-out offensive" (Richard Nixon Foundation, 2016). The press interpreted it as a "declaration of war on drugs," a term he used later and became associated with him.[87]

These developments motivated the 1971 Convention on Psychotropic Drugs. Almost all the substances controlled by this Convention are synthetic drugs produced by the pharmaceutical industry. In contrast to the Single Convention that was motivated by a simple belief in the prohibition of non-medical psychoactive drug uses as the fundamental drug control policy, the new treaties were reactive to the growth of global illegal drug markets that occurred despite that prohibition.

The 1971 Convention followed the model of the 1961 Single Convention, and many of its features are similar:

---

[87] For example, in the movie *The House I live in* (2012) directed by Eugene Jarecki there is a short from a later Nixon speech, in which he declares a "war against all drugs".

CND/INCB administrative authority, schedules distinguishing levels of control for different drugs, mandatory transaction documentation and licensing, an import/export control system, illicit trafficking, and penal provisions. Although a light reading may reveal minor difference between the two Conventions, they are extremely different. The Psychotropics Convention imposes significantly weaker controls. The reason for this becomes evident when the positions of the negotiating stakeholders are revealed and selected parts of the two treaties are carefully compared.[88] The overwhelming influence of the multinational pharmaceutical industry on the Psychotropics Convention was particularly noticeable [89] (Sinha, 2001, 24-25).

Sinha (2001, 25-26) compares the preambles of the two conventions and points out that in contrast with the Single Convention, the 1971 Psychotropics Convention makes no mention of the "serious evil" of "addiction," that "the use of psychotropic substances for medical and scientific purposes is indispensable and that their availability for such purposes should not be unduly restricted."

The 1971 Convention, as the Single Convention, has four schedules with distinct levels of control. Regarding tranquilizers in

---

[88] McAllister (1991), Kuševic (1977). McAllister's comparison is highly detailed and recommended; Kuševic adds useful context and insight. See also, Chatterjee, (1988), for a more technical and rudimentary comparison of the two Conventions.
[89] The key author of the preparatory draft, Arthur Lande, had ended his career with the UN not long before the Vienna conference. He attended the conference as the representative of the U.S. Pharmaceutical Manufacturer's Association, one of many industry-related observers. Another example of blatant corporate influence involved a group of six small Latin American countries. They uncharacteristically supported weakening the treaty and were collectively represented by a Swiss man who spoke poor Spanish and was not a government official, diplomat, or technical drug expert. He worked for the European pharmaceutical giant, Hoffmann-LaRoche (McAllister (2000, p. 232; Kuševic 1977, p. 39).

95

schedule IV, some "manufacturing states tried to eliminate Schedule IV by arguing that such drugs were sufficiently regulated by national controls, rendering international control unnecessary. Schedule IV remained in the end, albeit with a much smaller number of drugs in it, but the underlying assumption used in 1961 regarding placement had been completely reversed, in particular by the U.S.: 'unless there was substantial proof that a substance was harmful, it should remain uncontrolled'"[90] (ibid, 26-27). This shifted the burden of the proof from producers to regulators.

The earlier drug treaties included the base substances and derivatives: salts, esters, ethers, and isomers. The latter were excluded from the 1971 Convention, a measure that helps pharmaceutical industries. This was a political decision to assure that countries with solid pharmaceutical industries signed the convention (McAllister, 2000, 233; Sinha, 2001, 27).

The process to include a new drug in the schedules follows the model of the Single Convention. WHO is charged with the studies of each drug and of making recommendations to the CND. However, the 1971 Convention instructs WHO to consider relevant economic, social, legal, and administrative factors missing in the 1961 Convention. In other words, while employment and income generated by poppy, coca, and other plants used to produce drugs should not be considered in the decision-making process, they should be considered in the case of the pharmaceutical industry.

In conclusion, the 1971 Convention on Psychotropic Substances is less restrictive than the 1961 Single Convention on Narcotic Drugs. This difference is substantially due to the different economic interests that were affected by the two conventions.

---

[90] McAllister (1991, p. 158).

3.2 THE 1988 CONVENTION AGAINST ILLICIT TRAFFIC IN NARCOTIC DRUGS AND PSYCHOTROPIC SUBSTANCES

The 1988 Convention was also a reaction against growing illicit drug markets and the violence associated with some of them. In 1984 the Colombian Medellin cartel generated a narco-terrorist attack on the State, killing many judges, politicians, journalists, and police officers that opposed the cartel. In December of that year, the UN General Assembly warned about the nocive effects of growing illegal drug markets on security and economic and social development (UNODC, 2008, 203). Other developments included the increased availability of cocaine in North America and Europe and the production of amphetamine-type stimulants in clandestine laboratories in North America, Europe, and South-East Asia.

> The situation was steadily and rapidly deteriorating, and drug abuse was described as reaching epidemic proportions in many parts of the world. All countries in the world seemed to be vulnerable to drug trafficking and abuse, regardless of geographical location, political orientation, and stage of economic development. [...] The problem was exacerbated by increasing levels of violence and sophistication among the transnational organized crime groups which were facilitating the transit and marketing of these drugs. The Medellin and Cali cartels, operating out of Colombia, controlled much of the cocaine trade from Colombia to the United States and other countries. They were not only trafficking ever larger amounts of cocaine to North America and Europe, but also started to become a serious threat to security and governance. [...] It threatened the sovereignty and security of States and disrupted the economic, social, and cultural structure of society (UNODC, 2008, 205-206).

These developments led to the 1988 Convention against Illicit Traffic in Narcotic Drugs and Psychotropic Substances. This Convention was directed at drug trafficking activities that were already punishable offenses in the 1961 Single Convention. Drug possession for personal consumption became a criminal offense, even though governments could choose not to punish it. The 1988 Convention paid particular attention to money laundering, which had been a punishable offense in the 1961 convention, "but this obligation, hidden in the text of the 1961 Convention, had been largely 'forgotten' by most countries prior to the more explicit formulations contained in the 1988 Convention" (ibid, 206).

The 1988 Convention also criminalized illegal trafficking in precursor chemicals, another punishable offense, included but "forgotten," even though it was part of the 1961 convention. The 1988 Convention established an international precursor control regime that the INCB monitors. It regulated extraditions and expanded the extraditable offenses to include money laundering and the manufacture, transport, distribution of equipment, and precursor chemicals. However, "it also provides for some escape clauses, notably if the authorities in a country believe that compliance would facilitate the punishment of a person 'on account of his race, religion, nationality or political opinions.' It also makes extraditions '...subject to the conditions provided for by the law of the requested Party...' In fact, a number of national legal traditions do not allow for the extradition of nationals to foreign countries, partly based on constitutional principles" (ibid, 207).

Besides, it regulated *controlled delivery*, that is, "the technique of allowing illicit or suspect consignments of narcotic drugs, psychotropic substances, substances in Table I and Table II annexed to this Convention, or substances substituted for them, to pass out of, through or into the territory of one or more countries, with the knowledge and under the supervision of their competent authorities, with a view to identifying persons involved in the commission of offences established in accordance with article 3, paragraph 1, of the Convention" (Article 1 (g) of the convention).

The 1988 Convention also sought to strengthen international cooperation among its Parties to fight increasingly complex international drug trafficking organizations.

3.3 IDCS ORGANS

3.3.1 The Economic and Social Council (ECOSOC)

The ECOSOC[91] was established in 1945 in the UN Charter as one of the six principal organs of the United Nations. It is responsible for coordinating the economic and social fields of the organization, specifically regarding the 15 specialized agencies, the eight functional commissions, and the five regional commissions under its jurisdiction.

The Council serves as the central forum to discuss international economic and social issues and formulate policy recommendations addressed to member states and the United Nations system. Some non-governmental organizations have been granted consultative status to the Council and participate in the work of the United Nations.

3.3.2 The Commission on Narcotic Drugs (CND)

The CND[92] is one of the nine functional commissions of the ECOSOC. It was established by ECOSOC resolution 9(I) in 1946 to assist the ECOSOC in supervising the application of the international drug control treaties. In 1991, the General Assembly expanded the mandate of the CND to enable it to function as the governing body of the UNODC. ECOSOC resolution 1999/30 requested the CND to structure its agenda with two distinct segments: a normative

---

[91] https://www.un.org/ecosoc/en/about-us
[92] https://www.unodc.org/unodc/en/commissions/CND/index.html

segment for discharging treaty-based and normative functions and an operating segment for exercising the role as the governing body of UNODC.

The work of ECOSOC and the CND is linked through the agenda of the Council. The reports of the Commissions are considered by the Council during the General Segment of its substantive session each year, held toward the end of July, under the agenda item entitled "Social and human rights questions."

The report of the CND is adopted at the end of their respective sessions. It includes several resolutions and decisions adopted by the Commission, some of which may be for adoption by the Council or for recommendation by the Council for adoption by the General Assembly. These resolutions and decisions appear in the reports under the Chapter "Matters calling for action by the Economic and Social Council or brought to its attention." Once adopted by the Council, these resolutions and decisions become ECOSOC resolutions and decisions.

3.3.3 The United Nations Office on Drugs and Crime (UNODC)

The UNODC is the technical cooperation branch of the IDCS, "[t]o improve the overall assistance to developing countries, an additional body was created in 1972, the United Nations Fund for Drug Abuse Control (UNFDAC). Its main task was to raise funds to implement various technical assistance activities, notably providing assistance to developing countries in order to help farmers stop cultivating illegal drug crops; such activities are now grouped together under the generic category of 'alternative development' or 'alternative livelihoods'" (UNODC, 2008, 197).

As international organized crime and drug trafficking grew and became more complex, countries required better technical cooperation beyond what UNFDAC could give. In 1991 the secretariats of the three drug control bodies (DND, UNFDAC, and INCB) were merged into the United Nations International Drug

Control Programme (UNDCP). The secretariats of the UNDCP and the Centre for International Crime Prevention (CICP) were unified in 1997 to become the Office for Drug Control and Crime Prevention (UNODCCP). In 2002, the office was renamed the United Nations Office on Drugs and Crime (UNODC) (ibid, 197).

Today UNODC is mandated to assist the Member States in their struggle against illicit drugs, crime, and terrorism. In recent years, the UNODC activities related to crime and terrorism have increased substantially. One may foresee that they will continue to grow relative to its activities against illegal drug production, trafficking, and consumption. It would not be surprising if, in a few years, this agency becomes UNOCD (United Nations Office on Crime and Drugs), as organized crime and terrorism become more extensive and complex, and drugs end up as a less critical part of the agency's activities. The three pillars of the UNODC work program are:[93]

1. Field-based technical cooperation projects to enhance the capacity of Member States to counteract illicit drugs, crime, and terrorism.
2. Research and analytical work to increase knowledge and understanding of drugs and crime issues and expand the evidence base for policy and operational decisions.
3. Normative work to assist States in ratifying and implementing relevant international treaties, developing domestic legislation on drugs, crime, and terrorism, and providing secretariat and substantive services to the treaty-based and governing bodies.

3.3.4 The International Narcotics Control Board (INCB)

The INCB is an independent, quasi-judicial expert body established by the Single Convention on Narcotic Drugs of 1961 by merging two bodies: the PCOB, created by the 1925 International

---

[93] https://www.unodc.org/unodc/en/about-unodc/index.html

Opium Convention, and the DSB, created by the 1931 Convention for Limiting the Manufacture and Regulating the Distribution of Narcotic Drugs. The INCB is a Convention Organ. It is a subsidiary United Nations organ that reports to ECOSOC. Its Secretariat is part of the United Nations that supports the Board, whose members are independent experts outside the United Nations system (See chapter 5). However, as noted above, its secretariat (support staff) is part of UNODC, which, as shown in Chapter 13, section 7, has been a source of frictions and raises questions whether it is fit for its purpose in the current psychoactive drug world environment.

CHAPTER FOUR. CHARACTERISTICS OF THE DRUG CONVENTIONS

The first section of this chapter summarizes the main characteristics of the drug conventions and some significant policy consequences. The second section explores the internal logic of the conventions. It highlights some of their logical weaknesses, the lack of definition concerning critical terms, and the existence of contradictory definitions in different official languages. These make ambiguous and uncertain the interpretation of the conventions.

4.1 SOME OBVIOUS ONES

The Conventions' prohibition of non-medical uses of all controlled drugs does not differentiate among drugs or drug categories. Indeed, there is no recognition of differences such as hard and soft drugs. The same policies and standards are applied to all of them. All non-medical human bodily consumption of controlled drugs is considered drug abuse and requires countries to design and follow policies to eliminate it.

However, alcohol and nicotine, the two psychoactive drugs that cause the most deaths and social costs, are excluded from the IDCS controls. This shows that despite the persistent efforts to exclude the non-medical uses of all psychoactive drugs, the IDCS proponents could not overcome the practical, economic, and cultural obstacles to eliminate non-medical or non-scientific uses of those drugs.[94]

The IDCS policies define all experimental, occasional, frequent, or addicted non-medical drug users as *abusers*. Since abusive behaviors should not be tolerated, a "world without drugs" has been an aspirational policy goal. This was frequently expressed in

---

[94] For example, Bishop Brent "believed that liquor had a 'beverage value' and therefore was in the class of nutrients" (Musto, 1999, 68).

the United Nations publications like the INCB annual reports for 1994 (INCB, 1995a, 3) and 1997, published a couple of months before the United Nations General Assembly Special Session of 1998 (UNGASS-1998) (INCB, 1998,1). Not surprisingly, Pino Arlacchi, the Executive Director of UNODCCP, proposed in UNGASS-1998 the slogan: "A drug-free world: we can do it," which was not formally adopted but remained engraved in the minds of all participants in that UNGASS (UNDCP, 1998). The Outcome Document of UNGASS 2016 maintains the same position: "We reaffirm our determination to tackle the world drug problem and to actively promote a society free of drug abuse" (United Nations, 2016b, 1), a policy purpose restated in the 2019 CND: "We further reaffirm our determination to address and counter the world drug problem and to actively promote a society free of drug abuse in order to help ensure that all people can live in health, dignity, and peace, with security and prosperity, and reaffirm our determination to address public health, safety and social problems resulting from drug abuse" (CND, 2019, 1).

As noted in the previous section, article 36 on penal provisions of the Single Convention commits countries to comply with the IDCS "subject to its constitutional limitations." It also requires that "cultivation, production, manufacture, extraction, preparation, possession, offering, offering for sale, distribution, purchase, sale, delivery on any terms whatsoever, brokerage, dispatch, dispatch in transit, transport, importation and exportation of drugs contrary to the provisions of this Convention" be made "punishable offences when committed intentionally, and that serious offences shall be liable to adequate punishment particularly by imprisonment or other penalties of deprivation of liberty." However, "when abusers of drugs have committed such offences, the Parties may provide, either as an alternative to conviction or punishment or in addition to conviction or punishment, that such abusers shall undergo measures of treatment, education, after-care, rehabilitation, and social reintegration." In 1961, during the cold war, the United

States and Western Europe could not agree with the Soviet Union, Eastern Europe, and China on penal sanctions for drug users and addicts. Later on, Article 3 paragraph 2 of the 1988 United Nations Convention against Illicit Traffic in Narcotic Drugs and Psychotropic requires to criminalize drug consumption: "Subject to its constitutional principles and the basic concepts of its legal system, each Party shall adopt such measures as may be necessary to establish as a criminal offence under its domestic law, when committed intentionally, the possession, purchase or cultivation of narcotic drugs or psychotropic substances for personal consumption contrary to the provisions of the 1961 Convention, the 1961 Convention as amended or the 1971 Convention" (UNODC, 2013, 129). However, the Convention does not establish what sanctions countries should impose on drug users and addicts. They may be treated as sick people or as vulnerable victims of drug traffickers, even though their drug use is illegal. Thus, the Convention allows drug use to be considered a public health issue or a contravention of the treaties that does not have to be penalized.

The IDCS establishes punishable offenses for drug crimes but does not require the harsh policies followed at several times by various countries' "wars on drugs." However, these policies could have been justified as consistent with the conventions. Article 39 of the Single Convention asserts that: "a Party shall not be or deemed to be precluded from adopting measures of control more strict or severe than those provided in the Convention." Article 23 of the 1971 Convention reaffirms this: "A Party may adopt more strict or severe measures of control than those provided by this Convention if, in its opinion, such measures are desirable or necessary for the protection of the public health and welfare."

The two convention articles mentioned in the previous paragraph generate a strong authoritarian policy bias to the IDCS. They also may be interpreted as the legal support for governments to apply harsher and stricter sanctions, not proportional to the drug crimes, when they believe that these sanctions are necessary to protect the health and welfare of their societies. The INCB, for a long time, did not oppose the governments' "war on drugs" efforts, although recently, it has rejected those drug control methods when they violate human rights (see chapter seven).

The IDCS was developed mainly to control the non-medical use of opium, cocaine, and other plant-based drugs. The 1971 Convention on Psychotropic Drugs was enacted in response to the surge of psychedelic and other synthetic drug use during the 1960s. As noted above, most drugs included in this Convention are synthetic products of the pharmaceutical industry that lobbied and obtained a more flexible treatment for production and marketing than the one required by the 1961 Single Convention.[95]

The IDCS requires countries to be inflexible regarding production and trafficking, although it allows some flexibility toward drug consumption. However, in practice, its approach is biased toward law enforcement vs. prevention, treatment, rehabilitation, and resocialization. The system was built on the premise that the best policy options were to cut supply at the source and to have strong international trade controls to limit the availability of illegal drugs. These actions fall mainly within the scope of the police and justice systems that are in place in each country. In many countries, health delivery systems are substantially underfunded and cover only part of the population. Besides, addiction tends to be stigmatized, and spending on addicts is not a high government priority. Not surprisingly, the value of the resources devoted to drug law enforcement is much larger than those devoted to drug use prevention, treatment, rehabilitation, and resocialization.

The contribution of the social sciences to the construction of the IDCS was nil. The IDCS builders were highly motivated and committed religious people (mainly priests and pastors), physicians, toxicologists, lawyers, chemists, pharmacists, diplomats, police officers, and other professionals with solid ideological positions about

---

[95] Bruum, Pan and Rexed (1973) and Sinha (2001) document this process in detail.

drug use. They either dismissed most social factors and policies as contributors to drug production, trafficking, use, and addiction or considered that they were beyond the realm of drug policies. Most did not have knowledge of the social sciences. Others thought that the social sciences were not valid or felt they could not solve complex social problems. Indeed, the social sciences were undeveloped at the beginning of the 20th century, and any serious cool-headed policy discussion was complicated because of ideological differences. The INCB has traditionally interpreted the conventions' terms "medical and scientific purposes" as including only those derived from the natural sciences and medicine while disdaining the social sciences as simple non-scientific speculations.[96]

The IDCS rejects any possible experimentation and tolerance of non-medical drug uses because it may not allow exceptions to the limitation of drug use to *medical and scientific purposes*. Those experiments are not legitimate because drug uses risk harm to the individual, and most health sector members have made a "do no harm" oath.[97] This oath defines harm only within the human body,

---

[96] For example, In May 2012 during the second day of the first session I attended as a Member of the INCB, an unquestionable brilliant and dynamic colleague that had been the leader of the Board for two decades, claimed that the social sciences were not real sciences but simple speculations. It was obvious that I had wasted 50 years of my life in the social sciences! (Thoumi, 2016, 29).

[97] It is worth pointing out that the 2005 United States Supreme Court decision on *Gonzales v. Raich*, judged against allowing cultivation of medicinal marijuana for personal medicinal use, but Sandra Day O'Connor, the first woman member to the United States Supreme Court (nominated by Ronald Reagan) dissented and defended the value of experimentation with drug policies: "This case exemplifies the role of States as laboratories. The States' core police powers have always included authority to define criminal law and to protect the health, safety, and welfare of their citizens. Exercising those powers, California (by ballot initiative and then by legislative codification) has come to its own conclusion about the difficult and sensitive question of whether marijuana should be available to relieve severe pain and suffering. Today the Court sanctions an application of the federal Controlled Substances Act that extinguishes that experiment, without any proof that the personal cultivation, possession, and use of marijuana for medicinal purposes, if economic activity in the first place, has a substantial effect on interstate commerce and is therefore an appropriate subject of federal regulation" (Thoumi, 2014).

not within society. Thus, its policy consequences on society are irrelevant.

The amendment procedures to IDCS conventions are complex and challenging.[98] The process requires the Secretary-General to refer to ECOSOC any amendment requested by a Party to the 1961 and 1971 conventions. ECOSOC then convene a Conference to decide the matter or ask the parties their comments, approval, or rejection. If no party objects within 18 months, the amendment enters into force. If not, ECOSOC may call a Conference or reject the proposal. The amendment process for the 1988 Convention is somewhat different. The Secretary-General communicates any amendment proposed by a Party to the other Parties. If no Party rejects it within twenty-four months, it is deemed to be accepted. If any Party rejects the amendment, and if a majority so requests, the Secretary-General "shall bring the matter, together with any comments made by the Parties, before the Council which may decide to call a conference in accordance with Article 62, paragraph 4, of the Charter of the United Nations. Any amendment resulting from such a conference shall be embodied in a Protocol of Amendment. Consent to be bound by such a Protocol shall be required to be expressed specifically to the Secretary-General" (Article 31 of the United Nations Convention against Illicit Traffic in Narcotic Drugs and Psychotropic Substances of 1988).

The conventions respect the parties' sovereignty and should be implemented according to their constitutions (Article 36 of the 1961 Single Convention on Narcotic Drugs). One unintended consequence of this provision is the difficulty of applying the conventions in federal countries, where their sovereign states limit the federal government's policy actions. As shown in footnote 36, this is the case of the United States, where the federal government prohibits

---

[98] See Article 47 of the Single Convention on Narcotic Drugs of 1961, Article 30 of the Convention on Psychotropic Substances of 1971, Article 31 of the United Nations Convention against Illicit Traffic in Narcotic Drugs and Psychotropic Substances of 1988.

non-medical uses of marijuana, but it cannot force the states to comply (Thoumi, 2014). It raises an interesting question: is there a different IDCS for centrally organized countries and federal countries? There is no single answer to this question because states' autonomy regarding drug policies varies substantially in federal systems. However, in the United States, they have greater autonomy than in other federal countries (See chapter 13 section 13.5).

4.2. INCONSISTENCIES, IMPORTANT UNDEFINED TERMS, LEGAL VOIDS AND GAPS IN THE DRUG CONVENTIONS

The development of the IDCS was a remarkable global policy experiment with the goal of establishing and enforcing a unique policy to limit all human bodily consumption of psychoactive drugs to *medical and scientific purposes* across the world. As shown above, the process to achieve that goal lasted over fifty years. This was a long political process in which diverse interests and ideologies frequently collided. At times, power and strong-arm tactics have been used by countries. For example, the Hague Opium Convention was included in the Versailles peace agreement to force Germany and Austria to sign the convention. The United States threatened to impose crippling non-tariff import barriers to Turkish exports to force the country to adhere to the convention.

The main sticking point that delayed a global drug agreement was the conflict between countries that wanted to prohibit any nonmedical and scientific uses and those that preferred more flexible regulated drug markets. Other issues like the distribution of market shares of legal opium markets, the regulations of those markets, and the conditions that users and addicts' treatments had to meet were also obstacles at various points of the process. These, however, were negotiated among countries. In the end, none of the main stakeholders that participated in the process was fully satisfied, but the result has been notably resilient despite their differences.

The Single Convention is a treaty (agreement) among countries. When drafting any good agreement, experienced drafters make sure that all parties understand what the agreement entails. To this end, the treaty should define all relevant terms. This is a standard practice in the United Nations conventions. Indeed, the first article of the three drug conventions defines many essential terms and concepts.[99] Other definitions concern the UN drug agencies' roles and their staff positions. "This list confirms that when negotiating the conventions, it was important to clarify what each term meant to avoid ambiguities and confusion" (Thoumi, 2016, 20). However, the IDCS does not define the main concepts required to understand the purposes of the conventions and the reasons for its cornerstone policy. The concepts *health, physical health, moral health,* and *welfare* are undefined and ambiguous. The conventions do not define either medical or scientific purposes or medicine and science. Therefore, the main policy instrument limiting drug use to "medical and scientific" purposes is ambiguous. "Meanwhile, the fact that article 4 Paragraph 'c' treats medicine and science as separate raises doubts whether medicine is considered a science because if medicine is a science, there would not have been a need to mention it separately" (ibid, 20).

When the main concepts of a law or a treaty are not spelled out, it is impossible to confidently assert what they are and whether the policies enacted are consistent with the treaty's purposes. The failure to define the essential concepts of the drug conventions creates a "legal void or gap" that leaves open the Convention's interpretation and, thus, the question of which policies comply with it.[100]

---

[99] The following is a partial list: cannabis, cannabis resin, coca bush, coca leaf, opium, medicinal opium, poppy plant, poppy straw, narcotic drugs, illicit traffic, exports, imports, preparation, production, product, special stocks, stocks, territory, region, premises, psychotropic substances, controlled delivery, confiscation, seizure, proceeds, transit state.

[100] The lack of definition of the terms *medical and scientific* and the difficulty to establish which policies comply with the drug conventions were the main issues studied in Thoumi (2016 and 2017a). A committee of advisers to the government

In many cases, the preamble of the conventions may help fill legal voids. In this case, the UN drug bodies have argued that the preambles' vague statements about the health and welfare of mankind are the evident object and purpose of the conventions. However, this proposition is questionable. First, as shown in chapter two, the purpose of the IDCS starting in the Shanghai Commission and followed by the 1912 The Hague Opium Convention, the three conventions of the League of Nations, and the 1953 Opium Protocol was always to limit drug use to medical and scientific purposes. And second, there are inconsistencies among the versions of the Convention in the six official UN languages. The preamble of the English version reads "concerned with the health and welfare of mankind" but, the Spanish and French versions are different: "Las Partes, preocupadas por la salud física y moral de la humanidad," and "Les parties, soucieuses de la santé physique et morale de l'humanité," which translate as "The parties concerned with the physical and moral health of humankind." Revising the Russian, Chinese, and Arabic versions, the prefaces refer to various types of well-being and caring for human health and welfare.[101] Article 40, paragraph 1 of the Single Convention adds to the ambiguity of these terms as it asserts that "This Convention, of which the Chinese, English, French, Russian and Spanish texts are equally authentic."[102] The 1971 Convention on Psychotropic Substances in English, French, and Spanish have replicated those assertions about the convention's motivational concerns (ibid, 21).

---

of Canada uses the same point to argue that the legalization of non-medical marijuana uses in that country complies with the drug conventions (Fultz et al., 2017).

[101] The following are some of the definitions encountered: "the good fortune, health, happiness, prosperity, etc., of a person, group or organization", "the state of doing well especially in respect to good fortune, happiness, well-being, or prosperity", "the health and happiness of people", "physical and mental health and happiness", "the health, happiness, and fortunes of a person or group".

[102] In 1961 Arabic was not an official UN language but it was added in 1973.

111

Despite the authenticity of the French and Spanish versions, the United Nations documents appear to have dropped all references to "physical and moral health." At least during the last decades, these terms have not appeared in official United Nations publications in French and Spanish, except in the texts of the conventions.[103] For example, the Spanish version of the UNGASS 2016 resolution reads: *"Reafirmamos nuestro compromiso con las metas y objetivos de los tres tratados de fiscalización internacional de drogas, entre los que figura la preocupación por la salud y el bienestar de la humanidad"* (United Nations, 2016, 1), which is a literal translation of the English version of the same document. This raises several questions: Were the translators of the resolution unaware of the French and Spanish texts of the conventions, and they translated the English version literally? Why is it that the official convention versions in French and Spanish are not literal translations of the English version? When the conventions were written, the use of the term "moral health" in the French and Spanish versions was a signal that the purpose of the conventions was to impose a unique global moral code for psychoactive drugs production, marketing, and human consumption? Or was it just an honest mistake of the translators into French and Spanish? If so, how come the United Nations had such unqualified translators? But if this was a mistake, why is there a coincidence in the French and Spanish versions? Or was this a political decision that appealed to Francophone and Spanish-speaking countries? If so, why the term welfare was not included in those languages? Was the term moral health a good substitute for welfare? I am afraid that these questions have no good answers.

---

[103] During my eight years' experience as an INCB Board Member I cannot recall any Spanish version of an INCB official document that says "la salud física y moral de la humanidad", they all say "la salud y el bienestar de la humanidad", except for the 1961 and 1971 conventions texts. It appears that there is an unwritten agreement to use the literal translation from English rather than the one found in the authentic Spanish version. The same can be said of the documents of the CND and the UNODC. I wonder if in today's world environment the staff of those agencies feel uncomfortable using a broad moral argument as a justification for the conventions.

The conference to draft the Single Convention was explicitly convened to limit the use of controlled drugs globally for *medical and scientific purposes*. It was likely assumed that these terms did not have to be defined because they were universally understood. I posit that by the 1960s, Convention drafting had advanced to the point of requiring a better-defined purpose than during the pre-World War II period. And that "the health and welfare" or the "physical and moral health" were just politically correct terms that satisfied the need to justify the limitation of controlled psychoactive drug uses to *medical and scientific purposes*. One wonders if promoting *moral health* in French and Spanish-speaking countries made the prohibition policy more acceptable. In any case, "the health and welfare of mankind" and "the physical and moral health of humanity" were not concepts discussed in the process of establishing the IDCS. They appear to be just convenient pretexts or contrived reasons to justify limiting all human consumption of controlled drugs to *medical and scientific purposes*.

On rare occasions, the INCB has gone beyond the "health and welfare of mankind" purpose. For example, arguing the need for a comprehensive, integrated, and balanced approach to drug policies, it claims that "the ultimate goal of such an approach must be to achieve the overall aim of the drug control conventions namely, to ensure the mental and physical health and welfare of humankind" (INCB, 2015, 2). As shown below, mental health is one of the three components of health posited in the first principle of the WHO, and it is an essential object of WHO's activities.

Another issue arises because the interpretation of "welfare" varies substantially across societies depending on their social mores and government political ideologies, which makes it impossible to apply a single definition across all societies, as each country may define it in its own way.[104]

---

[104] In some countries for example, the death penalty for small drug trafficking crimes has been applied to improve social welfare, that is, to get rid of socially undesirable members. In other countries this would be totally unacceptable.

113

Not surprisingly, the lack of clear definitions of the essential terms of the drug conventions has resulted in conflicting positions about some policies' compliance with the IDCS. As shown in chapter two, *quasi-medical* uses of opium were debated in the IDCS building process. The Single Convention appeared to prohibit them but allowed 15 years for countries to implement the necessary changes. However, the non-binding Commentary to the 1961 Single Convention suggests significant flexibility in interpreting *medical purposes*. The Commentary explains the term *medical purposes* (United Nations, 1973, 111).

> The term 'medical purposes' has not been uniformly interpreted by Governments when applying the provisions of the narcotics treaties containing it. Some have prohibited the consumption of narcotic drugs by all addicts excepting only, when necessary, to alleviate suffering during withdrawal treatment; a number of other countries have permitted consumption by persons whose addictions proves to be incurable to the minimum quantities required to prevent painful withdrawal symptoms and to enable them to lead a normal life. There have also been a few cases in which all consumption of narcotic drugs by addicts was prohibited, even in the course of withdrawal treatment.
>
> The term 'medical purposes' does not necessarily have the same meaning at all times and under all circumstances. Its interpretation must depend on the stage of medical science in the particular time in question; and not only modern medicine, sometimes referred to as 'western medicine,' but also systems of indigenous medicine such as those which exists in China, India, and Pakistan, may be taken into account in this connection.

The term 'medical purposes' includes veterinary and dental purposes.

The Commentary acknowledges that countries have interpreted the term *medical purposes* in many ways regarding some different practices. Some countries have used criteria from modern medicine and have accepted a few traditional medical practices and ways to treat addicts, including some addiction maintenance, which "may be taken into account in this connection."[105] A statement that is vague enough to require further interpretation (Thoumi, 2016, 20).

The lack of definitions of the essential terms listed implies that different people may arrive at different or opposite conclusions when considering whether a policy complies with the convention. Bewley-Taylor (2012a, 48) considers other reasons and concludes that the convention "provides considerable interpretative autonomy" to the INCB. Barrett (2008, 7) argues that this is particularly important because, during the INCB's existence, most of its members have lacked training in international law and interpretation theories and methods. The Board does not have a legal advisory section that would provide such guidance.[106]

As shown, the Commentary to the 1961 Single Convention discusses the meaning of *medical purposes*, but the meaning of

---

[105] The Spanish translation of the Commentary has a stronger assertion as it reads "deben tenerse en cuenta a este respecto" (United Nations, 1989, 121) which means that they *should be taken into account*. It adds another possible interpretation issue.

[106] The Board has not had its own legal counsel, and when necessary, it has sought outside legal opinions, mainly from the UNODC legal advisory team. Since I joined the INCB in May 2012, every year until November 2019 the Board unsuccessfully requested a staff position for a competent international lawyer with expertise in treaty interpretation. In February 2020, a mid-level position was approved for a lawyer, however, the United Nations budgetary problems during the pandemic has not permitted new appointments as of February 2021. Unfortunately, having a lawyer on board would not solve the problem because different internationalist lawyers would have varying opinions about many issues, and any good attorney would defend the positions of their clients, in this case, the INCB members. The question is whether it is possible to choose an impartial legal adviser, or whether the Board members should assume the responsibility to interpret the conventions.

science or *scientific purposes* is left unexplained. Following the guideline of article 31 of the Vienna Convention, Thoumi (2016, 22) surveyed the definition of science in several dictionaries and used contrasting definitions in the Cambridge University Dictionary and the Royal Academy of the Spanish Language to establish the ordinary meaning of the term.

> These definitions show that the attempts to define science, besides trying to answer the question of what science is, have also developed systems to classify sciences and scientific knowledge. The contrast between the definitions of the two dictionaries is striking. The Cambridge University Dictionary limits science to what could be considered as modern sciences emanating from the Enlightenment, while the definition of the Royal Academy of the Spanish Language covers also pre-modern fields such as infuse and occult sciences, which the theories of knowledge developed in the 20th century would consider as "epistemological obstacles" to the development of modern sciences and scientific knowledge.
>
> The attempts to classify sciences are innumerable and result in a wide variety of groupings. The following is presented to illustrate this point:
> - Natural sciences: physics, chemistry, ecology, oceanography, geology, meteorology, human biology, and botany.
> - Social sciences: anthropology, archaeology, business administration, communication, criminology, education, government (political science), linguistics, international relations, psychology, sociology, economics, law, history, and geography.
> - Formal sciences: decision theory, logic, mathematics, statistics, systems, and computer theories.

- Applied sciences: all engineering fields, applied mathematics, applied physics, medicine, and applied computing.

The definitions and classifications of science show that there are many possible definitions of science and that the term 'science' does not apply only to the fourth definition of the Royal Academy of the Spanish Language: 'Body of knowledge relative to exact, physics, chemistry and natural sciences,' which is perhaps close to what some scientists would refer to as 'basic' sciences. Therefore, without clearly defining the terms 'medical' and 'scientific' in the conventions, it is logically impossible to claim that there is a unique way to interpret them. Furthermore, to be logically consistent, any interpretation of the conventions should spell out which definition of science is used (ibid, 22-23).

As a result, the failure to define the key terms of the conventions and the inconsistencies in the official versions in different languages make uncertain and ambiguous the interpretation of the conventions. Thus, it may be argued that as agreements, the international drug conventions have wide legal gaps or voids that allow for very diverging but legitimate interpretations.

Interestingly, this approach to interpreting the drug conventions has been rejected by some very well-known drug policy critics and activists: "An argument has also been made (although not by any State parties) that legal regulation is possible within the bounds of the treaties by interpreting the Conventions' 'scientific purposes' language to include experimentation with alternative regulatory options, so long as these are researched. This, however, misunderstands the meaning of 'scientific purposes' within the treaties, confusing the uses to which substances may be put with the scientific or evidence base for policy. It also takes the phrase out of its context, both within the article concerned and the treaty as a whole, contrary to basic Vienna Convention rules on interpretation" (Bewley-Taylor, Jelsma, Rolles and Walsh, 2016, 14).

Also, Lines and Barrett devoted a full journal article to the impossibility of interpreting the terms medical and scientific to include the social sciences as scientific: "Treaty interpretation has long been a subject of interest for international legal scholars. However, it is only recently that advocates for drug policy reform have taken up these questions. This article examines the proposition put forward by several authors that a legally regulated market in cannabis may be permissible under the international drug control treaties if considered as a policy 'experiment.' These authors contend that such measures conform to the general obligation of the Single Convention on Narcotic Drugs to limit uses of cannabis 'strictly to medical and scientific purposes'. Reviewing this position using the formal methods set out in Articles 31 and 32 of the Vienna Convention on the Law of Treaties, we conclude the interpretation proposed is untenable. While we share with these authors the objective of wider drug policy reform, we find the arguments supporting this position weak, and based on absent, flawed, or incomplete interpretive methodology" (Lines and Barrett, 2018, Abstract).

These two criticisms are based on a commonly accepted way attorneys interpret laws which is commented in chapter twelve, section 12.2.3. These critics use a simple legal approach that seeks to convince, not to prove. Thus, they choose facts and studies that support their argument but disregard those that contradict or raise doubts about what they support.

PART TWO: A COMPLEX PROBLEM, A SIMPLE POLICY IN PURSUIT OF AN UNACHIEVABLE GOAL

CHAPTER FIVE. THE ROLE OF INCB AS INTERPRETER OF THE CONVENTIONS

5.1 THE INCB

As noted above, the INCB is an independent treaty organ of the 1961 Convention created by joining the DSB and the PCOB of the League of Nations. As such, the INCB is a subsidiary organ of the United Nations. The INCB is a quasi-judicial body mandated to oversee the parties' compliance with the drug Conventions. The Board frequently asserts that its mandate is to make sure that countries comply with the limitation of controlled drugs and precursors to medical and scientific purposes to promote the health and welfare of mankind. It comprises thirteen members that "[s]hall be persons who, by their competence, impartiality, and disinterestedness, will command general confidence. During their term of office, they shall not hold any position or engage in any activity which would be liable to impair their impartiality in the exercise of their functions. The Council (ECOSOC) shall, in consultation with the Board, make all arrangements necessary to ensure the full technical independence of the Board in carrying out its functions" (UNODC, 2013, 14).

Most members have come from diplomacy, public health, and law enforcement backgrounds. A few have been women, and two of them have been Board presidents. However, the number of women members has increased significantly in the last three years.[107] Board members should be independent and cannot work on any drug-related issue for any government. INCB members are not

---

[107] In 2019 there were three women members. Another two were elected for the 2020-2025 period. In the April 2021 election for the period 2022-2027 three women members were reelected and a new one was elected. In the election of May 2021 women had the top three Board positions: president, vice president and head of the Standing Committee on Estimates.

United Nations staff, although its supporting secretariat staff is part of the United Nations.

5.2 THE INCB AS THE INTERPRETER OF THE UNDEFINED CONVENTION TERMS

The Board was established in 1968, and during its first two decades, it mainly played the role of an overseer of the illegal drug industry and the countries' drug policies. It monitored and reported the development of psychoactive drug issues worldwide, and its annual reports did not have elaborated policy positions. They were surveys of the developments in the illicit drug markets across the world. Their policy comments tended to be limited to expressing the obligation of countries to comply with their commitments to the conventions: prohibiting non-medical drug uses, eliminating coca chewing before the 12 December 1989 deadline, and controlling the diversion of opium and other controlled substances from legal to illegal markets.

However, in 1992 the structure of the annual report changed in response to the new challenges. As discussed before, the remarkable growth of international drug trafficking from the 1970s, the epidemic expansion of HIV associated with illegal drug injections, and the remarkably high violence level associated with drug trafficking in some countries led to the 1988 Convention Against Illicit Traffic in Narcotics and Psychotropic Substances. It focused on attacking trafficking organizations and increasing cooperation across countries to control the international drug trade. Despite the new convention, the problems associated with illegal drug trafficking continued to grow. In the most affected countries, civil society groups and their governments started to question their countries' net benefits from prohibiting non-medical drug use.

The critics had diverse positions. Those concerned with HIV and drug addiction advocated for harm reduction programs. Latin American governments experiencing drug trafficking violence and those whose states were threatened by drug trafficking organizations and illegal drugs markets that funded subversive movements clamored for undefined "new drug policy approaches" or "strategies." It led to the UNGASS 1990, the first one on the world drug problem that "adopted a Global Programme of Action that committed the Parties to the drug conventions to increase the resources devoted to fight drug addiction and trafficking and to increase their cooperation with other parties. It expressed its alarm at the growing link of drug trafficking and terrorism, branded the years 1991-2000 as the United Nations Decade Against Drug Abuse, and established in 1991 of the United Nations International Drug Control Programme (UNDCP)".[108]

The INCB, at the suggestion of Board Member Hamid Ghodse,[109] responded to these developments, including a new chapter

---

[108] https://www.unodc.org/documents/commissions/CND/Political_Declaration/Political_Declaration_1990/1990_Political_Declaration_and_Programme_of_Action.pdf

[109] See Ghodse (Ed.) (2008, 2). Professor Hamid Ghodse was a remarkable Iranian psychiatrist who was a very prolific academic with a long career at the University of London. He was an INCB member for over 20 years (1992-2012). He was an undisputed dominant figure and leader of the Board that he presided 11 of those years (1993, 1994, 1997, 1998, 2000, 2001, 2004, 2005, 2008, 2010, 2011). His academic achievements were impressive. Wikipedia lists the following degrees and honors: Doctor of Medicine (MD), Iran (1965); Diploma Psychological Medicine (DPM), United Kingdom of Great Britain and Northern Ireland (1974); Doctor of Philosophy (PhD), University of London (1976); Fellow of the Royal College of Psychiatrists (FRCPsych), United Kingdom (1985); Fellow of the Royal College of Physicians (FRCP), London (1992); Fellow of the Royal College of Physicians of Edinburgh (FRCPE), Edinburgh (1997); Fellow of the Faculty of Public Health Medicine (FFPHM), United Kingdom (1997); Doctor of Science (DSc), University of London (2002); Fellow of the Higher Education Academy (FHEA), United Kingdom (2005). Wikipedia also lists the following positions held by Professor Ghodse at the time of his death in December 2012: Professor of Psychiatry and of International Drug Policy, **University of London** (from 1987); President of European Collaborating Centres for Addiction Studies (from 1992), Member of the United Nations **International Narcotics Control Board** (from 1992), Member of the Executive Committee of the Federation of Clinical Professors (from 1994); Director of the Board of International Affairs and Member of the Council, **Royal College of Psychiatrists** (from 2000); Member of the Scientific Committee on

in its annual report: "Traditionally, this report had previously focused on control issues. The idea of the new chapter was to expand the report so that it also covered contemporary and topical issues related to its mandate. Since 1992 therefore, a particular theme has been selected each year for in-depth consideration. [...] The Board and its secretariat then painstakingly prepared, debated, and revised various drafts [...] Expert advice has been sought when necessary, and consultation with appropriate international organizations has also been part of the process. However, the final decision of every aspect of the chapter, as of the Annual Report as a whole has been that of the Board" (INCB, 2008b, 2).

The INCB, however, does not have a formal drug policy model. One reason for that is that the main assumptions required for such a model and the concepts that spell out the purpose of the IDCS were never made clear. It leaves the Board's mandate ambiguous, and, as shown below, it has allowed the INCB to change its policy positions over time. It may be argued that the failure of the IDCS to clarify the meaning of their most important concepts was necessary to achieve almost universal support among the world governments. Thus, practical reasons required the drug conventions' internal logic to be weak.

In the past, the INCB members were aware of the importance of the lack of definition of the terms *medical and scientific uses and purposes*. The 2003 report raised that issue: "[w]hile the international drug control conventions require parties to limit exclusively to medical and scientific purposes the production, manufacture, export,

---

Tobacco and Health (from 2000); Non-executive director of the National Patient Safety Agency (from 2001); Director of the International Centre for Drug Policy, St George's, University of London (since 2003); Chairman of Higher Degrees in Psychiatry, University of London (since 2003); Member of the Medical Studies Committee, University of London (since 2003). There is no doubt that during his tenure he was very influential in shaping international drug policies through the thematic INCB annual report chapters that he promoted. His edited book (Ghodse, 2008) summarizes the 1992 to 2006 annual reports thematic chapters.

import and distribution of, trade in and use and possession of drugs, the conventions do not provide a definition of the term 'medical and scientific purposes' but leaves that up to parties" (INCB, 2004, 37, ¶227).

This important and remarkable statement could have opened several interpretative options for the INCB. First, to let countries (the parties) individually decide how to interpret those terms. Second, to raise the issue in the CND where the parties could have debated it and provided guidelines to handle it. Third, it could have requested the opinion of the International Law Commission (ILC), the United Nations organ charged with advising about such issues and with significant research experience on treaty interpretation. This body has concluded that there is no unique way to interpret international conventions.[110]

The Board followed a different path. It pointed out that the expressions of *medical use* and *medical purposes* appeared in the 1931 Convention for Limiting the Manufacture and Regulating the Distribution of Narcotic Drugs to *medical needs*. But "none of those terms has been precisely defined in the current international drug control conventions or in the commentaries to those conventions. However, the 1971 Convention requires from WHO an assessment of the 'usefulness' of a substance when it is considered for international control" (INCB, 2004, 37, ¶228). The following paragraphs of the 2003 INCB report summarize important opinions expressed in WHO (1969):

> [...] the type and degree of international control must be based on two considerations: (a) the degree of risk to public health; and (b) the usefulness of the drug in medical therapy. [...] The usefulness of the drug must take into account the balance between risk and benefit. In the absence of sound evidence of

---

[110] The book edited by Georg Nolte (2013), a former president of the ILC, surveys the many ways in which international conventions have been interpreted and adapted to changing world environments and arrives at that conclusion.

therapeutic usefulness, recourse must be made to a drug's reputation for usefulness, which reflects the general opinion of practitioners or expert panels. That opinion may change with time. For example, new effects, desired or undesired, may be discovered; and with new discoveries, a drug may find new applications or become obsolete. Therapeutic efficacy and safety are basic conditions that have to be established before the drug can be marketed. [...] The consideration of usefulness of a drug goes far beyond medical use and includes its availability and cost and the knowledge and experience of those prescribing it and administering it. [...] Drugs can have different effects on the population of different communities due to cultural, environmental, and genetic factors, and therapeutic efficacy and safety may be influenced by various factors including nutritional status and the presence of infections, lesions of the central nervous system and the digestive tract. [...] It seems that the drafters of the international drug control conventions did not purposely leave the term 'medical use' ambiguous, but it is that they could not reach agreement on a universal definition. This situation will probably remain true in the future. [...] Medical practice and the concept of health change continuously. The expectations of individuals, the public, professionals, and policy makers interact with advancements in science and technology, as well as with economic, environmental, and sociological changes. The concepts of health improvement, quality of life, well-being, and so on influence how basic terminologies are used and can be defined (INCB, 2004, ¶229, 230, 231, 232).

The INCB, despite having acknowledged that WHO could not arrive at an agreed universal definition of "medical use," proceeded to do so and interpreted that and other key conventions terms.

In the absence of a definition agreed upon by WHO, the Board, for the purpose of carrying out its own work under the international drug control conventions, defines the terms in the following way:

"A medicine (medicinal substance; that is, whether synthetic and/or natural, pure or in the form of a preparation) is a substance used, designed or approved for the following medical purposes:

(a) Improving health and well-being;
(b) Preventing and treating disease (including the alleviation of symptoms of that disease);
(c) Acting as a diagnostic aid;
(d) Aiding conception or providing contraception;
(e) Providing general anesthesia.

Medical use:

The 'medical use' of a substance can be stated as its utilization for the above-mentioned medical purposes in a given country. Such use should be approved by the competent regulatory authority of that country and usefulness recognized by the medical community.

Medicines work mostly by biochemical, endocrinological, immunological, metabolic, or pharmacological mechanisms. Recently, in the European Union, a fifth category has been added that covers "genomic use" (stem cell administration, gene transfer etc.).

Scientific purposes:

The designation of the use of a drug for 'scientific purposes' is appropriate when it is used as a tool for investigating mechanisms of health or disease or when investigating the use of a product as a medicine. In patients, the investigation would be done as part of a clinical trial, which requires prior approval from the research ethics committee.

Medical consumption:

'Medical consumption' refers to the medicine (or medicines) consumed by patients for the purpose of improving health and well-being, acting as a diagnostic aid, providing contraception, or aiding conception, providing general anesthesia, and preventing and treating disease (including symptom alleviation), as well as for scientific purposes. Medical consumption includes ingestion, inhalation, injection, topical administration and any other route of administration" (INCB, 2004, 37-38, ¶233, 234, 235, 236, 237).

The definition of *scientific purposes* adopted by the INCB clearly shows that the Board's interpretation of science is very narrow and limited to what professionals in medicine consider is the practice of their profession. This was consistent with the belief of the Board Members that social sciences were not scientific. However, this contradicts the WHO position, that as shown in chapter thirteen, section 13.2, defines health in a way that includes *social health* and the *social determinants of health*. These are all part of the social sciences, which were unworthy to be accepted as sciences by the INCB.

5.3 THE LEGALIZATION OF NON-MEDICAL DRUG USES

In the 1992 report's thematic chapter one - "The legalization of non-medical use of drugs"- the INCB confronted the "legalizers" and, for the first time, sought to justify the IDCS policy to limit drug use absolutely to *medical and scientific purposes*. It starts explaining that the Parties, to comply with the 1961 Convention, are obliged to limit the production, manufacture, export, import, distribution of, trade in, use, and possession of drugs to medical and scientific purposes and to take such legislative and administrative measures as may be necessary or appropriate. It continues pointing out that "[n]one of the conventions requires a party to convict or punish drug abusers who commit such offences even when they have been established as punishable offences. The party may choose to deal with drug abusers through alternative non-penal measures involving treatment, education, after-care, rehabilitation, or social reintegration. Nevertheless, a party may choose to apply penal sanctions in such cases, since each convention permits a party to adopt more strict or severe measures than those provided by the convention if, in its opinion, such measures are desirable or necessary to prevent or suppress illicit trafficking" (INCB, 1992, ¶15c). The chapter then criticizes what the Board understood were the main arguments for legalization (ibid, ¶16).

> (a) 'Legalization is justified, since law enforcement has failed to control illicit supply or to reduce illicit demand': This argument, however, ignores the fact that legal sanctions have helped to deter or delay potential abusers, thereby limiting the growth of the illicit market.
> (b) 'Given current levels of access to illicit drugs, legalization would only have a minimum adverse impact on current drug abuse levels and would thus generate few additional health, safety or behavioural problems.' This argument, however, ignores the potential expansion of demand by individuals and society, particularly among young people, which could follow the removal of legal barriers, the freeing of entrepreneurial initiatives, and the lowering of market prices. It also ignores the possibility that there may be a substantial increase in economic and social costs, particularly to health-care systems (given the global experience with alcohol and tobacco abuse). This may include a sharp increase in costs resulting from accident-related injuries and other health-related problems.
> (c) 'Legalization would remove evils created by drug laws, such as corruption, violence, and drug-related crime, which are worse than the drugs themselves': This

argument assumes that drug-related black markets and corruption would significantly decline, but surely no community would accept making available, without any restriction, all drugs of abuse to all existing and potential abusers (including children) at sufficiently low prices. Even if one assumes that crime to support personal drug abuse may decline, crime committed under the influence of drugs, as well as chronic violence in the family and in the community, may increase. The assumption that organized criminal activity and related violence would significantly decrease may underestimate the capacity of organized crime to adjust to changing conditions without significant loss of economic, political, or social power.

The Board's chapter follows, undermining the credibility of the critics' arguments. The Board started mentioning valid policy issues that would appear within a complex policy framework. For example, what are the criteria to decide which drugs should be legalized, what potency levels would be permitted, what would be done to control the adverse consequences of their non-medical use? How would the marketing of such new drugs be dealt with? Would they be permitted without even a qualifying period and evaluation? What would happen with *designer drugs*? Would production and manufacture be limited? If so, how would the limits be enforced (e.g., limited to home production for personal use or to cottage industries or major enterprises)? What would market restrictions there be? Would the private sector or the public sector, or both be involved? How would price, purity, and potency levels be established and regulated? Would advertising be permitted? If so, what drugs would be advertised and by whom? Where would such drugs be sold (e.g., over the counter, through the mail, vending machines, or restaurants)? Would the sale of such drugs be limited to dependent abusers? If so, how many and from which cities or countries? What about experimenters and those not yet granted dependent status?

What would be the age limits for using legalized drugs and, if so, for which ones (e.g., access to cannabis at age 16, cocaine at age 18, and heroin at age 21)? Would there be restrictions on use because of function impairment (e.g., restrictions on use by transport, defense, nuclear power, and other workers)? For any necessary or desirable restrictions, what agency would enforce the law, what penalties and sanctions would be established for violations, and how would the risks of corruption and continued "illicit traffic" be dealt with? (ibid, ¶17).

All these are undoubtedly valid policy issues that have to be dealt with to regulate legal psychoactive drugs. However, the Board considered they would create unsurmountable policy problems and proceeded with a series of very revealing rebuttals. Indeed, the INCB appears to be seeking to attack a straw man who wanted a free uncontrolled market for all drugs: "It appears that the basic aim of the advocates of legalization is to allow the recreational use of narcotic drugs and/or psychotropic substances. It must be noted that such a step would create a legal demand for those drugs and, consequently, the current restrictions in respect of supply (cultivation, production, manufacture, trade, and distribution) would need to be abolished or fundamentally changed. History offers a good example of the consequences of such a change. The result would be similar to the situation of China in the nineteenth century, when, after the Opium War, the country was forced to accept the free availability of opium. Following that action, the number of opium addicts in the country increased drastically to an estimated 20 million" (ibid, ¶19).

According to the Board, legalization advocates had not yet presented a single valid argument: "The arguments put forward by advocates of legalization, although well-intended, can appear to be logical and simple when they are not; they do not withstand critical evaluation, and they tend to run contrary to general experience. The proposals in favour of legalization have tended to present possible legalization benefits against the costs of maintaining existing legal controls, without adequately addressing themselves to either the benefits of those controls or the social and economic costs of removing them. As the Board sees it, legalization advocates have not yet presented a sufficiently comprehensive, coherent, or viable alternative to the present system of international drug abuse control. The Board firmly believes that permitting the recreational use of drugs would have a substantial and irreversible adverse impact on public health, social wellbeing, and the international drug control system" (ibid, ¶23).

The Board firmly believed that permitting the recreational use of drugs would substantially and adversely impact public health, social well-being, and the international drug control system. The Board always pretended to be a technical body above politics, but this argument is fundamentally impressionistic: it has no references, does not provide evidence, and misrepresents the positions of most drug policy critics. Before 1992, as discussed above, the critics advocated for harm reduction policies to treat addicts and lower HIV risks. Critics in the Andean countries wanted to make coca chewing legal. Others insisted that anti-drug policies had to respect human rights. And some governments argued that they were overwhelmed by the violence and other harms associated with the growing drug trafficking.

By asserting that "it appears that the basic aim of the advocates of legalization is to allow the recreational use of narcotic drugs and/or psychotropic substances," the Board could have been referring either to a very small group of extreme libertarians, who argued that humans had the right to try psychoactive substances to enhance their human experience.[111] It could also have adhered to an unproven domino or slippery slope theory of government policies and social behaviors toward psychoactive drugs. For example, tolerating some non-medical use of marijuana would lead to extending that policy to all other psychoactive drugs.

Civil society and governments critical of the IDCS policies were not advocating a free market for those drugs. The question has

---

[111] Interestingly, what is perhaps the best know reference for the advocacy of free market for drugs was also published in 1992 (Szasz, 1992).

always been: what would be the best regulatory system? As the Board claimed, it is true that any system that would allow recreational psychoactive drug uses would be complex, and in many cases, very difficult to manage. But the Board dismissed the fact that this is also true for the current system, particularly in many vulnerable countries with weak governments, generalized and socially accepted corruption, or where governments lack territorial control over part of their land. In these cases, limiting drug production, trafficking and uses could be as complex and challenging to manage as regulating psychoactive drug markets by the State.

The INCB position is consistent with the implicit ideal United Nations country model discussed in the introduction: "The United Nations system is a child of modernity, and its drug conventions implicitly assume that all governments have full control of their territories, where they have a monopoly on power, force, and the law. It implies that current international norms are designed for nations, that is, for groups of humans with a common purpose and cohesive societies. Under these assumptions, societies are stable entities with legitimate norms and laws in which criminal acts are committed by a few socially dysfunctional individuals. Within this model, the current interpretation of the conventions is functional, and law enforcement agencies have a simple, clear job: to enforce the prohibition of social, ceremonial, recreational, and other 'non-medical and scientific' drug uses, without questioning policy legitimacy or effectiveness" (Thoumi, 2017b, 74).

This ideal model dismisses the messy and complex political realities that exist worldwide. It pretends that psychoactive drug consumption, production and trafficking are autonomous behaviors independent of many structural elements, including other social ills, harms, and policy constraining factors encountered in every country. Under these assumptions, illicit drug producers, traffickers, and users would be only a "few rotten social apples." And they could be "extirpated" by an effective and incorruptible law enforcement and judicial system and its agents.

The INCB 1992 Report triggered a reaction by a group of countries -Mexico and a few other Latin American and European countries, Australia and Canada- concerned with the need for harm reduction policies. It led to "a drug policy debate in the 1993 UN General Assembly in which resolution 48/12/ drafted by Mexico was adopted under which the General Assembly was to request the CND to monitor and evaluate the implementation of national and international drug control instruments, to identify areas of progress and weakness, and recommend to the high-level segment of the Economic and Social Council (ECOSOC) in 1995 'appropriate adjustments of drug control activities whenever required.' It was also to consider convening an ad-hoc expert group to contribute to the examination of the issues and identify 'concrete action-oriented recommendations'" (Jelsma, 2003).

Several initiatives followed, but the debate at the 1993 General assembly "clearly established the political limits of the search for 'appropriate adjustments' of the drug control system. Peru and Bolivia renewed diplomatic efforts to defend their traditional coca use. The WHO continued attempts to conquer ground within the UN system for a harm reduction philosophy and initiated several scientific studies. Discussions were opened about the need to review the classification of coca and cannabis products under the Conventions. Proposals were tabled to examine costs and benefits of Harm Reduction and decriminalisation strategies. And Mexico started in 1994 to rally support for a global summit of reflection, which eventually led to the 1998 UNGASS" (ibid).

The UNGASS-1998 was convened, to a substantial degree, in response to some countries' requests for better demand reduction policies. Before that, "the importance of demand reduction" was the topic of the Board's 1993 report. The report distinguishes between demand and supply reduction: "[i]It is evident that, at the national level, supply reduction and demand reduction cannot be separated from each other. There is, however, a major difference at the international level. Measures against the illicit manufacture, production, traffic, and diversion of drugs can be 'codified' in international treaties because their identical application constitutes the sine qua non-criteria for the functioning of the international drug control system. Demand reduction methods, however, cannot be 'standardized' by legal documents" (INCB, 1993, 3). This is a consequence of the flexibility that the conventions allow in the treatment of drug users.

The Board recognizes that demand reduction programs "should be carefully designed, taking into consideration not only the individuals concerned but also the socio-cultural and economic milieux. It follows, therefore, that programmes must be adapted to the society in question" (INCB, 1993, 4) and encourages governments to develop programs of education and community empowerment. The Board concludes that "[t]he success of demand reduction programmes depends on two factors: the political will of Governments to tackle the problem, as evidenced by, among other things, the provision of the necessary financial resources; and the community's willingness to cooperate" (ibid, 4). This is an overly optimistic statement that assumes demand reduction efforts could succeed if governments have "political will" and the involved communities would be willing to cooperate with the government. In other words, it assumes that psychoactive drug use is not related to unresolved structural social problems and that governments have the knowledge and capacity to eliminate drug uses.

However, regarding drug supply, the INCB is less optimistic and argues that traffickers take advantage of countries: "that suffer from civil war, terrorist activities, political instability, ethnic conflict, economic depression or social tension; that are not in a position to ensure governmental control over some parts of their territories; and that are not able to maintain adequate law enforcement, customs and pharmaceutical control services" (ibid, 1).

The Board then warns that countries that face those problems are a main obstacle to the IDCS success because "[t]he functioning of the international drug control system depends on the universal application of the provisions of the international drug control treaties. Deficiencies in national legislation and/or in the implementation of national laws and regulations create loopholes in the global network of protective measures" (ibid, 2).

The years before the UNGASS 1998 saw frequent debates at the CND meetings. WHO conducted research on the effects of marijuana and cocaine use that suggested that some non-medical uses could be allowed. The documents produced were suppressed and never published due to political pressures from some countries that argued that they had not been rigorous enough. This appeared to have deepened the drug policy divide.

The 1994 report's thematic chapter - "Evaluation of the effectiveness of the international drug control treaties" - defended the efficacy of the conventions, arguing that without them, the growth of drug use and addiction in the world would have been much greater. It continued expressing its trust in a simple policy solution to a complex social and medical problem: "the 'ideal' objective of a society free of non-medical use of drugs is a goal that should be aimed at, even though it may not be achievable" (INCB, 1995a, 3). However, as shown in Chapter ten section 10.3.2, in the supplement to the 1994 report, the INCB appeared ambivalent about non-medical uses of coca (1995b; ¶46 and ¶47). It requested the WHO a scientific review of the value and risks of coca chewing and the *mate de coca* (coca tea) to resolve whether these products would comply with the IDCS. Unfortunately, that study was never made.

But the drug-free society goal was re-stated again in the 1997 INCB report issued a few months before the 1998 UNGASS: "While the elimination of all forms of drug experimentation, use and abuse will never be achieved, it should not be a reason to give up the ultimate aim of all prevention efforts, namely a drug-free society. Most prevention efforts do have an effect and, like commercial advertising, reach enough of the market to have a positive impact. Prevention programmes should be considered successful even though they may not prevent all illicit drug use" (INCB, 1998, 1).

5.4 CONSEQUENCES

After 1992 the Board became a more active world drug policy actor. It argued that the international drug conventions were an important achievement in the history of international relations that all Parties should comply with. After all, treaties are contracts agreed in good faith, and they should be enforced. The fundamental INCB policy approach was quite simple: the drug conventions impose constraints on domestic and international drug policies that are non-negotiable. The Board will not accept any policy compromise. If governments encounter other constraints to their drug policies, they "shall take such legislative and administrative measures as may be necessary" to overcome them. Parties are committed to complying with article 4 of the 1961 Single Convention on Narcotic Drugs.[112] In other words, if governments face social, political, economic, etc., constraints, they are committed to overcoming them because they implicitly agreed to do so when they ratified the drug conventions. This is a "legalistic" approach that disregards the drug policies' social, political, economic, and cultural consequences. It is also an attempt to "depoliticize" drug policies, which would be an oxymoron.

The decision of the INCB to define some of the essential terms of the drug conventions turned a body charged with monitoring the countries' compliance with the conventions into a body that interprets the conventions. Not surprisingly, critics argued that the new thematic chapter of the annual report had been used to extend the INCB's mandate from watchdog to guardian of the conventions (Bewley-Taylor and Trace, 2006). Since then, many INCB members have claimed that they are indeed the "guardians of the conventions." It raises the millennia-old question of "who guards the guardians?" The following excerpt from an Economics Nobel Prize acceptance

---

[112] The INCB (1992, ¶14) also cites the 1971 convention that in article 5 requires Parties "of that Convention to take 'such measures as it considers appropriate'".

speech examines this issue, raised millennia years ago at the dawn of democracy.

> In posing the famous question, the Roman author, Juvenal, was suggesting that wives could not be trusted, and keeping them under guard is not a solution – because the guards cannot be trusted either.
>
> Half a millennium or so earlier, Plato, in *The Republic,* expressed a more optimistic view regarding the guardians or rulers of the city-state, namely that one should be able to trust them to behave properly; that it was absurd to suppose that they should require oversight.
>
> Socrates, referring to an earlier statement that 'drunkenness is most unbefitting guardians,' says: 'From intoxication we said that they must abstain. For a guardian is surely the last person in the world to whom it is allowable to get drunk and not know where on earth he is.' To which Glaucon, Socrates' interlocutor, replies: 'yes it would be absurd that a guardian should need a guard.' Instead of Juvenal's later pessimism, indeed cynicism, Plato - through Glaucon - expresses the optimistic view that one should be able to trust the city guardians and rulers to behave properly: that they should require oversight is and absurdity.
>
> A casual perusal of daily newspapers indicates that there is nothing absurd about the present day 'guardians' – by which I mean leaders and officials of political, economic and social entities – needing and indeed getting a great deal of oversight (Hurwicz, 2008, 377).

Because of the ambiguity of the conventions, the INCB policy positions depend on who the Board Members are and what they know and believe about drug policies. The INCB members have been primarily medical doctors and public health experts, law enforcement officials, penal lawyers, and diplomats. They have interpreted the Conventions from the perspective of their professions, colored by the ideology of their beliefs and perceptions of the State's role and the individuals' freedoms and liberties. Because of their background, the influence of the social sciences on those interpretations has been minimal.

Moreover, I posit that given the diverse ethnic, national, professional, and cultural backgrounds of the INCB members, the probability that when confronted with complex policy issues and problems, they all arrive at the same solution is virtually zero. Indeed, most people have strong feelings about psychoactive drugs' production, trade, and use that shape their views about those activities. Reason and logic play a role in shaping peoples' positions about drugs. Still, the fact that many cultures and professions generate different mindsets and worldviews presents a challenge to achieve a unique interpretation of the drug conventions and IDCS policies that could be successfully implemented worldwide.

The problems mentioned above are reinforced by a non-existent institutional memory (the Board does not keep detailed minutes of its sessions [113] and the lack of the required law interpretation skills among the INCB members and its staff. As a result, the interpretation of the conventions by the INCB is subjective and a function of the convictions, intuitions, and beliefs of whoever the Board members are at each point in time. Thus, it is not surprising that the INCB has not consistently interpreted the drug conventions over time and place. The following chapters are devoted to analyzing some of these inconsistencies.

---

[113] For example, some time back before publishing "Re-examining the 'Medical and Scientific. Basis for Interpreting the Drug Treaties: Does the 'Regime' Have Any Clothes?" (2016), I circulated the draft among all Board members and requested the Board's secretary to circulate it among the staff. The only comment I received was from the secretary of the Board who advised me not to publish it. However, apparently nobody had any recollection of the fact that 12 years earlier the Board had been concerned with the same issue and had defined the terms "a medicine", "medical use", "scientific purposes" and "medical consumption".

CHAPTER SIX. THE IDCS POLICY CHARACTERISTICS AND THE EVOLUTION OF ITS NARRATIVE

6.1 OVERVIEW

As noted above, the IDCS has not had a formal public policy model. It is based on a simplistic narrative: drug addiction is devastating for the addicted persons, families, the community, and the nation. To protect humans and society, after a lengthy process, the nations of the world agreed to prohibit all non-medical and scientific uses of the controlled psychoactive drugs and to "take such legislative and administrative measures as may be necessary" to succeed in implementing that prohibition.

As also shown above, after the 1988 Convention, the criticisms of the IDCS continued, and in 1992 the INCB changed the format of its annual report and used its chapter one to take a more active part in the drug policy debates. It became a thematic chapter in which the Board presented its positions on diverse, relevant topics.[114]

The 1992 annual report thematic chapter was a powerful attack on any possible legalization of non-medical drug uses. It made dire warnings that any such policy would have extremely high social costs. However, these statements were made without references to any scientific sources that supported them. They were presented as facts that every sensible person that had worked on drugs should know. The Board warned that any possible legal non-medical drug use was only a first step in a slippery slope that would lead to legal non-medical use of all other drugs. Not surprisingly, a couple of years later, in the 1994 report (INCB, 1995a, 3), the Board reiterated its

---

[114] This chapter reviews the thematic chapters of the INCB's annual reports that are most relevant to the main issues treated in this book, as well as the main political declarations and plans of action produced by the 1998 and 2016 UNGASS and by the CND meetings.

ideal goal of a "drug-free world," which was repeated in the 1997 report (INCB, 1998, 1) issued a few weeks before UNGASS 1998.

However, the Board's thematic chapters have not always raised issues related to the policy constrain to *medical and scientific purposes*. Topics like "the importance of demand reduction" (1993 report), "giving more priority to combating money-laundering" (INCB, 1996), "drug abuse and the criminal justice system" (INCB, 1997), "preventing drug abuse in an environment of drug promotion" (INCB, 1998), "freedom from pain and suffering" (INCB, 2000), "Alternative development and legitimate livelihoods" (INCB, 2006), "internationally controlled drugs and the unregulated market" (INCB, 2007), "shared responsibility in international drug control" (INCB, 2013), and others, expressed positions coherent with the Board's traditional interpretation of the conventions and tended to be well received and improved the knowledge of the conventions among the Parties to the treaties. Other thematic chapters discussed below were more controversial.

6.2 THE UNGASS 1998 POLITICAL DECLARATION AND THE CND 2009 ACTION PLAN

The UNGASS 1998 Political Declaration (United Nations, 1998a) supported the commitment to past IDCS policy positions and highlighted drug uses' adverse consequences.

> Drugs destroy lives and communities, undermine sustainable human development, and generate crime. Drugs affect all sectors of society in all countries; in particular, drug abuse affects the freedom and development of young people, the world's most valuable asset. Drugs are a grave threat to the health and well-being of all mankind, the independence of States, democracy, the stability of nations, the structure of all societies, and the dignity and hope of millions of people and their families; therefore:

We, the States Members of the United Nations,

Concerned about the serious world drug problem, having assembled at the twentieth special session of the General Assembly to consider enhanced action to tackle it in a spirit of trust and cooperation,

1. Reaffirm our unwavering determination and commitment to overcoming the world drug problem through domestic and international strategies to reduce both the illicit supply of and demand for drugs;

2. Recognize that action against the world drug problem is a common and shared responsibility requiring an integrated and balanced approach in full conformity with the purposes and principles of the Charter of the United Nations and international law, and particularly with full respect for the sovereignty and territorial integrity of States, the principle of non-intervention in internal affairs of States, and all human rights and fundamental freedoms. Convinced that the world drug problem must be addressed in a multilateral setting, we call upon States which have not already done so to become a party to and fully implement the three international drug control conventions. Also, we renew our commitment to adopting and reinforcing comprehensive national legislation and strategies to give effect to the provisions of those conventions, ensuring through periodic reviews that the strategies are effective" (United Nations, 1998a).

However, the United Nations also formulated a *Declaration on the Guiding Principles of Drug Demand Reduction* (United Nations, 1998b) that reiterate the importance of policies to limit demand. The **UNGASS** 1998 Political Declaration acknowledges that shared responsibility requires an integrated and balanced policy approach but shied away from making explicit the goal of a drug-free society. It advocated a balanced policy approach and set an action plan to achieve a significant drug demand reduction by 2008: the signing countries "[r]ecognize that demand reduction is an indispensable pillar in the global approach to countering the world drug problem, commit ourselves to introducing into our national programmes and strategies the provisions set out in the Declaration on the Guiding Principles of Drug Demand Reduction,[115] to working closely with the United Nations International Drug Control Programme to develop action-oriented strategies to assist in the implementation of the Declaration, and to establishing the year 2003 as a target date for new or enhanced drug demand reduction strategies and programmes set up in close collaboration with public health, social welfare, and law enforcement authorities, and also commit ourselves to achieving significant and measurable results in the field of demand reduction by the year 2008" (United Nations, 1998a, ¶17).

Following UNGASS 1998, the Board produced several thematic chapters that responded to some of the issues raised in that assembly. The thematic chapters of the 2002 (INCB, 2003) and 2003 (INCB, 2004) reports focused on "Illicit drugs and economic development" and "Drugs, crime, and violence: the microlevel impact." In both chapters, the Board argued that the consequences of the illegal drugs markets on societies, where they become entrenched, exceed any possible benefits of the income and wealth generated by the illegal trade.

In the 2002 report, the main point was that even when it appears that illegal drug revenues and profits produce economic development, in the long run, this is a mirage because the accumulated negative consequences of that development eliminate the possibility of achieving sustained economic, social development. Thus, governments should eliminate drug trafficking to achieve sustained economic development.

The same report stresses that micro-trafficking generates income for slum dwellers but leads to the development of local gangs that undermine the state's legitimacy in the affected areas and weaken

---

[115] See resolution S-20/3.

or destroy social cohesion harming social stability and development. The recommendation is to develop community-based initiatives to strengthen local societies and eliminate gangs and drug trafficking. These two chapters reflect the INCB's policy approach that underlines its position:

1. The prohibition of non-medical and scientific drug use cannot be subject to standard public policy evaluation. The possible benefits that the growth of the illegal drug industry and illegal markets could bring to a country would never exceed the social costs they generate.
2. The IDCS treaties are contracts that the Parties must respect. If the consequences of complying with these treaties are dire, countries should focus on eliminating the underlined factors that allow those consequences to take place in their societies.
3. In conclusion, limiting controlled drug use to medical and scientific purposes is an unmovable policy anchor. Countries must take measures to limit any possible negative consequence of the illegal markets without attributing any costs caused by those markets to that policy anchor.

In the 2007 thematic chapter on "The principle of proportionality of drug-related offenses" (INCB, 2008), it is argued that penal sanctions should be proportional to the crime. Proportionality in sanctions was mentioned before in the 1996 Report's thematic chapter on drug abuse and issue. This chapter presented an interesting dilemma to the Board because, as noted above, articles 39 of the 1961 and 23 of the 1971 conventions allow the Parties to apply stricter measures than those required by the conventions, which imply that governments can disregard the proportionality issue when sanctioning drug crimes. Furthermore, none of the drug conventions mention proportionality explicitly as a criterium for establishing the penal sanctions incurred by drug crimes. However, the Board, in this case, went beyond the conventions to argue for proportionality.

> Transposing the international drug control conventions into domestic law is subject to the internationally recognized principle of proportionality. The principle requires a State's response to anything that may harm peace, order, or good governance to be proportionate. In a narrower, criminal justice sense, the principle permits punishment as an acceptable response to crime, provided that it is not disproportionate to the seriousness of the crime. Variants of the broad principle are often enshrined in States' constitutions, with specific rules set out in more detailed national law. International and regional human rights instruments[116] and crime prevention and criminal justice instruments often develop or set the standards (INCB, 2008a, 2).

Here the INCB seems to acknowledge that proportionality in criminal sanctions is part of the individual drug producers, traffickers, and users' human rights, which was an issue that the Board avoided facing directly for a long time. The Board's implicit conflict between proportionality and the literal interpretation of articles 39 of the 1961 and 23 of the 1971 conventions was finally solved in the INCB's 2014 report (INCB, 2015). It states clearly that the drug conventions did not require "war on drugs" type policies and that countries should not apply the death penalty for drug crimes.[117] Before the 2014 report, the board members had interpreted the conventions narrowly, even denying any relation between drug policies and human rights on the

---

[116] For example, the Universal Declaration of Human Rights (General Assembly resolution 217 A (III)).

[117] It is interesting that until now no hard liner drug policy government has argued that requiring proportionality in drug crimes breaches the conventions.

basis that it would exceed its mandate (see the INBC President's statements in chapter seven).

Following the UNGASS-1998 mandates, the 2008 CND had to review the assembly's 10-year achievements. The years after UNGASS-1998 saw significant movements among civil society groups and governments with diverse and contradictory positions interested in evaluating the UNGASS's results. The disagreements among countries prevented the 2008 CND from having a rigorous evaluation of the UNGASS results. However, UNODC's Executive Director, Antonio Maria Costa, defended the IDCS, arguing that while the world drug problem had not been solved, it had been contained. He presented an interesting set of facts to support this statement (CND, 2008):

1. Illicit drug use has been contained to less than 5% of the world adult population, as opposed to 5 to 6 times this proportion for people addicted to tobacco or alcohol.
2. There are no more than 25 million problem drug users - that is less than 0.5% of the world population. There are more people affected by AIDS.
3. Deaths due to drugs are limited to perhaps 200.000 per year, namely 1/10 of those killed by alcohol and 1/20 of those killed by tobacco.
4. Worldwide, drug cultivation has been slashed (with the obvious exception of Afghanistan where the issue is insurgency, more than narcotics).
5. Adherence to the international drug control regime is practically universal, with the principle of shared responsibility unanimously accepted.
6. The regulatory system of production, distribution and use of drugs for medical purposes, functions well.

The comparisons used on deaths assume that a legal but regulated market for drugs like cocaine, methamphetamine, and the like, will produce addiction levels and deaths comparable to those of alcohol and tobacco. However, when presented with those figures, a curious researcher would ask why alcohol kills only one-half the number of those killed by tobacco. For this researcher, one question would be, what makes the social and economic costs of using those two drugs different? And another, how can we know that the costs generated by other drugs would be of similar magnitude to those of alcohol and tobacco? Researching this issue would provide lessons to improve market regulation of psychoactive drugs and lower their social costs.

Costa went on to argue that "even in the face of evidence to the contrary, the popular perception is that drug policy is not working as it should." For him, the policies were not the problem, but the bad image that people had of them because, unfortunately, they had "unintended consequences" (ibid). The first one "is the huge criminal market." It will not disappear with legalization because it only "may reduce the profits to criminals, but it will certainly increase the damage to the health of individuals and society. Drugs are not dangerous because they are illegal: they are illegal because they are dangerous. [...] It is a dangerous dialectic to call for *a world of free drugs* as opposed to *a world free of drugs*: they come with different degrees of collateral damage. With vision and resources, we can enforce the UN drug conventions in a manner that, on balance, represents by far the healthiest and the safest option" (ibid).

This statement assumes that in all societies, the collateral damage generated by illegal drugs illegal markets is always less than the social cost attributed to increased drug use. It, however, has never been demonstrated. Besides, it does not consider that the collateral damage varies significantly across countries depending on their vulnerabilities. Costa's assertion might be correct in some countries but very wrong in others.

Costa's second "(unintended) consequence has been policy displacement. [...] Fighting drug-related crime is expensive. So, despite the fact that promoting public health is the first principle of drug control, public security has received much greater investment at the expense of drug prevention and treatment (3:1 is the prevailing ratio). I fear this is political expediency: to focus on quick wins, like seizures and arrests (that reduce the problem), rather than on agents of slow change, like prevention and treatment (that solve the problem)" (ibid).

This statement puts public health above welfare as the primary purpose of the conventions. It disregards and denies the inherent hard-line authoritarian law enforcement bias of the IDCS, which makes it easier to apply harsh enforcement policies than a complex long-term policy approach to deal with the underlining social vulnerability factors.

Costa's third "consequence has been geographical displacement. Tighter controls in one region or on one product, produce a swelling of activity elsewhere. As a result of this *balloon effect*, the problem is displaced, but not solved" (ibid). This is a simple effect that any Ph. D. economist from a top university like Dr. Costa should have predicted rather than thinking of it as "unintended."

In summary, all the negative consequences of the IDCS policies that were unintended for Dr. Costa were so only because the narrow approach used to implement the policies did not allow the IDCS agencies to acknowledge their consequences. However, they were all expected by contemporary economics, criminology, and other social sciences. It, however, has a caveat: the development of those consequences could not have been forecasted accurately.

Despite these analytical weaknesses, the CND's document had interesting contributions to UNODC's policies. It argues first that law enforcement, while necessary, was not sufficient. Second, economic development, particularly for coca and poppy growing peasants, had to be a priority. Third, Costa also praised civil society organizations and the need to consider them legitimate participants in the drug policy debates and implementation. Fourth, another key point was the first-time recognition by United Nations drug agencies that the term *harm reduction* was legitimate, even though the document expanded the concept to include activities that those who have used the term might not have agreed with.

> I urge you not to get caught up in sensitivities about words. Everything we do at UNODC is meant to reduce harm: helping farmers switch to licit crops; assisting countries identify, monitor, and disrupt drug trafficking; developing educational campaigns in favour of drug prevention; helping governments to deal with drug law offenders in a humanitarian way. Let us not shy away from this jargon -- harm reduction - just because it has been appropriated by a vocal minority that has given to it a narrow and controversial interpretation (ibid).[118]

In another significant contribution, the document highlighted the importance of human rights and related it to harm reduction.

> Our work is guided first and foremost by *the UN Charter* that commits signatories to fundamental freedoms and by the *Universal Declaration of Human Rights* [...]. In Article 25 of the *Universal Declaration*, health is listed as a basic human right. As we emphasize the health aspects of drug control, it stands to reason that implementation of the drug Conventions must proceed with due regard to human rights. Thus far, there has been little attention paid to this aspect of our work. This definitely needs to be amended. Although drugs kill, I do not believe we need to kill because of drugs. The UN drug Conventions have left it to individual states to deal

---

[118] As a member of the civil society, I attended the 2008 and 2009 CND sessions. I had a copy of the CND originally distributed paper, but I misplaced it. Recently I found the final version in the UNODC web pages, but I could not find some of the quotes I had saved from the original, like the one I just quoted. The currently available version of the paper is less controversial than the original.

with health care and crime retribution, in relation with the specific cultural and judicial contexts. Mindful of this, today I propose that Member States extend the concept of harm reduction to include the need to give serious consideration to whether the imposition of capital punishment for drug-related crimes is a best practice (ibid).

These UNODC positions placed it ahead of the INCB in acknowledging the relevance of human rights for drug policies which, as noticed, the Board recognized only in its 2014 report.

The 2008 CND postponed a more rigorous evaluation of UNGASS 1998 results for one more year to allow a deep reflection period. The 2008 CND also induced civil society to act. A month after the CND meeting, former presidents Cardoso (Brazil), Gaviria (Colombia), and Zedillo (Mexico), jointly with a few other Latin American leaders and intellectuals, established the Latin American Commission on Drugs and Democracy. This Commission published in 2009 a report on time for that year's CND. This overly critical report declared that the war on drugs was dead and recommended exploring the possibilities to de-penalize marijuana consumption (Latin American Commission on Drugs and Democracy, 2009).

Civil society groups that defend the drug policy status quo also became active with the support of Sweden and many NGOs in the United States, Australia, and other countries. A significant part of them had links with religious groups. In September 2008, they met in Stockholm in the First World Forum Against Drugs, attended by over six hundred delegates from more than 80 countries. In that event, the World Federation Against Drugs (WFAD) was established. UNODC appears to have supported this meeting as Executive Director Antonio Maria Costa and Christina Ogüz, the head of UNODC's office in Afghanistan, were two main speakers.

The acceptance of a broad harm reduction concept in the UNODC document at the 2008 CND motivated a movement of 26 countries within the European Union to formally have the CND's recognition of the role of *harm reduction* as a legitimate drug policy. This movement was also supported by NGOs in the United Kingdom, the Netherlands, Spain, Portugal, Switzerland, and other countries. However, their proposal ran into trouble when the United States, Russia, Japan, Sweden, Italy, the Holy See, Cuba, Colombia, and others argued that the term *harm reduction* was too broad. When one of those countries insisted on a clear definition of *harm reduction*, it was impossible to arrive at a consensual definition. The group opposed to *harm reduction* vetoed any mention of it in the political declaration of the 2009 CND. The CND members have no problem, as amply discussed above, with the lack of definitions for its most essential convention terms, but they could not accept the same criterium for *harm reduction*.

The Drug-Free America Foundation, a founding member of WFAD, organized a side event at the 2009 CND in which they advocated strict drug abstinence. The INCB President, Prof. Hamid Ghodse, was a prominent speaker. When someone from the audience asked if to be consistent, they should also advocate total abstinence of alcohol and tobacco, the answer from some of the panelists was clear: "we would like to do so, but we do not think it is practical at this time."

In the end, the Political Declaration and Plan of Action of the 2009 CND (UNODC, 2009) reaffirmed the 2008 CND positions on human rights and abstinence: "the ultimate goal of both demand and supply reduction strategies and sustainable development strategies is to minimize and eventually eliminate the availability and use of illicit drugs and psychotropic substances in order to ensure the health and welfare of humankind."

It also welcomed "the important role played by civil society, in particular non-governmental organizations, in addressing the world drug problem." These assertions were followed by reaffirmations of traditional positions like the need for a global and multidisciplinary policy approach, the need for cooperation among state Parties and between them, the INCB and the WHO, and "reiterate our commitment to promote, develop, review or strengthen effective, comprehensive, integrated drug demand reduction programmes, based on scientific evidence and covering a range of measures, including primary prevention, early intervention, treatment, care, rehabilitation, social reintegration, and related support services, aimed at promoting health and social well-being" (ibid).

The political declaration also acknowledges "the continuing efforts made and progress achieved in countering the world drug problem, note with great concern the unprecedented surge in illicit opium production and trafficking, the continuing illicit cocaine manufacture and trafficking, the increasing illicit cannabis production and trafficking and the increasing diversion of precursors, as well as the related distribution and use of illicit drugs, and stresses the need to strengthen and intensify joint efforts at the national, regional and international levels to tackle those global challenges in a more comprehensive manner, in accordance with the principle of a common and shared responsibility, including by means of enhanced and better coordinated technical and financial assistance" (ibid).

After acknowledging the persistence of other significant problems, the political declaration decided to repeat the goals of earlier decades.

> To establish 2019 as a target date for States to eliminate or reduce significantly and measurably:
>
> (a) The illicit cultivation of opium poppy, coca bush, and cannabis plant;
>
> (b) The illicit demand for narcotic drugs and psychotropic substances; and drug-related health and social risks;
>
> (c) The illicit production, manufacture, marketing, and distribution of, and trafficking in, psychotropic substances, including synthetic drugs;
>
> (d) The diversion of and illicit trafficking in precursors;
>
> (e) Money-laundering related to illicit drugs" (ibid).

The plan of action of the 2009 CND was highly complex, comprehensive, and very detailed, but from a public policy perspective, inapplicable and unrealistic. The plan focused on three broad types of activities: a) demand reduction measures to lower drug abuse and dependence through a comprehensive approach; b) supply reduction and related measures, subdivided into three parts; and c) countering money-laundering and promoting judicial cooperation to enhance international cooperation. Each activity spelled out broad and undefined actions that the Member States should undertake. Their number exceeded two hundred, and each one starts with the word "should" followed by pursue, encourage, develop, promote, deliver, undertake, consider, strengthen, invest, support, ensure, involve, provide, establish, reassess, monitor, implement, address, enhance, harness, identify, cope, focus, endeavor, etc. Most of these actions are vague and leave the actual policy measures to be decided by each government. Any government that took them seriously would have had to make great institutional and structural reforms and make drug control a principal, if not the central issue in the country's policy agenda. Unfortunately, this Plan was destined to be a lengthy list of good intentions with few practical consequences. (Box 1)

BOX 1: 2009 CND PLAN OF ACTION

ACTIVITIES	ACTIONS AND MEASURES	
Demand reduction measures to lower drug abuse and dependence through a comprehensive approach	– Enhancing international cooperation. – Comprehensive approach to drug demand reduction. – Human rights, dignity, and fundamental freedoms in the context of drug demand reduction. – Measures based on scientific evidence. – Availability of and accessibility to drug demand reduction services, – Mainstreaming community involvement and participation, – Targeting vulnerable groups and conditions, – Drug use and dependence care in the criminal justice system. – Quality standards and training of staff. – Data collection, monitoring and evaluation.	
Supply reduction and related measures	Reducing the illicit supply of drugs	– Enhancing cooperation, coordination, and law enforcement operations to reduce supply. – Addressing new trafficking trends. – Reducing violence related to drug trafficking. – Addressing supply and demand reduction together. – Strengthening of anti-corruption measures and provision of technical assistance and capacity-building.
	Control of precursors and of amphetamine-type stimulants	– Improving understanding of the phenomenon of amphetamine-type stimulants. – Targeting the clandestine manufacture of

BOX 1: 2009 CND PLAN OF ACTION		
ACTIVITIES	**ACTIONS AND MEASURES**	
		amphetamine-type stimulants. – Preventing illegal sale and diversion. – Raising awareness and reducing demand. – Emerging issues in precursor control.
	International cooperation on eradicating the illicit cultivation of crops used to produce narcotic drugs and psychotropic substances and on alternative development	– Strengthening research, data collection, and assessment tools. – International cooperation on development-oriented drug control. – A balanced, long-term approach to addressing the illicit cultivation of crops used to produce narcotic drugs and psychotropic substances. – Innovative strategies to support alternative development.
Countering money-laundering and promoting judicial cooperation to enhance international cooperation	Countering money-laundering	
	Judicial cooperation	– Extradition – Mutual legal assistance – Transfer of proceedings – Controlled delivery – Witness protection – Complementary measures

Source: ibid (summary by the author)

6.3 THE INCB POLICY RESPONSES TO THE 2009 POLITICAL DECLARATION

The first INCB policy response was to continue promoting past policy frameworks. The 2010 and 2011 reports thematic chapters "drugs and corruption" and "social cohesion, social disorganization, and illegal drugs" are clear examples of an important consequence of focusing on an inflexible non-medical use policy anchor.

The chapter on drugs and corruption discusses the nature of corruption and its impact. It explains how organized crime intimidates and corrupts public officials, police, customs, and other law enforcement officials, the military, the judicial system, and how it has very damaging effects in countries with weak social controls and those in post-conflict situations. Then makes it clear that the vast profits generated by illegal drug markets are why corruption is prominent in some countries (INCB, 2011, 1). "The huge profits generated by illicit drug markets fuel the growth of powerful criminal organizations, whose financial resources sometimes exceed those of state institutions" (ibid, 9). And "dismantling the criminal organizations involved in drug trafficking or, at the very least, disrupting their activities is a prerequisite for successful drug control strategies" (INCB, 2011, 9). But is it viable?

This approach is consistent with the fact that the drug conventions require the prohibition of non-medical and non-scientific drug uses. However, the purposes of the Convention Against Corruption are only:

> (a) To promote and strengthen measures to prevent and combat corruption more efficiently and effectively.
> (b) To promote, facilitate and support international cooperation and technical assistance in the prevention of and fight against corruption, including asset recovery.

(c) To promote integrity, accountability, and proper management of public affairs and public property (UNODC, 2004 Article One).

Governments are required to eliminate non-medical or scientific drug uses, but the Convention Against Corruption only requires them to take measures to weaken corruption. But since corruption promotes illegal drug production, trafficking, and consumption, governments must also eliminate corruption to comply with the drug conventions.

In the 2011 chapter on social cohesion, the argument is that in communities where social cohesion has weakened, drug trafficking and consumption increase, but there are no references to the role of the illegal drug markets in weakening the communities' social cohesion. In the report's foreword, Board's President, Professor Ghodse, summarizes the chapter's main argument.

> The Board, while recognizing the importance of personal responsibility, describes how, in some communities, drug abuse has become almost endemic, part of a vicious cycle involving a wide array of social problems relating to violence, organized crime, corruption, unemployment, poor health and poor education. Those communities pose a risk not only to the persons living in them, but also to the wider society of which the communities are a part. Social cohesion — the ties that bind people together in communities and society — can be an indicator of the health of communities, and drug abuse and criminality can be a symptom of a 'fractured' society — a society suffering from lack of cohesion. Threats to social cohesion can include social inequality, migration, political and economic transformation, an emerging culture of excess, the growth of individualism and consumerism, shifting traditional values, conflict, rapid urbanization, a breakdown in respect for the law, and the existence of an illicit drug economy at the

local level. While a combination of those threats can be seen in many communities throughout the world, their existence does not mean that marginalization and drug problems are inevitable. It is important to respond to the needs of communities experiencing social disintegration before a tipping point is reached, beyond which the capacity for effective counteraction becomes insufficient. (INCB, 2012, iii-v)

The argument is like the earlier one on corruption and other social problems: drug abuse causes exceptionally high social costs. Therefore, it should be eliminated. But to achieve this, it is necessary to solve other social problems that contribute to addiction.

Social disintegration is a factual occurrence that must be attacked. The Convention Against Corruption seeks to promote anti-corruption programs while the drug conventions require the prohibition of all non-medical and non-scientific drug uses. Drug conventions' Parties are committed to eliminating all non-medical and non-scientific drug uses. Therefore, they should firmly apply the Drug Conventions policies and take measures to strengthen social cohesion to help drug conventions to achieve their goal of a "drug-free world."

The 2010 and 2011 reports acknowledge the circularity between illegal drugs, corruption, and social cohesion phenomena. Still, they refuse to recognize that they must be treated as a complex whole and disregard the contributory role of the illegal drug markets to generate or trigger those other social problems.

The thematic chapter of the 2012 INCB Report was on "Shared responsibility in international drug control." This chapter is less controversial than earlier ones because "[t]he clearest indication of the commitment of Governments worldwide to address the drug problem in a coordinated concerted and shared manner is the fact that almost all States have acceded to the international drug control conventions" (INCB, 2013, 4). Indeed, in principle, all governments would argue that they are willing to cooperate with the rest to control illegal drugs markets. The chapter has examples of good practices of shared responsibilities in the control of licit drugs, demand reduction measures, supply reduction and interdiction, and judicial cooperation" (INCB, 2013, 4-6).

It also warns that for them to be effective, "support for the principle of shared responsibility in drug control must go beyond rhetoric. As a cross-cutting issue, drug control and its legal framework — the international drug control system — have the power to effectively mobilize many actors in government departments, non-governmental organizations, the private sector, professional health-care, and consumer organizations and regional and international organizations" (ibid, 7).

The chapter restates the international character of psychoactive drug markets and the need for cooperation among all countries to achieve the global drug policy goals of the IDCS.

The 2013 thematic chapter (INCB, 2014), "Economic consequences of drug abuse," develops an interesting argument: drug abuse inflicts immeasurable harm on human societies that unfortunately cannot be estimated, but society must devote large amounts of resources to lower the costs that drug addiction generates on health, public safety, crime, productivity, and governance. The Board's analysis acknowledges the complexity of the problem: "The effects of drug abuse on those domains depend upon a host of interconnections within and outside these fields, including other factors such as those discussed in chapter I of the annual report of the Board for 2011, e.g., social structures, cultural values, and government policies" (ibid, ¶2).

It then proceeds with a series of policy recommendations that countries should implement to reduce the costs of addiction. This also follows the traditional argument of the Board, which attributes the costs generated by the drugs' illegal markets to drug addiction. That is why the policy solution is to treat addicts and fight to eliminate the black drug markets. The INCB recommends better drug prevention, treatment programs, rehabilitation, resocialization programs, and strengthening government institutions to confront drug trafficking. The chapter also argues that drug policies should consider the externalities they generate, in other words, their consequences outside drug markets. The question of how to do it is left to the governments to decide. These recommendations are impractical because they implicitly apply the United Nations policy model that assumes that States have effective law enforcement and justice systems, enough fiscal resources, unquestioned legitimacy, and territorial control in societies with strong social cohesion. But if that were the case, they would already have taken care of their drug consumption problems.

The thematic chapter of the 2014 Report on "Implementation of a comprehensive, integrated and balanced approach to addressing the world drug problem" started changing how the INCB looked at the drug phenomenon. Even though the chapter replicates the standard Board's position describing all the social ills generated by addiction to psychoactive drugs use, it explains the circularity and interdependence of social ills: "At the same time, the world drug problem is itself the result of the weak rule of law, unstable socioeconomic and political conditions, poverty, marginalization, and corrupt political, juridical and economic institutions. The fact that the world drug problem can be both a reason for and a result of difficult economic, social and political conditions is what makes addressing it so challenging" (INCB, 2015, 1).

The Board argues that drug policies should be in "full compliance with, and universal application of the provisions of the three international drug control conventions; and the implementation of two fundamental principles, namely a common and shared responsibility for tackling the world drug problem, and a comprehensive, integrated and balanced approach to addressing the problem. [...] None of these elements represents an incitement to an undefined 'war on drugs,' nor do any of them impose a purely prohibitionist regime or condone the repression of human rights" (ibid,1).

Those two principles require "Member States to ensure that controlled substances are available for medical and scientific purposes. Member States should place equal emphasis on supply and demand reduction strategies" (INCB, 2015, 2) in cooperation with the IDCS to address comprehensively its drug policy issues, limiting "the availability of controlled substances exclusively to medical and scientific purposes, while preventing and significantly and measurably reducing, or eliminating, the illicit production of, trafficking in and use of such substances" (ibid, 2).

The paragraphs on the socioeconomic and sociocultural, security and stability issues assert that the drug phenomenon does not have direct causes and that vulnerable societies can suffer significant negative consequences from the existence of illegal drug markets. They also insist that those issues should play a role in the formulation and implementation of drug policies and that the stability and security of the political system "are basic requirements for solving national and international problems that are of an economic, social, cultural or humanitarian nature and in promoting and encouraging respect for human rights" (ibid, 7-8). Furthermore, the Board states that human rights norms and the international drug control conventions are coherent. The core objective of the IDCS is supportive of the critical elements of the human rights conventions (ibid, 8-9).

The argument is that addressing the world drug problem requires policies to follow those two basic norms. And these require limiting drug uses to medical and scientific purposes. Indeed, illegal drug markets sometimes have substantial negative social, political, and economic consequences. Still, under no circumstances could these consequences be big enough to justify any non-medical psychoactive drug uses. One key question raised by the argument of this chapter is simple: if drug phenomena are complex and do not have direct causes, how can one be so sure that seeking zero non-medical drug use is always the best policy? Confronting this question appears to have been avoided relying on the belief in the immeasurably of drug addiction social costs.

The 2015 annual report's thematic chapter (INCB, 2016a), "The health and welfare of mankind: challenges and opportunities for the international control of drugs," was issued a few weeks before UNGASS 2016. It asserted the need for market controls of addictive substances over which addicted consumers lose their ability to decide their consumption levels. It ratified the flexibility that the conventions give the governments to formulate their addiction treatment programs if they maintain the same standards as other medical treatments (ibid, 2). The Board advocates a comprehensive approach to drug control that should take into consideration "Socioeconomic factors such as poverty, hunger, economic inequality, social exclusion, deprivation, migration and displacement, limited access to education and employment prospects, and exposure to violence and abuse. [...] States must look deeper at socioeconomic factors such as poverty, marginalization, gender, and child development. The role and responsibility of families and society in protecting children by creating environments that are conducive to the prevention of drug abuse cannot be overemphasized" (ibid, 2).

The Board also discusses the social harms resulting from the illegal drug markets, including the development of *failed narco-states*, the challenges of law enforcement programs to avoid corruption and human rights violations, and warns about the growing power of organized crime. But the question of whether the restriction of drug use to medical and scientific purposes has been or may be a vital contributor to *failed narco-states* is never posited (ibid, 2).

Until 2016 the Board treated some critical negative consequences of implementing drug policies as "unintended collateral damages." In this chapter, the Board takes a different position.

> There are a number of unintended consequences that can flow from a variety of factors, including the unbalanced

implementation of national and international drug control measures. However, the argument that the unintended consequences of implementing the drug control system are evidence that currently scheduled substances should be authorized for non-medical purposes is based on the incorrect assumption that those undesired consequences cannot be addressed within the framework of the international drug control system. While these consequences are unintended, they are expected, and they may be prevented and managed. The challenge that States parties face is to implement their treaty obligations in a balanced way that minimizes the negative impact of drug abuse and measures to control drug trafficking and to educate and treat the victims of such trafficking (ibid, 6).

The positions developed in the last few thematic chapters were the basis for the INCB presentation at the plenary and side events of UNGASS 2016.

6.4 THE UNGASS 2016

UNGASS 2016 was convened at the behest of Colombia, Guatemala, and Mexico to promote a drug policy debate before the scheduled 2019 CND meeting when drug policy results were evaluated. The aim was not to reform or rewrite the drug conventions.

Once UNGASS was convened, an argument arose within the UN about which branch would write the agenda and the basic document of the conference. On one side, the UN organs dealing with human rights, environment, and economic development, and countries like Colombia, Mexico, and Uruguay wanted the document to be written in the New York United Nations offices, where the human rights and environment programs are located and where the 2030 SDG were negotiated. On the other side, China, Russia, the United States, Peru, Cuba, Nicaragua, Singapore, and other countries argued that the document had to be written in Vienna, where the UN drug organs are located. The latter won, and the document was written in Vienna. The site selection was not neutral. It benefited the countries that supported the drug policy status quo while lowering the influence of those that sought reforms. A committee was established to draft the outcome document (UNODC, 2016). It was made of CND and UNODC staff who consulted governments, other UN agencies, and NGOs.

The outcome document reaffirmed the traditional drug policy approach recognizing that "while tangible progress has been achieved in some fields, the world drug problem continues to present challenges to the health, safety, and wellbeing of all humanity, and we resolve to reinforce our national and international efforts and further increase international cooperation to face those challenges" (UNODC, 2016, 1). The following paragraph spells out the underlining goal:

> We reaffirm our determination to tackle the world drug problem and **to actively promote a society free of drug abuse** in order to help to ensure that all people can live in health, dignity, and peace, with security and prosperity, and reaffirm our determination to address public health, safety and social problems resulting from drug abuse (ibid, 1; bolds added).

The document also affirms its concern about the lack of availability of pain relief drugs in many parts of the world. It acknowledges the governments' shared responsibility and the need for "an integrated, multidisciplinary, mutually reinforcing, balanced, scientific evidence-based and comprehensive approach." It states that all drug policies should be in "full conformity with the purposes and principles of the Charter of the United Nations, international law and the Universal Declaration of Human Rights,[119] with full respect for the

---

[119] Resolution 217 A (III)

sovereignty and territorial integrity of States, the principle of non-intervention in the internal affairs of States, all human rights, fundamental freedoms, the inherent dignity of all individuals and the principles of equal rights and mutual respect among States" (ibid).

Governments are committed to implementing "effectively the provisions set out in the Political Declaration and Plan of Action." The document expresses confidence that efforts to achieve the Sustainable Development Goals for 2030 and "to effectively address the world drug problem are complementary and mutually reinforcing." It recognizes the existence of "many persistent, new and evolving challenges that should be addressed in conformity with the three international drug control conventions, which allow for sufficient flexibility for States parties to design and implement national drug policies according to their priorities and needs, consistent with the principle of common and shared responsibility and applicable international law" (ibid).

These statements reject any need for policy change or convention amendments. However, they recognize the need to mobilize resources to effectively implement the Political Declaration and Plan of Action and the operational recommendations contained in the document. The document acknowledges that "civil society, as well as the scientific community and academia, play an important role in addressing and countering the world drug problem, and note that affected populations and representatives of civil society entities, where appropriate, should be enabled to play a participatory role in the formulation, implementation, and the providing of relevant scientific evidence in support of, as appropriate, the evaluation of drug control policies and programmes, and we recognize the importance of cooperation with the private sector in this regard" (ibid). The question here is how to interpret "appropriate."

Other statements refer to the need for cooperation between United Nations agencies and government agencies. Most of the UNGASS outcome document (UNODC, 2016, 4-26) is devoted to 104 operational recommendations on a lengthy list of drug policy issues. Each one of these, like the policy recommendations of the 2009 Plan of Action (UNODC, 2009) commented above, starts with "governments should" plus words like pursue, encourage, develop, promote, deliver, undertake, consider, strengthen, etc., etc. The successful implementation of these recommendations would require governments, as noted for the 2009 Plan of Action, to make great institutional reforms and make drug control a principal if not the central issue in the country's policy agenda.

The INCB's President statement in the UNGASS plenary (Sipp, 2016) concurred with the outcome document. It highlighted the positive achievements of the IDCS, the policy flexibility afforded by the drug conventions, and the need to increase demand reduction efforts. It exhorted governments to apply law enforcement measures proportional to drug offenses and respect human rights. It pointed out the importance of many social factors that make countries vulnerable to developing drug problems. It also trusts the comprehensive, integrated, and balanced approach spelled out in the 2014 Report (INCB, 2015) to provide an adequate policy framework to the IDCS and follows the traditional rejection of any possible non-medical controlled drug uses.

The INCB's reference to social issues and human rights was a positive change. Still, its primary position did not deviate from the past as it dismissed any possible non-medical or non-scientific use of controlled drug substances.

6.5 THE POST UNGASS 2016

The 2016 report's thematic chapter on "Women and drugs" expanded the positions of the INCB to include a gender perspective in its policies. The chapter surveys the social, biological, and environmental differences of drug use patterns, risks, and harms between women and men. It explores co-morbid depression, the risks, and problems of incarcerated women, the effects of sexual violence on drug use, the links between lack of education and participation in the drug trade, the consequences of women's drug abuse and their incarceration on their children, the links between drug use and sex work, and the consequences on babies of drug use during pregnancy. In conclusion, drug policies must have a gender perspective and consider all the women's issues associated with their participation as drug producers, traffickers, and users. To do so, governments must overcome strong cultural and institutional obstacles to eliminate traditional discrimination against women.

The thematic chapter of the 2017 annual report "Treatment, rehabilitation and social reintegration for drug use disorders: essential components of drug demand reduction" acknowledges that "the use of mood-altering psychoactive substances has been part of human civilizations for millennia" (INCB, 2018, 2) and that societies have treated it in quite different ways, some tolerant, others repressive. The chapter moves away from the traditional terminology and distinguishes between drug use, drug abuse, harmful drug use, drug dependence, and drug addiction to avoid stigmatization and discrimination: "Harmful drug use is understood as a pattern of drug use that causes damage to the physical or mental health of the individual. Drug dependence is a condition in which drug use becomes one of the highest priorities in the user's life and carries with it a range of associated behaviours" (ibid, 3). The traditionally used term *drug addiction* is replaced by *dependence* and *drug abuse* by *harmful drug use* or *drug use disorders*. Given that context, the terms mainly used in this chapter are *drug use* and *drug use disorder*.

The new terms are part of the Board's efforts to shift the emphasis of drug policies from law enforcement to public health (ibid, 3). The chapter presents a complex picture of factors associated with drug use disorders that "are best viewed as biopsychosocial in origin. There is no single factor that causes an individual to use drugs. A variety of risk factors and protective factors interact with each other and may result in drug use and subsequent dependence" (ibid, 4). They include the individual's personality, genetic, biological, and environmental factors (ibid, 4). This position concurs with WHO

(2008) nine principles for treating drug dependence to increase the effectiveness of treatment and rehabilitation interventions.

The Board restates its evidence-based position that drug dependence treatment is socially very cost-effective compared to other drug policies. The chapter also discusses treatments for special populations: children and adolescents, women, people in prisons and other custodial settings, people with co-occurring drug use and other health disorders, and other special population groups. It also argues that treatment, rehabilitation, and social reintegration for drug use disorders are part of the human rights to health.

In the special topics section of chapter two of the report, the Board for the first time asserts that drug policies should always comply with the human rights conventions, as shown in length in chapter seven below. From the perspective of drug policies, the 2017 INCB report will be remembered more for its discussion on human rights in chapter two than for its thematic chapter one. The policy consequences of the statements in chapter two are more important than those of chapter one.

6.6 THE 2019 CND: A THIRD TRY WITH THE SAME RECIPE

The March 2019 CND meeting was required to evaluate the results of implementing the 2009 Action Plan. The UN created the "UN system coordination Task Team on the Implementation of the UN System Common Position on drug-related matters" to comply with that requirement. The task team included members from sixteen different organizations that produced a document detailing the lessons "learned over the last ten years: a summary of knowledge acquired and produced by the UN system on drug-related matters" (United Nations, 2019). The study was submitted by the UN Secretary-General, Antonio Guterres, to the CND. Its introduction highlights the significant challenges confronting current drug policies.

Drug markets are evolving at unprecedented speed. The range of substances and combinations available to users has never been wider, and the amounts produced have never been greater. Cultivation and manufacturing of heroin and cocaine have reached record highs, synthetic drugs continue to expand, and the market for NPS remains widely diversified with a growing interplay with traditional drug markets. The non-medical use of regulated prescription drugs (either diverted from licit channels or illicitly manufactured) is becoming a major threat: in addition to the ongoing opioid epidemic in North America, there are signs of an opioid epidemic due to the non-medical use of tramadol in North and sub-Saharan Africa, as well as in the Middle East. Drug-related deaths are on the rise. At the same time, access to controlled drugs for medical purposes remains a dramatic problem in most low-and middle-income countries.

Reasons for blooming drug markets are complex and diversified. A combination of poverty and limited social and economic opportunities of rural communities, political instability, lack of government control, and changed strategies of trafficking organizations has driven the high level of illicit crop cultivation. There remain multiple factors at individual, micro and macro level that affect the vulnerability to drug use and its path to harmful use. While progress has been made by some countries to increase the accessibility to human-rights and evidence-based policy interventions, challenges remain with insufficient investment and implementation of schemes to prevent, treat, and reduce the potential harms posed by drug use. In contrast to an increasing trend of donors' commitment for overall international assistance, assistance in the sectors of alternative development and 'narcotics control' has significantly declined since 2008.[120] Punitive drug policies

---

[120] UNODC (2016).

continue to be used in some communities, despite being ineffective in reducing drug trafficking or in addressing non-medical drug use and supply, and continue to undermine the human rights and well-being of persons who use drugs, as well as of their families and communities.

The SDG 2030 Agenda is putting the dignity, health and rights of people and planet at the center of sustainable development.

Drug matters are intertwined with all aspects of sustainable development. All areas of the 17 Sustainable Development Goals shape the nature and dynamic of the drug problem. At the same time, the impact of the drug problem and the response thereto on development can be observed at individual, community, and national levels. For example, ensuring healthy lives and promoting well-being for all (SDG 3) requires effective measures to address the world drug problem, while the lucrative drug trade compounds corruption risk and undermines responsive, accountable, and transparent institutions at all levels (SDG 16).

When well-designed drug policy interventions directly or indirectly result in an improvement in the level of development of their target populations, operations designed to improve sustainable development can address the vulnerability of people or communities affected by the drug problem and can ultimately help address it. However, if not based on human rights standards and a solid evidence base, drug policies can have a counterproductive effect on development. Abusive, repressive, and disproportionate drug control policies and laws are counterproductive, while also violating human rights, undercutting public health, and wasting vital public resources (United Nations, 2019, 5-6).

The Task Team report covers a wide array of health issues, including gender-related policies and the right to health, prevention, treatment of drug use disorders, measures to minimize adverse consequences of drug use, and the factors affecting the cost-effectiveness of drug policies. It also discusses effective law enforcement and protection of vulnerable communities, including prevention of and response to drug-related crime and how to counter-trafficking. It advocates proportionate and effective policies and responses (including evidence on alternatives to incarceration and decriminalization/depenalization of drug use) and legal guarantees and safeguards pertaining to criminal justice proceedings and the justice sector (including legal aid and the right to a fair trial). The paper discusses the problems presented by vulnerable societies, the links between drug trafficking and peace and security (money-laundering, corruption, armed conflict, and political fragility and stability), the challenges presented by NPS, the growing non-medical use of pharmaceuticals, the use of the internet for drug-related activities and the need to increase social inclusion and of improving information (monitoring, epidemiology, and statistics). The document acknowledges that:

> The multifaceted nature of the problem requires a comprehensive, multidisciplinary approach that includes targeted law enforcement efforts to dismantle organized crime and ensure the physical security of people, alongside efforts that promote health, good governance and sustainable development underpinned by the drug control conventions, human rights laws, principles and standards, such as the principles of equality and non-discrimination. [...] The drug control conventions allow countries sufficient flexibility to design and implement national drug policies according to their priorities and needs, consistent with the principle of common and shared responsibility. As emphasized by UNGASS, the 2030 Agenda for Sustainable Development and the international drug control conventions, international human rights treaties and other relevant instruments are complementary and mutually reinforcing. [...]

By working together through the Task Team [...] the UN system can provide the kind of multidisciplinary support to Member States that can deliver more effective, evidence-based, and humane drug control policies that help rather than hinder a country's efforts to achieve its Sustainable Development Goals and to 'leave no one behind' (ibid, 42-43).

There is no question that the multi-UN agency Task Team produced an interesting document that presents arguments that recognize the complexity of legal and illegal drug phenomena. The issue is whether they will be sufficient to develop policies to cope effectively with the "world drug problem." This document was consistent with the 2019 CND Ministerial Declaration that renewed trust in the 2009 CND Action Plan. The signers of the 2019 CND Ministerial Declaration reaffirmed their "[...] commitment to effectively addressing and countering the world drug problem in full conformity with

- the purposes and principles of the Charter of the United Nations, international law, and the Universal Declaration of Human Rights,[121]
- full respect for the sovereignty and territorial integrity of States,
- the principle of non-intervention in the internal affairs of States,
- all human rights, fundamental freedoms, the inherent dignity of all individuals, and the principles of equal rights and mutual respect among States" (CND, 2019, 1).

They also reaffirmed their commitment "to actively promote **a society free of drug abuse** in order to help ensure that all people can

---

[121] General Assembly resolution 217 A (111).

live in health, dignity, and peace, with security and prosperity, and reaffirm our determination to address public health, safety and social problems resulting from drug abuse" (ibid, 1; bolds added).

They recognize "that there are persistent, new and evolving challenges that should be addressed in conformity with the three international drug control conventions, which allow for sufficient flexibility for States parties to design and implement national drug policies according to their priorities and needs, consistent with the principle of common and shared responsibility and applicable international law" (ibid, 2), and reaffirm their commitment "to a balanced, integrated, comprehensive, multidisciplinary and scientific evidence-based approach to the world drug problem, based on the principle of common and shared responsibility, and recognize the importance of appropriately mainstreaming a gender and age perspective into drug-related policies and programmes and that appropriate emphasis should be placed on individuals, families, communities and society as a whole, with a particular focus on women, children and youth, with a view to promoting and protecting health, including access to treatment, safety and the well-being of all humanity" (ibid, 2).

The document also reiterates the strength of the support to the IDCS as an adequate mechanism to cope with the complexity of the "world drug problem."

> [...] our resolve, in the framework of existing policy documents, inter alia, to prevent, significantly reduce and work towards the elimination of illicit crop cultivation and the production and manufacture of, trafficking in and abuse of narcotic drugs and psychotropic substances, including synthetic drugs and new psychoactive substances, as well as to prevent, significantly reduce and work towards the elimination of the diversion of and illicit trafficking in precursors, and money-laundering related to drug-related crimes; to ensure access to and the availability of controlled substances for

medical and scientific purposes, including for the relief of pain and suffering, and address existing barriers in this regard, including affordability; to strengthen effective, comprehensive, scientific evidence-based demand reduction initiatives covering prevention, early intervention, treatment, care, recovery, rehabilitation and social reintegration measures on a non-discriminatory basis, as well as, in accordance with national legislation, initiatives and measures aimed at minimizing the adverse public health and social consequences of drug abuse; to address drug-related socioeconomic issues related to illicit crop cultivation and the production and manufacture of and trafficking in drugs, including through the implementation of long-term comprehensive and sustainable development-oriented and balanced drug control policies and programmes; and to promote, consistent with the three international drug control conventions and domestic law, and in accordance with national, constitutional, legal and administrative systems, alternative or additional measures with regard to conviction or punishment in cases of an appropriate nature (ibid, 2-3).

The document also continues supporting the SDG goal that no one affected by drug problems should be left behind, "by enhancing our efforts to bridge the gaps in addressing the persistent and emerging trends and challenges through the implementation of balanced, integrated, comprehensive, multidisciplinary, and scientific evidence-based responses to the world drug problem, placing the safety, health, and well-being of all members of society, in particular our youth and children, at the centre of our efforts" (ibid, 4).

Finally, the document concludes by repeating the formula of the 2009 evaluation of the IDCS: "Following up to this Ministerial Declaration, we resolve to review in the Commission on Narcotic Drugs in 2029 our progress in implementing all our international drug policy commitments, with a mid-term review in the Commission on Narcotic Drugs in 2024" (ibid, 6).

This chapter reviewed the United Nations drug agencies' narrative through time and the way it has evolved. The following five chapters focus on how the INCB's positions have evolved regarding drug control issues related to human rights, harm reduction policies (distribution and change of needles and syringes, drug consumption rooms, and addiction and heroin maintenance programs), non-medical marijuana uses in The Netherlands and Uruguay, and coca chewing and other traditional coca uses in Bolivia. These chapters highlight the significant policy inconsistencies across time and place.

CHAPTER SEVEN. THE INCB AND HUMAN RIGHTS: OLD AND NEW POSITIONS

Until recently, one of the main criticisms of the IDCS has been its lack of concern with human rights. By the late 2000s, several critics pointed out the INCB's failure to disapprove and criticize drug policies contrary to the human rights conventions, and its claim that those issues did not apply to international drug policy (Barret et al., 2008; Barret, 2008; Csete and Wolfe, 2007; Small and Drucker, 2007)[122].

Most criticisms focused on the Board's skepticism toward needle and syringe exchange and distribution programs and its rejection of injection rooms as harm reduction policies to cope with the HIV/AIDS epidemic. The Board has also been cautious about opioid and heroin maintenance treatments. Criticisms were also made to the human and environmental damage caused by forced poppy and coca eradication programs. Further criticisms were made to the INCB's passivity in response to "war on drugs" actions that violated human rights, like extrajudicial executions, social cleansing programs, and the misuse of drug policies to suppress political dissent or segregate some ethnic or racial groups. United Nations Special Rapporteur on the Right to Health, Paul Hunt, pointed out the disconnect between the IDCS and the human rights conventions. He claimed that the IDCS and the Human Rights Conventions operated in parallel universes (Hunt, 2008).

For a long time, the INCB avoided taking a position about human rights because it was a technical body whose members were elected because of their technical capabilities. They were neither political appointees nor United Nations staff. The INCB argued that it anteceded the Human Rights Conventions as a technical organ

---

[122] Barrett, et al (2008) is the most comprehensive criticism. Some of these criticisms are somewhat repetitive, for example, Csete and Wolfe (2007) and Small and Drucker (2007) are almost identical. Barrett (2008) presented in a more detailed way some of the arguments developed in Barrett, et al (2008).

established by the 1961 Convention. Human rights were not mentioned in the drug conventions, and therefore, they were beyond its mandate.

The drug conventions aim to deal with drug addiction problems, and their fundamental policy relies heavily on criminal law enforcement. Even though the original motivation was to eliminate a health problem, repressive policies were not constrained by human rights considerations. As noted above, article 39 of the Single Convention and Article 23 of the 1971 Convention assert the right of any Party to decide what is its society's welfare and what repressive policies to apply. Therefore, based only on the drug conventions, the INCB would have nothing to say about actions such as the death penalty for drug crimes if the government claimed it was done to protect or improve its country's welfare.

In the text of the three drug conventions, there is only one reference to human rights. Because of pressures, mainly from Bolivia, article 14 ¶2 of the 1988 Convention reads: "Each Party shall take appropriate measures to prevent illicit cultivation of and to eradicate plants containing narcotic or psychotropic substances, such as opium poppy, coca bush, and cannabis plants, cultivated illicitly in its territory. **The measures adopted shall respect fundamental human rights** and shall take due account of traditional licit uses, where there is historic evidence of such use, as well as the protection of the environment" (Bolds added). This requirement to respect fundamental human rights and traditional coca uses could have had significant consequences for international drug policies. However, as shown below, the Board's interpretation nullified it (See chapter ten).

The INCB's claim that it was a technical and not a political body led it to interpret the conventions strictly and refuse to criticize harsh drug policies. For example, "[i]n a dialogue with civil society leaders in early March 2012,[123] Hamid Ghodse, president of the INCB, was asked, 'Legal sanctions in different countries include

---

[123] At the 2012 CND meeting (author's note).

extrajudicial murder, extrajudicial killings, torture – (is) there no atrocity large enough that you could possibly step outside your mandate and say something?' To which Ghodse replied, 'No, 100 percent not. Because, just basically, we are not there to express our opinion.' [...] Asked for its view on the death penalty for drug offences several weeks ago, the INCB said that such sanctions were the 'exclusive prerogative' of States" (Gallahue, 2012).[124] Even though the Board dodged human rights issues, on occasions argued that its policies did consider them.

> Limiting the use of narcotic drugs to medical and scientific purposes is motivated by humanitarian considerations, such as protecting the individual from the slavery of drug dependence and protecting society from the irresponsible behaviour of intoxicated individuals. The provisions of the international drug control treaties aimed at limiting the use of drugs to medical and scientific purposes should be regarded as 'limiting' free choice in human behaviour in the same way as traffic regulations, restrictions on the availability of weapons or poisons or other dangerous substances, or regulations on prescribing, dispensing, and using pharmaceutical products. (Thus, promoting the non-medical using drugs can be compared to promoting the violation of traffic regulations, free access to weapons or poisons, or the use of pharmaceuticals (such as antibiotics) without medical diagnosis.) Protecting the well-being of the individual and society is the purpose of prohibiting the non-medical use of drugs, which is certainly not an attempt to limit human rights. The Board wishes to draw attention to the confusion created by some advocates of legalization of the non-medical use of drugs with their statements about human rights. The

---

[124] Professor Ghodse reiterated this position at a private lunch in Vienna in November 2012.

prevention of drug abuse problems, by means of national and international drug control, and demand reduction activities, can be regarded as a basic right of the individual and society (INCB, 1995a, ¶18, 3-4).

This statement starts affirming the governments' duty to protect individuals from themselves. It ends by asserting that limiting drug uses to medical and scientific purposes is necessary for governments to fulfill that duty. Then, the protection against drug use is presented as a basic right of the individual who the State must protect against itself. Three years later, President of the Board Hamid Ghodse, in his speech at UNGASS 1998, restated this position: "humans have the right not to be exposed to addictive drugs and to have a life free of drugs."[125] However, at the launching of the INCB 2011 annual report, Professor Ghodse further expressed children have a right to be protected from contact with drugs (INCB, 2012b).

Human rights conventions have only one reference to psychoactive drugs. Article 33 of the Convention on the Rights of the Child reads: "States Parties shall take all appropriate measures, including legislative, administrative, social and educational measures, to protect children from the illicit use of narcotic drugs and psychotropic substances as defined in the relevant international treaties, and to prevent the use of children in the illicit production and trafficking of such substances."

In the press release at the launching of the 2011 Annual Report (INCB, 2012b, 3), the Board's President Hamid Ghodse argued that "youth have a right to be protected from drug abuse and dependence" and proceeded to stress the need to "break the vicious cycle of social exclusion and drug problems, Helping marginalized communities experiencing drug problems must be a priority [...] In communities the world over, in developed and developing countries,

---

[125] I was watching the UNGASS side event where Professor Ghodse made this statement.

drug abuse and drug trafficking has become virtually endemic, part of a vicious cycle involving a wide array of social problems such as violence, organized crime, corruption, unemployment, poor health, and poor education [...] It is crucial that the needs of communities experiencing social disintegration are urgently tackled before the tipping point is reached, beyond which effective action becomes impossible. Fractured communities, with little sense of social cohesion, are more likely to experience multiple problems, including drug abuse, and these problems can contribute to the social disorder and violence that have been seen in cities around the world and which can impact the wider society. Such communities not only place their own residents at risk but can also threaten the stability of the wider community. In the Report, the Board outlines a number of threats to social cohesion—including social inequality, migration, political and economic transformation, emerging cultures of excess, shifts in traditional values, rapid urbanization, conflict, growth in individualism and consumerism, breakdown in respect for the law, and the local drug economy."

This paragraph is remarkable because it was made one month before Professor Ghodse's interview at the CND mentioned above. In that interview, however, he failed to connect the social determinants of the "drug economy" with the human rights in society.

The May 2012 INCB session was the first one attended by several new members, who had doubts and questions about the IDCS policies formulation and implementation and the traditional consensus in the Board. They started to promote a less ideological debate within the Board, resulting in significant changes in the Board's interpretation of the conventions.

The INCB position on human rights issues began to evolve significantly, starting with the 2014 report. It points out that "the full compliance with, and universal application of, the provisions of the three international drug control conventions; and the implementation of two fundamental principles, namely a common and shared responsibility for tackling the world drug problem, and a comprehensive, integrated and balanced approach to addressing the problem. None of these elements represents an incitement to an undefined 'war on drugs,' nor do any of them impose a purely prohibitionist regime or condone the repression of human rights" (INCB, 2015, 1).

The following 2015 INCB report stressed that drug law enforcement policy "needs to be carefully designed keeping in mind both the objective of drug control and the possible unintended results. It is not the case that the world must choose between 'militarized' drug law enforcement and the legalization of non-medical use of internationally controlled drugs. The conventions do not mandate a 'war on drugs' [...] national law is subject to the internationally recognized principle of proportionality. [...] When applied to the criminal justice system, the principle permits punishment at an acceptable response to crime, provided that it is not disproportionate to the seriousness of the crime" (INCB, 2016a, 5).

Regarding human rights, the same report affirmed that "drug control action should be consistent with international human rights standards. State parties need to make full use of international legal instruments to protect children from drug abuse and ensure that national and international drug control strategies are in the child's best interest. The Board has also advised all countries that continue to retain the death penalty for drug-related offences to consider abolishing capital punishment for this category of offences" (INCB, 2016a, 6).

This interpretation established human rights limits to articles 39 of the 1961 Single Convention and 23 of the 1971 Convention. Until that time, both articles had allowed countries to implement tougher policies than those required by the drug conventions. The Board also highlighted that "[i]n addition to indirect and unintentional consequences for human rights via lawless, corrupt and arbitrary governance, violence can threaten efforts to safeguard human rights. It is especially true when drug trafficking and corruption weaken legitimate institutions of governance and contribute to the failure of national authorities or prevent weak States from developing robust structures" (ibid, 6).

The thematic chapter of the 2017 INCB report ("Treatment, rehabilitation and social reintegration for drug use disorders: essential component of demand reduction") elaborates further the Board's position on human rights (INCB, 2018):

- The Board emphasizes that for drug control action to be successful and sustainable, it must be consistent with international human rights standards (ibid, ¶251).
- The Board promotes national and international measures to strive towards an adequate availability of internationally controlled drugs for medical purposes that is not unduly restricted (ibid, ¶252).
- The Board stresses the importance of protecting the rights of persons with mental illness and improving mental health care. The Board also highlights the need to protect children from drug abuse and prevent children's participation in the illicit production of and trafficking in illicit substances (Ibid, ¶253).
- All human rights of alleged drug offenders and drug users at all stages of the criminal justice process must be protected as provided for in the international human rights instruments" (ibid, ¶254).
- The states are obliged under the international drug control conventions to establish certain types of conduct as punishable offences and to ensure that serious offences are liable to adequate punishment is subject to the constitutional principles of States and to the principle of proportionality. States are encouraged to provide alternative measures such as education, rehabilitation, or social reintegration, for persons affected by drug abuse (ibid, ¶255).
- Extrajudicial responses to drug-related criminality violate the international drug control conventions, which require

adherence to internationally recognized due process standards (ibid, ¶256).

- Although the determination of sanctions is a prerogative of States, the Board continues to encourage all States that retain the death penalty for drug-related offences to commute death sentences that have already been handed down and to consider the abolition of the death penalty for drug-related (ibid, ¶257).

The same chapter also has a long section on drug dependence treatment as a human right: "The International Covenant on Economic, Social and Cultural Rights sets out the right to health, which is described as 'the right of everyone to the enjoyment of the highest attainable standard of physical and mental health.' Since the treatment of drug dependence does improve the physical and mental health of affected individuals, such treatment is justifiably considered an element of the right to health" (ibid, ¶30). The INCB 2017 Report continues:

> The UN Committee on Economic, Social, and Cultural Rights[126] interpreted that the right to health contains a set of interrelated and essential elements in all its forms and levels. For treatment and rehabilitation services, those conditions include:
> (a) Availability: treatment services should be available in sufficient quantity taking into consideration the expected requirements, including the adequate amounts of medicines required for the treatment of drug dependence;
> (b) Accessibility: include non-discrimination, physical and economic accessibility, and confidentiality;

---

[126] 5HRI/GEN/1/Rev.9 (Vol. I), chap. I.

> (c) Acceptability: all treatment services should be culturally appropriate for beneficiaries and must be respectful of medical ethics;
> (d) Quality: implies the provision of medically and scientifically appropriate treatment services delivered by skilled treatment providers using evidence-based methods such as the prescription of medication with scientifically proven effectiveness (ibid, ¶31).

The Board took a critical position on mandatory drug dependence treatment: "Only in certain rare and limited cases may short-term treatment without consent be warranted, such as the legally sanctioned, involuntary hospitalization of individuals with severe mental health problems" (ibid,33). The report follows:

> Compulsory treatment, i.e., treatment administered without the expressed consent of the affected individual, should be discouraged for the following reasons:
> (a) The evidence for their effectiveness is poor;
> (b) They threaten the health of people undergoing the treatment, including through increased vulnerability to HIV and other infections;
> (c) They are in direct conflict with the human rights principles as stated in the International Covenant on Economic, Social, and Cultural Rights (ibid, ¶34).

It continues:

> An essential component of quality and availability of treatment services is access to the medications required to treat drug dependence. Certain medications that are demonstrated to be unequivocally effective in the treatment of drug dependence, such as methadone and buprenorphine, are internationally controlled substances. Many national drug

control policy frameworks make it difficult for treatment facilities to provide treatment using such controlled medications. Many controlled substances play a critical role not only in the treatment of drug dependence but also in, for example, pain relief, anaesthesia, surgery, and the treatment of mental disorders. The obligation to prevent their diversion, trafficking and abuse has received much more attention than ensuring that they are available in adequate quantities for medical and scientific purposes. Some countries explicitly prohibit the use of such medications. Elsewhere, even if the medications are available, service providers are reluctant to use them owing to cumbersome regulatory requirements. While the inappropriate prescription of controlled medications by health-care professionals must be discouraged, the Board has clearly recommended removal of legal sanctions for unintentional mistakes in handling opioids (ibid, ¶36).

And,

It is in the spirit of the international drug control conventions to ensure access to controlled narcotic drugs and psychotropic substances for medical and scientific purposes. States should therefore take measures to remove the legal and policy barriers that prevent access to them. It is essential that national laws governing the availability of pharmaceutical products in general are in line with the drug control treaties in that they curb illicit use and facilitate access to medicines for use in treatment. [...] Controlled medications must be equally accessible for all the health conditions for which they are needed, as required by the international drug conventions and consistent with scientific evidence. Undue restrictions on providing treatment using controlled medications is a violation of the right to health (ibid, ¶37).

Perhaps the most significant INCB policy position change in the 2012-2018 period was regarding human rights. There is no question that the Board's narrative distanced itself from a simple punitive law enforcement position and recognized that drug policies should be part of the complex overall social policy strategy of any government. However, governments may still argue that their drug policies that restrict human rights comply with the conventions because article 39 of the Single Convention does not deem or precludes parties "from adopting measures of control more strict or severe than those provided in the Convention" and article 23 of the 1971 Convention on Psychotropic Substances states that: "A Party may adopt more strict or severe measures of control than those provided by this Convention if, in its opinion, such measures are desirable or necessary for the protection of the public health and welfare." It means again that the ambiguity of the terms of the conventions allows for diverse interpretations depending on who are the INCB's members and how the Parties interpret the conventions (see chapter 5 section 5.2).

CHAPTER EIGHT. THE HARM REDUCTION CHALLENGE

8.1 OVERVIEW

Harm reduction policies, in general, acknowledge the fact that governments that seek to maximize social and economic welfare must be concerned with the multiple dimensions and complexity of welfare. And in doing so, their best policy regarding psychoactive addictive drugs should not be focussed only on pursuing an "ideal" and unattainable drug-free world. This approach accepts that drug use cannot be eliminated completely; government policies should seek to minimize the total harms of drug use plus those resulting from the anti-drug policies themselves. The argument is simple: a society should tolerate some drug use when it prevents greater social harms. In the psychoactive drug policy jargon, *harm reduction* refers mainly to:

- *opioid substitution therapy* based mainly on methadone and buprenorphine, designed to lower risky behaviors of heroin users;[127]
- *needle and syringe programs* that provide, distribute, or exchange those products to drug injecting users to lower the risk of HIV and hepatitis C transmission among injecting drugs users;
- *controlled heroin prescription* to heroin addicts considered incurable by their doctors; and

---

[127] Methadone is a synthetic opioid that has been used as a substitute of heroin to wean addicts from that drug. The problem is that unless its use is strictly controlled, it can also become addictive. Buprenorphine is an opioid partial agonist which means that its risk of addiction is lower that of methadone.

- *drug consumption rooms* where addicts can bring their drugs to be tested to avoid intoxications and overdoses, and clean needles and syringes are also supplied.

Supporters of these policy interventions have presented substantial evidence of their positive results.[128] From the INCB traditional perspective, *harm reduction* policies have been considered very risky, and in many cases, contrary to the conventions. Some INCB members have argued that many of these programs turn the government into an accomplice of drug trafficking.

The Board's skepticism about harm reduction was expressed even in its 1993 report after countries had faced the HIV epidemic. It: "Acknowledges the importance of certain aspects of 'harm reduction' as a tertiary prevention strategy for demand reduction purposes. The Board considers it its duty, however, to draw the attention of Governments to the fact that 'harm reduction' programmes are not substitutes for demand reduction programmes" (INCB, 1993, 4).

Some years later, the Board's position appears to have hardened. The foreword of the 2002 INCB report (INCB, 2003) by President Phillip O. Emafo, a pharmacist, is a very revealing example of the strong INCB position against some harm reduction policies.

> The Board continues to serve the international community in line with its mandate. Some distractions, however, come from groups that advocate the legalization or decriminalization of drug offences, and others come from groups that favour a crusade focusing only on 'harm minimization' or 'harm reduction.' Contrary to all available evidence, such lobbyists have persisted in proclaiming that there are safe ways to abuse drugs.

---

[128] See for example Bewley-Taylor, (2012a, 41-43), MacCoun and Reuter, (2001, Ch. 11, 12, 13).

Supporters of such legalization pursue their goals through aggressive, well-funded campaigns and with missionary zeal. Their arguments, however, do not reflect the truth. The truth is that there are no safe ways to abuse drugs. The truth is that drug abuse creates problems for the drug abusers, for their immediate environment and, ultimately, for society as a whole. Most people are all too familiar with the pain experienced by the family members of a drug addict and with the disintegration of families as a result of drug abuse. And many people are aware of the loss of productivity that occurs in companies whose employees abuse drugs.

The sight of unkempt drug abusers on street corners and in train stations, begging for money to finance their drug habits, cannot be ignored by responsible Governments. States have a moral and legal responsibility to protect drug abusers from further self-destruction. States should not give up and allow advocates of legalization to take control of their national drug policies. Governments should not be intimidated by a vocal minority that wants to legalize illicit drug use. Governments must respect the view of the majority of lawful citizens; and those citizens are against illicit drug use.

Persons in favour of legalizing illicit drug use argue that drug abusers should not have their basic rights violated; however, it does not seem to have occurred to those persons that drug abusers themselves violate the basic rights of their own family members and society. Families and society also have rights that should be respected and upheld (ibid, iii-iv).

There is no question that Mr. Emafo meant good. Still, while he claims that harm reduction policy supporters do that "contrary to all available evidence," he did not provide evidence or references to the contrary. He assumes that his position is based on proven findings accepted by all serious researchers. But what he provides as evidence is an impressionistic educated guess of someone who has been in contact with addicts, who has witnessed the pain of drug addicts and their family members, and who has been exposed to the sight of unkempt drug addicts in (European?) train stations. Mr. Emafo argues that those with positions contradictory to his are zealots who, unfortunately, are very well funded by some harm reduction supporters. This statement attempts to delegitimize those that have an opposite position. Mr. Emafo then argues that States have the duty to protect citizens from their wrong decisions and advocates for the imposition of a majority rule, dismissing the fact that in a true democracy, a primary duty of the government is to protect minorities from the dictatorship of the majority.

8.2 NEEDLE AND SYRINGE EXCHANGE AND DISTRIBUTION PROGRAMS (NSEDP)

A critical issue with syringe and needle distribution and exchange programs is that those are supplied to users of illegally obtained drugs who, according to the law, would have committed a crime purchasing them. The lack of clear definitions about *medical purposes* and *health* in the drug conventions leads to a situation in which different, intellectually honest people may arrive at contradictory positions. In this case, public health policymakers must choose between two social ills: an increase in HIV/AIDS and hepatitis C incidence or tolerating and perhaps even legitimizing an illegal activity. Supporters of the NSEDP consider them a preventive medicine effort to avoid the spread of fatal infections and, as such, satisfy the conventions' medical purposes requirement. However, their opponents argue that supplying needles and syringes knowing that they will be used to inject illegally obtained drugs makes their suppliers accomplices to illegal transactions and promotes drug trafficking. Despite these objections, NSEDP have proliferated.

UNODC (2018) reports that NSEDP were available in 93 of 179 countries with evidence of injecting drug use.

The INCB has cautiously supported NSEDP. The conventions do not contain, refer to or define *harm reduction*. Still, as noted in its 1993 report, the Board acknowledges the importance of certain aspects of *harm reduction* as a tertiary prevention strategy for demand reduction purposes. The Board considers its duty to draw the attention of Governments to the fact that *Harm reduction* programmes are not substitutes for *demand reduction* programmes (INCB, 1993, ¶29). In its report for 2000, the Board reiterated that *harm reduction* programs could play a partial role in a comprehensive drug demand reduction strategy. However, such programs should not be carried out at the expense of other essential activities to reduce the demand for illicit drugs, for example, drug abuse prevention activities.

In the 2003 report, the Board also noted that since some *harm reduction* measures were controversial, discussions of their advantages and disadvantages had dominated the public debate on drug policy. The Board regretted that the discussion on some *harm reduction* measures had diverted the attention (and, in some cases, funds) of "[g]overnments from important demand reduction activities such as primary prevention or abstinence-oriented treatment. [...] In a number of countries, Governments have introduced since the end of the 1980s programmes for the exchange or distribution of needles and syringes for drug addicts, with the aim of limiting the spread of HIV/AIDS. The Board maintains the position expressed by it already in 1987 that Governments need to adopt measures that may decrease the sharing of hypodermic needles among injecting drug abusers in order to limit the spread of HIV/AIDS. At the same time, the Board has been stressing that any prophylactic measures should not promote and/or facilitate drug abuse" (INCB, 2004, 36). This is an ambivalent statement because it does not clarify whether distributing needles and syringes did or did not promote or facilitate drug abuse.

8.3 DRUG CONSUMPTION ROOMS

To prevent overdoses, supervised drug consumption or injection rooms, provide clean needles and syringes and test drugs before use. These present similar issues to NSEDP, although they add a complicating point: does testing illegally obtained drugs with public funds turn the State into an accomplice to drug trafficking?

It posits the classical conflict between consequentialists versus deontologists. The former would believe that drug policies should evaluate all their consequences even if they break some laws. It means that societies should be allowed to have innovative policies towards psychoactive drugs and drug addiction. The latter would believe that certain moral obligations hold irrespective of their empirical consequences (MacCoun and Reuter, 2001, 56). The issue is how to weigh the social benefits and costs of both positions. Opponents implicitly make a cost-benefit evaluation of the policy's effects on social health and conclude that the negative costs exceed the benefits of drug users' physical and mental health. At the same time, supporters argue that the social benefits are positive and thus reinforce the support for such programs. However, these evaluations are frequently only impressionistic because of the difficulties of applying evidence-based criteria to determine the effects of each policy.

For a long time, the INCB argued that injection rooms were not acceptable according to the drug conventions. Its 1998 report demeans those practices: "Some States in Europe have established so-called 'shooting galleries,' where drug abusers can administer drugs under supervision and supposedly hygienic conditions. The Board urges those States to consider carefully all the implications of such 'shooting galleries,' including the legal implications, the congregation of addicts, the facilitation of illicit trafficking, the message that the existence of such places may send to the general public and the impact on the general perception of drug abuse" (INCB, 1999, 53).

The following year's INCB report rejects injection rooms as being against the conventions, but it appears to have a less aggressive tone.

> Drug injection rooms, where addicts may inject themselves with illicit substances, are being established in a number of developed countries, often with the approval of national and/or local authorities. The Board believes that any national, state, or local authority that permits the establishment and operation of drug injection rooms or any outlet to facilitate the abuse of drugs (by injection or any other route of administration) also facilitates illicit drug trafficking. The Board reminds Governments that they have an obligation to combat illicit drug trafficking in all its forms.
> Parties to the 1988 Convention are required, subject to their constitutional principles and the basic concepts of their legal systems, to establish as a criminal offence the possession and purchase of drugs for personal (nonmedical) consumption. By permitting drug injection rooms, a government could be considered to be in contravention of the international drug control treaties by facilitating in, aiding and/or abetting the commission of crimes involving illegal drug possession and use, as well as other criminal offences, including drug trafficking. The international drug control treaties were established many decades ago precisely to eliminate places, such as opium dens, where drugs could be abused with impunity. [...] The Board, recognizing that the spread of drug abuse, human immunodeficiency virus (HIV) infection, and hepatitis are serious concerns, encourages Governments to provide a wide range of facilities for the treatment of drug abuse, including the medically supervised administration of prescription drugs in line with sound medical practice and the international drug control treaties,

instead of establishing drug injection rooms or similar outlets that facilitate drug abuse (INCB, 2000, 26-27).

However, a few pages down, the Board turns back its tone: "The Board regrets that draft laws introduced in Germany and Luxembourg would allow for the establishment of drug injection rooms, also known as 'shooting galleries'" (ibid, 57). In the following years, the INCB was very persistent on this issue. For example: "The Board wishes to reiterate that the establishment of drug injection rooms, where addicts can abuse drugs obtained from illicit sources, under direct or indirect supervision of the Government, is contrary to the international drug control treaties" (INCB, 2002, 74). The INCB then proceeded for more than a decade in a manner consistent with this statement:

- The Board regrets that local authorities in the Australian state of New South Wales have permitted the establishment of a drug injection room, setting aside the concerns expressed by the Board that the operation of such facilities, where addicts inject themselves with illicit substances, condones illicit drug use and drug trafficking and runs counter to the provisions of the international drug control treaties. The Board notes that the national policy in Australia does not support the establishment of drug injection rooms. The Board urges the Government to ensure that all of its states comply fully with the provisions of the international drug control treaties, to which Australia is a party" (ibid, 80).
- Establishing drug injection rooms, where drug abusers can inject drugs that they have acquired from illicit sources, is contrary to the international drug control treaties (INCB, 2003: 70),
- In some countries, facilities have been established where injecting drug abusers can inject drugs that they have acquired illicitly. That practice has been allowed by national drug

control legislation or Governments have simply allowed or tolerated such initiatives by local governments or institutions. The Board has stated on a number of occasions, including in its recent annual reports, that the operation of such facilities remains a source of grave concern. The Board reiterates that they violate the provisions of the international drug control conventions (INCB, 2004, 37), and

– The Board urges all Governments to refrain from establishing 'drug consumption rooms' and to pursue alternative ways to increase access to health and social services, including services for the treatment of drug abusers (INCB, 2009, 103).

In recent years, the INCB's position has evolved as the Board's membership changed. The 2016 INCB Report asserts:

With respect to 'drug consumption rooms,' the Board wishes to reiterate its frequently expressed concern that, in order for the operation of such facilities to be consistent with the international drug conventions, certain conditions must be fulfilled. Chief among those conditions is that the ultimate objective of these measures is to reduce the adverse consequences of drug abuse through treatment, rehabilitation, and reintegration measures, without condoning or increasing drug abuse or encouraging drug trafficking. 'Drug consumption rooms' must be operated within a framework that offers treatment and rehabilitation services as well as social reintegration measures, either directly or by active referral for access, and must not be a substitute for demand reduction programmes, in particular prevention and treatment activities (INCB, 2017a, 91).

With this position, the Board implicitly hopes that all addicts must always continue their efforts to stop their addiction. Thus, for the INCB, there are no incurable addicts to whom controlled drug use may be tolerated.

8.4 OPIOID ADDICTION MAINTENANCE

Addiction maintenance programs are designed to supply drugs, through the health system, to addicts physicians believe that cannot be rehabilitated. This is a very complex issue that requires a definition of medical purposes. Without that, deciding whether addiction maintenance is a legitimate medical practice will depend on individual opinions.

Regarding opiate addiction in the United States, the Center for Substance Abuse Treatment explains (2005, Ch. 2): "This debate centers on two different views: (1) opioid addiction is a generally incurable disease that requires long-term maintenance with medication; or (2) opioid addiction stems from a weak will, lack of morals, other psychodynamic factors, or an environmentally determined predilection that is rectified by the criminalization of uncontrolled use and distribution and measures promoting abstinence".

The INCB's position was to accept drug opioid "[...] substitution and maintenance treatment as one of the forms of medical treatment of drug addicts, whereby a drug with similar action to the drug of dependence, but with a lower degree of risks, is prescribed by a medical doctor for a specific treatment aim. Although results are dependent on many factors, its implementation does not constitute any breach of treaty provisions, whatever substance may be used for such treatment in line with established national sound medical practice. The Board has, over the years and in line with its mandate under the estimate system of the 1961 Convention, discussed and confirmed quantities Governments have needed for such purpose. As is the case with the concept of medical use, treatment is not treaty-defined; therefore, the parties and the Board are provided with some flexibility" (INCB, 2004, 36-37).

These programs that generally use methadone or buprenorphine as a replacement for heroin have become common.

8.5 HEROIN ADDICTION MAINTENANCE

Heroin maintenance has long been used sparsely but persistently in the UK. In 1920 and 1923, the Ministry of the Interior promoted the Dangerous Drug Act that restricted the amounts of opiates that a doctor could prescribe during addiction treatment. It sought to strengthen a criminal approach to treating the problem of opium and its products. The medical establishment reacted and succeeded in having the Ministry of Health established in 1924 a committee led by Sir Humphrey Rolleston to study the matter. The Rolleston report, published in 1926, recommended allowing doctors to cautiously prescribe morphine and heroin in small, controlled amounts to their patients. In addition, it acknowledged that there were incurable addicts who should receive these drugs in the long run. This practice was adopted and maintained with ups and downs (Berridge, 1980; Mars, 2003).

The number of heroin addicts was not significant, and "the system was not very controversial. When the government in 1955 considered banning heroin completely, in response to international pressures rather than because any domestic complaints about the system, the British medical establishment fought back effectively, and the government eventually abandoned the effort" (MacCoun and Reuter (2001, 297).

In the 1960s, some doctors were lax prescribing heroin, and by 1967 the number of addicts increased to about 1,500. And "[i]n response, to the increase, the Dangerous Drugs Act of 1967 greatly curtailed access to heroin maintenance, limiting it to a small number of specially licensed drug-treatment specialists" (ibid, 297). It raised the number of addicts that sought help in specialized clinics, and "[a]t the same time oral methadone became available as a substitute pharmacotherapy. British specialists became as enthusiastic about this alternative as did their U.S. counterparts. [...] By 1975, only 4 percent of maintained opiate addicts were receiving heroin alone" (ibid, 297).

Switzerland is another country that has had a significant history of heroin maintenance. It is not clear why, but during the early 1980s, it experienced a sharp increase in heroin addiction. Heroin markets and use spread through several Zurich neighborhoods. After several years of law enforcement efforts to control illegal heroin markets, the city government opted to establish a tolerance zone in the Platzspitz, a traditional park in a small peninsula where it allowed drug selling and use outside the view of non-drug user residents. It was de facto a harm reduction location policy that reflected a decision of the city council to minimize the negative externalities of drug trafficking and use on nonusers. Concentrating illegal drug activities in one place also facilitated health services to addicts at a time of high prevalence of AIDS in the country. But that illegal market concentration also attracted users and traffickers from other areas. The concentration of addicts converted the once beautiful park into a dirty slum that attracted the attention of Swiss and international media and generated a social backlash. In January 1992, the city closed the park, but addicts did not go away. The police faced a more significant problem than the one before the park had been opened. In mid-1993, the city had to open again another tolerance zone, this time an informal one (ibid, 281-286).

The Zurich government opted in January 1994 to try a three-year heroin maintenance program that responded to the citizenry's dislike for tough enforcement and open drug use and trade scenes. This program complemented an extensive methadone maintenance program already in place. The program was limited in scope and was extended to other cities. It required heroin injections to take place only in designated clinics. Drugs could not be taken out. It also included control groups that received methadone instead of heroin. Patients had a minimum age requirement, a record of failure in at least two previous treatment attempts and could choose the required dose to avoid their possible need to continue using the illegal market (ibid, 288-290).

The program covered only a small proportion of heroin addicts as most were treated with methadone. The trial results were generally positive compared to those of the methadone programs: "69% of the participants remained in treatment 18 months after admission. About half of those recorded as dropouts in fact moved to other treatment modalities [...] Crime rates were very much reduced as compared to treatment entry [...] Self-reported use of nonprescribed heroin fell sharply, and the percentage with jobs that were described as 'permanent' increased from 14 to 32 percent and unemployment fell from 44 to 20 percent [...] though many addicts were able to detach themselves from the heroin subculture, they were unable to develop other attachments" (ibid, 291).

However, these results were not conclusive because the better results of heroin vs. methadone maintenance could have been because the heroin maintenance trial participants received substantially more psychosocial services than the typical methadone patient. Besides, heroin maintenance is a lot more expensive than methadone maintenance because it requires three times a day professional attendance compared to once a day for methadone. The trials generated a domestic debate and an international reaction. The INCB, applying article 14 of the 1961 Single Convention on Narcotic Drugs, approved the heroin imports required for the trials only if the government of Switzerland agreed to an independent evaluation by WHO. This evaluation concluded that heroin maintenance is feasible and may obtain positive social results, but it did not demonstrate a superior policy option (ibid, 292-295).

The INCB used WHO's evaluation to discourage other governments from following the Swiss example.

> One of the key conclusions in the report is that the 'Swiss studies were not able to examine whether improvements in health status or social functioning in the individuals treated

> were causally related to heroin prescription per se or a result of the impact of the overall treatment programme.' It is also stated in the report that the Swiss studies did not provide convincing evidence that, even in cases where methadone treatment has persistently failed, the medical prescription of heroin generally leads to better results than further methadone-based treatment. In view of the conclusions of the External Panel and mindful of the responsibilities accorded to it in the international drug control treaties, the Board remains concerned over the Swiss heroin programme and policy of heroin prescription. The Board does not encourage other Governments to allow heroin to be prescribed to opiate addicts (INCB, 2000, 57).

After other countries developed heroin maintenance programs, the INCB softened its position.

> Heroin is prescribed in a few countries to a small proportion of long-term opiate addicts, and in some other countries research on prescription of heroin for the treatment of such addicts is under way. The Board reiterates its reservations concerning the medical prescription of heroin. The Board wishes to emphasize the importance of formally involving WHO in the evaluation of the results of all projects on the medical prescription of heroin to addicts (INCB, 2005, 33).

The INCB, following WHO's criteria, recognizes heroin and opioid maintenance as long as "[...] those measures include supervised consumption, application of appropriate conditions for drugs to be taken home, treatment according to clinical standards, prescription monitoring systems and mandatory training of health-care professionals. The Board reiterates its request to the Governments concerned to establish a mechanism for the systematic collection of information on the diversion and abuse of drugs prescribed for substitution treatment, using, inter alia, statistics on emergencies related to drug abuse and statistics on drug-related deaths" (INCB, 2007a, 89).

In more recent years, other countries developed similar programs: Australia, Denmark, the Netherlands, Spain, Germany, Canada, England. The European Monitoring Center on Drugs and Drug Addiction (EMCDDA) evaluated the randomized controlled trials (RCTs) and the costs of supervised injectable heroin (SIH) treatment in the six countries where evaluations were available[129] (Strang, Groshkova and Metrebian, 2012). This evaluation concludes that:

> Two common features characterise the new approach to heroin treatment. Firstly, SIH is not a first-line treatment, but rather is an option for patients who have not responded to standard treatments such as oral MMT[130] or residential rehabilitation. Secondly, all injectable doses (typically, approximately 200 mg of diacetylmorphine per injection) are taken under direct medical or nursing supervision, thereby ensuring compliance, monitoring, safety, and prevention of any possible diversion of prescribed diacetylmorphine to the illicit market: this requires the clinics to be open for several sessions per day, every day of the year (ibid, 11-12).

The main results of the EMCDDA evaluation were:

− Major reductions in the continued use of "street" heroin occurred in those receiving SIH compared with control groups (most often receiving active MMT).

---

[129] Switzerland (Perneger et al., 1998); the Netherlands (van den Brink et al., 2003); Spain (March et al., 2006); Germany (Haasen et al., 2007), Canada (Oviedo-Joekes et al., 2009) and England (Strang et al., 2010). Australia stopped it heroin maintenance program and today has a methadone maintenance one.

[130] Methadone Maintenance Treatment (author's note)

- Smaller reductions occurred with the use of a range of other drugs, such as cocaine and alcohol. However, the difference between reductions in the SIH group and the various control groups was not as great as those in 'street' heroin.
- Reductions in the criminal activity of SIH patients were evident and were substantially greater when compared with patients under control conditions.
- The efficacy of heroin provision as a treatment modality on several outcomes (retention, mortality) was corroborated by a systematic review conducted by the Cochrane Group. However, more serious adverse events have been reported to occur in patients receiving SIH than oral methadone. It suggests that SIH may be less safe and require more resources and clinical attention to manage greater safety issues.
- Countries that have conducted longer-term (up to six years) follow-up studies have seen high retention in SIH (55 % at two years and 40 % at six years), with patients sustaining gains in reduced 'street' heroin use and marked improvements in social functioning.

This study confirmed the findings of MacCoun and Reuter regarding costs. SIH was up to ten times more expensive than MMT in the trials surveyed.

In conclusion, heroin maintenance programs are consistent with the drug conventions. Still, the evidence shows that they should be used with caution and should only be an option to treat patients that have failed to respond to other addiction treatments.

CHAPTER NINE. COFFEE SHOPS IN THE NETHERLANDS VS MARIJUANA LEGALIZATION IN URUGUAY

9.1 OVERVIEW

This chapter compares the INCB's reaction to the coffee shops' experiment in the Netherlands with its reaction to the non-medical marijuana legalization in Uruguay. This exercise shows that the INCB has applied the conventions in a different way to both countries. In The Netherlands, coffee shops can sell small amounts of marijuana, an illegal product, to their customers. They were, however, not allowed to grow or purchase marijuana. Their customers have not been sanctioned, even though they bought an illegal product. The local governments have made informal arrangements to collect taxes from the coffee shops even though their product's costs are not in the books. The government has tolerated, although officially not condoned, marijuana production and sales to coffee shops. On the other hand, Uruguay has established a very controlled legal marijuana production and a market that requires users to register with the government and strictly limit their purchases. At the same time, it has strict sanctions on those that sell and purchase in the illegal market.

9.2 THE INCB AND THE COFFEE SHOP POLICY IN THE NETHERLANDS

In the early 1970s, the INCB was concerned with the Netherlands being the main point of European drug entry and distribution to the continent. Its 1974 report expressed these concerns.

> The situation in the Netherlands seems to have been deteriorating for some time, mainly owing to the illicit traffic.

[...] Considerable quantities of cannabis are entering the country, partly for onward routing to neighbouring countries, especially the Federal Republic of Germany, but increasingly for local consumption as well. [...] In the last two years, there has been a steep increase in the heroin traffic. Much of the heroin appears to come from Asia, which indicates that traffickers have been benefiting from the economic ties between the Netherlands and Southeast Asia. Their activities have also been facilitated by the presence of an Asian colony in the Netherlands (INCB, 1974, 26).

Domestic drug use was also an issue: "Moreover, the Netherlands authorities have adopted a liberal attitude towards cannabis. There can be little doubt that the ease of access to supplies of cannabis draws consumers to the Netherlands. This movement is extending to other dangerous substances as well, such as heroin and LSD. [...] The Netherlands authorities are not alone in their concern about the situation, which is causing alarm in several neighbouring countries. While it is confident that the authorities will do all that is necessary, the Board has decided to keep the problem under permanent observation" (ibid, 26).

In 1975, concern about the Netherlands being the leading illegal importer and the center of drug distribution for Europe was reaffirmed (INCB, 1975, 15). In 1976 in response to this issue, the Netherlands enacted a new Opium Act that included all substances classified in the 1961 Single Convention on Narcotic Drugs, and introduced two lists of substances:

1. *substances with an unacceptable risk*; and
2. *cannabis products* (Grund and Breeksema, 2017)

Besides, "possession of 30 grams of cannabis or less could either be dismissed or charged as a petty offence or misdemeanour (comparable to a traffic ticket) and, importantly, would not result in a criminal record. In addition, another distinction was made between possession for personal consumption and possession with intent to distribute, formalising the 1969 Public Prosecutor's office enforcement guidelines" (De Kort, 1995).[131]

The 1976 Opium Act did not legalize the production and sale of marijuana, but it authorized the Prosecutor-General to issue directives allowing the establishment of coffee shops. These directives defined the Dutch prosecution policy in drug cases.

> The directives address, among other issues, the conditions of operating coffee shops, the different approaches in cases involving hard drugs and soft drugs, and what constitutes a small quantity of drugs for personal use.
>
> Technically, it is illegal to buy and sell soft drugs, but the Dutch government tolerates the sale of soft drugs in coffee shops to prevent users of soft drugs from coming into contact with hard drugs. Coffee shops are establishments where cannabis may be sold and used but no alcoholic drinks may be sold or consumed. As long as certain conditions and guidelines are met (discussed below), the public prosecutor's office will not prosecute, under a policy of tolerance (*gedoogbeleid*). In addition, if anyone is caught with small quantities of drugs for personal use outside of a coffee shop, he or she will not be prosecuted.
>
> A. Coffee Shops
>
> The Opium Act Directive sets out the rules for the toleration policy applicable to the operation of coffee shops. Coffee shops are prohibited from
> - advertising,
> - possessing or selling hard drugs,
> - causing a nuisance,

---

[131] Cited by Grund and Beerksema (2017).

- allowing minors to enter the premises or selling soft drugs to them,
- selling more than a limited amount of soft drugs per transaction and having more than 500 grams in stock
- allowing nonresidents of the Netherlands to enter the premises and to buy soft drugs. (Gesley, 2016, 21-22)

The Board's 1976 report referred to the enacted legislation but did not mention the coffee shops.

> Taking into account the gravity of the situation the Government of the Netherlands has taken steps against the illicit traffic. In the spring of 1976, a National Drug Unit was formed within the Ministry of Justice, particularly to co-ordinate information on this traffic throughout the country. The bill to which the Board referred in its last report was submitted to Parliament in 1976. Under this new legislation, the penalties that can be imposed on persons using drugs will be reduced while those relating to traffic, particularly that in drugs 'involving unacceptable risks' - such as opiates and amphetamines - will be more severe. [...] It is to be hoped that these steps will help to improve a situation which remains serious, not only for the Netherlands but also for all its neighbours" (INCB, 1976, 18).

In its Report for 1977, the Board appears to make a general reference to the marijuana issue without referring to The Netherlands and quotes its 1975 report: "the Board again considered this question and concluded that ... 'Parties are ... obliged to take the necessary measures to prevent any non-medical consumption. However, according to the provisions of the Convention, non-medical use - although prohibited - need not necessarily be subject to penal sanctions. In other words, apart from authorizing its use licitly, each Government is free to decide, in the light of the particular conditions existing in its country, on the most appropriate measures for preventing the non-medical consumption of cannabis. However, in reaching its decision, the Government must, of course also take into account the international implications which may result from it. With regard to the illicit traffic in cannabis, Governments must prevent it and punish the traffickers severely'" (INCB, 1977, 3).

The following five annual reports did not have any reference to the coffee shop issue. The 1983 report retakes the cannabis consumption issue in a general way: "The Board has previously stated and reaffirms that each Government is free to decide in the light of the particular conditions existing in its country on the most appropriate measures for preventing non-medical consumption of cannabis. However, each Government must also take into account the international implications which could result from its decisions. At the same time, the Board stressed, and also reaffirms now, that non-medical consumption of cannabis is illegal under the 1961 Convention and that no Party to the Convention can authorize such use without being in violation of the Convention. Parties must limit the use of cannabis to medical and scientific purposes and are obliged to take measures to prevent non-medical consumption, including the confiscation of the drug found in the unauthorized possession of the individual concerned" (INCB, 1983, 2).

However, further down the report, there is a remarkable reference to the Netherlands: "The Board has been following with interest recent developments in the Netherlands regarding narcotics control which had given rise to concern on the part of other countries in the region. The Board's dialogue with the Government revealed that the legislation is in conformity with the requirements of the 1961 Convention and that the Government is determined to maintain and carry out this legislation. The Board understands that the developments which gave rise to international concern are to be considered exceptional and are not likely to recur" (ibid, 23).

The question is whether this paragraph applied to the coffee shops. The answer is no because the Board's position was consistent with the new Opium Act that did not formally condone the coffee shops. This is technically accurate, but by allowing the Prosecutor-General to set the policy directives, the 1976 Opium Act created a legal loophole for establishing the coffee shops. Remarkably, seven years after the Netherlands started the coffee shops experiment, the INCB reports had never raised this loophole issue.

In the following five reports, there is no mention of the Netherlands. The 1989 report has two references to that country. The first one was about the country's vulnerability to drug smuggling and the measures to control it (INCB, 1990, 23). The second praises the country's anti-drug policy.

> The drug policy of the Netherlands emphasizes the prevention of abuse and the rehabilitation of drug addicts. In evaluating their efforts, authorities point to the unique situation in Amsterdam, which plays unwilling host to large numbers of drug addicts from other countries. For the country as a whole, overall abuse of cannabis and heroin have remained stable and even decreased in some parts of the country. While the abuse of cocaine has increased among multi-drug abusers in particular, authorities indicate that widespread abuse of 'crack' has not developed to date. They attribute this to an information campaign which targets addicts, most of whom are known to the authorities (ibid. 23).

In the 1990 report, the INCB presents a very positive picture of drug policies in the Netherlands. However, at the end of its comments, it indicates that its marijuana policy attracts foreign abusers.

> The Netherlands reports that indicators, such as the decline in the number of drug-related deaths, the increase in the

average age of drug abusers and the stabilization of the number of drug abusers for several years, reveal a positive trend. Efforts to contain drug abuse have centered on education, prevention, and treatment programmes. With respect to law enforcement, emphasis has been placed on combatting cocaine and heroin trafficking. Criminal law is designed to enable the administration to pursue a flexible drug policy towards abusers to avoid their going underground and becoming even more difficult to integrate socially. The aim is to ensure that abusers can continue to be reached for counselling and treatment. The authorities have concluded that the methadone and needle exchange programmes have provided effective ways of establishing treatment contacts, thus diminishing the spread of AIDS. The fact that less than 10 per cent of AIDS patients are drug abusers is attributed to the country's health and drug policies. The Board notes, however, that these policies have also led to easy availability of cannabis, controlled under the 1961 Convention, as well as to the influx into the Netherlands of drug abusers from neighbouring countries. The authorities regard cannabis as less dangerous for public health (INCB, 1991, 28-29).

The praise for the country's drug policies is reaffirmed in the 1991 report.

The authorities of the Netherlands continue to apply the guidelines which were adopted in 1976 for the detection and prosecution of offenses under the country's Opium Act and take a relatively tolerant attitude towards small-scale dealing of cannabis conducted in cafes, while at the same time restricting trafficking in other drugs as much as possible. This policy is designed to reduce the involvement of young people with criminal elements. Abuse of cannabis is reported to have been stable since the beginning of the 1970's. The Netherlands is one of the few countries in Europe where the number of drug-related deaths continues to decline (INCB, 1992, 33).

The 1992 report finally mentions coffee shops explicitly. Still, it presents a positive picture of the country's marijuana policy and the social costs of marijuana use. However, it raises the issue concerning the use of coffee shops to distribute other drugs.

A mission of the Board visited the Netherlands in October 1992. On the basis of its opium law of 1976, which distinguishes between 'hard drugs' and 'soft drugs' with regard to law enforcement measures, the Government has a policy of tolerating cannabis abuse and the sale of up to 30 grams of cannabis products in so-called coffee-shops. The public health authorities have estimated that there are between 550,000 and 600,000 regular cannabis abusers in the Netherlands. It is believed that the public health problems associated with cannabis abuse are not significant and that the penalties of its abuse should not be more damaging than the effect of the drug itself. It is also believed that the abuse of cannabis has not drastically increased despite the fact that the number of coffee-shops in the country appears to have increased to between 1,000 and 2,000. There is evidence that some coffee-shops are increasingly being used by traffickers and that, in some of those shops, other drugs are being sold in addition to cannabis products. A number of coffee-shops have been closed down for that reason. The Government is concerned about these developments and is investigating the situation with a view to reviewing its policy (INCB, 1993, 36).

The 1993 report also reviews the trends of marijuana use in various regions and warns about the increased THC content of the marijuana available in the Netherlands. Again, it raises questions about the coffee shops.

> Cannabis remains the main drug of abuse in Europe. No changes have been observed concerning the extent of cannabis abuse in Europe as a whole, with the exception of formerly socialist countries, where cannabis abuse has been increasing. Whereas in the United States, the number of cannabis abusers has decreased in the last few years, no such trend has emerged in Europe. More and more Governments have taken a position against the liberalization of cannabis smoking; even experts who were inclined to exempt from narcotics control measures marijuana with a THC content of 1 or 2 per cent no longer regard as 'soft' drugs the cannabis varieties cultivated in the Netherlands, which may be ten times more potent. The dialogue between the Government of the Netherlands and the Board has led to lively discussion among the general public and at the governmental level in that country. The Board is confident that the Government of the Netherlands will take the necessary measures to limit the cultivation of cannabis and the expansion of so-called coffee-shops, in which a person may purchase up to 30 grams of cannabis products (INCB, 1995a, 48).

Here the issue is the coffee shop expansion, not the contradiction of that policy with the drug conventions, which finally raised two years later. In the 1995 report, there is a follow-up of the concerns expressed two years earlier.

> The Board notes recent initiatives taken by the Government of the Netherlands in an effort to bring its drug policy more in line with the international drug control treaties.[132] It notes with satisfaction that the Government and the parliament of

---

[132] This statement contradicts earlier ones because the country's policy had not changed, and it had been deemed acceptable before.

> the Netherlands are taking into consideration, during their discussions, the provisions of the international drug control treaties, the impact of their decisions on the drug control policy of other States and on the illicit traffic situation and the views expressed in the report of the Board for 1993. At the same time, however, the Board expresses its continued concern at the persistence of certain practices, only slightly altered, which call into question the Government of the Netherlands' fidelity to its treaty obligations. This includes continuing the failed policy of 'separation of markets,' tolerating the continued cultivation of nederwiet[133] provided that it is of lower THC content, permitting the operation of so-called coffee shops, many of which have fallen under the control of criminal elements, and continuing to stockpile narcotic drugs for nonmedical purposes. The Board will continue to observe closely the progress made by the Government of the Netherlands in fulfilling its treaty obligations (INCB, 1996, 58).

In other words, it took twenty years for the INCB to question the coffee shops' fidelity to the country's treaty obligations. In 1996 there was a Board's mission to the Netherlands, and its conclusions are summarized in that year's report.

> The Government and Parliament in 1995 and 1996 reviewed the national drug policy, concluding that it had been successful from the point of view of health but had had a number of negative consequences for the Netherlands and other countries. The Board appreciates the recent commitment of the Government to address those consequences with a more stringent policy and in cooperation

---

[133] Nederwiet is a term that refers to marijuana grown in the Netherlands that has a high THC content (author's note).

with other Governments. The Board notes with satisfaction that government officials are conscious of the importance of maintaining the existing international consensus on drug control issues and are against the adoption of unilateral measures which are not in line with such consensus. [...] Noting the increased prevalence of cannabis abuse in the Netherlands, the Board is following with interest the specially targeted prevention campaign on the health damages produced by that narcotic drug. [...] While the Board has taken note that the Government of the Netherlands is determined not to allow henceforth a permissive attitude vis-à-vis certain promotional activities of coffee shops and that their number has already been reduced significantly, the Board reaffirms its position that the toleration of coffee shops, buying, stocking, and selling cannabis products for non-medical use does not conform with the provisions of the 1961 Convention. [...] The Government of the Netherlands concluded from the findings of studies that prevalence of heroin abuse in the Netherlands is relatively low and that the level of cannabis abuse is not significantly higher than in other European countries and is much lower than in North America. In addition, the heroin abuse population is rapidly ageing in the Netherlands. [...] The Board will follow closely the developments and will maintain its excellent dialogue with the Government of the Netherlands (INCB, 1997, 61-62).

It was the first reference by the INCB about the fact that the coffee shops did not comply with the drug conventions. The following 1997 report mentions the coffee shops as an indirect incitement to drug use but fails to refer to the Netherlands.

A certain amount of discretion is inevitable when implementing the law. Prioritization takes place regarding which types of crime are pursued more vigorously than others because of limited financial and human resources. The seriousness of the crime must also be considered. Thus, there are areas in most cities, in both developed and developing countries, where drug transactions are known to take place. This is formally tolerated in some countries, for example, where cannabis is openly sold in coffee shops, an activity that might be described as indirect incitement. This is not in accordance with the spirit or the letter of the international drug control treaties (INCB, 1998, 6).

For some years, the INCB was quiet regarding marijuana in the Netherlands. The Board returned to the marijuana issue in the Netherlands only at the beginning of the 2000s, when some countries and organized international civil society groups began challenging the IDCS policies, as shown in the introduction of this book.

In January 2012, amendments to the national framework of the Netherlands for policy related to so-called 'coffee shops' as contained in the Opium Act Instructions came into force, with the aim of reducing the size of such sites, facilitating control, and combating drug tourism. Access to 'coffee shops' is to be restricted to residents of the Netherlands aged 18 years or older who are members of a 'coffee shop,' with membership to each site limited to 2,000 individuals per calendar year. The restrictions were applied in three southern states (Limburg, North Brabant, and Zeeland) as from May 2012, and were to be implemented nationwide from January 2013. The amendments also increase the minimum distance between 'coffee shops' and secondary schools and secondary vocational institutions. While the Board has taken note of this development, its position continues to be that such 'coffee shops' are in violation of the provisions of the international drug control conventions (INCB, 2013, 100).

The following report (2013) also commented on the coffee shops issue.

> [...] a rule limiting access to so-called 'coffee shops' to residents of the country came into effect nationwide, after having been introduced in three southern provinces (Limburg, Noord-Brabant, and Zeeland) on 1 May 2012. However, municipalities were permitted to implement the new rule gradually and in accordance with local 'coffee-shop' and security policies. The Government announced that, as of June 2013, 70 per cent of the 103 municipalities of the country were already implementing or were planning to implement the residency criterion. Planned restrictions that were to enter into force in January 2013 to limit access to such venues to a maximum of 2,000 'members' per year were revoked by the Government in November 2012. The Government also announced in November 2012 that the planned increase in the minimum distance between such venues and secondary and vocational schools to 350 meters would not be imposed by national rules. While noting those developments, the Board reiterates its position that such 'coffee shops' are in contravention of the provisions of the international drug control conventions (INCB, 2014, 79-80).

These comments on the Netherlands were descriptive and not judgmental of the country's new policies.

9.3 THE INCB AND MARIJUANA LEGALIZATION IN URUGUAY

As soon as the government of Uruguay started to move toward non-medicinal marijuana legalization, this became an important issue for the INCB. Its concern was first expressed in its 2011 report: "In 2011, the National Drug Board of Uruguay approved the national drug control strategy for 2011-2015. The strategy, among other things, proposes to promote international debate on current drug control policies" (INCB, 2012a, 68).

In the following report, the INCB expressed again its concerns: "The Board noted with concern that in August 2012, the Government of Uruguay presented to its national congress a proposed law to legalize the production and sale of cannabis in the country. According to the proposed law, the Government would assume control and regulation over importing, producing, acquiring title to, storing, selling, and distributing cannabis herb and its derivatives. If adopted, the law could be in contravention of the international drug control conventions to which Uruguay is a party. The Board, in line with its mandate, has sought a dialogue with the Government of Uruguay to promote the country's compliance with the provisions of the international drug control treaties, in particular the 1961 Convention" (INCB, 2013, 71-72).

The President of the Board did have a dialogue with the Government of Uruguay although not a mission to that country: "[i] the margins of the 2013 Commission on Narcotic Drugs (CND) session in March in Vienna, the Uruguayan Minister for the Presidency ('prosecretario', equivalent to "Prime Minister") Diego Cánepa had extensive meetings with Raymond Yans. But it is true that there was a certain reluctance on the Uruguayan side to receive Yans in Montevideo before the Parliamentary process was concluded. Yans' attitude raised concerns that the already polarised and politicised national debate in Uruguay might be further 'polluted' by his unsubstantiated personal opinions if they were presented as official UN positions. Uruguay expressed its willingness to engage in further dialogue with the Board once the legislation had been approved" (Jelsma, 2013).

Marijuana legalization was supported only by less than 40% of the Uruguayan population. An open dialogue with the INCB or an INCB mission to Uruguay could have been detrimental to the government's enactment hopes. Thus, "[t]he Board notes with concern that in July 2013, the lower house of Uruguay approved new legislation that would allow the State to assume control over and regulate activities related to the importation, production or acquisition of any title, storage, sale or distribution of cannabis or its derivatives, under terms and conditions to be determined by a regulation, for the purpose of nonmedical use. The law has yet to be approved by the Senate. The Board wishes to point out that such legislation, if approved, would be contrary to the provisions of the international drug control conventions" (INCB, 2014, 57).

After this development, the Board's president requested an audience with Uruguayan President José Mujica in which he expected to dissuade Mujica from his project to legalize marijuana. The government agreed to send a delegation to the November session of the Board, where it would explain the country's position. However, 48 hours before the scheduled meeting, the government canceled it.

Then, "on 20 December 2013, the Legislative Power of Uruguay passed Act No. 19.172, establishing a legal framework applicable to the control and regulation by the State of the importation, exportation, planting, growing, gathering, production, purchase, stocking, sale, distribution, and use of cannabis and its derivatives" (INCB, 2015, 25).

The INCB staff, following diplomatic protocol, had prepared a press release to respond to this expected development.[134] The INCB president's reaction to the enactment of the law was unfortunate and in a press conference, deviating from the press release, "accused Uruguay of negligence with regard to public health concerns, deliberately blocking dialogue attempts and having a 'pirate attitude' towards the UN conventions" (Jelsma, 2013).

---

[134] See:

http://www.incb.org/documents/Publications/PressRelease/PR2013/press_release_111213.pdf

The next day, the "pirate attitude" accusation was the top first-page headline across the Uruguayan press and important drug news across Latin America.[135] Unfortunately, the president's words offended Uruguay. A Board member[136] apologized for his colleague's words to the Uruguayan Ambassador to the Organization of American States (OAS) and the Secretary-General of the National Drug Board.[137]

This action lowered the tension between the Government and the Board. Uruguay then sent a mission to the Board's 109th session, held in February 2014, where "[t]he representatives of the Government of Uruguay reported on recent measures taken in the field of drug control in that country and assured the Board of the Government's commitment to drug control and full and unconditional cooperation with the Board. The Board will continue its dialogue with the Government of Uruguay, with a view to promoting the country's compliance with the international drug control treaties, including through the sending of a high-level mission of the Board to Uruguay" (INCB, 2015, 26).

After the Uruguayan visit, the INCB changed its tone: "In December 2013, the Senate of Uruguay approved new legislation, previously approved by the lower legislative chamber, that allows the State to assume control over and regulate activities related to the

---

[135] See:https://www.elobservador.com.uy/onu-eleva-el-tono-actitud-uruguay-marihuana-es-propia-piratas-n267322, https://www.lainformacion.com/asuntos-sociales/interes-humano/sociedad/la-legalizacion-de-la-marihuana-en-uruguay-es-una-actitud-de-piratas-dice-la-onu_ggwg5ijgvhjscfzfyryej3, http://en.mercopress.com/2013/12/14/pot-fumes-mujica-calls-un-officil-liar-after-he-accused-uruguay-of-pirate-attitudes

[136] The conventions require every INCB member to be independent, and there are no hierarchies among them. The President is the regular voice of the Board, but he/she is not the boss of the Board. To operate effectively, in most situations, no prior consultation takes place before issuing press releases, and members rely on the political and diplomatic sensitivity of the President.

[137] See: http, http://www.montevideo.com.uy/Noticias/JIFE-se-excuso-con-Uruguay-uc221353. As noted above, the Board has not kept official records of its meetings. However, to my knowledge, this was the first time that a member challenged publicly a statement of an INCB Board's president.

importation, production, storage, sale or distribution of cannabis or its derivatives, or the acquisition of any title related thereto, under certain terms and conditions, for the purpose of nonmedical use. The regulations governing the implementation of this law were fleshed out in a presidential decree in May 2014. Sales of cannabis to consumers were delayed, however, owing to difficulties in implementing the law. Such sales are expected to start in 2015. The Board notes that this legislation is contrary to the provisions of the international drug control conventions, specifically article 4, paragraph (c), and article 36 of the 1961 Convention as amended by the 1972 Protocol and article 3, paragraph (1) (a), of the 1988 Convention" (INCB, 2015, 62).

Since then, the dialogue between the INCB and the Uruguayan government has improved. In the following 2015 report, there is a minor neutral reference to Uruguay: "the further regulation of a market for cannabis for non-medical use, as is the case of Uruguay" (INCB, 2016a, 61).

In the 2016 report, the Board reiterates in a couple of places that Uruguay's marijuana policy contradicts the conventions, but "in November 2015, INCB carried out a mission to Uruguay. The objective of the mission was to discuss the legislation on the non-medical use of cannabis and its implementation in Uruguay. During the mission, the INCB delegation held consultations with senior officials from the Ministries of the Interior, Health, and Foreign Affairs, as well as with the Attorney General. Meetings were also held with officials from the newly established Institute for the Regulation and Control of Cannabis and the Scientific Advisory Committee. The INCB delegation also had the opportunity to visit drug abuse treatment facilities. [...] During the mission, the implementation of Law No. 19.172, permitting the non-medical use of cannabis, was discussed with the national authorities of Uruguay. The discussions were focused on the inconsistency of that law with the provisions of the 1961 Convention. The Board expressed its intention to continue to monitor the situation and the compliance of the Government of

Uruguay with the international drug control treaties. To that end, it requested the Government to keep it informed of all relevant developments in that area and to be provided with information on the public health consequences of the implementation of Law No. 19.172" (INCB, 2017a, 33-34).

Regarding the Netherlands, in the 1917 report, the Board expresses that it "has continued its dialogue with the Government of the Netherlands on several drug-related developments, including its 'coffee shop' policy and legislative initiatives related to the cultivation of cannabis. In order to discuss matters pertaining to drug control in the country, [...] The Board received communications from the Government of the Netherlands providing further explanations on the issues discussed. [...] In February 2017, the lower house of parliament of the Netherlands narrowly voted to approve a bill regulating the cultivation of cannabis for non-medical purposes. [...] According to the information available to the Board, the public prosecution office of the Netherlands has raised concerns that legalizing cultivation of cannabis for non-medical purposes would put the Netherlands in contravention of the international drug control treaties. [...] While noting the efforts of the Government to contain the number of its 'coffee shops' and their effects, the Board reiterates its call upon the Government to take steps to close its 'coffee shops,' because that policy contravenes the provisions of the international drug control treaties" (INCB, 2018, 33-34).

The Board has also continued its dialogue with Uruguay: "In March 2017, Uruguay submitted a report to the Board on the status of implementation of Law No. 19.172 adopted in December 2013, which had created a regulated market for the non-medical use of cannabis. Uruguay continued to develop its institutional and regulatory framework for the implementation of the law, covering such areas as the sale of cannabis for non-medical purposes in pharmacies; the establishment of the procedures to be followed in the event of consumption of cannabis and other drugs in the workplace; and the registration, sale and dispensation of cannabis for non-medical use [...] In July 2017, pharmacies in Uruguay started selling cannabis to registered users for non-medical use. The Board takes note of the Government's plans to assess the public health consequences of the law in the near future and inform the Board about the outcome of the assessment. At the same time, the Board reiterates that the legalization and regulation of cannabis for non-medical purposes is contrary to the relevant international legal framework, which categorically restricts the use of controlled substances such as cannabis to medical and scientific purposes" (INCB, 2018, 36).

There is no question that the INCB non-medical marijuana uses in the Netherlands were treated for a long time with kids gloves and that in Uruguay, at first, some Board members may have been somewhat aggressive. However, after 2014 the treatment of both countries became very balanced.

As other countries legalize non-medical; marijuana uses, the Board will have a complex challenge because simply arguing that non-medical marijuana use violates the drug conventions does not seem significantly dissuasive. This is an issue that either sooner or later (hopefully sooner) the CND, that is the organ that should discuss international drug policies, must confront.

CHAPTER TEN. BOLIVIA AND THE COCA CHEWING CONUNDRUM

10.1 OVERVIEW

Since the INCB was established, coca chewing has been a concern of the Board. The 1961 Single Convention prohibited non-medical ingestion of coca leaves and established in article 49 ¶2e) that: "Coca leaf chewing must be abolished within twenty-five years from the coming into force of this Convention as provided in paragraph 1 of article 41." This provision de facto applied mainly to Bolivia and Peru, where that practice was generalized among Amerindian communities. It was a minor issue in Colombia, where the habit was restricted to a small population. And in the northern regions of Argentina and Chile, where coca is not cultivated, coca chewing is common among some social groups.

The 25-year deadline (December,12,1989) to eradicate coca destined for all non-medical uses, except supplying Coca-Cola, was not enforced anywhere. For a long time, coca chewing has been prevalent in parts of the Andean countries in varying intensities. When the Single Convention was signed in 1961, the region's governments supported the elimination of coca chewing. However, this support weakened as the Amerindian cultures' status, which frequently was dismissed as uncivilized, improved in the Andean countries.

This section summarizes the evolution of the beliefs about coca chewing in those countries and the frequently conflicting relationship of the INCB with Bolivia. This country has taken the most independent position. It illustrates the problems that arise from attempts to impose a unique policy that restricts human behaviors globally in a multicultural and diverse world.

10.2 THE EARLY INCB POSITION ON COCA CHEWING

The First INCB report in 1968 devotes seventeen of its 22 analytical pages to explaining what the Board is and its functions and five pages to important policy issues. The discussion of coca and cocaine covers almost two of those pages. There is no question that coca chewing was a main issue for the Board. Its positions reflected closely those taken by the 1950 Report of the UN Commission of Enquire on the Coca Leaf (United Nations, 1950).[138] Coincidentally, Dr. Marcel Graxier-Doyeaux, one of the four members of that commission, was a founder INCB Member, where he served six years (1968-1973).[139]

As noted above, the commentaries to the 1961 Convention recognize traditional medicinal opium in China, India, and Pakistan. Still, there is no recognition of legitimate traditional medicinal coca in the Andean countries. The INCB 1968 (INCB, 1968) report analyzes the coca situation in Bolivia and Peru. It dismisses all traditional coca chewing as illegitimate and states that it should be eliminated in the interest of the world, coca-growing countries, and their coca chewers. These are victims of a harmful habit amongst the Andean Indians, many of whom live in precarious economic conditions and resort to chewing the leaves to quell the pangs of hunger (ibid, ¶71). Coca chewing habit is a local public health problem of concern only to the countries of the Andean Highlands (ibid, ¶72). The Board points out that legitimate medical cocaine uses are declining and likely to disappear except for the small amount of coca needed to supply Coca-Cola. Besides, in practice, the supply of coca for traditional uses cannot be controlled, and clandestine manufacturers of cocaine have been able to produce for the international illicit cocaine market (ibid, ¶73). Thus, it considers that any tolerance of coca cultivation for

---

[138] Analyzed in chapter two section 2.6.
[139] At the time he was the Board's vice-president and Member of the World Health Organization Expert Committee on Dependence-Producing Drugs (INCB, 1969, 2). See also footnote 67.

traditional uses is dangerous for the international community because the governments where coca grows could not be trusted to control the diversion of coca to the production of cocaine.

To proceed, the INCB argued that action is required on two fronts: to reduce the areas of organized production to manageable proportions and, in parallel, progressively reduce and eventually eliminate the coca-chewing habit (ibid, ¶74). The goal was to wean the Andean Indians from the chewing habit by intensive and sustained public health and educational programs and improving their living standard (ibid, ¶75). The Board recommended the Governments of Bolivia and Peru to continue to concentrate their immediate efforts in the following sectors: the active prohibition of any new coca leaf planting; the application of measures to restrict authorized cultivation to specified districts; and a strengthening of the enforcement services employed in the drive against clandestine cocaine manufacture and in the pursuit and prosecution of illicit traffickers (ibid, ¶80). The Board acknowledges that implementing these policies entails a radical change in the agricultural economy, for which substantial administrative, technical, and financial resources will be needed. Such a significant change can only be achieved with international technical and financial support (ibid, ¶83).

From the perspective of the Amerindian communities and those that support traditional coca uses, the presence in the Board of one of the authors of the questioned 1950 study, which argued against coca chewing, politically weakened the INCB argument. Unfortunately, the INCB relationship with Peru and Bolivia started on the wrong foot, which has persisted, especially with Bolivia.

In the 1969 report, there is again an encouragement to the Bolivian government to comply with the 1961 Convention and start the progressive elimination of coca chewing (INCB, 1969, 17). In the report's section "Other countries of interest," Bolivia and Peru are reminded again of their obligation to eliminate the coca chewing practice. The 1970 report (INCB, 1970) reasserts the coca chewing elimination issue.

In the absence of official reports from the competent national authorities the Board is unable to judge what progress, if any, has been made towards implementing the formal Agreements entered into with the Permanent Central Narcotics Board during successive missions to Bolivia in 1964 and 1966, whereby the Government undertook to embark on a positive programme designed to bring about the ultimate elimination of production and chewing of coca leaves. The Government must surely agree that this is essential for the health and welfare of the Bolivian people. Early steps in this direction are also urgently necessary from the international standpoint, because of the persistent outflow of crude cocaine into illicit channels" (ibid, ¶86).

In its first reports, the INCB position reflects a profound belief in the socially devastating effects of coca chewing addiction. The 1971 report reminded Bolivia and Peru of their commitment to eliminate coca chewing before 12 December 1989, when the 25-year deadline established in the 1961 convention was to be met. However, as illegal cocaine production, trafficking and consumption increased, after the mid-1970s, the focus of the INCB reports shifted from coca chewing to cocaine and drug trafficking. The 1971 report (INCB, 1971) also devotes several paragraphs to the topic, as follows:

¶67. In its 1970 Report, the Board observed that at last it seemed to be some possibility of action to cope with the abusive consumption of coca-leaf in Peru, and it welcomed the intention to incorporate coca restrictions in the comprehensive land reforms planned by the national authorities. A formal assurance by the Government that any land grants made under the reform programme will include a ban on coca-bush cultivation would be a useful first step, but what is clearly required is a determined drive to reduce existing coca plantations. This could well form part of a regional campaign, planned and carried out in concert with Bolivia and other countries in the Andean region. Peru is well-placed to take the initiative in such a regional approach while at the same time reducing its domestic production, and the Board looks to the Government to recognize and respond to this challenge.

[...] ¶85. Coca chewing appears to be an important concern because their harmful effects on those that chew coca and the Bolivian and Peruvian governments' impossibility to regulate the coca chewing market.

¶86. The chewing of coca leaves as an indulgence has been practised for centuries in and around the Andean uplands of Peru and Bolivia where the coca bush is indigenous and where it is cultivated in extensive plantations. Under the authoritative rule of the Incas the phenomenon had perhaps no particular social significance. In more recent times, however, it has been increasingly recognized as having a debilitating effect on those who practise it and, accordingly, to be detrimental to the economic and social welfare of the region."

[...] ¶89. So long as coca leaf chewing continues to be widely practised it will be virtually impossible to prevent the clandestine manufacture and the subsequent outflow of cocaine from this region into the illicit traffic. This fact alone gives this form of abuse a more than local relevance; and it will attract yet greater international concern if, as now seems not improbable, cocaine becomes more generally an ingredient of multi-drug abuse."

[...] ¶93. During the twenty years which have elapsed since coca-leaf-chewing was authoritatively recognized to be harmful, corrective measures have been sadly deficient, and it is to be hoped that, from now on, a greater strength of purpose will be displayed by the governments concerned, aided by a greater degree of international co-operation.

After the early 1970s, for both the United States and the United Nations, the importance of coca chewing declined sharply relative to the need to attack cocaine production and international trafficking. Because of the growing importance of international cocaine trafficking in Bolivia, Colombia, and Peru, the focus of drug policies also shifted from traditional uses in native communities to the production of cocaine and trafficking for exports.

10.3 THE PERSISTENT IMPORTANCE OF COCA

While the importance of coca in the global drug debates declined, the economic and social development of the Andean countries after WWII made it more important domestically. Some native peasant communities became organized, particularly in Bolivia. Their level of education increased substantially, the government's investment in infrastructure in transportation, electricity, water, sewer, and in the education and health sectors contributed to improving life expectancy. By the 1960s, these changes had led to fast population growth, a large rural-urban migration, and very fast urban growth. Radio, and later television, became widespread. These developments changed the traditional social structures across the Andean countries, and particularly in Bolivia, they had important consequences regarding coca and cocaine issues.

10.3.1 Relevant Changes in Bolivian Society

The Bolivian population has always been predominantly Amerindian. The 2001 census shows a population of 62% Amerindian, 30% mestizo (mixed race), and the balance a blend of diverse "whites." Until recently, Amerindians were a large underclass with limited political power. From independence in 1825 until 1982, the country was politically very unstable, and military coups and governments were frequent. For a long time, economic power was concentrated among large landowners and mining companies that dominated the economy and the country's exports.

In 1952 the country experienced a left-wing revolution that implemented a significant land reform. Amerindian workers in the haciendas received land and became organized in *sindicatos* (Unions). Since the 1950s, health improvements have generated a population explosion across Latin American countries. Responding to the population increase, the Bolivian government promoted the settlement of uninhabited areas, mainly lowlands, which were particularly adequate for coca plantings. The Chapare region was the primary receptor of settlers.

With the revolution, literacy rates in the Amerindian community started to increase, and their education improved. Through time, their leaders started to participate in the Indigenist movement and became their leaders. As noted above, in the 1940s, most indigenists opposed coca chewing. Still, over time this paradigm changed, and the current Indigenist movement made coca a symbol of Amerindian identity and an instrument for its social cohesion.

Bolivia's mineral sector had been diverse, but tin, a product subject to unstable global prices, became its most important product and export. Following the 1952 revolution, the government nationalized the tin mines, and mining workers developed strong labor unions. However, the international tin price boom and busts induced some miners migration to Chapare, which increased sharply when the tin price crashed in 1985. The revolution also broke down the hacienda system in the highlands and promoted peasant migration to Chapare.

Following their experience in the high lands, the peasants and former miners who settled in Chapare developed local worker *sindicatos* whose main cash crop was coca. These *sindicatos* formed federations and a large, very well-organized confederation that became very politically active. The confederation negotiated with the government concerning the provision of schools, energy, roads, health, etc. Indeed, Chapare has received a lot of investment, and it is likely to be the rural region with the best infrastructure and public utilities and services in the country.

The confederation became the instrument through which native Bolivians, belonging to 36 recognized ethnic groups, gained political power and made coca and coca chewing the main symbol of their different identity from that of the non-native Bolivians. For example, in July 1988, under pressure from the United States, Bolivia enacted a new coca law (Law 1008) that "decreed stiff penalties for drug-trafficking activities and regulated coca cultivation. It established three coca-planting categories. First, legal coca, grown in traditional Yungas of La Paz and Yungas of Vandiola areas. Second, 'surplus' coca grown in Chapare, to be eradicated gradually after compensating peasants. And third, illegal coca plantings in other regions subject to rapid eradication without any compensation to peasants. The debate on this law was most acrimonious. Law opponents advanced extensive nationalistic arguments against imperialism and on behalf of the defense of cultural values" (Thoumi, 2003, 115).

The enactment of Law 1008 required a substantial accommodation among the different stakeholders.[140] The Law banned aerial spraying of coca plantings and required international donor funding of a $2,000 compensation to the peasants for each hectare of coca eradicated. The alternative development programs in Chapare were justified as part of the international *shared responsibility* approach to fighting drugs (Thoumi, 2003, 328-330). Peasant compensation was tough to accept among significant American political sectors that viewed it as equivalent to paying someone not to commit a crime. Law 1008 confirmed the legality of coca chewing and other traditional and industrial uses and declared

---

[140] The main scholars of the Bolivian illegal drugs at the time acknowledge the role of the United States in formulating and passing Law 1008. See for example (Léons and Sanabria, 1997), Gamarra (1994) and Painter (1994).

coca cultivation legal in the "traditional production zone" in the Yungas.

Technically, Law 1008 breached the drug conventions, but the $2,000 compensation per hectare eradicated paid by international donors, mainly the United States, validated to all Bolivian society that policy. Thus, the legal commitment that Bolivia had made in the 1961 Single Convention to eliminate all coca by 12 December was de facto a dead letter that had outlived its relevance over one year earlier.

10.3.2 The 1988 Convention and the Bolivian Reservation

During the drafting of the 1961 Single Convention, Bolivia lobbied unsuccessfully against including the coca leaf in schedule I of the Convention and eliminating traditional coca uses. Bolivia renewed its efforts during the conference that drafted the 1988 Convention and apparently, achieved its goal. As noted, this Convention has only one reference to coca. Article 14 ¶2 reads: "Each Party shall take appropriate measures to prevent illicit cultivation of and to eradicate plants containing narcotic or psychotropic substances, such as opium poppy, coca bush, and cannabis plants, cultivated illicitly in its territory. The measures adopted shall respect fundamental human rights and shall take due account of traditional licit uses, where there is historic evidence of such use, as well as the protection of the environment." However, ¶1 of the same article says: "Any measures taken pursuant to this Convention by Parties shall not be less stringent than the provisions applicable to the eradication of illicit cultivation of plants containing narcotic and psychotropic substances and to the elimination of illicit demand for narcotic drugs and psychotropic substances under the provisions of the 1961 Convention, the 1961 Convention as amended and the 1971 Convention".

Any unsuspecting reader of Article 14 ¶2 would think it guarantees indigenous communities' human rights, traditional uses of coca, welfare, and environmental protection considerations in implementing drug policies. Despite this paragraph, to protect traditional coca uses, the Bolivian government signed and ratified the 1988 convention with a reservation on Article 3, paragraph 2 that reads: "Subject to its constitutional principles and the basic concepts of its legal system, each Party shall adopt such measures as may be necessary to establish as a criminal offence under its domestic law, when committed intentionally, the possession, purchase or cultivation of narcotic drugs or psychotropic substances for personal consumption contrary to the provisions of the 1961 Convention, the 1961 Convention as amended or the 1971 Convention". The scope of this article and its reservations are much broader than those of article 14 and its possible reservations. The Bolivian reservation is clear about the legitimacy of traditional coca uses in the country.[141]

> *Reservation made upon signature and confirmed upon ratification:*
> The Republic of Bolivia places on record its express reservation to article 3, paragraph 2, and declares the inapplicability to Bolivia of those provisions of that paragraph which could be interpreted as establishing as a criminal offence the use, consumption, possession, purchase or cultivation of the coca leaf for personal consumption.
>
> For Bolivia such an interpretation of that paragraph is contrary to principles of its Constitution and basic concepts of its legal system which embody respect for the culture, legitimate practices, values, and attributes of the nationalities making up Bolivia's population.
>
> Bolivia's legal system recognizes the ancestral nature of the licit use of the coca leaf which, for much of Bolivia's population, dates back over centuries. In formulating this reservation, Bolivia considers that:

---

[141] See: https://treaties.un.org/Pages/ViewDetails.aspx?src=TREATY&mtdsg_no=VI-19&chapter=6&clang=_en#EndDec

- The coca leaf is not, in and of itself, a narcotic drug or psychotropic substance;
- The use and consumption of the coca leaf do not cause psychological or physical changes greater than those resulting from the consumption of other plants and products which are in free and universal use;
- The coca leaf is widely used for medicinal purposes in the practice of traditional medicine, the validity of which is upheld by WHO and confirmed by scientific findings;
- The coca leaf can be used for industrial purposes;
- The coca leaf is widely used and consumed in Bolivia, with the result that, if such an interpretation of the above-mentioned paragraph were accepted, a large part of Bolivia's population could be considered criminals and punished as such, such an interpretation is therefore inapplicable;
- It must be placed on record that the coca leaf is transformed into cocaine paste, sulphate and hydrochloride when it is subjected to chemical processes which involve the use of precursors, equipment and materials which are neither manufactured in or originated in Bolivia.

At the same time, the Republic of Bolivia will continue to take all necessary legal measures to control the illicit cultivation of coca for the production of narcotic drugs, as well as the illicit consumption, use and purchase of narcotic drugs and psychotropic substances.

The 1988 Convention was followed by the first UNGASS on drug problems in 1990 that adopted a Global Programme of Action and branded 1991-2000 the United Nations Decade Against Drug Abuse. In 1991 also the United Nations International Drug Control

Programme (UNDCP) was established. These developments were followed by a high-level three-day meeting of the General Assembly in 1993 "to examine urgently the status of international cooperation" in drug control. A letter from the Mexican government to the Secretary-General requested more attention focused on demand reduction as the most effective way to solve the drug problem. This letter was supported by the frustrations of other Latin American countries with the prevailing drug policy results. The INCB 1992 report, for the first time, devoted its chapter one to a specific topic and chose the legalization debate and the need to continue the prohibition of drug uses, including for marijuana.[142] These two documents determined the 1993 meeting agenda (Jelsma, 2003, 182-183).

Following the 1993 General Assembly debates, the INCB 1994 Report focused on the "effectiveness of the international drug control treaties." It concluded that only minor adjustments were necessary to improve their workings. One of the possible adjustments was regarding coca. Paragraph 21(c) is clear about it: "The conflict between the provisions of the 1961 Convention and the views and legislation of countries where the use of the coca leaf is legal should be solved. There is a need to undertake a scientific review to assess the coca - chewing habit and the drinking of coca tea."

The Board also published a Supplement to the 1994 Report (INCB, 1995b) with a long section, "Coca leaf: a need to clarify ambiguities." There the Board requested the CND a study on the effects of coca chewing and coca tea. Unfortunately, that study never took place.[143]

---

[142] As shown above, the 1992 report was the first time that the INCB indicated that the coffee shops of the Netherlands were breaching the drug conventions.
[143] The following two paragraphs of that report expressed the Board's position about the need to revisit the coca chewing issue: "There is a need to examine the situation regarding States parties to the 1961 Convention that have made reservations under article 49 of that Convention. Traditional drug use that had been temporarily

In the same supplementary report (INCB, 1995b), the Board expressed the need for "clarification of the long-standing misunderstanding of the provisions of article 14 of the 1988 Convention, which has had some bearing on the debate on coca leaf. Article 14 deals with measures to eradicate illicit cultivation of narcotic plants and to eliminate illicit demand for narcotic drugs and psychotropic substances. Paragraph 2 of article 14 states that parties to the 1988 Convention, when taking such measures, should take due account of traditional licit use, where there is historic evidence of such use. But that provision should be seen in the light of article 25 of the 1988 Convention, which stipulates that the provisions of that Convention should not derogate from any obligations undertaken by parties to the Convention under the previous international drug control conventions. Furthermore, the drafters of the 1988 Convention enhanced the non-derogatory clause by including in paragraph 1 of article 14 a provision stipulating that any measures taken pursuant to that Convention should not be less stringent than the provisions applicable to eradication of illicit cultivation of plants containing narcotic drugs and psychotropic substances under the provisions of the previous international drug control conventions" ¶49.

It is interesting that not only this requested clarification did not occur, but also that the Bolivian reservation to Article 3, ¶2 was not mentioned.

---

permitted under the 1961 Convention should be assessed, with a view to making a decision on what the approach of the international drug control system should be to that problem. A true assessment of the habit of coca leaf chewing is urgently called for" ¶46. "There is also a need for WHO to undertake a scientific review of the value and risks of mate de coca. That would provide a basis for Governments to make the necessary policy-related decision to resolve the conflict between the provisions of the conventions and the ways in which the Governments and societies concerned view mate de coca and deal with it in legislation" ¶47.

10.3.3 Traditional Coca Uses and the Bolivian Rebellion

In 2006 Evo Morales, a former miner, a coca grower, and the president of the confederation of coca growers' *sindicatos,* was the first Amerindian elected president in Bolivian history. Since then, the government's position has been that coca is a native plant, a gift from *Pachamama* (mother earth), with many good uses that should be exploited, and that cocaine was a Western capitalist product that should be controlled. One of the main projects of the Morales government was to socially revalue coca that, according to him, has been despised by the capitalist West. His goal was to have coca recognized worldwide as a symbol of Amerindian identity and solidarity in Bolivia and as an especially useful plant in the world. This campaign sought to differentiate coca, a mother earth gift to the world, from cocaine, a Western invention that is very destructive. This campaign revived the old: "coca is not cocaine" lemma of the 1930s and 1940s debates in Peru and Bolivia. These statements raised the INCB's concern with the Morales' government coca positions.

The 2007 INCB Report (INCB, 2008a) issued a few days before the CND session was important because that CND was expected to evaluate the UNGASS 1998 Plan of Action results. The INCB stated its concern with the failure of Bolivia and Peru to comply with their coca eradication commitments.

> The Board is concerned that the cultivation of coca bush for purposes that are not in line with the 1961 Convention is continuing in some countries. Uses of coca leaves contrary to the provisions of the 1961 Convention are also continuing, and some of those uses are even being expanded [...] Governments should ensure that the production, export, import, distribution, use and possession of, as well as trade in, coca leaf are limited to medical and scientific purposes, just as they would be limited in the case of any other narcotic drug. In addition, coca leaves may also be used for the preparation

of a flavouring agent that should not contain any alkaloids[144] [...] Governments permitting the cultivation of coca bush should set up an agency to carry out certain functions, as required under articles 23 and 26 of the 1961 Convention. [...] The practice of chewing coca leaves continues in Bolivia and Peru and, on a limited scale, in some other countries. The Board wishes to point out that, within 25 years following the entry into force of the 1961 Convention, coca leaf chewing should have been abolished in those countries where it was taking place. As the 1961 Convention came into force in 1964, coca leaf chewing should have come to an end in 1989. [...] In addition, coca leaf is used in Bolivia and Peru for the manufacture and distribution of mate de coca (coca tea). Such use is also not in line with the provisions of the 1961 Convention. The Board again calls on the Governments of Bolivia and Peru to consider amending their national legislation so as to abolish or prohibit activities that are contrary to the 1961 Convention, such as coca leaf chewing and the manufacture of mate de coca (coca tea) and other products containing coca alkaloids for domestic use and export.[145] [...] The Board calls upon the Governments of Bolivia and Peru to initiate action without delay with a view to eliminating uses of coca leaf that are contrary to the 1961 Convention and to strengthen their efforts against trafficking in cocaine in the region. [...] The 1988 Convention requires Governments to establish as criminal offences under domestic law, when committed intentionally, activities involving coca leaf that are contrary to the provisions of the 1961 Convention. [...] The provisions of the 1988

---

[144] This is the exception to supply coca leaves to Coca-Cola (Article 27 of the 1961 Single Convention on Narcotic Drugs). This is the only non-medical coca human ingest recognized by the drug conventions.
[145] Report of the International Narcotics Control Board for 1993 (United Nations publication, Sales No. E.94.XI.2), ¶211.

Convention, including reservations made under that Convention, do not absolve a party of its rights and obligations under the other international drug control treaties. It is therefore important that States fulfil their obligations under those treaties in spite of any reservations they may have made. [...] The Board calls upon the Governments of Bolivia and Peru to initiate action without delay with a view to eliminating uses of coca leaf that are contrary to the 1961 Convention and to strengthen their efforts against trafficking in cocaine in the region (INCB, 2008, 37-38).

The same year, UNODC (2008, 207) supported the INCB position: "The reference to 'traditional licit uses' was interpreted by some countries in the Andean region (Bolivia and Peru) as an acknowledgement by the international community that such 'traditional licit uses' still existed and that 'due account' for such 'traditional licit uses' would have to be taken, including for sufficient production to satisfy these 'traditional licit uses' (coca chewing, 'mate de coca' tea). In contrast, the 1961 Convention had already outlawed the habit of coca leaf chewing, opium smoking, the quasi-medical use of opium and the non-medical use of cannabis, and the production of drug crops for such purposes. [...] Under Article 14 ¶1 of the 1988 Convention, however, it is made explicit that 'Any measures taken pursuant to this Convention by Parties shall not be less stringent than the provisions applicable to the eradication of illicit cultivation of plants containing narcotic and psychotropic substances ... under the provision of the 1961 Convention."

Here UNODC repeated the position expressed by the INCB in the Supplement to its 1994 Report discussed above. Besides, it contradicts the acceptance of quasi-medical uses of opium expressed in the Commentary to the 1961 Single Convention mentioned above (United Nations, 1973, 111).

The INCB's interpretation of Articles 14 and 25 of the 1988 Convention contradicts "the principle that 'the later law supersedes the earlier law' (*lex posterior derogat priori*) which is taken to be one of the 'general principles of law recognized by civilized nations' and, as such, applicable to conflicts between earlier and subsequent treaties" (Aufricht, 1952).[146] The INCB argued that ¶1 of article 14 states that "any measures taken pursuant to this Convention by Parties shall not be less stringent than the provisions applicable [...] under the provision of the 1961 Convention". This denies that ¶2 may supersede or modify ¶1. Thus, ¶2 would have no meaning or usefulness and should not have been written, except to trick those that wanted the exception into believing that they had obtained it. In a contract (a treaty) signed in good faith, a clause like the one on ¶2 would not be included unless it could be applied. If the Board was convinced of the legitimacy of its interpretation and had been acting in good faith, it should have requested the Convention's amendment to repeal ¶2.

Furthermore, the Board asserts that according to Article 14 ¶2, policies "should take due account of traditional licit use, where there is historic evidence of such use" (INCB, 1995b, ¶49). But this is an incomplete sentence that eliminates essential contextual elements that have crucial implications. The complete sentence in Article 14 ¶2 reads: "The measures adopted shall respect fundamental human rights and shall take due account of traditional licit uses, where there is historic evidence of such use, as well as the protection of the environment." In this sentence, the main point is the respect of fundamental human rights. Article 14 ¶2 requires that policies dealing with the peasants that grow coca for traditional uses must respect their fundamental human rights and the environment. As noted above, article 14 ¶2 is the first and only mention of "fundamental human rights" in the three IDCS conventions.

By hiding the references to fundamental human rights and the environment and appealing to Article 25 of the 1988 Convention on

---

[146] This article presents the history of this principle and a substantial literature about it.

241

the "non-derogation from earlier treaty rights and obligations," the INCB implied that policies that take into consideration fundamental human rights and the environment would be less stringent than the ones required by the earlier conventions. Thus, article 14 ¶2 should be disregarded as inapplicable.

It also contradicts the contemporary public policy approach that recognizes that every policy faces political, economic, social, cultural, environmental, and other restrictions. In this case, article 14 ¶2 introduces new policy restrictions: respect of fundamental human rights, traditional coca uses, and protection of the environment. It makes drug policies more stringent as they diminish the number of policy options that comply with the conventions. Article 14 ¶2 reflects the complexity of the drug policy issues. It is more demanding from governments and more stringent than simple punitive law enforcement policy approaches. In response to these developments, President Evo Morales led the Bolivian delegation to the 2008 CND, where he formally requested:

- To take the coca leaf off the 1961 Single Convention schedule I.
- That traditional coca chewing, and coca tea should be accepted as legitimate coca uses.
- To explore other possible industrial coca uses.

Then in a very theatrical act, he chewed some coca leaves, insisting that this practice was not a problem for native Bolivian communities. At the same time, cocaine, a Western invention, had created a global problem.

On February 7, 2009, under Morales's leadership, Bolivia adopted a new Constitution that, as shown by the following excerpts, from its preface was drastically different from the earlier ones:[147]

---

[147] An Oxford University English version of the new constitution is available online at Constituteproject.org (2018)

[...] We populated this sacred Mother Earth with different faces, and since that time we have understood the plurality that exists in all things and in our diversity as human beings and cultures. Thus, our peoples were formed, and we never knew racism until we were subjected to it during the terrible times of colonialism.

A State based on respect and equality for all, on principles of sovereignty, dignity, interdependence, solidarity, harmony, and equity in the distribution and redistribution of the social wealth, where the search for a good life predominates; based on respect for the economic, social, juridical, political and cultural pluralism of the inhabitants of this land; and on collective coexistence with access to water, work, education, health, and housing for all.

We have left the colonial, republican and neo-liberal State in the past. We take on the historic challenge of collectively constructing a Unified Social State of Pluri-National Communitarian law, which includes and articulates the goal of advancing toward a democratic, productive, peace-loving, and peaceful Bolivia, committed to the full development and free determination of the peoples.

Article 1 of the Constitution formulates the new political structure for the country: "Bolivia is constituted as a Unitary Social State of Pluri-National Communitarian Law,[148] that is free, independent, sovereign, democratic, intercultural, decentralized and with autonomies. Bolivia is founded on plurality and on political, economic, juridical, cultural and linguistic pluralism in the integration process of the country."

---

https://www.constituteproject.org/constitution/Bolivia_2009.pdf
[148] *Estado Unitario Social de Derecho Plurinacional Comunitario*

Article 384 spells out the country's position regarding coca: "The State shall protect native and ancestral coca as cultural patrimony, a renewable natural resource of Bolivia's biodiversity, and as a factor of social cohesion; in its natural state it is not a narcotic. Its revaluing,[149] production, commercialization, and industrialization shall be regulated by law."

Immediately after enacting the new Constitution, the Bolivian Government, following article 47 of the Single Convention, proposed an amendment to Article 49 of the Convention to allow traditional coca chewing in the country without changing coca plantings and cocaine control production and trafficking. After the 18-month period allowed for challenges to the proposal, eighteen countries objected, including all the members of the G8. Only five countries supported the amendment: Ecuador, Uruguay, Costa Rica, Venezuela, and Spain. Most of the Parties to the Convention abstained. Given this result, ECOSOC had several options: it may have allowed the amendment to be valid only in Bolivia, it could have made it valid across the world except in the countries that objected to it, it may have called a conference to debate the issue, or it could have rejected the amendment. ECOSOC chose the last option.

From the Bolivian perspective, the issue was clear. In the 1988 Convention, Bolivia assumed that the 1988 Convention had recognized the legitimacy of their traditional coca uses because they were part of the Bolivians' fundamental cultural human rights. But the INCB and the UNODC turned that down with questionable arguments. Bolivia had ratified the Convention with reservations to article 3 ¶2 to allow traditional coca uses, a fact that was silently dismissed. Then it proposed an amendment to allow coca chewing, and that was rejected.

After this result, Bolivia denounced the 1961 Convention and, following the procedure specified in the Single Convention's

---

[149] This reflects the government's belief that coca has been despised by the capitalist west and should be revalued (author's note).

Article 46, proceeded to apply to re-accede to the convention with reservations. The reaction of the INCB was strong. In the foreword of its 2011 report Hamid Ghodse, the president of the Board, expressed the Board's position (INCB, 2012, v).

> One major challenge to the international drug control system is the recent decision by the Government of the Plurinational State of Bolivia to denounce the Single Convention on Narcotic Drugs of 1961 as amended by the 1972 Protocol. While it announced its decision, the Government made known its intention to re-accede to the Convention with a reservation. The Board has noted with regret that unprecedented step taken by the Bolivian Government and is concerned that, inter alia, while the denunciation itself may be technically permitted under the Convention, it is contrary to the fundamental object and spirit of the Convention. If the international community were to adopt an approach whereby States parties would use the mechanism of denunciation and re-accession with reservations, the integrity of the international drug control system would be undermined, and the achievements of the past 100 years in drug control would be compromised.

It is an interesting comment that reflects a peculiar way to interpret international drug treaties. It asserts that in this case, the denunciation process is only a technicality that may be dismissed because it is "contrary to the fundamental object and spirit of the Convention." Thus, article 46 should not be applied. One question is then, what is the purpose of having article 46 if there are cases when sovereign Parties to the 1961 Convention cannot apply it? If so, the Convention should have listed the criteria for preventing countries from denouncing and re-accessing the Convention. Another question is, what would be the object, spirit, and integrity of the Convention? These concepts were not made clear in the drug conventions and were not interpreted by the Board, creating uncertainty. For example, integrity may mean that every convention article should be respected, or perhaps that sovereign Parties should not be allowed to change their minds about drug policies. Is the object of the conventions to protect and promote the health and welfare of humankind as the INCB has proclaimed, or to limit drug use to medical and scientific purposes? The spirit of the conventions is a more metaphysical concept. Does it mean that policies should always pursue the unobtainable goal of a world without drugs disregarding the social, political, or economic costs that may arise from those actions?

The Bolivian reservation to re-accede to the 1961 Single Convention was short and straightforward:[150]

> *Reservation:*
>
> The Plurinational State of Bolivia reserves the right to allow in its territory: traditional coca leaf chewing; the consumption and use of the coca leaf in its natural state for cultural and medicinal purposes, such as its use in infusions; and also the cultivation, trade, and possession of the coca leaf to the extent necessary for these licit purposes.
>
> At the same time, the Plurinational State of Bolivia will continue to take all necessary measures to control the cultivation of coca in order to prevent its abuse and the illicit production of the narcotic drugs which may be extracted from the leaf.

For Bolivia's reservation to be rejected, at least 61 States Parties (a third of the 183 States parties to the Convention at that time) had to object within one year after the Secretary-General circulated the proposed reservation among States parties. The deadline for objections expired on 10 January 2013. Only 15 countries objected:

---

[150] https://treaties.un.org/Pages/ViewDetails.aspx?src=TREATY&mtdsg_no=VI-18&chapter=6

United States, Mexico, Japan, Russia, Canada, the UK, Germany, France, Italy, the Netherlands, Sweden, Finland, Portugal, Israel, and Ireland.

In the 2012 annual report, the Board reaffirmed its concerns about the Bolivian actions on the integrity of the IDCS.

> The denunciation of the Convention took effect on 1 January 2012. In 2012, the year the Government launched an international campaign to solicit the support of States parties to the 1961 Convention for its strategy to re-accede to that Convention with a reservation. The Board expressed its concern in its annual report for 2011 that if the international community were to adopt an approach whereby States parties would use the mechanism of denunciation and re-accession with reservations to overcome problems in the implementation of certain treaty provisions, the integrity of the international drug control system would be undermined (INCB, 2013, 71).

The Bolivian experience raises a question about the strength of the global support of some of the IDCS policies. The most powerful countries rejected Bolivia's denunciation of the 1961 Convention and its re-accession (all the G8), and a few others objected. However, 92% of the Parties to the Convention did not object despite pressures from the G8 countries. Besides, Argentina and Chile, countries where coca is smuggled for chewing purposes, have tolerated this traffic for a very long time without pressuring Bolivia to control that trade. These results suggest that many countries might not accept domestic non-medical coca uses but realize that in a diverse world, others could do so, and if those uses do not present a threat to them, they will not object. The lack of support of the G8 position on coca may have also been a strategy followed by many countries to prevent a precedent of successful G8 pressure. They feared it could be applied when countries might choose policies that the G8 countries would oppose.

These facts are consistent with the reality that the United Nations parties have vastly different power, cultures, ideologies, development levels, and ethics that determine their interests and responses. That is why the IDCS may be somewhat flexible, and many countries could accept drug policy experiments in other places when they do not affect them directly.

PART THREE. THE CHALLENGES FOR DRUG PUBLIC POLICIES

CHAPTER ELEVEN: COMPLEXITY, PUBLIC POLICY, SOCIAL VULNERABILITY AND POLICY EFFECTIVENESS

11.1 OVERVIEW

Governments commonly follow a course of action to deal with problems or issues in their countries. It usually takes the form of a public policy. The gaps between policy design, implementation, and success have always been a challenge. Public policy implementation always has obstacles. Many policies have sought behavioral changes throughout history, and governments have relied on moral suasion, support from other organizations like religions, families, peer groups, tribes, etc. These provide social controls that induce people to behave according to each society's mores and conventional wisdom. When these fail, the threat of governments' sanctions has been the main deterrent used to seek the desired behavioral change.

Drug policies based on fear and sanctions, applied with varying degrees of force, have been prevalent with few exceptions. Implementing the drug use restriction for medical and scientific purposes followed a simple law enforcement pattern that prevailed worldwide when the IDCS was created: a law was enacted, and the government sought ways to enforce it. In the case of prohibition, the problem was always preventing the development of illegal markets and contraband. Its solution depended on the police, the security, and the judicial systems to dissuade or sanction the concerning behavior.

In post-WWII, civil liberties and rights were strengthened in some societies, and new policymaking and implementation approaches were developed. These new approaches explore and analyze the effectiveness of different policies, identify their unexpected consequences, and evaluate policy implementation's social and economic costs. They also show that policies must rely on market incentives and cooperation with diverse civil organizations to promote policy compliance. It is imperative to make sure that citizens feel that they share in the policy's ownership. In other words, the success of any policy that seeks to influence behaviors requires a partnership between the citizenry and the government. Simple top-down (deter and use force) or bottom-up policies that arise from a community without governmental support are bound to fail sooner or later. The interaction of the government with citizen organizations in policy formulation and implementation is a necessary condition for policy success (Colander and Kupers, 2014, Ch. 1 and 2). Policy success requires the co-creation among all stakeholders in the policy formulation and implementation processes.

The industrial revolution that started around 1760 and accelerated since then has changed the effectiveness of top-down policies. People became educated, developed professional skills, and became aware of the world beyond the community in which they were born. They got in contact with goods, services, and ideas generated in distant places, etc. The transportation revolution that expanded markets and the more recent explosion of communication technologies transformed the world. The traditional drug policy model became obsolete and incapable of dealing with many issues that have become increasingly complex. The dynamic of this phenomenon has become exponential in recent decades, increasing the complexity of drug issues and the drug policies' challenges.

The IDCS is inspired by the social problems associated with psychoactive drug addiction and is part of the international law treaty system developed to regulate the relationships among countries. As noted above, the UN system was designed to deal mainly with borders, international wars and security, migration, tariffs, and other international trade issues. However, the IDCS treaties differ from other treaties because they go beyond regulating international trade of controlled drugs and their chemical precursors and require the Parties' commitment to regulate personal drug use and behaviors. To achieve this, it restricts governments from freely establishing their regulations of domestic drug use. An overly ambitious international law experiment that imposes a unique drug use constrain to all humans, independently of their life experiences, culture, traditions, and beliefs. The success of this experiment must face many obstacles and constraints because international law has feeble enforcement capabilities. It cannot force domestic social and individual behavioral changes. The IDCS has relayed mostly on naming and shaming to motivate governments to enforce its policies.

The drug conventions aim to alter human behavior and eliminate drug addiction. To achieve these goals, drug policies have trusted the deterrent effect of law enforcement even though there is no evidence that it is significant across the world. They have also trusted the ability of the health sector to prevent addiction and treat, recover, and re-socialize addicts. Those policies might be effective under some circumstances in some locations. Still, although they are well-intentioned and might be supported by most people, they end up being an unending struggle pursuing an unachievable ideal drug-free world, as the IDCS agencies have frequently acknowledged.

Post-WWII developments in the social sciences have highlighted the complexity of social policies and the need to understand the relationships among people, governments, and other social institutions that regulate individual behavior. These relationships show that individual behaviors do not have direct causes and effects, making it difficult to establish causality in the development of psychoactive drug production, marketing, and use. Furthermore, the determinant factors of those developments are often hidden, and in other cases, the relationship among factors is not stable. Drug-related problems do not have unique solutions or can be solved with universal *best practices*. This chapter explores these issues.

11.2 LAWS, SOCIAL NORMS AND SELF CONTROL

Humans are selfish (i.e., self-interested) but also social. Throughout history, there has been tension between these two drivers of individual behavior. People are moved by their desire to achieve individual goals such as wealth and power but belonging to a community also generates personal satisfaction and meaning to life. If everybody follows only their drive to compete for individual materialistic supremacy accumulating wealth and power, without behavioral constraints imposed by social organs, the result would be a dog-eats-dog pre-Hobbesian society. Few will achieve success, and most will fail because success requires being on top and frequently stepping down hard on the rest. But if competition is mitigated by cooperation, most people could benefit. Every society today has a mix of competitive and cooperative legitimate behaviors. Individual behavior has three types of controls, imposed by:

- The government.
- Other social organs like family, religion, etc., generate identity and cohesion and reflect society's culture.
- The third kind of controls are the internalized norms that persons develop through the socialization process of learning their societies' culture, attitudes, beliefs, language, and behavior. These norms generate internalized behavioral norms and constraints (self-control) that depend on the individual's natural inclination and life experiences (Thoumi, 2012, 979).

In societies in which the formal rules and norms of the State are reinforced by the informal or social norms stressed by family, religion, peer groups, schools, etc., a low level of lawbreaking is achieved with relatively little law enforcement efforts. In these societies, lawbreaking would tend to be done by a few "bad apples" (the law of large numbers means that there will always be some outliers in the distribution of individual behavior) that law enforcement could take care of.

On the other hand, when legal and social "norms differ significantly, law enforcement efforts are counterbalanced by informal norms, and enforcing state laws is very difficult [...] The socialization process molds people and, in some societies, adults are more prone to lawbreaking than in others" (Thoumi, 2012, 980). When the gap between legal and social norms is small, the socialization process generates internalized behavior constraints that support legal and social norms. But when that gap is large, a common situation in segmented, stratified, and polarized societies, anti-crime policies, and formal and informal norms are prone to conflict, producing highly counterproductive results. "The conflict and confusion among norms tend to produce people with low self-control because, first, people realize that formal norms could be easily broken. Second, it creates uncertainty about what the norms are. Third, it weakens the possibility of sanctions"[151] (ibid, 980). Furthermore, when a group feels excluded from the legal norm elaboration process, breaking them is frequently a form of gaining status within the excluded group.

In today's world, anti-drug policies face many obstacles. First, in countries with segmented societies and low empathy and cohesion across social groups, law enforcement may be easily corrupted and used by the group that controls the enforcement mechanism against the others. Second, laws frequently must be enforced by individuals who are part of the same social group in which lawbreakers have grown. They may share with criminals the same disdain for the law

---

[151] "The social and internal sanctions could prevent or encourage the illegal action. When there is no gap or a very small one between social and formal norms, the social sanctions are an obstacle to illegal activities. But when there is a large gap, they encourage them. For example, family and friends might praise a successful tax evader or smuggler. Guissarri (1988) found that tax evaders in Argentina bragged about their success. In the 1980s in Medellin, the 'crowning' (safe arrival) of a cocaine shipment to the U.S. was openly celebrated with big parties, firing shots in the air and great fanfare. In the United States some young ghetto males have considered going to jail as a rite of passage into adulthood (Jones-Brown, 2014, 342). In these cases, the formal and informal norms work in opposite directions" (Thoumi, 2012, 980).

and easily end up helping the criminal organizations they are supposed to attack. These factors increase the risk of corruption and police involvement in drug trafficking.

The gaps between state and social norms and between them and those internalized by individuals are necessary preconditions for people to break the law and for drug criminal organizations to develop. Still, they are not sufficient conditions for that to happen. These gaps "increase the probability of law-breaking but do not necessarily lead to crime for individual economic benefit. For organized crime to develop, one of two other conditions is necessary. First, the informal social norms of behavior should allow individuals to disregard the effect of their actions on other people. In other words, the negative effects that drugs may have on consumers and society at large should not be an obstacle for an individual to engage in illicit production or trafficking. That is, people should be individualistic and self-interested. Second, a divided society may have a marginalized group whose informal norms might deviate greatly from the legal ones. But if there is a strong social cohesion, solidarity, dignity and respect and empathy for human life within the marginalized group, it would not produce or traffic in a product or service that is perceived as being damaging to fellow humans[152]" (ibid, 980).

To have successful drug policies, governments must accept that there are social groups in today's multicultural and pluralistic societies in which there is no coincidence between legality and legitimacy. Indeed, from the perspective of any individual, actions may fall into four categories: legal and legitimate, legal but

---

[152] In Nepal, for instance, there is a large gap between the country's laws and the behavior norms of Buddhist monks. Nepal might have appropriate land and weather to produce opium and heroin, but it does not produce them. In other contexts, individuals or social groups may feel justified producing drugs because they can be used to achieve or fight for a higher cause. such as defending or overthrowing the government or liberating the country. This is the case of many national security agencies that end up involved in drug trafficking.

illegitimate,[153] illegal but legitimate[154], and illegal and illegitimate. These categories are determined by socially accepted norms within the group of which the individual is part. For example, cocaine exports are considered legitimate by many Colombians (and some residents of other Latin American countries). They justify these exports as part of capitalism. For many, this belief is a proven truth that cannot be refuted. These people have very strong beliefs and, in terms of Haidt (2012, xiii), have a *"Righteous Mind."* They are convinced of the accuracy and validity of those beliefs. People with "righteous minds" are fundamentalists and do not accept that their beliefs may be false or questioned. These beliefs are moralistic, blinding, and differ across societies.

I posit that the main challenge in discussions about the IDCS arises because many of the positions for and against its policies are formulated by *Righteous Minds,* absolutely convinced of their validity. Therefore, successful drug policies must focus on changing blind drug policy beliefs that exist in each society. For example, simply arguing that an international treaty prohibits the behaviors condoned by blind policy beliefs falls on deaf ears. That is why if drug policies want to alter drug production, trafficking, and use, they must focus on understanding the norms and behaviors that either promote or condone drug use, trafficking, and production irrespective of their consequences. It requires changes in the mindset prevailing in society. In other words, policymakers should understand the internalized individual behaviors of the actors, that is, the etiology of the behaviors that the policy wants to change.

---

[153] For example, abortion that contradict deeply held religious beliefs.
[154] Like coca and poppy growing in some communities of poor peasants.

11.3 THE CHALLENGE OF COMPLEXITY

There is no question that the current drug markets have many of the characteristics of complex systems. Even though there is no consensus about what a complex system or complexity is. The most common definitions focus on systems in which many variables interact in ways that are difficult to see and understand and where frequently the feedbacks among variables are unpredictable. In this section, there are no attempts to discuss the many ways in which complexity has been studied. It selects one existing methodology used to analyze complex systems applicable to IDCS subject matter: the Cynefin framework. It is an excellent model to categorize the evolution of drug markets and an outstanding tool to understand drug policy problems.

11.3.1 The Cynefin Framework

The Cynefin[155] Framework is a conceptual model which was developed at IBM during the early 2000s. This framework has continued to evolve through the applications of a group of scientists. The central idea of the framework is to offer decision-makers a "sense of place" to view their perceptions in dealing with a situation or problem (Browning and Latoza, 2005). This model has been widely applied as a problem-solving tool to formulate and implement effective policies in a variety of organizations. This framework posits that policy issues arise within "five contexts defined by the nature of the relationship between cause and effect. Four of these—simple, complicated, complex, and chaotic—require leaders to diagnose situations and to act in contextually appropriate ways. The fifth - disorder- applies when it is unclear which of the other four contexts is predominant [...] Simple contexts are characterized by stability and clear cause-and-effect relationships that are easily discernible by

---

[155] Cynefin (kun-ev-in) is the Welsh word for habitat.

everyone. [...] Simple contexts, properly assessed, require straightforward management and monitoring. [...] Directives are straightforward, decisions can be easily delegated, and functions are automated. Adhering to best practices or process reengineering makes sense" (Snowden and Boone, 2007). But problems may arise in simple contexts. Understanding the issues at hand may be misunderstood or simplified, and policymakers may react using "*entrained thinking*, a conditioned response that occurs when people are blinded to new ways of thinking by the perspectives they acquired through past experience, training, and success" (ibid). That is, they are victims of their epistemological obstacles.

They may also become complacent: "the most frequent collapses into chaos occur because success has bred complacency [...] Complicated contexts, unlike simple ones, may contain multiple right answers, and though there is a clear relationship between cause and effect, not everyone can see it. It is the realm of 'known unknowns.' [...] It's important to remember that best practice is, by definition, past practice" (ibid). Thus, it is likely to be less effective when the context changes. The various competing solutions and the lack of clarity of the causality result in several 'good practices,' but not a 'best practice.' Policymakers 'in a complicated context must sense, *analyze*, and respond'" (ibid). There often is a need to bring in new expertise and try a few options in these cases.

In a complex context, many factors may trigger the problem, and there is no simple cause and effect relationship, "right answers can't be ferreted out. This is the realm of 'unknown unknowns.' [...] In this domain, we can understand why things happen only in retrospect. Instructive patterns, however, can emerge if the leader conducts experiments that are safe to fail. That is why, instead of attempting to impose a course of action, leaders must patiently allow the path forward to reveal itself. They need to probe first, then sense, and then respond" (ibid). Complexity "involves a large number of interactive elements. The interactions are nonlinear, and minor changes can produce disproportionately major consequences. The system is dynamic, the whole is greater than the sum of its parts, and solutions cannot be imposed; rather, they arise from the circumstances. It is frequently referred to as *emergence*. The system has a history, and the past is integrated with the present; the elements evolve with one another and the environment; and evolution is irreversible. Though a complex system may, in retrospect, appear to be ordered and predictable, hindsight does not lead to foresight because the external conditions and systems constantly change. Unlike in ordered systems (where the system constrains the agents), or chaotic systems (where there are no constraints), in a complex system, the agents and the system constrain one another, especially over time. This means that we cannot forecast or predict what will happen" (ibid).

Solutions within complex contexts require an open discussion and allow for innovation and experimentation with diverse ideas. "Dissent and formal debate are valuable communication assets in complex contexts because they encourage the emergence of well-forged patterns and ideas" (ibid). In complex contexts, outcomes are not predetermined and may arise unexpectedly. Thus, there is a need for constant monitoring: "In a chaotic context, searching for right answers would be pointless: The relationships between cause and effect are impossible to determine because they shift constantly, and no manageable patterns exist—only turbulence. This is the realm of unknowables. [...] The immediate job is not to discover patterns but to stanch the bleeding" (ibid). The first challenge is to stabilize the situation before seeking solutions.

An excellent solution to a problem is great but applying it in the wrong situation or context can lead to more complicated or harmful outcomes. Using the framework can help structure the approach towards finding the correct solution that matches the conditions of the problem. Then our more traditional problem-solving tools can be used for the appropriate categories: "Different problem situations warrant different approaches to find the right solution" (ibid). Figure 1 summarizes the framework.

Figure 1. Cynefin Framework

Complex
- There are unknown unknowns
- Even the starting point requires experimentation
- The right questions to ask need exploration
- The solution is only apparent once discovered
- The sector of emergence ideas
- Routine solutions don't apply
- Higher levels of interaction and communication are essential

Complicated (Good Practices)
- Multiple right answers are available
- A general idea of the known unknowns
- You know the questions you need to answer
- Don't know how to obtain the answers
- The problem is more predictable than unpredictable
- Cause and effect relationship is not immediately known but is discoverable given enough time

Disorder
The problem does not fit in other 4 cathegories. Strong personal preferences are in place. No time to correct the situation

Chaotic
- The immediate priority is containment. The solution does not have to be the best, as response time is more important
- Sector for novel solutions
- No one knows what the answer may look like with certainty
- Many decisions to make, no time to think
- Immediate action to reestablish order

Simple (Best practices)
- Clear cause and effect relationship are evident to everyone
- A single, correct answer exists
- A fact-based approach is required
- The problem statement is understood, and solution is evident
- Simple problem solving methods can be applied
- The situation requires minimal expertise to resolve

Source: https://txm.com/making-sense-problems-cynefin-framework/
Adapted by the author

11.3.2 Drug Markets as a Complex System

The Cynefin framework is helpful to understand the development of illegal drug markets from the beginning of the 20th Century on. The history starts with what many might have thought was a straightforward, simple problem of controlling opium, and to a lesser degree, cocaine and marijuana, in a few locations in the world. With hindsight, it can be claimed that at the beginning, policymakers could have argued that the policy to limit drug uses to medical and scientific purposes could have been what today is called a *best practice*. However, the policy was formulated because it was morally good, but it was unknown how effective it was. As time went by, the drug policy problem became complicated, drug issues became relevant in more countries, and new drugs were developed and used. The world became increasingly more integrated, and drug markets started to grow. In some countries, they became endemic and occasionally violent, and what could have been a best practice of the past became increasingly ineffective.

As this process expanded, the development of illegal drug markets varied greatly depending on each country's physical, social, political, and economic structures. In some societies, their consequences have been mild, in others more pronounced, in some bad, and others devastating. Within countries, some groups have benefited from the revenues, profits, and wealth generated illegally, and others have suffered increases in drug addiction that at times have been epidemic. Incarceration levels increased in some communities, and high levels of violence in some places, at times, reached levels only experienced in conventional wars among countries.

The dynamic effects of illegal drug market profits have also varied. In some places, they have corrupted many of the State's institutions, to the point that it is possible to talk about narco-states or narco-regions controlled by drug criminal organizations. In some places, illegal drug monies have funded subversive organizations that want to overthrow the State and paramilitary groups that act against reformist movements. In countries like Afghanistan and Colombia, illegal drugs have played vital roles in changing behaviors that trapped those countries in drug production and trafficking. In some slums, mainly in Latin American and the United States, drug-related violence became extremely high and endemic, and local trafficking organizations acted as de facto governments.

At the international level, there have been other significant consequences. NPS appeared in the drug markets every year. More countries produced precursors and, recently, pre-precursors of psychoactive drugs. The drug trafficking revenues grew, and money laundering corrupted the financial sector of many countries.

These consequences would not have been achieved in all these places without social support networks that either condoned or directly supported illegal drug activities. Drug money corrupted the political and law enforcement systems, and drug-driven corruption became accepted in many countries or regions. These conditions show that the illegal drug markets have become extremely complex, and thus, traditional policies formulated to cope with simple drug problems cannot succeed. To provide long-term solutions to the "drug problem," it is necessary to develop a new drug policy paradigm. However, in places where the drug market situation has become chaotic, and the relations among variables are not knowable at the moment, the situation calls for social stabilization efforts before searching for effective long-term policies.

The Cynefin framework leads us to conclude that the IDCS policy to eliminate all non-medical drug uses may be the best policy for the societies that may be placed in the southeast quadrant of figure 1. This may be reasonably good for those in the northeast quadrant, but that policy should not be used in societies in the other two quadrants or the disorder rectangle. Furthermore, the development of illegal drug markets shows that societies in the two east quadrants are always at risk of evolving toward the other areas. Thus, even when the prohibition looks like a best practice, it does not guarantee long-term policy success.

11.3.3 The IDCS Agencies accept Complexity, but only when it does not challenge IDCS Policies

The narrative in the recent INCB annual reports, in the United Nations Task Team on the Implementation of the UN System Common Position on drug-related matters (United Nations, 2019) and that of the UNODC documents have increasingly acknowledged the complexity of drug phenomena defined by the interactions of many social, political, economic, and cultural policy issues. But this narrative has also restated the ideal goal of a drug-free world, an interpretation of the conventions that denies any scientific value to the social sciences because these might support some non-medical drug uses. However, the IDCS drug agencies also acknowledge that the drug issues are complex and that the ideal goal of a drug-free world is unachievable. Thus, it may not be argued that prohibiting all non-medical drug uses is necessarily the best and only appropriate policy. A necessary condition for this policy to be correct is that no conceivable social harms associated with illegal drugs markets could ever be sufficient to merit a change in a prohibition policy presumably taken for the "health and welfare" or for "the physical and moral health" of humanity.

In the real world, there are economic restrictions imposed by the always limited resources available. This constraint forces policymakers everywhere to make tradeoffs among goals such as eliminating corruption, drug use, violence, social, economic, and political stability, increasing national defense and security, etc. Given that restriction, the best possible policy should aim to minimize total social harms, not simply eliminate the harms attributed to one social ill like drug addiction (This point is elaborated mathematically in chapter 13, section 2.3).

Other obstacles to policy effectiveness: social, cultural, institutional, geographical, religious, ethnic, racial, etc., also force policymakers to make policy tradeoffs. Under realistic conditions, it is easy to conceive situations where the best possible solution would require the IDCS to compromise and tolerate some restricted non-medical drug uses. Situations like this arise not only in the social sciences. Indeed, in many of the so-called "hard" sciences, it is recognized that to achieve the best solution to any problem, it is necessary to understand all the constraints faced and overcome them. Focusing on what appears to be the shortest or apparently more direct way to solve a problem, in most cases, is the wrong way to go about it. That is why controlled experimentation is required to find adequate ways to solve any complex problem. Furthermore, most complex problems do not have a unique solution.

The IDCS agencies may accept that there are limits to their public policies' effectiveness. Still, they do not accept any non-medical and scientific uses of the controlled drugs, even when confronted with reliable evidence that the harms resulting from the possible increase in controlled non-medical use are lower than the harms of prohibiting such use. The IDCS frequently argue that controlled non-medical use is intolerable because the harm created by drug addiction is immeasurable. The disdain by the IDCS agencies for the scientifically obtained knowledge in the social sciences impedes them from accepting that there may be cases where social science-based knowledge may show that tolerating some non-medical uses would increase social welfare. The rejection of these types of options would condemn societies to an everlasting inferior policy option. From the perspective of contemporary public policy, the absolute prohibition of non-medical drug uses, and totally free drug markets are both extreme policy options that may be considered and either chosen or rejected, depending on the welfare consequences empirically expected in each case. Neither of these two possible policies should ever be dogmas. In virtually all cases, the best policy is likely to be an intermediate one that should be changed or adapted as the social, political, economic, and environmental contexts change.

However, the IDCS mindset rejects this point because any tolerance of non-medical psychoactive drug use will start a slippery slope to legalize all drug uses. Thus, the absolute prohibition of all non-medical and non-scientific drug uses is the only option. Since this is not an evidence-based position, it is a dogma, so it may not be refuted.

Not surprisingly, even though the INCB and UNODC reports, as well as the report of the Task Team on the Implementation of the UN System Common Position on drug-related matters, have used the results of contemporary social sciences' evaluations to support their policies, they have never used the same tools to evaluate the drug use restriction to medical and scientific purposes.

Several decades ago, economists started analytical cost and benefit evidence-based policy evaluations. These have been used to compare drug policy alternatives. For example, "[t]he cost of achieving a 1 percent reduction in consumption through domestic enforcement is predicted to be 7.3 times the cost of achieving the same reduction through treatment of heavy users. The costs of achieving this reduction through source-country control and interdiction policies are predicted to be even higher, 23.0 and 10.8 times the cost of treatment, respectively" (Rydell and Everingham, 1994).

Rand Corporation (1995) confirms these results: "[t]reatment is seven times more cost-effective in reducing cocaine consumption than the best supply-control program and could cut consumption by a third if it were extended to all heavy users, according to the study. Such a strategy could also substantially reduce the number of users and the costs they inflict on society through crime and lost productivity."

A later study using a similar model (Caulkins et al., 1997) estimated that $1 million spent on treatment could reduce U.S. cocaine consumption by 104 kilograms. This figure is much higher than spending the same amount of money on trying to lock up more dealers (26 kilograms) or providing longer sentences to convicted dealers (13 kilograms). Notably, these estimates are based on a reasonably pessimistic estimate of treatment effectiveness (MacCoun and Reuter, 2001, 34).

These studies clearly showed that shifting resources from supply control to prevention, treatment, rehabilitation, and resocialization would increase total health and welfare and lower the costs of reducing cocaine consumption in the United States. The IDCS has not only accepted these results, but it has internalized them to the point that they have become part of their conventional drug policy wisdom. For example, the INCB 2013 report chapter one uses the same type of arguments.

> The phenomenon of drug abuse requires societies to dedicate resources to evidence-based prevention, education, and interventions, including treatment and rehabilitation. Although such activities can be resource-intensive, studies have shown that for every $1 spent, good prevention programmes can save Governments up to $10 in subsequent costs. [...] Heroin, cannabis, and cocaine are the drugs most frequently reported by people entering treatment worldwide. It is estimated that only one in six problem drug users worldwide, some 4.5 million people, receives the required treatment, at a global cost of about $35 billion annually. [...] Research Findings clearly show that investment in treatment is cost-effective compared with the cost of untreated and continuing abuse. Research conducted in the United States of America reveals that every $1 invested in treatment yields a return of between $4 and $12 in reduced crime and health-care costs (INCB, 2014, 1-2).

However, as shown in chapter six, section 6.3, the same report dismisses the possibility to estimate the costs of drug addiction because "drug abuse inflicts immeasurable harm on public health and safety around the world each year and threatens the peaceful development and smooth functioning of many societies." The recent Task Force Lessons Learned Report concurs as follows:

> Services aimed at reducing the harm caused by non-medical drug use are also cost effective. For example, each dollar spent in a needle-syringe programme can return up to $5.50 in averted health-care costs. By comparison, incarceration appears expensive and ineffective. [...] Although the overall costs of scaling up programmes to minimize the adverse health consequences of drug use will be high, it will be a worthwhile action; not only do the societal benefits of programmes to minimize the adverse health consequences of drug use exceed their treatment costs, but they also have the potential to provide significant returns on investment for governments. These interventions can be cost-effective by most thresholds in the short term and cost-saving in the long term[156] (United Nations, 2019, 21-22).

According to the IDCS, the immeasurability of the social costs of drug addiction makes it impossible to compare the social costs and benefits of any controlled non-medical use system of a drug such as marijuana with those of prohibiting drug uses. Unfortunately, none of the IDCS agencies has ever explained why those costs of addiction are immensurable.

In conclusion, the IDCS has advanced in recognizing the complexity of drug issues and currently accepts standard evaluation methods to measure policy effectiveness, except when those methods question their narrow interpretation of the drug use limitation to medical and scientific purposes. In other words, it accepts the consequences of the complexity of drug policy. Still, it is trapped by a treaty-agreed policy that is an unchangeable simple solution to an overly complex policy issue that the IDCS drug agencies acknowledge is unachievable. This has led the IDCS agencies to advocate a

---

[156] Wilson et. al., (2015).

comprehensive, integrated, and balanced approach to lower drug demand and supply, but always within its inadequate context to solve the complex drug problem.

11.4 DIVERSE SOCIETIES, DIFFERENT GOVERNMENTS, DIFFERENT POLICIES

The great diversity of drug-related experiences in different societies reflects the influence of historical, cultural, institutional, technological, and geographical factors, etc., on the policy effectiveness in each society. Every government has a type of governance: the method, strategy, and system used to govern. These can vary broadly depending on the political ideology and the organizational structure of each government and country. Governance determines how governments relate to their people, how they expect people to relate with them and among themselves. One may look at governance in a broad spectrum ranging from various forms of extreme authoritarianism to very liberal and open democracies. However, all societies have governments that are a mixture of those two extremes. For example, a government may have a liberal governance toward religion and an authoritarian one toward drug use.

The World Bank (2017, 4), focusing on the United Nations 2030 SDG, defines governance as "the process through which state and non-state actors interact to design and implement policies within a given set of formal and informal rules that shape and are shaped by power." This way to look at governance transcends the original simple definition and focuses on the complexity of public policies. Successful policy formulation and implementation require a deep understanding of power structures. This condition applies to all human organizations, not just to States. For example, a successful business, academic, bureaucratic, military, or religious career is achieved by understanding those power structures and using that knowledge to succeed. Governments that want to confront drug issues successfully must also do so. The issue is whether the government uses that understanding to promote the common good or only the good of social groups that have enough power to influence policy formulation and implementation to benefit their interests

Governability is the extent to which it is easy or difficult to govern a country. It depends on the degree of its racial, cultural, and ethnic homogeneity, the age structure and education of the citizenry, the extent of government's territorial control, the degree of social capital and cohesion, the degree of government's legitimacy among the population, and other social and structural factors like the degree and social acceptance of wealth, income, and social status inequalities. Depending on these factors, some countries are easier to govern than others. Whether a policy is effective and works or does not work in a society depends on its governmentality and governance.

Governability problems have been persistent throughout history, and most governments have used authoritarian methods to establish and maintain social order. They have used force or religious and ideological arguments to impose behaviors desired by the person or group that controlled the government. They decided what laws and social norms were legitimate and used their power to force people to comply. Policies in such traditional systems have been justified to comply with theories about controlling predatory human behavior or imposing social order. These policies appeal to revelations by divine forces or ideologies developed by wise humans convinced of their knowledge of how a society should be organized for the good of the country, nation, tribe, race, ethnic group, humankind, mother nature, the glory of God, etc. This authoritarian policy formulation model has prevailed throughout history. The people's compliance is based on fear of sanctions or their acceptance of the imposed norms as part of a "normal" or natural social order.

Under purely authoritarian governments, sovereignty rests at the top of society, and policies, individual rights, and freedoms are decided from the top down. The modernization process induced by the enlightenment that accelerated globalization, and increased technology, urbanization, education levels, migrations, communications, etc., produced significant social cleavages. Many individuals sought new individual freedoms, while traditionalists fearing structural social changes that would lead to disorder or violence, reacted attempting to block or turn back those changes. For them, the past, frequently just an idealized mirage of it, was a better reality than the changing present leading to an unknown and uncertain future. Thus, politicians often appeal to tradition, national, racial, or religious identity, promising to revive that mirage.

The policy model of The Enlightenment proclaimed that The People were sovereign. It rejected the legitimacy of aristocratic, monarchic, and imperial systems. It promoted equality and democracy and radically changed societies' beliefs about individual freedoms, human rights, governability, and governance. Societies have evolved and adapted in different ways to the accelerated social, economic, cultural, and political developments of the last two centuries. These produced new challenges to all country governments. In fact, in most countries today, the State must cope with pre-modern, modern, and post-modern social sectors with varying worldviews or mindsets that could undermine some policies and increasingly modern technologies that the State and people use to achieve power.

The prevalence of the rule of law varies substantially from country to country and among country regions. In some, "corruption is widespread, and large corporations, religious groups, political parties, NGOs, the media, subversive and paramilitary groups, tribes, and other social organizations challenge the states' power, legal monopolies, and territorial control, and the legitimacy of many laws. These organizations vary in different countries and regions" (Thoumi, 2017b, 75). Their decisions can have substantial effects on any country. Today it is difficult, or perhaps impossible, to find a country with a purely authoritarian or democratic government. On the one hand, democracy is an ongoing project that constantly expands or shrinks. On the other hand, authoritarian regimes might seem stable, but they also face the forces of change that have grown exponentially with technological development, globalization, and information technology.

Because of those differences and the post-modern nature of the current State, successful public policies must respond to each country's social, political, and economic structures and local jurisdictions. In authoritarian societies, policy implementation relies on law enforcement agencies that seek to sanction and punish lawbreakers and deter potential ones. Frequently this mechanism is also used to suppress political dissent, racial or religious minorities.

Irrespective of the type of government's ideology and strategy, policies always face some significant constraints that must be considered for policy success. There is no unique way to classify those constraints, but commonly scholars refer to social, economic, political, institutional, cultural, geographical, technological, and international constraints, including globalization pressures.[157] Any of these factors may lead to policy formulation or implementation failure.

Every organization: -family, school, religious organization, business enterprise, political party, social club, government, etc.- has a power structure that determines a governance approach to influence what every person should, can, and may do. Every post-modern state has a political system shaped by its power structure that constrains and influences policy implementation.

> Power is the ability of groups and individuals to make others act in the interest of those groups and individuals and to bring about specific outcomes. [...] Depending on the context, actors may establish a government as a set of formal state institutions (a term used in the literature to denote organizations and rules) that enforce and implement policies.

---

[157] This list is not exhaustive and different authors may have a longer and more complex list of factors.

Also, depending on the context, state actors will play a more or less important role with respect to non-state actors such as civil society organizations – or business lobbies. In addition, governance takes place at different levels, from international bodies to national institutions, to local government agencies, to community and business associations. These dimensions often overlap, creating a complex of actors and interests (World Bank Group, 2017, 3).

Globalization pressures to a significant extent, depend on forces outside the countries. It expands every person's worldview and integrates individuals from closed societies with the outside world, influences their values and beliefs, and challenges many traditions. It also challenges many traditional governments and their governance and is an increasing obstacle for implementing top-down policies. That is why strongly authoritarian governments seek to control the exposure of their citizens to outside ideas. In the past, they vetoed and burnt books. Today they censor the internet.

Technological developments are also frequently beyond State control. But advances in marketing techniques that influence consumer behaviors have been adapted to the political realm. Now political parties and governments use information technologies and psychology to seek changes in their citizenry's and opponents' political opinions. These mindset-changing techniques appeal to deeply held individuals' beliefs and sentiments and are increasingly used to influence behaviors, elections, and obtain power. Today, politicians who may be ignorant about many policy complexities but have the social intelligence to sense peoples' feelings can manipulate the electorate using *alternative facts* and *fake news*.

The technologies designed to change individuals' mindsets may be used to modify some policy constraints. Still, physical constraints must be confronted independently of the governance strategy or ideology: economic resources are limited, all governments have budgets, and countries have gross national incomes that limit what they can do. Economics, a social science, is part philosophy and part physics. It is the philosophy of material life: it deals with the material needs of humankind and the ways to satisfy them.[158] As part of physics, economics studies the limitation imposed by the physical world on the satisfaction of human needs. From this perspective, economics seeks to engineer the systems and processes by which humankind copes with physical scarcities. It seeks to manage the scarce resources available to humankind to achieve specific goals determined by the ideology or philosophy of each society and its government. As is the case with any crucial philosophical issue, economics does not have a unique answer. That is why there are communist, socialist, capitalist, communitarian, etc., paradigms and schools of thought in economics, each of which has its way to engineer and manage physical scarcity.

Unfortunately, in the drug policy discussions, the principles or assumptions underlining the economic engineering philosophies that inspire the policy positions of each discussant are not made explicit, and everyone justifies their position by giving reasons for it. Societies with more deontological leanings will produce policies that could not be accepted in societies with more liberal inclinations and vice versa. These conflicts are the main reason why some dismiss a possible contribution of the social sciences to drug policy formulation and implementation as unscientific.

11.5 SOCIAL HARMS, SOCIAL VULNERABILITY AND CRIMINAL POLICY EFFECTIVENESS

The literature on criminology and law enforcement has many references to social harms and events that encourage the development of illegal economic activities: corruption, economic crises, growing income and wealth inequality, social exclusion, racial,

---

[158] In his classic history of the ideas of modern economics thinkers Heilbroner (1953) coined the term, "The Worldly Philosophers" that reflects these two aspects of economics.

ethnic, sexual, and other forms of discrimination, the existence of subversive and paramilitary groups, violence, the decline of the traditional extended and nuclear families, the weakening of traditional religious beliefs, rural-urban migrations (including forced displacements), rapid urbanization, etc. These risk factors make countries vulnerable to criminal organizations' development and illegal drug production, traffic, and consumption. But while all of these factors may be important in particular situations, the development of illegal economic activities does not have direct causes. The evidence shows that most poor, socially, and politically excluded people do not become criminals. The same is true about racial, religious, sexual minorities, and migrants. Risk factors increase the probability that something will happen. Like anything based on risk, the development of criminal organizations and illegal drug use and markets are probabilistic events that cannot be forecasted accurately (Thoumi, 2017b, 75-76).

Social harms and risk factors are interrelated, and frequently these relations are circular. They feed on each other and may produce a vicious circle. For example, corruption encourages criminal activities like drug trafficking, which in turn encourages corruption. When property rights are not well defined, or the State cannot protect them, activities to capture, extract, or appropriate wealth may become socially accepted, weakening property rights. In many cases, government budgets become bounties to be captured, increasing people's attempts to evade taxes. It harms governments' budgets. When illegal economic productive activities like cocaine refining and trafficking get established and become socially accepted, illegal income and wealth become socially legitimate. These developments weaken social and self-controls that protect from the development of other criminal activities like extortions, kidnappings for ransom, smuggling, private protection of property rights. These weaken the State's efforts to define and protect those rights. This circularity among harms implies that once drug trafficking organizations get established in a country, they become one more risk factor. They are prone to diversify their criminal activities and encourage the development of groups that will follow suit and engage in illegal mining, extortion, kidnapping, corruption to capture government budgets or change laws in what may become a kleptocracy. In a vicious circle of this nature, a society falls into a dishonesty and illegality trap from which it is exceedingly difficult to get out (Thoumi, 1987, 45).

On the positive side, social and economic structures and events lower the risk of harm and protect societies against crime. These include good accessible education programs, strong families, strong religious beliefs, stable economies, low unemployment, etc. They help to create or contribute to virtuous circles.

The presence, absence, and intensity of risk-promoting or protecting factors determine a society's vulnerability and risk of developing illegal drug production, traffic, and consumption.

> Because these factors are dynamic and change over time, the degree of vulnerability of any country also varies in time, as does the possibility for the development of criminal organizations. The social, political, and economic developments and the globalization process of the last 70 years increased dramatically or made evident the vulnerability of many societies. The consequences of the prohibition of non-medical drug uses have varied significantly depending on each country's vulnerability.[159] This is why societies with authoritarian traditions and strong social cohesion, empathy, and other protective factors, could comply easily with the conventions, while liberal or extreme individualistic societies have had great difficulties doing so. Some have implemented

---

[159] For example, Colombia has paid an exceedingly high social price producing, trafficking, and fighting illegal drugs. There is no doubt that the Single Convention of 1961 has been the most important international document signed and ratified by the country; but drug issues were so irrelevant in Colombia in 1961, that it did not even send a delegation to the Conference that negotiated and drafted the Convention (Thoumi, 2015, 379).

'harm reduction' policies contrary to the conventions' prevalent interpretation, and others are clamoring for world drug policy changes. But since the risk factors do not predict when a country will have a drug consumption, trafficking, or production crisis, it can only be asserted that countries must be vigilant because always there is a risk to develop those problems[160] (Thoumi, 2017b: 76).

Unfortunately, because many vulnerabilities are latent and not easily perceived, governments do not give them a high priority in their policy's agendas until they trigger significant drug problems.

The inability to forecast the development of organized crime raises complex causality issues that make it exceedingly difficult to formulate effective policies and design policies to lower the vulnerability of each society. It is a particularly challenging task. Political reforms challenge society's mindsets and ingrained beliefs that have influenced the status quo. That is why the political systems are not designed to implement policies that require significant social reforms unless internal or external pressures develop. The physical, political, economic, social, cultural, and institutional risk factors that affect the effectiveness of all government policies are part and parcel of contemporary public policy analyses.

In traditional societies, the common good might be defined by those at the top of the power structure, and their main goal is maintaining the status quo that is attributed to natural selection (survival of the fittest), a God-given order, the conquest by a superior race or culture, etc. These are always ideological reasons that have been used to justify the social structure that frequently has a high concentration of wealth, income, and power in the hands of traditional elites, political parties, ethnic or racial groups.

---

[160] For example, the current drug addiction problems of Pakistan and the drug related violence in Honduras and Mexico were expected given those countries vulnerabilities, although they could not have been predicted accurately. Similar developments are likely to arise in some high-risk sub-Saharan countries.

Formulating complex public policies implies agreeing on a common good that requires commitment, coordination, and cooperation among all the policy's stakeholders. It also requires that different government agencies and non-state actors act in sync with the policy. Political will by the government is necessary, but it is not sufficient because policy implementation must confront the power asymmetries among existing stakeholders. These asymmetries exclude some groups from the policy arena and allow others to capture policies, that is, to influence their formulation and implementation to benefit their narrow interests. They also may allow for clientelism to develop, a system by which political organizations "purchase" the electorate's support distributing goods or services. In these cases, politicians choose their voters rather than the other way around. Participation in the political arena is determined by power asymmetries, incentives to participate, preferences, and beliefs of each stakeholder (World Bank Group, 2017, 7-12).

The stakeholders of the psychoactive drug policies are not just IDCS agencies and the countries' governments that ratified the drug conventions. The list of important stakeholders in this process is impressive: peasants that grow drug source plants, drug users and small dealers and producers, pharmaceutical and chemical companies, financial institutions, international donors (countries and foundations), local religious and social leaders, members of the different branches of the governments, companies that participate in eradication programs, etc. Some of these groups have had some minor roles in the drug policy arena, but many have not had roles. Furthermore, the drug policy perspectives of every one of these groups present some policy constraints or obstacles to drug policy efficiency. Every constraint and obstacle restrict the number of possible solutions that would satisfy all groups. The larger the number of constraining factors, the smaller the number of those solutions, which very frequently may be zero.

Policy success requires expanding access to the policy arena and establishing a respectful dialogue among all stakeholders to the point that they are willing to make compromises among the goals of the different power groups that generate the constraining factors. It also requires generating incentives for those groups to adapt to changing conditions. A successful drug policy should come from a dialogic process of mutual respect between drug policymakers and all stakeholders aiming for each group to understand the reasons of the others. It, of course, is challenging to achieve because drug policies have always been top-down and have generated very substantial distrust among all actors. Therefore, the first policy step should be to establish mutual trust among stakeholders. It is a prerequisite because successful drug policies require to be co-created by all stakeholders.

When this is not done, countries have a high risk of persisting with ineffective policies that might seem reasonable at first sight. These tend to be based on intuitions, feelings, and perceptions. But not on an understanding of the complexity of the concerning problem. Unfortunately, cases of this nature are common. For example, the wars on drugs policies do not consider why different people produce, traffic, and consume drugs. And also, the war on terrorism fails to understand when terrorism is just an effective strategy of aggrieved groups that feel they have nothing to lose. Wars against political dissent can censor and punish, but they do not eliminate the dissenting ideas and the sources of dissent.

Drug policy co-creation presents unique problems when the main stakeholders are large drug cartels, subversive, or paramilitary criminal organizations. The drug policy problem transcends drug issues and becomes part of conflicts that threaten the State itself when they are present. In these contexts, drug policy success is virtually impossible without solving the power conflicts within the society.[161]

---

[161] This has been a key factor for the resiliency of the industries of illegal poppy-heroin in Afghanistan and coca-cocaine in Colombia (Thoumi, 2005). Because of this, it looks as if Afghanistan had a patent to produce heroine and Colombia one to produce cocaine. These two export markets are the only ones in which the two countries appear to have a near monopoly.

Once it is accepted that the drug markets have evolved and become complex, an important corollary is that the IDCS was developed backward. It started with the proposition that the best and only possible policy worldwide was the prohibition of all non-medical or scientific uses of controlled psychoactive drugs. After promoting this global policy for over 50 years, it was enacted in an international convention. All countries were prompted to comply with that treaty and enforce the policy taking all "legislative and administrative measures as may be necessary."

However, from the perspective of contemporary public policy and complexity, the first step to formulating a global drug policy should be to identify and understand the nature and characteristics of drug production, marketing, and consumption worldwide. The annual World Drug Reports present maps of drug production, trafficking, and use worldwide that show remarkable differences in the complexity of their patterns among countries. Those differences should be studied to identify the triggering and the protective factors of illegal drug production, trafficking, and use. The findings of those studies could be the basis for designing policies that consider each country's complexity and complement the traditional law enforcement approach. Because complex problems do not have direct causality and require considering multiple factors, the IDCS should tolerate some policy experimentation.

The top-down backward construction of the IDCS can be described as a policy in search of a justification provided by the statements of concern with the "health and welfare of mankind" or "the physical and moral health of humanity" in the preamble of the 1961 Single Convention. Once the Convention was ratified, it became a legal contract, and this allowed everyone to forget about questioning the fundamental underlining reasons why a drug policy was necessary. However, this policy that appears practical to its supporters is also impractical because it would never achieve its purpose.

I am aware that a process that considers complexity would be deemed impractical by almost any policymaker. Even though the current prohibition may be defended as an expedited and practical policy option, it is not evidence-based. The current policy is a dogma that cannot be questioned, but it is only a placebo to cure the "world drug problem."

CHAPTER TWELVE: PROPOSALS TO TACKLE DRUG POLICY REFORM

12.1 OVERVIEW

As noted above, the Parties to the drug conventions, analysts, and other observers frequently acknowledge that since the IDCS was established, the non-medical use of controlled drugs has increased substantially and that illegal drug markets generate other social ills. Still, they also agree that changing the conventions is virtually impossible. Despite this perception, several studies, including this one, have developed new possible policy approaches and options. Some of them are presented in this chapter.

12.2 MEDICAL AND SCIENTIFIC PURPOSES AND THE LACK OF DEFINITIONS

One way to update old rules to changing situations is by reinterpreting them. This would be possible by expanding the meaning of "medical and scientific uses" in the conventions to include non-Western medicine and the knowledge of the social sciences obtained using recognized scientific methods. However, this approach faces obstacles. First, it is difficult to establish authentic dialogues across sciences and academic disciplines, and second, epistemological obstacles may arise from religious, cultural, political, and ideological beliefs. This section examines these issues.

12.2.1 Lack of Definitions and the Need for Consensus

The purpose of any treaty, like that of any law, is to protect a social good. However, the IDCS conventions are unclear about what social good is protected and appear to appeal to vague concepts like the health of the society, its moral health, or its welfare to justify its goal to eliminate all non-medical drug uses. Reaching a consensus about the protected social good or the policies to achieve it were the main reasons it took fifty-two years to agree on a drug convention.

The purpose of the IDCS was to limit the use of drugs. It was always the main goal for those that promoted the creation of the IDCS. But this was a policy goal, not a protected social good. The preamble of the drug conventions indicates that the protected social goods were health, moral health, and welfare. However, achieving a worldwide consensus about those terms was virtually impossible given the world's political, cultural, religious, and ideological diversity.[162] However, a consensus was feasible about a policy goal: to limit psychoactive drug uses to *medical and scientific purposes*. It was still vague but allowed all governments to agree with it.

As shown above, the lack of definitions of the main terms of the conventions allowed the INCB to interpret the Parties' obligations in ways that resulted in inconsistencies through time. Their application has varied depending on the country and on the Board's composition across time. That is why it is crucial to explore the consequences of the vagueness of the main definitions and the factors that influence how people develop their own beliefs and interpret the evidence about psychoactive drugs.

The cultural and institutional diversity across countries has been the main obstacle to a clearly defined worldwide consensus about a standard individual drug use behavior that an international treaty could successfully impose. First, even though mores, institutions, and social controls vary widely worldwide, some social uses of psychoactive drugs have been controlled within every society. And second, because the enforcing capacity of many governments is

---

[162] The concept of social welfare used to estimate the social cost of drug use in an authoritarian regime would be quite different in a liberal one. The same would apply to the violence related to drug trafficking or the need to apply very harsh sentences to eliminate illegal markets. Thus, it is impossible to achieve a consensus among the governments of all the countries of the world about the costs and benefits of drug policies and their consequences because they depend on the rights and obligations that people have in each society, that is, on the individual human rights and responsibilities that are socially and legally accepted in each country.

fragile. Thus, the current IDCS policies are likely to encounter significant cultural and institutional obstacles in many societies.

Limiting psychoactive drug use to *medical and scientific purposes* led to seeking an unachievable "ideal drug-free world." Consequently, the convention's drafters emphasized what the world "should be" and did not consider any evidence-based viable policy applicable worldwide. They expected that all Parties to the Conventions would enact laws and establish the necessary public institutions to eliminate non-medical and non-scientific drug uses successfully. This expectation swept under the rug all the actual policy implementation problems that any government would face enforcing the prohibition of *non-medical and scientific* drug uses.

Once this policy was established, it was assumed as a common-sense proposition that it did not have to be justified. It was accepted as correct by most policymakers, religious leaders, health sector professionals, and law enforcement agencies and received broad support among governments worldwide. This acceptance did not require defining or explaining the key terms medical, scientific, health, physical health, moral health, and welfare.

In 1961, drug control policies had not been a priority in most countries' governments' policy agendas. The drug-uses restriction to medical and scientific purposes was accepted because knowledgeable health sector professionals recommended it. It implied that the drafters of the conventions were wise and knew what was either morally or socially right for humankind. Thus, the core policy adopted by the IDCS was a dogmatic rule that had to be enforced globally through international treaties.

As discussed above, the main challenges to that policy are a) the strength of the punitive law enforcement efforts that violate human rights, b) the lack of proportionality in criminal sentencing, c) the harm reduction issues concerning how to cope with addicts, d) the traditional coca uses, and e) the recent legalization of non-medical cannabis in some countries and the American states where public opinion or the government consider that social or government controls can regulate the drug-markets better than the current prohibitions. However, in these cases, the supporters of policy flexibility, a "new strategy," or "legalization," present only local facts as reasons for world drug policy change. They do not spell out a process to build a new worldwide consensus.

12.2.2 A Policy Discussion among Activists

In most policy debates, the lack of definition of key concepts is prevalent. Today all citizens have opinions about the public policies of their interest. Most people might not express their opinions about some policies, but they have ideas or questions about them. Many policy issues are complex, and most people do not have the knowledge and the skills required to arrive at a rigorous position. For example, in electoral systems, people must choose among candidates that frequently promise great results without explaining the actual policies to achieve them. Many people choose based on party affiliation, the recommendation of an authority figure, their own experience, or their intuitions, beliefs, and feelings. Not surprisingly, in open electoral systems, successful politicians must understand how people feel about the world and adapt their campaigns accordingly. They should have the emotional intelligence to feel their electorate.

Everybody alive must live and explain life to themselves and their role in society. Most of these explanations require acts of faith. When people face those that support positions that contradict theirs about what they consider essential, they frequently appeal to explanations that involve human conspiracies or interventions by evil powers. For example, some defenders of the IDCS argue that their opponents are zealots funded by an "evil man," presumably George Soros,[163] or mercenaries with hidden interests, and not honest people convinced of the validity of their arguments. On the other side, in Latin American countries, many people frustrated with the high level

---

[163] As suggested by Mr. Phillip O. Emafo, the president of the INCB, in the foreword of the 2003 INCB annual report discussed above.

of violence associated with drug trafficking argue that the drug use prohibition is promoted by hidden economic and political interests in the center of the "empire." In these arguments, evil always wins! The following is a non-exhausting list of reasons provided in those discussions or debates.

Reasons supporting the IDCS:
- There is a consensus at the World Health Organization and similar regional and national health organs that physicians should decide how and when to use addictive psychoactive drugs.
- Can you imagine a world in which pharmacies could dispense cocaine over the counter but require a medical prescription for antibiotics?
- Religions sometimes use psychoactive drugs ceremonially, under very restrictive conditions, but they do not condone their free or recreational non-medical use.
- Drugs destroy the dignity and humanity of addicts.
- Drug addiction destroys the youth's futures and has immeasurable social and economic consequences.
- Limiting drug use to medical and scientific purposes is such a great idea that 187 countries where 99.5% of the world's population lives have supported the 1961 Single Convention on Narcotic Drugs.
- Selling addictive drugs for non-medical uses is immoral.
- Addictive drugs generate violence within families and society and should be prohibited.
- The current IDCS is not perfect, it cannot eliminate drug addiction, but it is better than other alternatives.
- Current drug policies are good, but their problem is the lack of political will to implement them correctly.

- Drug policies have unintended consequences caused by the evil they are fighting (addiction or drug trafficking), not by the policies' implementation, which should be strong.
- Drug policies have prevented more significant harms. They have not eliminated drug addiction but have controlled its growth, which would have been much greater otherwise.

Reasons against the IDCS:
- The prohibition of non-medical drug use violates the human rights of those that use them without negative consequences to other people.
- Prohibition and the war on drugs have not prevented a large increase in the volume of drugs produced and consumed and have generated incentives for developing **NPS**.
- Drug policies attack the weakest link in the illegal drug chain, and they have been used to incarcerate small producers, users, and dealers that frequently are addicts themselves.
- Drug policies have been implemented to segregate and discriminate against some social minorities and stifle political dissent.
- The prohibition of non-medical drug uses has benefited the world financial sector that profits from their money laundering business. The world financial sector depends on these amounts of money to generate its profits.
- The United States prohibits cocaine and heroin to obtain huge profits that are kept in the country.
- The prohibition of non-medical and scientific drug uses is a pretext of the imperialist forces to dominate and control the natural resources of the countries that grow coca and poppy.
- The private jail industry in the United States needs drug prohibition to fill its jails and make large profits.

- Prohibition is the cause of the extremely high violence in countries like Colombia, Mexico, and Honduras, among others.
- Lobbies from the chemical industry support prohibition to sell the herbicides issued to eradicate coca and poppy plantings. They also benefit from selling precursor chemicals at inflated prices.
- The promoters of prohibition want to keep illegal drug profits high and do not allow countries to legalize soft drugs like marijuana.
- One never hears of American or European drug trafficking kingpins captured. These policies are used only against Latin American drug kingpins.
- The United States could not maintain alcohol prohibition. Why did it prohibit cocaine? This proves that it has a double moral!
- The United States is a capitalist country that knows that when there is demand, there is supply. Therefore, they should not require coca eradication programs.[164]

All reasons of those who support limiting drug uses to *medical and scientific purposes* and of those who oppose them appeal to facts,

---

[164] This is a widespread position in Colombia that is used to justify cocaine exports. An anecdote illustrates this point: a high-level Colombian diplomat that worked on international drug policy issues in Vienna argued that "under capitalism, when there is demand, there is always a supply." I replied that if so, how come Colombia has much less competition in the international market of cocaine, by far its most profitable export than in all its other exports? Was it that the entrepreneurs in all other countries that can grow coca and produce cocaine were stupid?" The diplomat's answer was that John Maynard Keynes had proved that "when there is demand, there is supply." There is no question that the opinion of the most famous economist of the first half of the XX century is a lot more authoritative than mine. The critical point from the diplomat's perspective was the appeal to a very famous authority. The difference between the context in which current illegal cocaine markets operate, and the great depression in the United States when Keynes made his assertion, was irrelevant.

some of which are partially real or imagined. The IDCS defenders do not prove that its drug-use restriction is reasonable or the best psychoactive drug policy for all countries of the world under all circumstances. Similarly, their critics do not prove that more flexible drug use policies would always be better independent of the drug in question and the circumstances of the drug markets where their preferred policies would apply.

It is striking that most drug policy positions on both sides of the drug debate pretend to promote social welfare. Still, the arguments only express policy beliefs with a fragile evidence base. On both sides, reasons are treated as unquestionable proofs, but their opponents' reasons are dismissed as false or dishonest. Current IDCS policy supporters only defend what to them is good. The system's detractors argue that current policies do not work because they have not eliminated illegal drug use and many negative consequences. Still, neither one presents a policy model that explains under which circumstances their preferred position would be good and under which ones it would not be satisfactory.

The scientific method, including when applied in the social sciences, requires the possibility to disprove empirically any position or accepted conclusion. It has been absent in virtually all drug policy arguments. Until now, a constructive dialogue has been extremely difficult and virtually impossible in most cases. Those who favor current policies fear a more liberal approach to drug use will produce a devastating drug addiction epidemic. For example, they frequently argue that any relaxing of non-medical marijuana use will lead to a "slippery slope" that will legalize non-medical use of other psychoactive drugs. This argument assumes that if it were not for the IDCS, country governments would not control drug uses independently, even though they support those control policies every year at the CND. And those against the IDCS policies argue that current policies have failed because they have not significantly reduced illegal drug markets. They argue that prohibition policies cause many social ills and should be changed. They simply assume that the social costs of increased addiction associated with a lax drug policy market will be smaller than the current costs due to the IDCS controls.

Not surprisingly, drug policy debates most frequently end up as deftly presented monologues in which everyone gives reasons, but nobody refutes those who disagree. These seminars and debates are meetings of activists convinced of their "truths." Drug policy seminars tend to be meetings among the converted, those who support one point of view, have powerful feelings about it, and express reasons for their support. In these events, people preach to the choir. Activists always promote a policy that they "know" is correct. When they present their ideas before their opponents, they speak past each other without establishing a dialogue.

Every society develops consensuses about how people should behave, but individual members always have differences regarding substantive policy issues. Societies may achieve a broad consensus about a particular issue, for example, the superiority of the market economy over a centrally planned one, or vice versa. But rigorous empirical studies that measure political leanings and opinions along a dimension or axis in which "liberal" and "conservative" ideas are at the two extremes have shown that the distribution tends to be normal in every society, with a high concentration in the center. Surveys using the same methodology in ninety-seven countries that ask people to identify themselves from right to left on a scale ranging from 1 to 10 result in distributions very close to the normal. Few individuals describe themselves as extreme liberal or conservative. This is valid even in countries with authoritarian governments where dissent is restricted (Tuschman, 2013, 28-31).

Another interesting conclusion is that even though the distribution tends to be normal, in some countries, it is placed more to the left or the right than in others. This shows that the policy leanings of the members of each society are determined by factors associated with their personalities, their life experiences, and the society's culture.

In fact, most people do not care to understand most political issues because their main problem is to survive or have a good life. Most respond adopting the common beliefs (conventional wisdom, common sense) prevailing in the environment in which they are born, including their family, religion, philosophy, political ideology, and education. These provide facts, beliefs, and knowledge that people interiorize and use to identify themselves as members of a society or group. These are used to respond to the question, who are you? The persons' responses show that societal beliefs regarding sex and sexual orientation, religion, nationality, ethnicity, race, profession, employment, group memberships, and political affiliation are highly determinants of individuals' identity. It appears that humans tend to be herd animals, and the deeper explanations of life are left for a minority of thinkers to seek.

The reasons provided by supporters and opponents of the IDCS and the evidence about the distribution of political positions within every society raise two fundamental questions: why intelligent, educated, intellectually committed, and honest people, when confronted with the same empirical evidence, arrive at different conclusions that frequently are contradictory? And why do they fail to acknowledge the legitimacy of their opponents' positions? These questions have to be answered to understand the drug policy discourses and debates.

12.2.3 A Good Example of a Paradigm Conflict about Drug Policies

The Lines and Barrett (2018) article, mentioned at the end of chapter four, section 4.2, is, without doubt, a coherent legal piece elaborated within the framework for treaty interpretation used by the IDCS organs. They reject the argument developed in Thoumi (2016), Collins (2016), and Fultz et al. (2017). They argue that these authors extend the meaning of scientific purposes to include non-medical sciences and propose that a legally regulated market in cannabis may be permissible under the international drug control treaties if it is considered a "policy experiment." Lines and Barret appeal to articles 31 (General Rule of Interpretation) and 32 (Supplementary Means of Interpretation) of the Vienna Convention on the Law of Treaties of 1969 (VCLT). These articles provide formal procedures to interpret the conventions, and they conclude that the interpretation proposed by those authors is untenable and their arguments are very weak. Good lawyers are like chess players, they can play with white or black pieces, and they must simultaneously attack and defend any side of a legal issue, keeping within the game's rule book or framework. Their goal is to convince, not to prove. The Lines and Barrett article is entirely devoted to the impossibility of interpreting the terms medical and scientific in the way proposed by those authors and this book.

> While increased scholarship on the interpretation of these long-standing, and in many ways outdated, agreements are necessary and welcome, in order for drug reform proposals to be credible, we must ensure the clarity of interpretive theory and method adopted. With this in mind, this article examines the proposition put forward by a number of writers that a legally regulated market in cannabis[165] may be permissible under the drug treaties if considered as a policy 'experiment.' Considered in this way, these authors contend that such measures conform to the general obligation of the Single Convention on Narcotic Drugs to limit uses of cannabis "strictly to medical and scientific purposes" (Lines and Barrett, 2018, 438-439).

> They continue, each author "proposes an expanded and novel understanding of the norm as it has been typically applied within international drug control law and resulting State practice: in

---

[165] For the purposes of this paper, we use the term 'legally regulated market' as shorthand to describe a policy environment that allows for legal production, transport, sale, possession and use of cannabis for recreational, cultural, or religious uses.

effect, a new interpretation of a key treaty provision" (ibid, 439) but "the interpretation they propose is untenable. While we share with these authors the objective of wider drug policy reform, we find the arguments supporting their position week, and based on absent, flawed, or incomplete interpretive methodology" (ibid, 439). And "this concept has therefore been central to international drug control law for over one hundred years and is widely acknowledged as prohibiting legally regulated markets in controlled substances that allow for recreational, cultural or religious uses.[166] Key scholars of international drug control law have argued that limiting controlled drugs strictly to medical and scientific purposes constitutes the object and purpose of the regime" (ibid, 439-440). The authors then appeal to respected academic authorities and provide names of international law scholars to support their point.

These assertions are interesting. As shown in chapter two, the limitation of drug uses to medical and scientific purposes was first proposed by the United States at the Shanghai Commission at the prompting of religious missionaries in China and The Philippines and could not be agreed upon in the following four international drug conventions. The United States achieved its goal to enact that principle only in the 1961 Single Convention on Narcotic Drugs. Thus, the assertion: "this concept has therefore been central to international drug control law for over one hundred years" is questionable because it was contended and challenged for a long time before 1961 and in recent years.

The authors proceed to criticize Thoumi (2016) in some detail: "Francisco Thoumi suggests that because the treaties offer no concrete definition of 'medical and scientific purposes,' it creates what he describes as a 'legal void' or 'legal gap.'[167] According to Thoumi, 'This ... presents a logical dilemma since the terms 'medicine' and 'science', that are the key determinants of the allowed drug uses, are

---

[166] See Leroy, Bassiouni and Thony (2008).
[167] Thoumi, *supra note* 18, at 20

not defined. Thus, it is logically impossible to know if any specific policy complies with the conventions and it is not possible to rule out any policy as 'unscientific.'"[168] Thoumi's primary interpretive resource is the dictionary, noting that 'definitions of science provided by the most recognised dictionaries are extremely diverse.'[169] Based upon these divergent dictionary definitions, Thoumi concludes that 'The failure to define and clarify the term 'science' implies that there is no unique way to interpret the conventions. For instance, it may be logically possible to accept that the policies of Uruguay and the States of Colorado and Washington that have allowed non-medical and research uses of marijuana comply with the conventions if those policies are based on scientific evidence from both medicine and the social sciences.'[170] In his article, Thoumi makes no reference to the literature on treaty interpretation and does not discuss the Vienna Convention on the Law of Treaties. That there are many ways to interpret the text is, of course, clear. However, a key issue is whether a given is sufficiently adherent to a clear interpretive method so as to be sufficiently persuasive argument.[171]" Here, their argument seeks to persuade, if not to prove or refute logical positions.

However, Thoumi's argument took at face value the first sentence of Article 31 of the Vienna Convention on the Law of Treaties of 1969: "A treaty shall be interpreted in good faith in accordance with the ordinary meaning to be given to the terms of the treaty in their context and in the light of its object and purpose." That is why, since there were no definitions for the terms *medical and scientific*, the ordinary meaning provided by the dictionaries' definitions of science is consistent with the pretended purpose of the conventions: the physical or moral health and the welfare of humankind, which as noticed above, is the social good that the conventions claim to protect. This concept is evident in European

---

[168] Ibid., page 21
[169] Ibid., page 26
[170] Ibid., page 26-27
[171] Tobin, 2010.

Continental Law, in which the concepts used in the law must be spelled clearly but not in the common law legal system based on precedent decisions. Furthermore, from Thoumi's perspective and contemporary public policy, the limitation of drug uses to medical and scientific purposes is a policy instrument, not the underlining policy goal. For Lines and Barrett, Thoumi's position is only a "creative interpretation of medical and scientific purposes" (Lines and Barrett, 2018, 444).

Thoumi's (2016) argument does not necessarily lead to the legalization of marijuana as the authors claim: "[t]here is no question that conventions should be complied with, but there is also no question that the conventions should be clear and logically consistent because otherwise, they would lead to contradictions and confusion. To avoid these problems, the conventions generally define their most important terms carefully, and in this respect, the drug conventions are flawed because they fail to define their two most important concepts 'medical and scientific purposes'. In legal parlance, they have a 'legal void' or 'legal gap.'" (Thoumi, 2016, 20).

This flaw in the conventions is essential. As shown in this book, it has led to varying interpretations, depending on the professional background, beliefs, and ideologies of the INCB members and the countries and times where they have been applied. Thoumi's argument may lead to the legalization of some non-medical marijuana uses, if and only if a rigorous evidence-based study could prove that the social costs generated by anti-drug policies exceed the costs of increased addiction that the tolerance of non-medical marijuana uses would cause. Social sciences have developed scientifically based methods that are applied widely worldwide to estimate the costs of crime, pollution, human displacement, the value of human life, etc. They are used across many agencies part of the United Nations system and are at the core of evaluating the SDG-inspired policies.

The positions of Lines and Barrett on one side, and Thoumi on the other, also differ regarding the contextual interpretation. In

Article 31 of the Vienna Convention, the interpretation of the conventions should consider the context in which they are created. For Lines and Barrett, this context is defined only by lawyers.

> Significantly, the title of Article 31 is in the singular ('General Rule' rather than 'General Rules'), implying that all the interpretive elements contained within it must be applied collectively, rather than selectively, in order to arrive at a proper interpretive conclusion. The International Law Commission has long approached the methods in Article 31 as a 'single combined operation,'[172] a view that has been adopted, for example, at the European Court of Human Rights.[173] When these sources cannot resolve the question, the Vienna Convention allows recourse under Article 32 to 'supplementary means' such as treaty drafting history and debates (*the travaux preparatoires*). As John Tobin notes, Articles 31 and 32 may be summarised as including various forms of interpretation: 'textual, contextual, teleological, and historical.'[174] In short, treaty interpretation is done by applying specific sources of law within a specific interpretive framework. To be sure, many interpretations can be put forward. It is not about finding 'the' definitive answer, but 'an' interpretation that is more persuasive than others, which must include its formal legal method[175] (Lines and Barrett, 2018, 447).

Again, the argument's goal is to persuade. As noted in chapter 1, 2, and 11 of this book, the process to limit drug uses to medical and scientific purposes started in the context of a strong European

---

[172] International Law Commission, 1966.
[173] *Witold Litwa v Poland* App no 26629/95 (4 April 2000) para. 58; See also *Golder v United Kingdom* App no 4451/70 21 (21 February 1975) para. 30. '... the process of discovering and ascertaining the true meaning of the terms of the treaty is a unity, a single combined operation'.
[174] Tobin, *supra note* 24, p. 17.
[175] Tobin, Ibid.

colonialism and ended when the United States and the USSR were the two superpowers and the European colonies in Asia and Africa were becoming independent. At the time, the addiction problem to be tackled appeared to be simple, and so did the policy instrument to be implemented. Besides, even in 1961, drug addiction issues were not important in most countries' policy agendas. Drug policies were not thought to have significant global social welfare implications because drug use and addiction were concentrated in a few countries. From today's public policy perspective, drug production, trafficking, and consumption are complex issues, and as Lines and Barret acknowledge, the IDCS is "in many ways outdated." Unfortunately, it is not just outdated. It is also dysfunctional for its aims.

As shown by the legal approach based on precedent, the absolute restriction of drug uses to medical and scientific purposes is based on arguments of authority and on what judges and juries have decided. It does not require definitions of the main terms of the drug conventions. That is why they cite Tobin again:[176] "Straying too far outside of formal methods, or 'cherry-picking' individual elements while excluding others, compromises any conclusions reached, which is where the above authors fall short" (ibid, 447- 448). This approach implies that anyone who wants to study and understand the IDCS must hire highly qualified lawyers to explain the conventions. However, these explanations will be about how the conventions have been interpreted, not how they can be used to solve the complex drug issues of today. Precedents, as best practices, frequently become past practices, and what has worked to solve a simple problem of the past is unlikely to work when the problem evolves and becomes complex.[177] As more technological and social changes occur, the more

---

[176] Tobin (2010, 17).

[177] For example, Cartwright and Hardie (2012) survey the experience of Randomized Controlled Trials (RCT), the golden instrument of evidence-based research, and find that in many cases, what works in one place might not work somewhere else. This is particularly so in the case of social policies.

the context of human life changes, and the more likely past best policies become obsolete.

Additionally, article 32 of the VCLT determines that a term of the conventions should be reinterpreted if "(a) Leaves the meaning ambiguous or obscure, or (b) Leads to a result which is manifestly absurd or unreasonable." However, the Lines and Barrett argument not only dismisses the importance of the ambiguity in the key terms of the conventions, but it makes it impossible ever to find a situation in which current drug policies would lead to a "manifestly absurd or unreasonable" result.

To conclude, I know I will not convince Professors Lines and Barrett, and they would not convince me. Our paradigms are too different. I accept that their analysis may have the support of many international lawyers. I am also confident that sometime in the future, the policy evaluation systems developed by the social sciences will be applied to all psychoactive drug policies, including the limitation of drug uses to *medical and scientific purposes.*

12.3 POLICY REFORM VIA "INTER SE" TREATY MODIFICATION

As noted in chapter 4, section 4.1, the drug conventions are exceedingly difficult to amend, a point confirmed by the experience of Bolivia and its efforts to take the coca leaf out of schedule I of the Single Convention or to obtain the legitimacy of the traditional coca uses in that country. This difficulty is common to international conventions, "[d]ue to the conflicting interests prevailing at an international level, amendments of multilateral treaties, especially amendments of treaties with a large number of parties, prove to be an extremely difficult and cumbersome process; sometimes an amendment seems even impossible" (Dörr and Schmalenbach, 2012, 719).[178] These authors indicate that the 1969 Vienna Convention on

---

[178] Quoted by Jelsma (2017).

the Law of Treaties a group of countries to permit countries to countries "to modify the treaty as between themselves alone" (Jelsma, 2017).

Bewley-Taylor, Jelsma, Rolles, and Walsh (2016, 11) argue that the "inter-se" clause provides an option to modify the drug conventions: "The 1969 Vienna Convention on the Law of Treaties (VCLT) also allows for the option to modify treaties between certain parties only, offering in this context an intriguing and under-explored legal option somewhere between selective denunciation and a collective reservation (see below). According to Article 41 of the VCLT, 'Two or more of the parties to a multilateral treaty may conclude an agreement to modify the treaty as between themselves alone,' as long as it 'does not affect the enjoyment by the other parties of their rights under the treaty or the performance of their obligations'". It is not "incompatible with the effective execution of the object and purpose of the treaty as a whole[179]" (ibid, 11).

Inter-se modifications are not easy. In the case of marijuana, for example, they:

> [...] would require that the agreement include a clear commitment to the original treaty obligations vis-à-vis countries not party to the inter se modification agreement, especially concerning prevention of trade or leakage to prohibited jurisdictions. All the provisions in the treaties—including those pertaining to cannabis—would remain in force vis-à-vis the treaty's State parties that are not part of the inter se agreement. Over time, such an inter se agreement might evolve into an alternative treaty framework to which more and more countries could adhere, while avoiding the cumbersome (if not impossible) process of unanimous approval of amendments to the current regime.[180] In theory, modification

---

[179] For more details on scheduling, see Hallam, Bewley-Taylor & Jelsma (2014).
[180] Article 41, Vienna Convention on the Law of Treaties of 1969.

inter se could be used by a group of like-minded countries that wish to resolve the treaty non-compliance issues resulting from national decisions to legally regulate the cannabis market, as Uruguay has already done, and Canada appears poised to do. Such countries could sign an agreement with effect only among themselves, modifying or annulling the cannabis control provisions of the UN conventions. This could also be an interesting option to explore in order to provide a legal basis justifying international trade between national jurisdictions that allow or tolerate the existence of a licit market of a substance under domestic legal provisions, but for which international trade is not permitted under the current UN treaty obligations (ibid, 11).

To support their case, the authors then appeal to "[a] leading authority on international treaty law, J. Klabbers, describes the inter se option as 'perhaps the most elegant way out,' but also notes that though inter se modification is based on an ancient principle of international law, 'practical examples are hard to come by.'[181] Indeed, it seems this is essentially uncharted legal territory, but a good case could be made that the increasing tensions between cannabis policy trends and the frozen drug treaty system provides a clear example of circumstances for which this exceptional option was designed and deemed to be of crucial importance. Indeed, though its use has been rare, the inter se option has been understood since the outset of the UN system as a means of reinforcing treaty regimes, not undermining them. Where regimes are exceptionally resistant to reform, and therefore liable to become brittle and antiquated, an option such as inter se modification could actually strengthen the regime by demonstrating that it is capable of modernization" (ibid, 11).

The argument for inter se treaty modification as a solution for the cannabis legalization movements has continued to be supported

---

[181] Klabbers, (2006).

by Boister and Jelsma's (2018) article in a law journal devoted to that issue. In the same issue, Van Kempen, Hein, and Fedorova (2018) strengthen the argument incorporating human rights.

> Although the UN narcotic drugs conventions do not allow states parties to legalize cannabis cultivation and trade for recreational use, there are possibilities for states to do so anyhow while staying within the boundaries of international public law. A first option concerns positive human rights obligations, *i.e.,* obligations that require states to take measures in order to offer the best protection of human rights. If a state convincingly argues that with cannabis regulation positive human rights obligations to protect society can be more effectively achieved than under a prohibitive approach, the priority position of human rights obligations over the drugs conventions can justify such regulation. The second option regards the modification of the drugs conventions through an *inter se* agreement on cannabis regulation between certain of the states' parties only. The positive human rights approach and the *inter se* possibility can strengthen each other and are a supreme combination (Van Kempen and Federova, 2018, abstract).

The proponents of inter se treaty modification coincide with Lines and Barrett (2018) (see chapter 4, section 4.2) and with Bewley-Taylor, Jelsma, Rolles, and Walsh (2016, 14) in their limited definition of the terms *medical and scientific purposes.* They criticize the argument developed in this book because it "misunderstands the meaning of 'scientific purposes' within the treaties." They assume that contracts are not required to make clear their essential terms. And that in the case of international treaties, only well-trained international lawyers are allowed to interpret the meaning of the treaties' undefined terms.

Inter se modification experiments may be encouraged, and their viability should be explored. These experiments should undoubtedly be an option, but not the only one in a complex system that requires significant adaptation to a changing world context.

12.4 SHOULD DIFFERENT DRUGS BE TREATED DIFFERENTLY?

As shown in chapter 6, section 6.1, the INCB (1992) devoted its first analytical chapter to argue against non-medical controlled drug use acceptance. Its arguments were based on the complexity and difficulty of establishing different policies for different drugs. Hall (2018)[182] acknowledges that those uses breach the drug conventions. It is also necessary to explore the consequences of allowing some non-medical drug uses of different drugs and consider their possible positive and negative consequences.

Hall warns that this is not easy because of significant disagreements about the harms that different drugs cause on users. However, the problem goes beyond establishing what harms different drugs cause on users. The consequences of psychoactive drug use are not just on the users' bodies and also affect social health, a field in which causality is very frequently hidden. Despite these limitations, Hall summarizes the evidence available in public health studies about the different effects that various drugs have on individual users. Based on his extensive experience, he suggests ways in which that evidence should inform drug policymaking. A significant part of the evidence comes from the estimates of the global burden of disease. This figure combines the estimates of the years of life lost from premature death plus the years lived with disability attributable to drug use. The latter

---

[182] Hall's paper is important not only because of his arguments, but also because he is a former INCB Member (2012-2014), and a respected academic known for his rigorous empirical studies, and he cannot be branded an activist for or against "legalization". His paper reflects his concerns with the rigidity of the IDCS interpretation of the drug conventions.

is adjusted depending on the degree of disability to produce the total disability-adjusted life years (DALY) lost (Institute for Health Metrics and Evaluation, 2013).

This measure, used in health policy analyses, is very democratic and egalitarian because it equally values the year lost by any human being, independent of personal wealth, sex, income, social status, etc. A year lost by a particularly important and rich person is valued equally to a poor or unemployed female. It is certainly not a concept used in costs and benefits analyses by economists. The result of these estimates shows that the global burden of disease caused by illegal drugs is 1% of the total from all diseases, and pales compared to those of alcohol (3.9%) and tobacco (6.3%) (Hall 2018, 5). The rest (about 88%) is attributed to other illnesses suffered by humans.

Hall also explores the problems that arise in trying to evaluate alternative drug policies: "in an ideal world, we would like to conduct randomized control trials (RCT) that compare how current and alternative policies operate in comparable countries. Unfortunately, RTCs are only feasible for drug policies of very limited scope, e.g., comparing different treatments for problem drug users, evaluating different types of school-based drug-prevention programmes or comparing different interventions for drug-related offenders" (Hall, 2018, 6). To this obstacle, one may add that finding comparable countries or, in many cases, even regions within countries is challenging. As shown in chapter eleven, the vulnerability of each society tends to be unique to it, and the governability and policy success possibilities vary substantially across countries and regions.[183]

---

[183] Economists for example, are prone to argue that countries with similar income per capita, history and religion are comparable. But complexity models show that the causality factors are frequently hidden. Acemoglu and Robinson (2012 chapter 4) in what has been perhaps the most widely used economic development text during the last decade, show that throughout history, what appeared to be small differences among countries may end up producing very different economic development results.

The lack of solid evidence has led proponents of the legalization of non-medical controlled drug uses to underestimate their policy proposals' risks frequently. Thus, governments should be pretty cautious about non-medical drug uses, but precisely because there is no good evidence, policy experiments may be valuable. Hall concludes that cannabis is a viable candidate for non-medical use experiments, although with caveats. Cannabis legalization has the risk of focusing states' efforts on maximizing tax revenues, with terrible consequences on drug users. However, he considers that "the major risk that cannabis poses to non-users is a modest increase in accident risk if users drive while intoxicated" (Hall, 2018, 7). Users have other risks if the government fails to control the THC content, which may be very high today in some marijuana plant varieties. Other risks are the failures to prevent access to marijuana to young people whose brain development can be affected. Hall warns about the risks that "a for-profit cannabis industry will behave like the alcohol and tobacco industries in promoting heavy use among existing users and recruiting new, younger, users.[184] A legal cannabis industry may also become powerful enough to resist public health-orientated cannabis regulation[185]" (ibid, 6).

Hall discusses the consequences of legalizing non-medical use of MDMA and other "party drugs." MDMA has a much lower dependence risk than other drugs, and the people that use these drugs are more educated and less criminally involved than other drug users. Hall claims that "few users of these drugs report serious harms in drug surveys, but we are less certain about how this may change if more people use these drugs under legalization or if legalization changed the characteristics of users and their patterns of use; e.g., it increased the number who used multiples of usual recreational doses, in combination with other drugs, such as alcohol and the stimulants, or via injection" (Hall, 2018, 8).

---

[184] Caulkins, (2016), Kleiman, (2015).
[185] Kleiman, 2015.

Legalizing opioids and cocaine present more problems and raise more questions. Hall argues for the *mitigated prohibition* of opioids, maintaining their prohibition, but providing effective harm reduction programs to prevent overdoses and blood transmitted diseases.

The legalization of cocaine and other stimulants like amphetamines presents other problems because their dependence increases aggression and assaults: "The history of failures to control stimulant drugs misuse via prescription systems does not encourage optimism about the success of those systems" (Hall, 2018, 9).

Hall's conclusions emphasize that the United Nations policy goal of a "drug-free society" has made it easy for critics to claim that the IDCS has failed because it has not achieved its goal. It has also allowed critics to advocate legalization without looking at the possible implications of such policies. Hall warns that any tentative conclusion of his paper should be taken with caution. Some specific issues like the potential problems high THC cannabis may generate in a legal market should be carefully evaluated. The main contribution of this paper is that it cautiously explores the need to evaluate social and economic costs and benefits of non-medical drug uses. It suggests ways to evaluate proposals to regulate the markets of different drugs and how social sciences can improve psychoactive drug policy formulation and implementation.

CHAPTER THIRTEEN. OTHER INESCAPABLE DRUG POLICY ISSUES

The recent developments in the United Nations system and how some countries deal with drug policies challenge the IDCS. The IDCS is facing a dilemma. It may continue with its business-as-usual attitude and risk becoming increasingly irrelevant in important world regions or explore possible forms of cooperation with countries interested in drug policy reforms. This chapter illustrates some of the main challenges faced by the IDCS and some of the inescapable policy issues that it must confront.

13.1 SUSTAINABLE DEVELOPMENT GOALS (SDG): THEIR CONFLICTS WITH AND CHALLENGES TO IDCS POLICIES

On 25 September 2015, the United Nations Sustainable Development Summit adopted the 2030 Agenda for Sustainable Development, the most ambitious United Nations development agenda ever. Indeed, the first sentence in its title is no less than "transforming our world." Its preamble states, "this Agenda is a plan of action for people, planet and prosperity. It also seeks to strengthen universal peace in larger freedom. We recognise that eradicating poverty in all its forms and dimensions, including extreme poverty, is the greatest global challenge and an indispensable requirement for sustainable development" (United Nations, 2015, 1).

It set 17 Sustainable Development Goals and 169 detailed targets, which "seek to build on the Millennium Development Goals and complete what these did not achieve. They seek to realize the human rights of all and to achieve gender equality and the empowerment of all women and girls. They are integrated and indivisible and balance the three dimensions of sustainable development: the economic, social and environmental" (ibid, 1). The SDG focus on:

People We are determined to end poverty and hunger in all their forms and dimensions and to ensure that all human beings can fulfil their potential in dignity and equality and in a healthy environment.

Planet We are determined to protect the planet from degradation, including through sustainable consumption and production, sustainably managing its natural resources, and taking urgent action on climate change, so that it can support the needs of the present and future generations.

Prosperity We are determined to ensure that all human beings can enjoy prosperous and fulfilling lives and that economic, social, and technological progress occurs in harmony with nature.

Peace We are determined to foster peaceful, just, and inclusive societies which are free from fear and violence. There can be no sustainable development without peace and no peace without sustainable development.

Partnership We are determined to mobilize the means required to implement this Agenda through a revitalized Global Partnership for Sustainable Development, based on a spirit of strengthened global solidarity, focused in particular on the needs of the poorest and most vulnerable and with the participation of all countries, all stakeholders, and all people (ibid,1).

The SDG are a policy program based on many United Nations conferences and summits "which have laid a solid foundation for sustainable development and have helped to shape the new Agenda. These include the Rio Declaration on Environment and Development; the World Summit on Sustainable Development; the World Summit for Social Development; the Programme of Action of the International Conference on Population and Development, the

Beijing Platform for Action; and the United Nations Conference on Sustainable Development" (United Nations, 2015, ¶11).

The 2030 agenda is exceptionally ambitious. Indeed, the SDG seek drastic structural changes in human societies that require profound policy changes to respond to humankind's main current problems.

> We are announcing today 17 Sustainable Development Goals with 169 associated targets which are integrated and indivisible. Never before have world leaders pledged common action and endeavour across such a broad and universal policy agenda. We are setting out together on the path towards sustainable development, devoting ourselves collectively to the pursuit of global development and of 'win-win' cooperation, which can bring huge gains to all countries and all parts of the world. We reaffirm that every State has, and shall freely exercise, full permanent sovereignty over all its wealth, natural resources, and economic activity. We will implement the Agenda for the full benefit of all, for today's generation and for future generations. In doing so, we reaffirm our commitment to international law and emphasize that the Agenda is to be implemented in a manner that is consistent with the rights and obligations of states under international law (United Nations, 2015, ¶18).

The document that formulates the 17 SDG and the 169 associated targets (United Nations, 2015) reflects the weak relationship that has existed between the IDCS and most United Nations agencies, especially those related to population, human rights, social and economic development, and the environment (see Box 2).

Box 2 THE SEVENTEEN SDG

1. End poverty in all forms everywhere.
2. End hunger, achieve food security and improved nutrition, and promote sustainable agriculture.
3. Ensure healthy lives and promote well-being for all at all ages.
4. Ensure inclusive and equitable quality education and promote lifelong learning opportunities for all.
5. Achieve gender equality and empower all women and girls.
6. Ensure availability and sustainable management of water and sanitation for all.
7. Ensure access to affordable, reliable, sustainable, and modern energy for all.
8. Promote sustained, inclusive, and sustainable economic growth, full and productive employment, and decent work for all.
9. Build resilient infrastructure, promote inclusive and sustainable industrialization, and foster innovation.
10. Reduce inequality within and among countries.
11. Make cities and human settlements inclusive, safe, resilient, and sustainable.
12. Ensure sustainable production and consumption patterns.
13. Take urgent action to combat climate change and its impacts.
14. Life below water: Conserve and sustainably use the oceans, seas, and marine resources for sustainable development.
15. Life on land: Protect, restore, and promote sustainable use of terrestrial ecosystems, sustainably manage forests, combat desertification, and halt and reverse land degradation and halt biodiversity loss.
16. Promote peaceful and inclusive societies for sustainable development, provide access to justice for all and build effective, accountable, and inclusive institutions at all levels.
17. Strengthen the means of implementation and revitalize the global partnership for sustainable development.[186]

Source: ibid. Summary by author

---

[186] This SDG requires policies on finance, technology, capacity building, trade, and systemic issues that include policy and institutional coherence, multi-stakeholder partnerships, and data monitoring and accountability.

The SDG document references conferences and summits that helped formulate them, but they do not include any IDCS reference. Indeed, addictive drugs are mentioned only in two of the 169 associated targets. The fifth target of goal three "strengthen the prevention and treatment of substance abuse, including narcotic drug abuse and harmful use of alcohol," and the target 9b of the same goal "strengthen the implementation of the World Health Organization Framework Convention on Tobacco Control in all countries, as appropriate." Thus, on addictive drugs, the SDG's primary focus is on alcohol and tobacco, the two legal psychoactive drugs that account for most of the deaths and social costs associated with drug addiction worldwide.

Despite the lack of references to the IDCS, its policies impact several SDG. For example, the manual and aerial eradication of poppy and coca plants; precursor controls; drug producers and sellers' penal sanctions, and other anti-drug policies have consequences on the environment, poverty, health, income inequality, families' well-being, employment, and other factors related to SDG. The IDCS agencies have only recently begun to exhort governments to consider these factors. The Task Team on the Implementation of the UN System Common Position on drug-related matters (United Nations, 2019) emphasizes the role of drug policies on SDG goal 3 (the right of health), and goal 8 (inclusive and sustainable economic growth), a common goal with alternative development programs in areas of illegal crops.

Drug policies also impact other SDG goals. For instance, goals 4 and 5, the empowerment of excluded peoples (4) and women (5), to reduce inequality. And the first six targets of goal 16 (reducing significantly all forms of violence and related death rates everywhere; ending abuse, exploitation, trafficking, and all forms of violence against and torture of children; promoting the rule of law at the national and international levels and ensuring equal access to justice for all; reducing illicit financial and arms flows, strengthening the recovery and return of stolen assets and combat all forms of organized crime, reducing corruption and bribery in all their forms; and developing effective, accountable and transparent institutions at all levels).

However, the Task Team also acknowledges that those targets are far from being achieved. In a way, the SDG are a blueprint for an ideal world that should be a model to improve policies. Both the IDCS and the SDG seek ideal and unachievable goals. The SDG are overly ambitious and innovative, but their implementation would require extraordinary institutional, political, economic, social, and cultural changes. The SDG seek to eliminate poverty, hunger, social exclusion, and discrimination, protect the environment, redesign urban and rural life, make health and education universal, etc. And send a clear message that United Nations agencies should depart from their business-as-usual attitude. The question is whether that would be feasible. The SDG are so ambitious that the best that can be hoped for is a few advances to lower hunger, poverty, inequality, education, and health, protect the environment, and improve governability and the quality of life on earth. Unfortunately, the achievements of the SDG depend critically on achieving changes in the power structures of all countries, and that will probably be their primary obstacle.

The challenge for the IDCS is to adapt its policies to become an active participant in the SDG project. To advance towards the SDG goals, the United Nations must use social sciences evaluation methods that recognize the necessary tradeoffs among some of those goals. But the IDCS is stuck on its position that the harms caused by drug addiction are immeasurable. The only legitimate policy option is the prohibition of non-medical drug uses because the harms caused by this policy will always pale compared to the immeasurable harm of addiction. Unfortunately, it is improbable that the IDCS will overcome this blind policy belief.

13.2 THE WHO'S DEFINITION OF HEALTH AND ITS CONSISTENCY WITH THE IDCS

13.2.1 WHO and the Definitions of Health

The definition of health is essential for the IDCS because its requirement to limit controlled drug uses to *medical and scientific purposes* involves knowing what those purposes are. As noted, the IDCS does not define health, but WHO has a broad definition that is helpful. Besides, WHO plays a key role in the IDCS: first, it advises the CND about what drugs to include or eliminate from the convention schedules. Second, three of the thirteen positions at the INCB are filled by experts elected among candidates submitted by WHO. Third, it provides valuable support to the INCB, the CND, and the UNODC regarding many drug and health issues.

WHO's Constitution, which antecedes the 1961 Single Convention on Narcotic Drugs by 15 years, defines three components of health.[187] This definition is valid within the United Nations, and the IDCS policies should be consistent with it. The first principle of WHO's Constitution defines health as "a state of complete physical, mental and social well-being and not merely the absence of disease or infirmity." It implies that the three health components, physical, mental, and social well-being (or welfare), are integral parts of health. They must be considered to decide whether a policy meets the medical purposes criterium. Physical, mental, and

---

[187] WHO's Constitution was adopted by the International Health Conference held in New York from 19 June to 22 July 1946, signed on 22 July 1946 by the representatives of 61 States (Off. Rec. Wld Hlth Org., 2, 100), and entered into force on 7 April 1948. Amendments adopted by the Twenty-sixth, Twenty-ninth, Thirty-ninth, and Fifty-first World Health Assemblies (resolutions WHA26.37, WHA29.38, WHA39.6 and WHA51.23) came into force on 3 February 1977, 20 January 1984, 11 July 1994, and 15 September 2005 respectively and are incorporated in the present text
(http://www.who.int/governance/eb/who_constitution_en.pdf)

social well-being issues are also an integral part of WHO's goals and policies.

Despite postulating three components of what may be called total health, WHO's Constitution did not initially define any of them. It might be possible for the medical and public health professions to reach a consensus about physical and perhaps mental health definitions. However, a consensus about healthy social well-being (which to simplify may be called "social health") could be exceedingly difficult to achieve. It is not surprising that in the late 1940s, at the end of the Second World War and the start of the Cold War, defining social health was certainly an unsurmountable challenge for WHO's founders. This challenge persists today as it would require an agreement among countries about the role of the State in society and the rights and duties of individuals in all countries. This also implies achieving an agreement about a unique set of civic rights and civic ethics across the world is a virtually impossible task.

As mentioned, the INCB is a treaty organ limited to monitoring compliance with the drug treaties. But WHO is a policy organ of the United Nations that has more flexibility to formulate and implement its policies. Its function is more practical than the INCB's, and to facilitate its work, after a few years of experience, it defined mental health as "a state of well-being in which every individual realizes his or her own potential, can cope with the normal stresses of life, can work productively and fruitfully, and is able to make a contribution to her or his community."[188] While WHO did not define social health, it identified the "*social determinants of health*" (SDH) that "are the conditions in which people are born, grow, live, work and age. These circumstances are shaped by the distribution of money, power, and resources at global, national, and local levels. The SDH are mostly responsible for health inequities - the unfair and

---

[188] http://www.who.int/features/factfiles/mental_health/en/ Updated in August 2014.

avoidable differences in health status seen within and between countries."[189]

In other words, social health is a function of a myriad of social, political, economic, and physical factors that determine the environment in which people live. The SDH transcend traditional health policy issues and go to the core of political, social, and economic development policies, which become part of WHO's medical issues as social health determinants.

13.2.2 WHO's Principles, Constitution, and Policies

The principles stated in the preamble of WHO's Constitution are:[190]

- "health is a state of complete physical, mental and social well-being and not merely the absence of disease or infirmity."
- "the enjoyment of the highest attainable standard of health is one of the fundamental rights of every human being without distinction of race, religion, political belief, economic or social condition."
- "the health of all peoples is fundamental to the attainment of peace and security and is dependent upon the fullest co-operation of individuals and States."
- "the achievement of any State in the promotion and protection of health is of value to all,"
- "unequal development in different countries in the promotion of health and control of disease, especially communicable disease, is a common danger."
- "healthy development of the child is of basic importance; the ability to live harmoniously in a changing total environment is essential to such development."

---

[189] http://www.who.int/social_determinants/en/
[190] https://www.who.int/governance/eb/who_constitution_en.pdf

- "the extension to all peoples of the benefits of medical, psychological and related knowledge is essential to the fullest attainment of health."
- "informed opinion and active co-operation on the part of the public are of the utmost importance in the improvement of the health of the people."
- "governments have a responsibility for the health of their peoples which can be fulfilled only by the provision of adequate health and social measures."

WHO is a large organization of problem-solving professionals that deals directly with sick people and those at risk of illness and the ways to improve total health. Following a realist and practical approach, WHO (2008) has advanced in its challenge to meet its mandate developing four strategies to advance policies that public health systems can deliver.

WHO's strategy starts focusing on efforts leading to universal medical health coverage (WHO, 2013) and requires social organizations' cooperation with the government to provide adequate health and support social measures. Its focuses on assuring that people have access to health services and that the governments provide a good healthy environment. In practice, WHO has sought to promote public health services accessible to the population, including a healthy physical environment to prevent disease.

WHO recognizes that the power structure, the income and wealth distributions, the casts and classes that discriminate and exclude, the lack of information and education, and other social issues are important SDH that may frustrate health policies.[191]

WHO has continuously made efforts to learn about and overcome obstacles to their goals. There is no question that WHO's

---

[191] WHO's October 2011 Rio Political Declaration on SDH is a most important policy statement
https://www.who.int/sdhconference/declaration/en/

quest to meet its mandate faces many political, economic, social, cultural, and physical constraints. As noted above, when any decision-making organ confronts a problem, every policy or action faces constraints that limit the set of possible solutions. The more constraints imposed on the solution of a problem, the more limited is the set of possible solutions. In cases where there are many constraints, the probability of conflicts among some constraints is very high.

It makes it impossible to find a solution to a policy problem that does not breach one of the constraints. In such situations, the set of solutions that satisfy all constraints is nil. For example, WHO faces political issues that arise from the power structures of the countries where it operates and from international powers. The examples of the suppressed marijuana and cocaine studies before UNGASS 1998 and its lack of response to the INCB request for a study on coca chewing and coca tea attest to these pressures (see chapter five section 5.3).

WHO is aware that political and other constraints prevent it from achieving its universal good quality health coverage goal. However, its capacity to organize research gives WHO a critical advantage over the INCB and UNODC because it allows WHO to find ways to overcome some of the obstacles it faces in its efforts to fulfill its mandate. When WHO confronts a complex and challenging problem, it develops practical programs to comply with its mandate. For example, to respond to epidemics and pandemics, WHO develops protocols to overcome threats like those used to confront security threats, natural disasters, and other risky situations. These threats must be managed by applying prevention and mitigation policies. For example, the threats of measles and polio are always latent. Universal vaccination may lower these risks and appear to eradicate them, but if some people refuse to vaccinate their children, the illnesses appear again. Epidemiologists understand that preventive measures can lower risks but never completely eliminate them. To lower the risks, they should identify the vulnerabilities of each population and take measures to lower or, if possible, eliminate them. Once the threats materialize, the policies should first mitigate their consequences, understanding that they might not eliminate the problem but aim to lower it to a socially acceptable level. Preventive measures must be applied, including efforts to develop a vaccine to prevent a recurrence.

This approach forces WHO to confront all the social, cultural, political, economic, etc., constraints that limit their policies. And follow a viable policy that minimizes risks. For example, it must always confront the consequences of the physical-economic constraint determined by its budget. According to the second WHO's principle, its policies should be formulated to maximize health for everybody. And as noted, according to its first principle, health has three components: physical, mental, and social. The total health to be maximized is a function of those three different dimensions of health. Taking these two principles at face value, mathematical optimization methods widely used across many sciences can be applied to find the characteristics of effective policies that maximize total health given a budget limitation.

Health and psychoactive drug production, marketing, and consumption are overly complex issues. The concepts of physical, mental, and social health are fundamental in WHO's principles, but WHO does not rank them according to their importance. The discussion of SDH indicate that the three variables of total health are interrelated, that is, that changes in one affect the others. The following exercise is a simplified version of reality that assumes that the three types of health are independent. Attempts to incorporate the interdependence among the three health variables would complicate the mathematics but not change the fundamental conclusions.

13.2.3 The Reality of Scarcity and the Mathematical Conditions for Total Health Maximization

To start, let us posit that WHO aims to maximize total health (H), that is a function of physical health (P), mental health (M), and social health (S). This function varies depending on each government ideology, the level of social cohesion, and other structural factors of each society. For example, there might be societies where physical health is highly valued, but not mental health. This would happen if, for example, mental illness is associated with a punishment or a test sent by God to a person, or when it is conceived as a failure of the individual's personality, in which case he or she should be punished or disposed of to protect society. The concept of social health would vary enormously depending on the mindset and worldview prevailing in each society. There is no doubt that every society may have a health function $H = f(P, M, S)$ different from those of all other societies. Still, independently of the actual form of that function, all governments must confront a physical resource constraint.

Of course, without an exact formula for H, it is impossible to find the ideal policy solution in a specific situation. However, standard mathematical optimization techniques identify some basic conditions that should solve any specific policy optimization problem. Once this is done, it is possible to check if a policy meets those conditions.

To proceed, it is necessary to identify the constraints or restrictions that impose limits to the feasible values of H. Independently of other constraints (social, cultural, political, etc.), each type of health requires physical resources such as health professionals, medicines, hospitals, equipment, research, etc., which are always limited. Indeed, health sector leaders are always clamoring for more resources to satisfy health needs. Therefore, the physical resource constraint faced by policymakers is an economic constraint that is binding.

To illustrate the optimization problem, one may use a simple model of three total health producing variables, P, M, and S, that use costly resources and formulate a simple optimization problem:

Maximize $H = f(P, M, S)$ subject to a budget constraint that can be written as:
$$\lambda(B - cpP - cmM - csS)$$

Where λ is a Lagrange multiplier, **cp, cm,** and **cs**, are the costs of one unit of P, M, and S, and B is the total available funds to spent in P, M, and S. The problem is then:

$$Max\ H = f(P, M, S) + \lambda(B - cpP - cmM - csS)$$

As explained in any calculus textbook, adding $\lambda(B - cpP - cmM - csS)$ to the function, H does not change it or affect it because $[(B - cpP - cmM - csS) = 0]$, and adding 0 to $f(P, M, S)$, does not change it.

A situation that maximizes or minimizes a function must meet certain "first and second-order conditions." The "first-order conditions" apply to both maximization and minimization solutions. The "second-order conditions" allow to differentiate between the characteristics of a solution that minimize from those that maximize a function. For the argument of this essay, there is no need to go into the second-order conditions. The first-order conditions to maximize $f(P, M, S)$ are:

$$\frac{\partial H}{\partial P} = \lambda cp, \quad \frac{\partial H}{\partial M} = \lambda cm, \text{ and } \frac{\partial H}{\partial S} = \lambda cs$$

From where:

$$\frac{\frac{\partial H}{\partial P}}{cp} = \lambda, \quad \frac{\frac{\partial H}{\partial M}}{cm} = \lambda, \quad \text{and} \quad \frac{\frac{\partial H}{\partial S}}{cs} = \lambda, \quad \text{or:} \quad \frac{\frac{\partial H}{\partial P}}{cp} = \frac{\frac{\partial H}{\partial M}}{cm} = \frac{\frac{\partial H}{\partial S}}{cs}$$

That is, the partial derivative of H with respect to P, M, and S divided by the cost of producing the last unit of P, M, and S should be equal.[192] This simply means that for any policy to maximize H, the last unit of money (peso, dollar, ruble, euro, renminbi, etc.) spent on the production of physical, mental, and social health must make the same contribution to total health. When this condition is not met, it is possible to increase total health by transferring resources spent in one type of health to others. This requires coordinated policies among all agencies and actors that oversee physical, mental, and social health to assign resources where they would have the most significant impact on overall health.

Of course, suppose the types of health are interrelated. In that case, the conditions for maximization get more complex because they require figuring out the contribution of the resources devoted to one type of health and adding or subtracting the positive and negative indirect contributions to other types of health. But independently of the form of the total health function to be maximized and whether the three types of health are interrelated, the budgetary constraints require to assign limited resources to balance the expenditures in physical, mental, and social health so that the contribution to the total health of the last monetary unit spent on each type of health (physical, mental, and social) is the same.

The conditions for total health maximization derived from WHO's principles imply that if economic resources are limited, there are tradeoffs among physical, mental, and social health that the optimal WHO policies must consider. This requires a holistic approach that is much broader and evidence-based than the IDCS drug use limitation to *medical and scientific purposes.* That means

---

[192] The partial derivatives of the dependent variable H are its changes caused by the changes in each one of the independent variables -P, M, or S-, while maintaining the other two variables constant.

that a single-minded policy to push for the elimination of a factor contributing to physical or mental health disregarding all other social factors that affect total health is not only not optimal, but furthermore, it cannot be the only policy to be applied under all circumstances.

13.2.4 Is There a Conflict Between the IDCS Policies and WHO's Principles?

As noted above, UNGASS 2016 and 2019 CND outcome documents, following the long-standing IDCS position, reaffirmed the "determination to tackle the world drug problem and to actively promote a society free of drug abuse." And jointly, INCB, UNODC, and WHO (2018) asserted that the three United Nations drug agencies complement each other. These statements assume that there are no conflicts between WHO's principles that aim to maximize total health and how the prohibition of non-medical drug uses has been interpreted by INCB and promoted by UNODC, the CND, and the UNGASS on the world drug problem.

The conditions for maximization of total health show that if resources are limited, to maximize total health, the WHO must estimate the contribution to the total health of the marginal expenditures on each of the three components of total health. It means that WHO must focus on coping with the world health problem, using mitigation and preventive measures. Unfortunately, the WHO has not recognized the full scope of actions necessary to promote social health. Its application of social health has only been based mainly on factors that directly affect the human body. It is not surprising given the origins of the organization and the professional backgrounds of WHO's staff. They have focused on medical preventive measures and vaccines. However, to eliminate health problems, it is necessary to attack the factors that increase social vulnerability and strengthen those that protect society. In other words, it is necessary to seek social vaccines. Despite this weakness, the WHO is aware that its drug policies cannot be focused only on eliminating the threat of addiction caused by some drug uses or eliminating addiction at any cost.

The current INCB policy position argues that all sectorial policies should be coordinated, but only if the constraint to limit drug use to non-medical and scientific purposes is maintained. The INCB argues that the text of the conventions established that limiting drug use to non-medical and scientific purposes is the best possible policy to maximize either the *health and welfare* or *humankind's physical and moral health*. However, as shown above, that approach does not maximize total health. A priori rejects some health policy options that could be superior to those obtained by prohibiting all non-medical drug uses. That is why constraining drug uses to medical and scientific purposes, disregarding the contributions of the social sciences, and seeking a drug-free world independent of social costs become obstacles to total health maximization and the concordance of IDCS policies with WHO's principles and epidemiological practices.

For this not to be the case, it would be necessary that the resources (B in the equations in 13.2.3) needed to implement the drug and health policies were available at no cost. This would mean that they were either infinite or so large that they would become public goods like the air humans consume without paying for it. In other words, for the IDCS to be consistent with the WHO principles, the prices of all resources used to implement health policies must be zero, which of course, is non-sense.

WHO has other obstacles that prevents it from meeting the conditions for total health maximization because political, cultural, religious, institutional, and other factors also restrict its policies. WHO finds these constraints in all its activities, not just in those related to psychoactive addictive drugs, and it has tried to do the best it can within those limits. By understanding and recognizing its constraints, WHO's policy approach is analogous to harm-reduction drug policies. For example, the WHO knows that in the short run, it cannot eradicate most illnesses. Thus, it must focus on the locations and illnesses where they can achieve the most harm reduction given its constraints. It should identify the most vulnerable societies and social groups and concentrate on the most illnesses that cause the most harm.

As noted above, the INCB's policy position is uncompromising against any non-medical drug uses. This position is periodically ratified in meetings like UNGASS 2016 and the 2019 CND that reaffirm the pursuit of the ideal unachievable goal of a drug-free world. This approach has prevented the Board from recognizing any tradeoffs between total health components (especially its mental and social dimensions). It has also led to a rejection of any non-medical drug uses independently of any social health consequences. The 2017 INCB annual report (2018, 4) states that only 1 in 200 people that use drugs in their lifetime have drug use disorders, that is, become addicts. One may posit that many of the 199 out of 200 drug users use them to cope with their life problems and to feel better mentally and socially.

In liberal-leaning societies where governments are concerned about illegal drug use and its citizens' social health, they should inquire about the social health factors that lead their citizens to use those drugs. When these are established, drug policies should be formulated in a co-creative process with all stakeholders. In these societies, the top-down drug policies imposed by the government under the pretext of promoting the health and welfare of humankind are ineffective and, worse, could be socially invalid and rejected. However, in authoritarian societies, where the central authority imposes social norms seeking its ideal view of society, it decides what policies maximize social welfare and has no qualms about limiting human rights and eliminating or jailing the human "bad apples" in its midst. The question is, which approach would improve the social health and welfare of each society?

13.3 HEALTH SECTOR SERVICES AND LEGAL PSYCHOACTIVE DRUGS

The health sector presents several significant regulatory challenges. The health services market is peculiar because, in virtually all cases, there is a very significant asymmetry between the information available to the buyer (the patient) and the seller (the health sector's suppliers). It is a classic market power asymmetry that, in many cases, is extremely large. In the health services market, the consumers (patients), frequently under duress, do not know what services and medicaments to buy and pay someone to tell them what to buy and how to spend their money. Furthermore, when patients are in a hospital, doctors and other professionals decide the treatment. They have a very weak or absolutely no opportunity to shop around, bargain prices, or choose cheaper services or medicaments (generics, for example). At the end of the service, the consumers receive a bill they often cannot understand but must pay before they are released. In this case, the consumers are forced to purchase goods and services from a monopolist that sets its prices. Of course, many people treated in hospitals have insurance, and their bills are paid by either the private insurer or the government. In these cases, the patients know that the insurance would cover most services. It induces patients to seek the "best" services and pass the costs to the pool of insurance subscribers or the taxpayers. Not surprisingly, health costs have been out of control in many countries.

For WHO and the United Nations SDG goals, health services are a human right that people are entitled to, independent of their capacity to pay. This means that a considerable proportion of the health service pricing takes place outside competitive markets. In practice, these markets offer extractive revenue opportunities to many. For this system to work fairly, it would be necessary for all providers to be benevolent non-profit maximizers that would not take advantage of the knowledge differentials between themselves and their patients and their families. Not surprisingly, in many parts of the world, many health services have been provided, and are still provided, by charitable organizations.

The chemical-pharmaceutical sector also offers extractive income opportunities for the drug or precursor producers. Drugs are relatively cheap to manufacture once the knowledge to produce them is obtained. The cost of the research to generate the knowledge necessary to produce any drug is very high relative to its manufacturing cost. It is a classic case that approaches what economists call a *public good*, with very large fixed costs but very low marginal costs. In an ideal theoretical world, to maximize total health, a government (a global government?) would design a way to fund the research and make sure that the produced drugs would sell at their marginal costs. It would be a policy consistent with the second WHO principle that requires policies to maximize total health. In today's world, this is totally impractical. Countries have established an international patent system to solve the problem of generating knowledge and new drugs. It allows the private sector to produce knowledge, get a monopoly for a limited time, and sell drugs at prices substantially higher than their marginal costs to cover the pharmaceutical companies' research plus other fixed costs.

The international patent system has significant biases generated by the profit maximization goals of any rational monopoly. First, companies seek to separate markets to charge a higher price where people may afford to pay more. Second, pharmaceutical companies' research prioritizes the development of new drugs to treat illnesses that affect those more able to pay, people from rich countries and wealthy individuals in developing countries. Third, the system allows pharmaceutical companies to make minor changes to the molecules of the medicaments and get patents for "new drugs" that are like the old ones, de facto extending their monopolies. Fourth, pharmaceutical firms have been able to exploit the drug markets influencing the legislation that regulates them. For example, in the United States, they got Congress to enact legislation that prevents Medicare, the social security health program for retirees, from negotiating drug prices with the suppliers. Fifth, in almost all countries, pharmaceutical companies have strict limits on advertising. However, they can contact health sector professionals to inform them about their products' uses and benefits. Today's information technology allows these companies to precisely know which doctors and what they prescribe and use several incentive mechanisms to increase sales. These include funding doctors' participation in scientific seminars in luxury resorts where they can combine a few lectures with golf rounds, etc. In some cases, they compensate doctors with kickbacks under and above the table. These and other characteristics of the current system based on patents substantially increase the costs of health treatment and raise the pressure on the budgets of WHO and other official agencies that work to achieve social health goals.

The point is simple. Today humanity has the knowledge and resources to provide at least essential health services to almost all humans. However, the existing societies are not organized to do so. The recent opioid overdose epidemic in the United States is a clear example of this. The epidemic started with some pharmaceutical companies and health sector professionals providing services and medicaments to people suffering from pain. Either willingly or unwillingly, these actors underestimated the addiction risks, and in many well-known cases, they overprescribed addictive painkillers that resulted in many addicts and overdose deaths. Have these companies, along with public health sector professionals who dispensed their drugs, become the most successful drug cartel in the world?

The breakdown of the Soviet Union generated in some capitalist countries a triumphalist euphoria that has prevailed until now. Many capitalist leaders ended up believing that any free market is always better than any communist, socialist, or planned economy system. It resulted in a "greed is good mentality" that justifies any monopolistic or extractive market behavior. As shown by the opioid epidemic, there is no question that the markets of legal addictive psychoactive drugs must have stricter regulations to prevent socially dangerous drug uses. However, today these controls are deemed "socialistic" by some people (mainly in the United States) and should be avoided at all costs.

The use of legal drugs today has a very ironic pattern. Many affluent societies are overmedicated, and so are wealthy individuals worldwide. But, most humans do not have access to the drugs they need. In most of the world, the recent opioids epidemic has been concurrent with very low use of opioid analgesics, like morphine. One of the INCB's jobs is to obtain information about the use of legal opiates and analyze those data. For a long time, the Board has been concerned that the amount of statistically defined daily doses (S-DDD)[193] of morphine, codeine, and other narcotic pain killers available in many countries is very small. The Board has frequently urged countries to make more of those drugs available, and in 2016 it published an extensive study of the availability of opioid analgesics across the world that found that:

> Around 5.5 billion people still have limited or no access to medicines containing narcotic drugs, such as codeine or morphine, leaving 75 per cent of the world population without access to proper pain relief treatment. Around 92 per cent of morphine used worldwide is consumed in countries in which only 17 per cent of the world population lives: primarily the United States of America, Canada, Western Europe, Australia, and New Zealand. Inadequate access contradicts the notion of article 25 of the Universal Declaration of Human Rights,[194] including the right to medical care, which also encompasses palliative care. The inequitable use of opioid analgesics does not seem to be attributable to a lack of raw materials. Global production of opiate raw materials has exceeded global demand for many years. As a

---

[193] S-DDD applies to any drug. It is a number per certain number of inhabitants, most frequently 10,000, or 100,000 people.
[194] General Assembly resolution 217 A (III).

result, stocks have been increasing, albeit with some fluctuation. Over the past 20 years, global consumption of opioids has more than tripled. Available data indicate that the amount of opiate raw material that is available for the manufacture of narcotic drugs for pain relief is more than sufficient to satisfy the current level of demand as estimated by Governments. For psychotropic substances, the issue of supply is more complex. That topic is addressed in detail in the chapter devoted to those substances (INCB, 2016b, iii).[195]

This study identified the main obstacles to extending the use of opioids in the countries where the S-DDD was inadequate. In descending order, the reasons expressed in the questionnaires received by the Board from the responsible government agencies were: one. Lack of training or awareness among health professionals. 2. Fear of generating addiction. 3. Limited financial resources. 4. Problems in sourcing from industry or imports. 5. Cultural and social attitudes towards the treatment of pain. 6. Fear of diversion into illicit channels. 7. Fear of prosecution or sanction. 8. International trade control measures. 9. Onerous regulations (INCB, 2016b, 30-33).

Addictive pain killers present a complex policy challenge. On the one hand, the legal markets, including pharmaceutical companies, distribution marketing networks, prescribing health sector personnel, and users, need to be regulated to prevent fraudulent sales and overdoses. On the other hand, there is a global need to increase the use of those same drugs among the vast number of people who need them and prevent diversion to illegal markets. SDG 3.8 reaffirms the goal of universal health coverage, one of WHO's main goals, which includes palliative care. The obstacles to expanding analgesic opioids identified by the INCB (2016b) study illustrate a challenging future policy agenda.

---

[195] An academic article summarizing these results was published by some INCB members and staff in *Lancet* (Berterame, et al., 2016).

13.4 THE NEED TO CONTROL THE INTERNATIONAL TRADE OF PSYCHOACTIVE DRUGS AND CHEMICAL PRECURSORS

The IDCS originated from the concern with the international opium trade during the second half of the XIX century. Since then, the international trade of psychoactive drugs has been a permanent and essential policy issue. Countries are advancing toward a diversity of drug policies, including the legalization of some psychoactive drug uses. Still, they must operate in an environment where international trade of drugs and precursors can undermine domestic drug policies. Starting with the League of Nations' 1925 and 1931 drug conventions (See chapter two section 2.5), a system was developed to assure that the international trade of opium and other controlled substances was used to supply only legitimate medical requirements. This system was further developed and reinforced by the following international treaties. Monitoring the implementation of this is today a central function of the INCB. That is why the drug conventions require its parties to annually submit to the Board estimates of required controlled drugs produced and used and to report their imports and exports. The function of the INCB's Standing Committee on Estimates is to make sure that those estimates conform with countries' needs.

The United Nations conventions respect national sovereignty, but in a globalized world, all countries are interdependent. Therefore, any country's policy that tolerates non-medical drug uses may risk undermining other countries' sovereignty, regardless of how well the country justified it. Thus, any policy experiment of this kind should be strictly controlled to prevent diversion to markets in other countries. That is why legalization of cannabis use must have strict controls to prevent negative consequences on other countries.

The 1961 Single Convention on Narcotic Drugs and the 1971 Convention on Psychotropic Substances established the requirements to estimate the world's legal needs for all controlled substances and created a system to regulate their international trade. It has been a primary function of the INCB since its creation in 1968.

The drug conventions do not control many precursor chemicals. The INCB has developed guidelines for a voluntary code of practice for the chemical industry and for the laboratories of the competent national authorities to test those chemical precursors. "They are intended for use by laboratories that are in need of reference standards and by competent national authorities that are responsible for the control of drugs and precursors and that issue the import and export authorizations required to exercise that control." (INCB, 2007b, iii).

Article 12 of the 1988 Convention against Illicit Traffic in Narcotic Drugs and Psychotropic Substances on the precursors frequently used in the illicit manufacture of narcotic drugs oblige the governments of the exporting countries to provide notification to the INCB regarding exports of chemicals before such exports depart from their territory. To facilitate countries' compliance with this obligation of precursor chemicals exporting countries, the INCB established the Pre- Export Notification Online system (PEN Online) to alert the competent national authorities in the importing country with the export transaction details. The PEN Online System enables the easy online exchange of information between the Member States on shipments (export and import) of the chemicals required to manufacture illegal addictive drugs, such as heroin, cocaine, and amphetamines. And to provide the ability to raise alerts to stop suspect shipments before they reach illicit drug manufacturers. The system facilitates a full electronic reply to acknowledge receipt and notify the exporting country of clearance to export.[196] It is a fundamental tool for preventing the diversion of precursors from international trade.

---

[196] (https://www.unodc.org/unodc/en/global-it-products/pen.html)

Since then, the Board has developed other systems to facilitate information exchange among governments. A Precursors Incident Communication System (PICS) provides real-time communication and information sharing between national authorities on precursors incidents (seizures and other events). The Board has continued developing electronic communication systems about precursor chemicals and today has a tool kit available to all governments.[197]

Chemical precursors control presents other challenges. When a precursor is added to the controlled lists, chemical producers find pre-precursor chemicals whose molecules are remarkably similar to those of the previous precursor and can be used to make the same drug. For example, at INCB request, the CND fifty-seven session in 2014 scheduled in Table I of the 1988 convention alpha-phenylacetoacetonitrile (APAAN), an important "designer" precursor used to produce amphetamine-type stimulants. This led to a very sharp decline in seizures of APAAN. However, APAA (Alpha-phenylacetoacetamide), an unscheduled chemical close relative of APAAN, emerged in 2015 after APAAN was placed under control a year earlier. Chinese produced APAA started to be seized in several European countries and East and South-East Asia.

> In 2017, two additional developments occurred: a limited resurgence of APAAN and the emergence of MAPA as a substitute for APAA. MAPA is the methyl ester of alpha-phenylacetoacetic acid. Given the challenges associated with the proliferation of a series of closely related chemicals (to which has drawn attention in the past), the limited international special surveillance list was amended in 2013 to include the concept of extended definitions for such derivatives. MAPA is covered by that definition, and INCB encourages competent national authorities to make full use of

---

[197] https://www.incb.org/incb/en/precursors/precursors/tools_and_kits.html

the international special surveillance list and alert relevant sectors of industry to the possible misuse in illicit drug manufacture of chemicals on the list (INCB, 2019, 20).

This case illustrates the challenges of precursor chemicals control in domestic and international markets. That is why it is important to explore ways to amend the conventions to allow the scheduling of families of substances rather than individual ones that are the only ones that can be scheduled currently.

The concern with the precursor chemicals of the main internationally trafficking drugs led the Board to develop frameworks for international cooperation in matters related to trafficking in chemicals used in the illicit manufacture of drugs, specifically cocaine and heroin (Project Cohesion), and amphetamine-type stimulants, and other synthetic drugs (Project Prism). [198]

These projects "provide platforms for time-bound intelligence-gathering operations with a view to collecting information on potential gaps or weak links in international precursor control, on new trafficking trends, on modi operandi, on the actual use of the target chemicals in the illicit manufacture of drugs and on how those chemicals are diverted to enter the clandestine laboratory environment. The projects are thus aimed at assisting Governments in ensuring the necessary level of alertness and developing specific risk profiles to prevent future diversions and - ultimately - to identify the trafficking organizations involved. Participants in Project Cohesion and Project Prism are continually alerted to suspicious shipments and actual and attempted diversions of precursors, as well as newly emerging precursors. Alerts occur through Special Alerts, and automated push notifications via the INCB Precursors Incident

---

[198]

(https://www.incb.org/incb/en/precursors/special_projects/Prism_and_Cohesion.html).

Communication System PICS (for registered users only)" [199]. These two projects allow rapid and direct communication between the authorities concerned of different countries.

The persistent appearance of NPS led to the establishment of Project ION (International Operations on NPS) to support national authorities' efforts in preventing non-scheduled NPS from reaching consumer markets. Project ION activities are primarily the coordination, collection, and communication of strategic and operational information related to suspicious shipments of, trafficking in, or manufacturing or production of NPS. The project has focused on synthetic NPS with little or no known medical, scientific, or industrial uses. Its activities are primarily engaged in the coordination, collection, and communication of strategic and operational information.[200]

The growing volume of licit international trade in controlled substances continuously increased the workload of the national agencies required to provide information to the INCB. In 2015 the INCB, jointly with UNODC developed the International Import and Export Authorization System (I2ES), a web-based electronic system designed to facilitate trade in internationally controlled substances by facilitating the online exchange of import and export authorizations. This development was achieved with financial and technical support from the Member States, without which the UN drug agencies could not have overcome their financial constraints. I2ES is accessible and free to all governments. It is a safe and secure platform for generating and exchanging import and export authorizations between trading countries while ensuring full compliance with all provisions of the 1961 Convention as amended and the 1971 Convention.

The estimates of the requirements of narcotic drugs and the assessments of psychotropic substances established by States parties

---

[199] (https://www.incb.org/incb/en/precursors/special_projects/Prism_and_Cohesion.html).

[200] (https://www.incb.org/incb/en/project_ion.html)

and endorsed by the Board are automatically synchronized with I2ES. After an import authorization has been approved, the system calculates in real-time the remaining balance of the estimates or assessments available to the importing country. Trading partners registered with the platform can access that information at any time. The trading countries can also use the system to securely communicate and exchange information directly with their counterparts if a transaction request requires further clarification.

The online exchange of import and export authorizations using I2ES enables real-time data transfer between trading countries, thus facilitating a much faster approval process. To provide a fully electronic and paperless international trade system, the Board established the possibility for Governments to use electronic signatures and the import and export authorizations processed through the system.

Any drug policy reform effort must maintain rigorous international trade controls on all scheduled substances to safeguard other countries' sovereignty. In recent decades international organized drug trafficking has learned to produce new psychoactive drugs and chemical precursors that should be strictly controlled. In many instances, these developments could become a strong constraint on the countries domestic drug policy flexibility.

13.5 THE IDCS PROBLEMS IN FEDERAL GOVERNMENTS WHERE STATES ARE AUTONOMOUS REGARDING DRUG POLICY

As pointed out in the introduction, legal pluralism is common in many countries today, and it may prevent the equal implementation of the conventions across countries. Article 36 of the Single Convention provides:

> Subject to its constitutional limitations, each Party shall adopt such measures as will ensure that cultivation, production,

manufacture, extraction, preparation, possession, offering, offering for sale, distribution, purchase, sale, delivery on any terms whatsoever, brokerage, dispatch, dispatch in transit, transport, importation and exportation of drugs contrary to the provisions of this Convention, and any other action which in the opinion of such Party may be contrary to the provisions of this Convention, shall be punishable offences when committed intentionally, and that serious offences shall be liable to adequate punishment particularly by imprisonment or other penalties of deprivation of liberty.

Since constitutional limitations vary across the world, there is a possibility that the IDCS norms may vary depending on the country where they are applied. The issue is whether this possibility transcends criminal issues regarding illicit drug production, trafficking, and use.

The main current issue regarding federal governments is the cannabis non-medical use legalization in Canada and several states and other jurisdictions in the United States. The INCB made its position clear in a December 2017 Alert (INCB, 2017b, 1-2).

> The implementation of the drug control conventions requires States to act in good faith to adopt legislative, policy and regulatory measures in order to comply with the international obligations to which they have agreed to be bound. Given their different political, legal, and constitutional structures, the nature of the measures taken varies from one State party to the next.
>
> In seeking to comply with their international legal obligations, States with federal structures face unique challenges, related to the fact that the implementation measures may fall within the authority of the federal government, a sub-national constituent government, such as that of a state, province or territory or may be a matter of

shared authority. In this context, it is important to recall that the drug control conventions, like all international treaties, are binding in respect of the entire territory of a state party, 'unless a different intention appears from the treaty or is otherwise established' and that, as a rule, States cannot invoke their internal law as justification for their failure to perform a treaty.[201] [...]

Article 4(c) of the 1961 Single Convention on Narcotic Drugs, as amended by the 1972 Protocol, restricts the use of narcotic drugs subject to international control (including cannabis) to medical and scientific purposes. [...]

In some instances, sub-national Governments have taken measures towards legalizing and regulating the non-medical use of cannabis, despite federal law to the contrary and the strict prohibition of non-medical use set out in the 1961 Convention. Here again, the Board has engaged with the Governments of the State parties concerned in order to reiterate that these developments are in violation of the international drug control legal framework. Accordingly, the Board has requested that remedial action be taken in order for the national Government to honour the country's international obligations. The Board has repeatedly expressed that these developments have jeopardised the integrity of the international drug control system as a whole by undermining one of its fundamental principles. [...]

Finally, the Board wishes to remind the Governments of all State parties that they are responsible for ensuring the respect of their international obligations and that the effectiveness of the international drug control system depends upon their comprehensive implementation by all members of the international community.

---

[201] Vienna Convention on the law of treaties, United Nations, Treaty Series, vol. 1155, No. 18232; Articles 26, 27, 29.

This INCB Alert refers to articles 26, 27, and 29 of the 1969 Vienna Convention on the Law of Treaties (VCLT). Article 26 on the Observance of Treaties, Pacta Sunt Servanda,[202] reads "[e]very treaty in force is binding upon the parties to it and must be performed by them in good faith," and Article 27 on the Internal Law and Observance of Treaties "[a] party may not invoke the provisions of its internal law as justification for its failure to perform a treaty. This rule is without prejudice to article 46 section 2". It is then helpful to read article 46 on Provisions of Internal Law Regarding Competence to Conclude Treaties:

> 1. A State may not invoke the fact that its consent to be bound by a treaty has been expressed in violation of a provision of its internal law regarding competence to conclude treaties as invalidating its consent unless that violation was manifest and concerned a rule of its internal law of fundamental importance. 2. A violation is manifest if it would be objectively evident to any State conducting itself in the matter in accordance with normal practice and in good faith.

Article 29 on Territorial Scope of Treaties reads: "Unless a different intention appears from the treaty or is otherwise established, a treaty is binding upon each party in respect of its entire territory." The real issue is whether these articles apply not only to domestic laws but also to constitutional norms.

The United States is an excellent example that raises many interesting issues. This country has a federal organization in which the States keep many functions transferred to the central government in other federal systems. According to the American Constitution, the 50 States are sovereign. They have not signed or ratified the

---

[202] Latin for "agreements must be kept" that is a basic principle of civil, canon, and international law.

conventions and are not obliged to enforce them. Article 1, section 8 of the American Constitution lists the *enumerated powers* that the sovereign States have transferred to the Federal Government. These powers limit what the Federal Government can do. It is a classic agent-principal case in which the Federal Government (the agent) can only exercise the powers that the States (the principals) give it. For example, in the case of psychoactive drugs, even though the United States enacted the 1970 Controlled Substances Act, it cannot force the state and local police and judicial systems to enforce it. When the states do not cooperate, the Federal Government may only use law enforcement agencies like the CIA, the DEA, the FBI, the National Guard, and the Federal Justice System (Thoumi, 2014). This situation posits several interesting questions. For example, what is the role of the VCLT regarding the constitutions of countries that ratify international conventions? Would there be a situation where the ratification of an international drug convention implicitly amends a country's constitution? Those are intriguing issues for international lawyers to debate, but they certainly are issues that transcend the role and capabilities of the INCB and its 13 Board Members. Many countries are organized as federal states. Even though their systems are different, the issue of the different compliance with the drug conventions will persist in those states.

The marijuana legalization process in some states in the United States and the incapacity of the central government to enforce its laws on these states posit an essential question: has the conventions' prohibition on non-medical marijuana uses become a dead letter in the United States? The almost total lack of references to the United Nations IDCS in the American government documents and the press suggests so. Ironically, for a century, the United States federal government was the leading force in constructing and implementing the IDCS. However, the country's federal structure has constitutional constraints for the central government to enforce international trade agreements. It explains why the central government cannot domestically apply what it pressures countries to apply abroad (Thoumi, 2014).

13.6 FACING NATIONAL POLICY POSITIONS THAT DEPEND ON STRONG AND BLINDING FEELINGS AND EMOTIONS: THE UNITED STATES AND COLOMBIA AS AN EXAMPLE

The literature about how the human mind's decision-making processes work shows that regarding essential issues like nationality, race, religion, liberties, freedoms, gender, individual profession, political parties, patriotism, and psychoactive drugs, etc., many individuals are convinced that their positions are based on solid scientific evidence, but they are greatly influenced by their life experiences and their feelings and emotions.

Most people's world view depends on the values of the family and society in which they grow up. Cultures tend to produce world views with some blind policy beliefs, that is, policy positions that are justified appealing to the unquestionable conventional wisdom in their societies, part of which may be considered today as *alternative facts* based on tradition and sentiments. The international relations between Colombia and the United States are an excellent example of how their different world views produce blinding policy beliefs and different *alternative facts* about cocaine production and trafficking.

Illegal drug policies in the United States and Colombia are a good example of countries whose vulnerabilities complement each other to produce a chronic illegal unsolvable drug problem. The solutions to their "drug problem" require significant changes in both countries' power structures and beliefs. Their political systems are unlikely to provide reforms because they are not designed to change the prevailing national mindsets and world views. Not surprisingly, during the last forty-five years, the international cocaine trade has been the central international relations issue between these two close political allies in the American continent.

The United States federal government has persecuted drug producers, traffickers, and consumers and incarcerated a vast amount of people (in 2019, the U.S. had 4.3% of the world's population and 22% of its incarcerated population), established anti-money laundering controls, funded education campaigns, and enacted extensive legislation at the federal and local levels. However, it has not been able to control its illegal demand for drugs like cocaine, the appearance of illegal markets for NPS, and recently a legal opioid addiction epidemic. Only the opioid epidemic diverted somewhat the focus on the United States anti-drug policy on eliminating foreign illegal drugs sources that were corrupting the country's youth.

This blind policy belief places the causes of drug addiction in the United States in alien societies. During his 2016-2020 presidential period, Mr. Trump took advantage of this blind policy belief. He persistently argued that undocumented and asylum-seeking migrants were bringing large quantities of illegal drugs to the United States despite evidence that almost all smuggled drugs come in through cargo ports of entry. These actions are consistent with another critical, American blind policy belief. Despite arguments about the United States being a cultural melting pot, the American Civil War did not end in 1865. A belief in white superiority has persisted among a significant group of white Americans, particularly those unskilled workers with poor education. They have been skillfully manipulated by politicians using *alternative facts* and *fake news* to attribute their economic instability and the source of their fears to Latin American mestizo immigrants and black citizens accused of drug crimes (Metzl, 2019). There is, however, another American blind policy belief, the personal right of guns ownership, including assault-type, which allows Latin American drug trafficking and subversive organizations to source their weapons in the United States.

Colombia did not export a single coca leaf or a gram of cocaine while they were legal. According to the conventional wisdom of most Colombians, the development of the illegal cocaine industry is the root of the country's very high levels of violence and many other critical social problems like corruption and the propensity to engage in many illegal economic activities. Despite massive traffickers' extraditions and eradication programs that some years have supposedly eliminated more coca plants than what was estimated to exist, the country has not been able to control cocaine production. When most Colombians are asked why the country cannot control cocaine output, the most common answer is "when there is demand, there is supply" in any capitalist system. And if one asks that if cocaine is by far the country's most profitable export, how come Colombia has a lot fewer international competitors than in any other export? They either shrug their shoulders, do not answer, or seek other justifications.[203] Their justificatory and exculpatory arguments are complemented by another blind policy belief, a complaint that "Colombia puts the dead bodies, and the United States keeps the money from the drug trade." When someone asks, how do many countries with drug trafficking and other organized criminal organizations have not similar violent experiences? They answer that violence in the United States was equally high during alcohol prohibition and led to legalization. Suppose one responds that the iconic case of violence associated with prohibition in the United States was the famous 1929 St. Valentine Day massacre that produced only seven deaths, a number that pales with the series of narco-massacres experienced in Colombia. In that case, they will stop talking or consider that the data about prohibition-related violence in the United States is just an "alternative fact" that must be rejected. If one gets bold and argues that the Colombian problem is not that it puts the dead bodies, but the assassins for whom it is natural to kill for large illegal profits. The most common reaction is to end the

---

[203] Some I heard are "that cocaine is the only product that the CIA or the DEA assigned us to produce" or the Americans tolerate their cocaine demand because Monsanto lobbies the American congress to profit from selling glyphosate for aerial spraying of coca. (By the way, since 2017 Monsanto has not been an American company, it is a subsidiary of Bayer, a German corporation.) Perhaps the most curious defense of the assertion "when there is demand, there is supply" is that of a Colombian diplomat commented in footnote 164.

conversation abruptly and consider the person who made the statement a traitor that must be shunned.

Concerning international drug policies, neither of these two countries has seriously focused its anti-drug policies on dealing with their vulnerability factors such as social exclusion, unemployment, weak family structures, frustrated upward mobility expectations, lack of territorial control by the state, racial discrimination, etc. Their policies try to mitigate the drug problem, but their political systems have not found the vaccine against drug production, trafficking, and consumption. Indeed, they have not even dared to ask the questions why they produce, traffic, and consume drugs, because they already have the answers. Most of their drug policy resources have been devoted to law enforcement, and both placed the root of their drug problems abroad.

Colombia's main explanation for its policy failure has been the existence of a vast, profitable, and irresistible international cocaine demand. Both countries feel they are victims of foreign evils and unable to solve their illegal psychoactive drug problem, but they continue the same drug policies. At times, policies appear to progress toward their goals, but these advances are not sustainable, and drug production, trafficking, and consumption go back to earlier or new highs. Thus, despite their political alliance for the last 45 years, the international relations between both countries have been narcotized by the cocaine issue.

Both societies implicitly reject the evidence that their drug production, trafficking, and consumption are mainly determined by their governance and governability structures. Illegal drug activities are symptomatic of unresolved social issues and are not the responsibility of foreign countries. Yes, if there were no cocaine demand, there would not be a supply, and if there were no supply, there would not be a demand. But neither cocaine demand nor supply can be eliminated without solving the structural vulnerability issues in both countries, that is, vaccinating them. As a result, both societies appear trapped in a marriage made in hell, with no possible divorce agreement.

Similar blind policy beliefs are present in other countries. Skilled political leaders use those beliefs to manipulate the masses and concentrate power. They all seek scapegoats for their policy failures. However, as shown in chapter twelve, the causality of those social harms is often hidden and difficult to determine, which makes the scapegoating official explanations credible to many people.

The challenge for drug policy success lies in tearing down the epistemological obstacles that create blind policy beliefs and asking fundamental questions about the countries' social structures that make them vulnerable to producing, trafficking, and consuming psychoactive drugs. It is the main obstacle to solving "the world drug problem" and achieving the SDG.

13.7 IS THE ADMINISTRATIVE STRUCTURE OF THE INCB FIT FOR PURPOSE?

13.7.1 Administrative Characteristics of the INCB

The Single Convention appears to have left the INCB administration to be developed by its members in cooperation with the Secretary-General. Article 11 of the Single Convention on rules and procedures of the Board is straightforward: "The Board shall elect a President and such other offices as it may consider necessary and shall adopt its rules and procedures." And article 16 on the Secretariat is equally simple "the secretariat services of the Commission and the Board shall be furnished by the Secretary-General. In particular, the Secretary of the Board shall be appointed by the Secretary-General in consultation with the Board."

This last sentence reveals that in 1961 the INCB was sufficiently important within the UN system to have the Secretary-General appoint the Secretary of the Board. However, today, the UN system is a lot bigger and more complex, and the time of the Secretary-General is a lot more valuable than in 1961. Besides, the INCB is a small UN organ little known in the New York UN offices.[204] These developments led to the Secretary-General delegating the appointment of the INCB Secretary to the Director-General of the UN Vienna office.

Every complex organization has front and back offices. In the INCB, its 13 Board Members are the front office that is the organization's face and respond for its actions. They are the ones that represent the Board and interact formally with high-level officials of other countries, multilateral organizations, and other relevant drug policy issues actors. They are elected for five-year periods and may be reelected. They meet every year in three sessions of one, two, and three weeks. They are independent experts in the various disciplines related to the IDCS issues. They do not represent any country and cannot work for any government or private organization in jobs that could end up questioning their independence and objectivity regarding drug control issues.

Board members serve pro bono.[205] In their country missions, they have the rank of UN Ambassadors and are expected to interact with very high-level government staff. They get paid transportation to and from Vienna and a daily subsistence allowance to attend the Board's sessions and official missions to countries, organizations like WHO, or international events related to the functions of the INCB. But they do not receive any benefits. For example, they must provide

---

[204] Indeed, in 2016 at the UN New Yok office I ran into an old Colombian acquaintance that at one time had presided ECOSOC and was surprised that he did not know about the INCB when I told him I was a Board Member.

[205] Article 10 paragraph 6 of the Single Convention of 1961 states: "The members of the Board shall receive an adequate remuneration as determined by the General Assembly". In the 1980s and 1990s they received $3,000 a year. However, a stoppage of the United States contribution forced a financial crisis in the UN and the General Assembly of 2002 (resolution 56/272 of March 27) lowered the remuneration to $1 a year that is never collected. It was agreed that this dollar legally complies with the convention's requirement to give INCB members an adequate remuneration.

their health insurance during official Board trips, including the INCB sessions in Vienna.

The back office is provided by United Nations personnel, appointed according to the United Nations procedures, which support the front office. They include experts on different issues related to the IDCS. Politics play a role in their appointment because the UN has implicit national and gender quotas. Thus, these appointments are made seeking some meritocratic criteria but also have political constraints.[206]

In 1968, the INCB resulted from merging the PCOB with the DSB, which originated in the League of Nations. It continued with the functions of those two organizations. These functions had to do with overseeing compliance with the drug conventions, estimating the needs for controlled substances, and monitoring the international trade of controlled substances.

The relationship between the front and back offices was never spelled out, and both the Board members and the supporting staff seemed to work relatively well with each other without many conflicts. No Party or civil society group questioned the IDCS policy consensus, which may explain why there was no apparent need to specify how front and back offices related to each other. However, the lack of records of the INCB sessions makes it impossible to establish if there were significant conflicts.

Article 11 ¶1 of the 161 Single Convention on the "rules of procedure of the Board" reads: "The Board shall elect its own President and such other officers as it may consider necessary and shall adopt its rules of procedure."

The Board did not pay much attention to regulating the relationship between its members or its staff. However, it developed

---

[206] For example, in July 1999 I was appointed to start the research work in the Global Program Against Money Laundering at UNODCCP (today UNODC) and I had to fill two vacancies to start that program. As soon as I arrived, I was informed that I had to seek women from underrepresented countries, which was an especially important constraint.

some guidelines for the conduct of the INCB members. A two-page typewritten document, which was distributed to all members at the beginning of each session in Vienna.[207] The purpose of these guidelines was "to assist Members on the discharge of their obligations to the Board. Members have a general duty to act in the interests of the international community as a whole, rather than to any particular section thereof, and on all occasions in accordance with the public trust placed in them. Their personal conduct is therefore of paramount importance, and Para. 2 of article 9 of the Single Convention on Narcotic Drugs, 1961, as amended by the 1972 Protocol, states that: 'Members of the Board shall be persons who, by their competence, impartiality, and disinterestedness, will command general confidence.' The above statement incorporates principles of selflessness, integrity, honesty, objectivity, and accountability" (INCB, n.d.). The guidelines focused on the conflicts of interest of the Board members with their activities outside the Board. This is because the front office positions are part-time, and the Board members, unless they are retired or independently wealthy, must have other paid jobs.

The lack of records of Board meetings has an important consequence. The INCB does not have an official institutional memory. Thus, it is not possible to find if there have been cases in which Board Members have been forced to resign for reasons of conflict of interest. Talking to old-timers who worked at the INCB or UNODC, some mentioned that around the 1970s, two members resigned because they had working links with pharmaceutical companies. They also mentioned that in the late 1990s, a Board Member was working informally for a national agency involved in drug issues. The concerned member raised the issue to the Board, but it did not consider this a source of conflict of interest because the member did not have a formal contract. Apparently, the person was paid under the table. These are simple hearsay rumors that stress the need for a formal historical archive of the Board. This shows that the

---

[207] It was never mentioned as confidential during my eight years at the board.

management of the Board has been flexible and inconsistent in the past.

The administrative structure of the INCB has one characteristic that has become problematic. The front office is independent, but the back office does not respond directly to it. As shown above, the Board's Secretary was supposed to be appointed by the UN Secretary-General in consultation with the Board. However, the Secretary-General delegated this task to the Executive Director of UNODC.

In practice, that means that the front office does not supervise the work of the back office. In fact, the Board does not supervise its Secretary, who is under the UNODC Executive Director (ED). The secretary supervises the rest of the staff that is also part of UNODC. It was not an issue for a long time. According to former Board members and staff, the INCB until recently always operated by consensus. Besides, as shown in chapter five, from 1992 to 2012, Hamid Ghodse became a charismatic leader recognized by UNODC Executive Directors and staff as a brilliant professor and researcher (which he was) whose positions about drugs were to be followed.[208] However, there is no way to find out if there were frictions between the INCB members and the staff, and in any case, Professor Ghodse would have solved them internally.

13.7.2 Vulnerabilities and Conflicts

In early 2012 there was an event that had a significant impact on the Board. The INCB secretary had retired, and after the search for candidates, the Board decided to vote to choose its candidate. As noted above, the Convention does not mention any vote within the Board to choose is secretary. It only says that the Secretary-General

---

[208] Indeed, I would argue that the history of the IDCS there have been three remarkable personalities: Bishop Charles H. Brent during the IDCS origins in the first two decades of the XX century, Harry J. Anslinger the director of the FBN from 1930 to 1962, and Hamid Ghodse who was the undisputed leader of the INCB from 1992 to 2012.

will appoint the secretary in consultation with the Board. As pointed out, in this case, the UNODC ED was delegated by the Secretary-General to make the appointment.

It is not clear how private this election was. Still, I could gather from old UNODC and INCB staff that the Board voted either 9-4 or 10-3 in favor of candidate A. Hamid Ghodse, the president of the Board, met with the UNODC ED to convey the support of the Board for candidate A. However, he argued that candidate B was better, and the ED appointed him. Because the Convention did not specify the consultation process, this meeting was accepted as the consultation required by the Convention. This event had significant consequences for the Board:

1. It pointed out the weakness of the front office relative to the back office. Candidate B understood that most of the Board had voted against him and that his support had come from the UNODC ED and the Board's president, whose period ended and died soon after. Besides, it was clear that the UNODC ED disregarded the candidate chosen by most Board members.
2. It divided the Board's staff. Some felt that the Secretary's election was compromised and unfair, even though it was argued that it followed the text of the 1961 Convention. The fact that candidate A ended up working directly under candidate B added negative feelings among staffers who felt that their career development paths were vulnerable.
3. It showed that the INCB, an independent subsidiary organ of the UN, cannot elect its own Secretary and evaluate his or her performance. Furthermore, hiring and evaluating personnel has been done through the Secretary in consultation with the INCB president. The rest of the Board does not participate in the process. In every

session, the Secretary informs ex-post any staff changes made.
4. UNODC manages the back office. Many of its staffers had worked at UNODC, and some INCB staffers have moved to the UNODC. They see moving from one to the other as a career advancement possibility under the same supervisory system. Board members are elected to five-year part-time appointments, and the staffers have permanent jobs that are part of their careers within the UN system. They are not evaluated by the Board Members but by the Secretary, which UNODC's ED evaluates. This arrangement raises important loyalty issues regarding the staff.

Despite the lack of explicit modern administrative norms, the INCB seemed to have worked rather well if the front and back offices shared a strong consensus about their tasks and the interpretations of the conventions. As explained in chapter five, the illegal drug industry and the international drug trade started to grow fast in the mid-1970s, a phenomenon that became exponential during the 1980s. This induced the INCB to become the interpreter and the guardian of the conventions. It changed its annual report to include a topical chapter to treat essential policy issues, and it became a leading actor in the drug policy debate. International drug phenomena continued increasing in complexity, and after May 2012, a few recently elected members began to question the traditional consensus of the Board cautiously. Some also had had managerial experience and began to question some of the staff's actions. One complaint had to do with the lack of information that the members received about what went on in the Board while it was not in session. Some Board members felt that parts of the staff were complacent and entrenched in their way of operating and did not respond effectively to their requests. As time went by, these feelings increased, and in 2017 some Board members requested to have private Board sessions with interpreters, but no staff presence. These sessions became more frequent in 2018 and 2019 after several Board members requested a private session after a staff member lobbied them not to vote for a candidate for Board president. This event reinforced the feeling expressed privately by some members that the INCB was an organization in which the back office had a Board that was expected to rubber-stamp their actions, rather than a Board with a supporting back office.

13.7.3 The Expanded Tasks of the INCB

As noticed above, for about four decades, the Board's administrative structure was not perceived as a source of problems for the INCB. The Board, its staff, and UNODC had a consensus about the drug conventions and policies and could work together without significant friction. But the scope and the complexity of drug issues grew, and so did the activities of the Board.

The publications of the Board are a good indicator of these developments. Article 15 ¶1 of the 1961 Single Convention instructs the Board to "prepare an annual report on its work and such additional reports as it considers necessary also containing an analysis of the estimates and statistical information at its disposal, and, in appropriate cases, an account of the explanations, if any, given by or required of Governments, together with any observations and recommendations which the Board desires to make. These reports shall be submitted to the Council through the Commission, which may make such comments as it sees fit."

The first annual report (1968) was typewritten in stencils and had twenty-two pages. The report size of the report grew slowly to thirty-eight pages in 1981 and 56 in 1991. After the Board started its thematic chapter, it grew to seventy-six pages in 1994, accompanied by a 34 pages supplement. The 2019 report in English has 146 pages. In 1998, the Board changed the format from a booklet to a European letter-sized book with a flat spine. It includes detailed maps, graphs, and other visual materials. The quality of the publication is excellent. Of course, the eBook format is also available.

The Board also publishes a treaty-mandated report on the implementation of article 12 of the 1988 convention, which is entitled "Precursors and chemicals frequently used in the illicit manufacture of narcotic drugs and psychotropic substances." It has a similar format to the Annual Report and contains a significant amount of data and analysis.

There are other Board reports on issues it considers crucial. For example, in 2016, the Board produced a comprehensive study on the inequitable use of opioid analgesics (INCB, 2016b). And on the need to expand the medical use of morphine to the vast number of sick people that need it worldwide, as argued in section 13.5 of this chapter.

The Board's publications and the policy statements of its presidents have been the face of the INCB and part of the drug policy debate. However, the INCB has other bread and butter tasks that sustain the organization. They do not attract the public eye, and the staff performs them quietly.

As mentioned before, in the 1925 Opium Convention, the IDCS created a system of import certificates and export authorizations designed to assure that every international transaction in controlled substances had to be known and approved by the competent authorities of the importing and exporting countries (See chapter two section 2.5.2). Then the 1931 Convention for Limiting the Manufacture and Regulating the Distribution of Narcotic Drugs established a compulsory system that required countries to estimate the volume of their drug needs, which could be modified in emergencies. Every importing country could seek the cheapest provider but could not import more than the amount reported as required to satisfy its needs. To manage this system, the DSB was created to establish the global drug needs. Governments were required to report import and export drug quantities to the DSB, but only after the selling order had been executed (See chapter two section 2.5.2). As the complexity of drug production, trafficking, and use grew, the Board had to develop complementary tasks to respond to the new realities.

These tasks consume a very significant staff time and resources. As noted in section 13.4, the Board developed Projects ION and I2ES in response to the growing challenges of the international trade of controlled substances and precursor chemicals and the appearance of NPS. These online systems allow real-time communications between the Board and the Parties of the conventions and among those Parties.

The expanded tasks of the INCB increased the complexity of the requirements for government officials that interact with the INCB. Complying with the drug conventions requires governments to have functionaries familiar with texts of the conventions and with the online systems developed by the INCB to facilitate their job. The Board has identified several obstacles to receive good quality data. Sometimes the people in charge of responding to the INCB data requirements are unfamiliar with those requirements and with the online systems explained above. Other times the INCB systems are new and unknown to the responsible functionaries. Furthermore, their jobs are often not stable, and frequently the INCB staff must interact with new employees.

To improve the quality of data received from the governments in 2016, the Board started the INCB Learning project to provide regional training seminars for officials of competent national authorities. These seminars bring together government officials from several countries to one location. As is also the case with the I2ES, INCB Learning has been viable only with financial support from the Member States such as Australia, Belgium, France, the Russian Federation, Thailand, and the United States.

Besides the tasks described in this section, the staff has other functions. They prepare and accompany Board members to country missions. They draft the mission reports, support, and accompany Board members in other official functions. For example, they draft the public positions of the Board and support members when they attend official meetings.

The INCB is a small UN agency with a staff of some forty professionals and a very tight budget. In recent years it has appealed to young interns to be able to advance its programs. As noted, some of the new activities of the Board have been possible only with financial and technical support from some country members. This is an issue that could raise doubts about the Board's impartiality and objectivity.

13.7.4 Consequences of the Administrative Structure of the INCB and a Need for Change

The administrative structure of the INCB worked well for a time, but as the activities of the Board increased and became more complex, the role of the back office grew. The fact that the Board meets only for a brief time in Vienna increased the responsibilities of the Secretary that struggled to do more things with basically the same human resources. The Secretary took on some front office roles. The Board members felt that the secretariat staff overstepped their functions, displacing them. From the perspective of the Board members, the Secretary should not be the CEO of the organization. Board members need to be aware of the daily activities of the Board, for example, the communications of the INCB with the Member States, and the annual evaluations of the staff, etc.

It is essential to explore ways to strengthen the connection between the front and back offices. The current pandemic has shown that virtual communications systems are much better than what people believed. Indeed, future work will be less presential and more virtual. Thus, INCB monthly virtual sessions could be a possibility. This, of course, will require Board members to devote more time to their INCB job. Without that commitment, their risk of frustration with the back office will not go away.

As the scope of drug issues becomes broader, the need for effective international drug policies increases. There is a need to rethink how the INCB and other drug agencies are organized to respond to the complexity of drug production, trafficking, and consumption. Relying only on the prescription "only for medical and scientific purposes" will not do.

CHAPTER FOURTEEN. FINDINGS AND THE DRUG POLICY CHALLENGE

14.1 A SUMMARY OF THE INTERNATIONAL DRUG CONVENTIONS' POLICY APPROACH

As shown in the first part of this book, establishing the IDCS was a long, and at times contentious process. While countries agreed about the need to control the international trade of psychoactive substances, it was difficult to agree on appropriate controls. It took over a half-century to reach a consensus. It resulted in the 1961 Single Convention on Narcotic Drugs that entered into force on December 13, 1964. This convention prohibits all human drug uses except for *medical and scientific purposes.*

Following the standard practices at the time, this policy was not evidence-based as required by contemporary public policy strategies and theories. Furthermore, despite its apparent clarity, the 1961 Single Convention and the two others that followed failed to define their most important terms: medical and scientific (medicine and science), health, moral health, social health, and welfare. This failure reflected the fact that there was, and still is, impossible to reach a global consensus about the meaning of these terms. The lack of definitions was a practical policy option and allowed for a diversity of interpretations.

The INCB and the CND have interpreted the conventions as absolutely prohibiting all non-medical and nonscientific human bodily drug consumption. This has been the basis for the United Nations drug organs promotion of the unachievable goal of a drug-free world. It became an unmovable anchor to which all other drug policies must be subjected.

This interpretation reflects the professional composition of the Convention drafters and the lack of social scientists' influence. For a long time, the INCB considered that the social sciences were not sciences, only speculations. It dismissed any possibility that the social sciences could ever find reliable evidence that under some circumstances, tolerating some controlled non-medical human uses of psychoactive drugs would be a better social policy.

As shown in chapter seven, as late as 2012, this narrow policy approach led the INCB to argue that human rights were not an issue in the formation of the IDCS, and international drug policies were unrelated to human rights. Thus, taking human rights when evaluating drugs policies was going beyond the mandate of the INCB. For a long time, the Board's position against getting involved with human rights was firm.

The Board recognized that illegal drug markets generate corruption, violence, weaken social cohesion, and prevent sustained economic development. It also urged governments to solve these problems because they were obstacles to reaching the drug policy's goal of eliminating non-medical or scientific drug uses. Thus, the policies to solve those social problems should reinforce and support the narrow prohibition of non-medical or scientific drug uses.

Until its 2014 annual report, it avoided taking a position about the need for drug policies to consider human rights. In this report, the Board, for the first time, insists on the need for drug policies to comply with all international human rights conventions. It also asserts that "war on drugs" type policies are not required to comply with the drug conventions, that drug sanctions should be proportional to the magnitude of the crime and that the death penalty should not be applied to drug crimes. Furthermore, based on the International Covenant on Economic, Social, and Cultural Rights, the Board stresses that the treatment, rehabilitation, and social reintegration for drug use disorders are part of the human rights to health.

Harm reduction issues, particularly needle and syringe distribution and exchange programs (NSEDP) and drug consumption rooms, have been controversial to the INCB that initially took a hardline position against them. The INCB has evolved and now accepts NSEDP and drug consumption rooms if the participants are encouraged to attend treatment programs.

Regarding marijuana, it is interesting that for a very long time, the INCB did not react to the sale of recreational marijuana in the Netherlands, which was wide open but technically illegal. This allowed the government to say that it did not support non-medicinal marijuana uses. However, the INCB reacted immediately and firmly to the very well-regulated and evidence-based Uruguayan project to allow recreational marijuana. From the perspective of the INCB, illegal recreational marijuana in the Netherlands was okay, but it was intolerable in Uruguay (where it was legal).

The traditional use of coca (coca chewing and coca tea) was another contentious issue for the INCB. The 1961 Convention required governments where coca grew to eliminate all human bodily coca consumption 25 years after entering into force. In the early INCB reports, there was always a reminder of that obligation to Bolivia and Peru. About a year and a half before that dateline, article 14 ¶2 of the 1988 Convention asserted that "the measures adopted shall respect fundamental human rights and shall take due account of traditional licit uses, where there is historic evidence of such use, as well as the protection of the environment." From Bolivia's perspective, this paragraph legitimized traditional coca uses. To protect this result, Bolivia signed the Convention with reserves to protect its traditional coca uses. However, both the INCB and UNODC argued that this paragraph of the 1988 Convention could not be applied because other articles of the Convention prevented those uses. As shown in chapter ten, the legal position of the United Nations drug agencies denying the legitimacy of traditional coca uses contradicts contemporary treaty theory.

In 2009 After Evo Morales, a former leader of the coca growers' confederation, was elected president of Bolivia, he successfully changed the country's Constitution. In 2009 the Bolivian government proposed an amendment to the 1961 Single Convention on Narcotic Drugs to allow coca chewing without altering other coca plantings and cocaine production controls. The amendment was rejected by the UN Economic and Social Council (ECOSOC), and

Bolivia denounced the 1961 Convention. Following the Convention's procedure, Bolivia applied to access again to the Convention, this time with reservations. Bolivia achieved its accession to the Convention on February 10, 2013 (see chapter ten).

The INCB had a strong adverse reaction to this development because it undermined the integrity of the IDCS. However, the United Nations drug agencies could not prevent Bolivia from legalizing traditional coca uses. After a couple of years of tensions between the INCB and Bolivia, their relationship smoothed out, becoming polite and non-confrontational.

The history of the INCB interpretation of the drug conventions clearly shows that it depends on who the INCB members are and what they think. This characteristic is reinforced by the INCB practice of not having records of its sessions. Traditionally the Board has acted by consensus, but there is no way to determine how those consensuses were achieved.

As shown in the last paragraphs, beginning around 2014, the position of the United Nations drug agencies evolved and became somewhat more tolerant and flexible of a few minor policy changes. Indeed, the United Nations drug organs have not been blind to the reality of the increasing complexity and growth of international and domestic drug markets. This change in attitude is reflected in a change in the INCB narrative that has increasingly acknowledged that:

- Many social harms are interrelated circularly with reciprocal feedback. For example, corruption facilitates the development of illegal drug markets that promote more corruption.
- That interaction between illegal drugs and corruption may lead to *failed State* situations and even *narco States* or *narco regions*.
- Illegal drug production, trafficking, and use are affected by many factors related to the individuals' psycho-social situation

and the political and economic environment in which people live.
- Drug policies must respect human rights without excluding drug users, traffickers, and producers, as well as addicts and those that are incarcerated.[209]
- Drug policies should have a gender approach to respond to the particular problems of women involved in the use, production, or traffic of drugs.
- The interaction of psycho-social factors like poverty, social exclusion, unemployment, etc., with drug phenomena has no direct causes. All those are only factors that increase the probability of involvement in illegal drug industries or the use of drugs.
- There are also protective factors like solid families, social cohesion, active religious participation, national pride, employment, and good education that lower the probability of involvement in illegal drug activities.
- It is impossible to predict when society will develop a drug problem, but the combination of risk and protective factors of each society determines its vulnerability.
- The so-called "unintended drug policy consequences" are expected. However, they may not be forecast accurately, should be considered part of the social and economic costs of the anti-drug policies, and governments should establish systems to prevent and respond to them.

---

[209] As shown in chapter four, the IDCS does not require the harsh policies followed at several times by various countries' "wars on drugs". However, Articles 39 of the 1961 and 23 of the 1971 conventions do not preclude countries from adopting more severe measures than those provided in the conventions when countries consider them desirable or necessary for the protection of the public health and welfare. Thus, the INCB refrained from criticizing the "wars on drugs" until it published its 2014 report (INCB, 2015, 1).

- Drug policies should move from their traditional emphasis on law enforcement to a public health approach.
- Drug policies must be evidence-based.

This narrative reasonably accurately describes the complex world psychoactive drug phenomenon resulting from a series of interrelated factors whose contribution to the outcomes depends on how all factors act and interact. There is no unique way in which those relations develop, and often the structure of the relations and the relevance of different factors are hidden. Furthermore, frequently when a factor appears to most people as an essential determinant of an event, they tend to assume causality. However, this could be simplistic and wrong. For example, the exceptionally high profitability of cocaine is considered the cause of the development of coca plantings in Colombia. But that high profitability fails to produce comparable results in other places, such as Ecuador, with the same physical possibilities to grow coca. To formulate effective policies to eradicate coca in Colombia is necessary to know why those plantings do not grow across the river in Ecuador.

14.2 POLICY CHALLENGES OF A COMPLEX "WORLD DRUG PROBLEM"

As pointed out in the introduction, recent worldwide developments have shown that many political decisions are based on emotions and feelings. This fact was corroborated by the booming industry that provides *fake news* and *alternative facts* to influence elections and political positions. An important conclusion of the recent academic literature is that when people take positions on what they care strongly about, they assume they are acting rationally. But they frequently are blinded by feelings and sentiments. That is why there is a growing political polarization in many societies and a great need to have consequential dialogues. As shown throughout this book, the main actors in the development and implementation of the IDCS and their main critics regarding at least some of their positions fit this description. Thus, it has been extremely difficult to have consequential drug policy debates that may result in more effective drug policies.

The IDCS has advocated a comprehensive, integrated, and balanced approach in drug policy formulation and implementation that includes the academic branches relevant to the drug issues (health, economics, law, agronomy, chemistry, finance, law, etc.). However, this IDCS approach produces programs and policies about psychoactive drug consumption, production, and trafficking within their current mindset. In their periodic meetings, the IDCS agencies evaluate their policy results, acknowledge that they fail to achieve their goals, and promise that they would obtain better future results ten years later by maintaining the same policy approach.

Simultaneously, the United Nations drug agencies have recognized a current broad consensus that the "world drug problem is complex," and its complexity has increased continuously and exponentially at times. As argued in chapter eleven, section 11.3, it is possible to identify cause and effect relationships and formulate best practice policies or solutions when problems are simple. As problems become more complicated, those policies might still be good (not best) practices but lose effectiveness. But when problems become complex, there are no apparent cause and effect relationships, and the processes to formulate policies should tolerate and encourage dissent and out-of-the-box thinking. Policies should allow for experiments not only for the continuous support of traditional goals but also for different policy instruments.[210] However, these changes require that policy paradigms also change. Otherwise, policies most likely will fail to achieve their sought results, and vulnerable societies, or parts of them, risk descending into chaos.

---

[210] For example, one possibility would be to allow some restricted non-medical drug uses but establishing an insurance system against addiction and its consequences. People require insurance to drive a car, the same concept may be used for drug use. The insurance would cover addiction treatment, rehabilitation, and resocialization for the addict and compensations to victims of the addicts' behavior.

A complex drug policy approach differs from the traditional one because it requires thinking out of the box and developing a policy formulation and implementation process that responds to the complexity of the problem at hand, not to what the world was sixty or worse, 120 years ago. The prohibition of non-medical and non-scientific drug uses is an unmovable policy anchor, but it is not designed to fight market forces in today's world. The IDCS has repeatedly acknowledged that its "drug-free world" goal is unachievable. As extensively shown in this book, this goal is a dogma that does not rely on evidence or scientific theories. The goal to eliminate all non-medical drug uses has been an IDCS "blind policy belief" that prevents policy effectiveness, which has trapped international drug policies since 1961. Besides, it has allowed some governments to use anti-drug policies for other purposes.

In the history of market controls, it has been extensively shown that anchors prohibiting all transactions or fixing prices and quantities might achieve satisfactory results for some time when the market problem is simple. Still, as markets become more complex, anchors become obsolete, and policies must be changed. When this is not done, they produce very large undesirable social and economic consequences. Price controls of staple goods and housing rents, and fixed exchange rates, are good examples. In all these cases, authoritarian governments have been able to maintain them by providing large subsidies. But in liberal market economies, they end up generating scarcities and illegal markets and very high economic and social costs. In the end, these societies have been forced to find better ways to deal with the problems at hand. Some argue that this was the case of alcohol prohibition in the United States, a policy that has been quite successful in some authoritarian societies.

Accepting a complex "world drug problem" implies that there are no unique or straightforward solutions. The drug-free world goal of the IDCS should be abandoned, but this requires a mindset change that is difficult to take place. Until now, the United Nations preaches the complexity of the "world drug problem" while vending backward, arguing that its current policy framework is fit for purpose and will eventually provide better results. This position is affirmed and reaffirmed while recognizing that its ideal of a "drug-free world" is unachievable. After over sixty years of trying, that ideal goal has become increasingly distant and elusive. Thus, *the best policy goal would be to learn how to live with regulated non-medical uses of psychoactive drugs. It would seek to minimize the total harm of drug use plus other social harms, including those generated by anti-drug policies.* This is not a moral issue. It is only a consequence of acknowledging the impossibility of achieving a drug-free world and the presence of weaknesses and vulnerabilities in many societies worldwide. An unpleasant but straightforward conclusion is that current policies are not fit for purpose in the complex world described in the public documents of the IDCS.

14.3 ARE THERE ANY STEPS THAT MAY BE TAKEN TO IMPROVE THE IDCS?

As with any complex problem, in the case of drugs, it is also necessary to accept that there is no single *optimum* policy and that several options should be allowed. Absolute prohibition or liberalization of non-medical drug uses are always conceivable policies. Still, the complexity of the drug phenomenon implies that in almost all cases, neither one of them would be optimal.

The precedent chapter thirteen discussed a non-exhaustive list of inescapable issues that the IDCS faces and will continue to face. It shows that the absolute prohibition of non-medical drug uses conflicts with the WHO's Constitution and some of the SDG. However, the conflicts between the IDCS and WHO or the SDG have not prevented them from operating. If the IDCS does not respond to the reality of the drug phenomenon complexity, it will at best become a system that an increasing number of countries will disregard. The IDCS needs to be more relevant. Adopting complex policy methods is a necessary step in that direction.

The IDCS adoption of WHO's definition of social health as part of a broader definition of health will improve the links of the IDCS with WHO and recognize that the social sciences have a fundamental role to play in drug policymaking. This, of course, would require moving away from the non-evidence-based assertion that drug addiction costs are immeasurable while the costs of other social ills and harms can be measured.

The IDCS should also extend its actions in legal psychoactive drugs and the international trade of illegal drugs and their chemical precursors because legal and illegal psychoactive drug phenomena are interrelated. The growing importance of non-state actors is a characteristic of this complex world. They include some private sector businesses and NGOs, illegal actors that seek to maximize illegal profits, and those that use force to change the political status quo or protect corrupt governments. The UNODC has increasingly been concerned with many of these issues and could help estimate the costs of crimes associated with the black markets generated by the prohibition of non-medical psychoactive drug uses.

The list of inescapable issues also includes the structural problems of the IDCS agencies, particularly the INCB. As shown in chapter thirteen, there is a need to modernize the INCB administrative structure and make it more responsive to the increasing complexity of the drug phenomenon. This would require changes in its relations to the UNODC and WHO. One may only wonder if the United Nations structure would permit that.

Complex drug problems require policies that focus on changing human behavior. The IDCS is designed to urge governments to comply with agreements that require changes in individual behaviors. However, most member states do not know how to make these changes or do not have the capabilities to implement them. Thus, anti-drug policies have relied chiefly on fear and harsh punishments that do not change the heart and minds of those that participate in illegal drug activities. Governments end up using law enforcement that does not have the public support of many groups. That is why many current drug policies fail.

As shown in this book, in many cases, drug policies are based on powerful and blinding feelings and emotions. It may be argued that while people want to act rationally, our unconscious plays a vital role in our decision-making processes. Because of this, to make effective drug policies, it is necessary to learn and understand what makes people prone to produce, traffic, and use legal and illegal drugs. Otherwise, without knowing these decision-making processes, it is impossible to formulate and implement effective policies to change individual behaviors.

As shown in chapter 5, section 3, in 1992, the first thematic chapter of the INCB reports offered a lengthy list of reasons why "the legalization of non-medical use of drugs" was impractical and impossible to implement. Today many would argue that the simple prohibition of non-medical drug uses is equally impractical and difficult to implement. The approach to solving the "world drug problem" requires confronting the difficulties of controlling drug markets. Advances in the social sciences, like cultural and social anthropology, have developed methods that identify diverse behavioral patterns across societies and how adequate policies can affect human behavior. The IDCS must take advantage of these developments.

With the help of social sciences, the IDCS may overcome its aversion to policy reform away from policymaking based on fear and punishment. It may try diverse ways to explore the possibility of having regulated, controlled, and limited uses of some drugs while at the same time limiting the social costs of the likely increase in addiction. Without multidisciplinary open and honest interaction and constant questioning of the basic assumptions of everybody's mindset models, there is no hope to solve complex problems.

This might sound radical to many who would accuse the author of being "pro drugs" or suggesting a free market for drugs, all of which is nonsense. Many drug policy experts come from the health sector in which there are many complex issues and where ways to deal with them are constantly being developed. The production, trafficking, and use of drugs are frequently referred to as social cancers. Following that analogy, the public health sector learned that simply attempting to extirpate cancerous cells might cure some less complicated cancers, but not most of them. Cancer research has shown that there is a wide variety of cancers, and their treatment requires understanding the DNA and structure of each type of cancerous cell. We must accept that without an adequate understanding of the etiology of psychoactive drug production, trafficking, and consumption, enacting laws to extirpate them will fail. It will force governments to appeal to dissuasive methods that are likely to threaten or apply force to drug producers, traffickers, and users but will not change "their hearts and minds," their mindset about their relationship with the government, State, and other humans.

One lesson of contemporary public policy in liberal open societies is that effective policies should be co-created by all stakeholders. To have grassroots support, all stakeholders must actively participate in the policy formulation and implementation process. Another lesson is that this alone is not enough. For example, peasant coca-growing associations should be promoted and encouraged to participate in the policymaking process. But to succeed, it is also necessary to generate trust and empathy among all stakeholders to agree that coca cultivation to produce cocaine to be sold in illegal markets somewhere else is ethically unacceptable. Many current policies toward coca-growing peasants seek to provide sustainable income sources, but they do not break stakeholders' cultural, ethnic, and class barriers. Peasants seek monetary benefits, but they perceive themselves as second-class citizens, who are not part of the state power structure. If this mindset persists among peasants, there is no hope to lower the size of the coca plantings because the structural social vulnerability that encouraged coca plantings would not be eliminated. It is the case in Colombia. The relative success in controlling coca plantings in Bolivia compared to Colombia and Peru is an example of the importance of community participation in policy agreements.

Policy success on the consumption side would require the participation of drug users to negotiate non-medical restricted drug uses. Many people maintain that drug use is part of their everyday life, some artists use it to enhance their creativity, and for the most vulnerable, drugs help them escape reality. In a sense, for them, this is a quasi-medical use, but of course, they take significant risks, and many may end up trapped by addiction. This is the case of slum artists that use drugs not to escape but to create new artistic realities in Medellín (Jaramillo-Escobar and Thoumi, 2012). In many places, social inequality and slum life are the primary triggers of illegal drug use. Unless policies focus on the structural social vulnerabilities, treating drug addiction does not eliminate the vulnerability factors. The resocialization of addicts is a process that, to be successful, also requires trust and mutual empathy between the addicts and the service providers.

The IDCS was developed when psychoactive drug issues were not significant in most countries, and the prohibition of non-medical uses appeared reasonable to almost all policymakers. Today the fear of drug addiction and other prevailing blind policy beliefs about the unknowns associated with drug policy changes are likely to prevent the acceptance of a complex drug policy control system in most countries.

Current world developments raise many doubts about the capacity of most governments to create mutual empathy among the drug issues' stakeholders. The growing social and economic inequality within many countries, the extraordinary increase in desperate migrations, and the sharp increase in racial and nationalistic conflicts, among other developments, have served as a breeding ground for authoritarianism across broad areas of the world.

The top-down traditional drug policies based on law enforcement are likely to be supported at the CND meetings. Some countries will legalize non-medical cannabis uses, and since many American states will also do so, some other countries in the American continent are likely to follow. Others will not.

The IDCS has recognized complexity. Its challenge is how to alter its policies to make them coherent with its narrative. This narrative accepts the interrelation among social harms such as corruption, addiction, violence, increasing inequality, weakening social cohesion, social, income, wealth inequalities, unemployment, etc. The IDCS and the governments must have a comprehensive policy approach to include all stakeholders. These policies require significant structural reforms.

Unfortunately, the most likely scenario for the IDCS is that the United Nations drug agencies will continue asserting that the purpose of the drug policies is to limit drug uses to medical and scientific purposes to protect and promote the health and welfare of humankind. This position would likely be reaffirmed at the next annual CND meetings. But the movement to legalize non-medical marijuana will weaken the IDCS. Some civil society groups may press for amendments or rewritings of the conventions, which would likely be rejected, increasing the risk of weakening the IDCS capacity to implement its policies.

I am aware that many readers will feel disappointed that this book does not provide specific drug policy recommendations. Unfortunately, the illegal drug markets conundrum has no unique, simple, and precise solution.

The cloudy future perspective motivates me to take care of myself to cheat life expectancy estimates to witness whether another UNGASS on the world drug problem will be convened before the 2029 CND. If I am still alive then, I would ask that, as an INCB alumnus, I will be allowed to attend such possible UNGASS and CND meetings.

EPILOGUE

Caminante no hay Camino

Caminante, son tus huellas
el camino y nada más;
Caminante, no hay camino,
se hace camino al andar.
Al andar se hace el camino,
y al volver la vista atrás
se ve la senda que nunca
se ha de volver a pisar.
Caminante no hay camino
sino estelas en la mar.

Antonio Machado

Wayfarer, there is no path

Wayfarer, the only way
Is your footprints and no other.
Wayfarer, there is no way.
Make your way by going farther.
By going farther, make your way
Till looking back at where you've wandered,
You look back on that path you may
Not set foot on from now onward.
Wayfarer, there is no way;
Only wake-trails on the waters.

Antonio Machado

REFERENCES

Acemoglu, D., & Robinson, J.A. (2012), *Why Nations Fail. The origins of power, prosperity, and poverty.* Random House. http://www.tinyurl.com/y57yqpy8

Adelman, J. (2013). *Worldly Philosopher: The Odyssey of Albert O. Hirschman.* Princeton University Press.

Anzola, M. (2014). *El paradigma de la seguridad jurídica en un Estado en transformación.* Universidad Externado de Colombia.

Arango, M. & Child, J. (1986). *Coca-Coca. Historia y manejo político y mafia de la cocaína.* Editorial Dos Mundos.

Aufricht, H. (1952). Supersession of Treaties in International Law. *Cornell Law Review,* 37(2), 655-700.

Barrett, D. (2008). *Unique in International Relations? A Comparison of the International Narcotics Control Board and the UN Human Rights Treaty Bodies.* [eBook edition]. International Harm Reduction Association. https://www.hr-dp.org/files/2013/09/23/Barrett-UniqueinInternationalRelations.pdf

Barrett, D., Lines, R., Schleifer, R., Elliott. R., & Bewley-Taylor, D. (2008). *Recalibrating the Regime: the need for a human rights-based approach to international drug policy.* The Beckley Foundation. https://www.hr-dp.org/files/2013/09/23/BarrettRecalibratingTheRegime.pdf

Berridge, V. (1980). The Making of the Rolleston Report: 1908-1926. *Journal of Drug Issues,* 10 (1), 7-28. https://doi.org/10.1177/002204268001000102

Berterame, S., Erthal, J., Thomas, J., Fellner. S., Vosse, B., Clare, P., Hao, W., Johnson, D.T., Mohar, A., Pavadia, J., Samak, A.K., Sipp, W., Sumyai, V., Suryawati, S., Toufiq, J., Yans, R., Mattick, R.P. (2016). Use of and barriers to access to opioid analgesics: a worldwide, regional, and national study. *The Lancet.* 387(10028), 1644. https://doi.org/10.1016/S0140-6736(16)00161-6.

Bewley-Taylor, D.R. (2012a). *International Drug Control. Consensus Fractured*, Cambridge University Press.

___. (2012b), Towards a revision of the UN drug control conventions. The logic and dilemmas of Like-Minded Groups. *Series on Legislative Reform of Drug Policies.* 19, 1-16. Retrieved September 13, 2021 from https://www.tni.org/files/publication-downloads/dlr19.pdf

Bewley-Taylor, D., Jelsma, M., Rolles, S. & Walsh, J. (2016). Cannabis regulation and the UN drug treaties: strategies for reform. *WOLA Briefing Paper.* Retrieved September 13, 2021 from https://www.wola.org/wp-content/uploads/2016/08/Cannabis-Regulation-and-the-UN-Drug-Treaties_June-2016_web.pdf

Bewley-Taylor, D., & Trace, M. (2006). *The International Narcotics Control Board: Watchdog or Guardian of the UN Drug Control Conventions?* The Beckley Foundation Drug Policy Program. https://www.beckleyfoundation.org/resource/the-international-narcotics-control-board-watchdog-or-guardian-of-the-un-drug-control-conventions/

Bicchieri, C. (2006). *The Grammar of Society. The Nature and Dynamic of Social Norms.* Cambridge University Press. https://doi.org/10.1017/CBO9780511616037

Boister, N. & Jelsma, M. (2018). Inter se Modification of the UN Drug Control Conventions. An Exploration of its Applicability to Legitimise the Legal Regulation of Cannabis Markets. *International Community Law Review,* 20(5). 456-492. https://doi.org/10.1163/18719732-12341385

Browning L, Latoza R. (2005) The use of narrative to understand and respond to complexity: A comparative analysis of the Cynefin and Weickian models. *Emergence: Complexity and Organization.* 2005, 7 (3-4),32-39. https://doi.org/10.emerg/10.17357.69421b2dab204467eb06670e53cc73e6.

Bruum, K., Pan, L. & Rexed, I. (1975). *The Gentlemen's club. International control of drugs and alcohol.* The University of Chicago Press.

Buxton, J. (2006). *The Political Economy of Narcotics. Production, consumption & global markets.* Zed Books.

____. (2010). The historical Foundations of the Narcotic Drug Control Regime. In P. Keefer & N. Loayza (Eds.), *Innocent Bystanders. Developing Countries and the War on Drugs* (pp. 61-93). The World Bank and Palgrave MacMillan.

Carter, W. E., & Mamani, M. (1986). *Coca en Bolivia.* Librería Editorial "Juventud".

Cartwright, N., & Hardie, J. (2012). *Evidence-Based Policy: A practical guide to doing better.* Oxford University Press.
https://doi.org/10.1093/acprof:osobl/9780199841608.001.0001

Caulkins, J.P. (2016). Legalising Drugs Prudently: The Importance of Incentives and Values. In J. Collins (Ed.), *After the Drug Wars* (pp.40-50). London School of Economics Expert Group on the Economics of Drug Policies. https://www.lse.ac.uk/ideas/publications/reports/after-drugs

Caulkins, J, Rydell, C.P., Schwabe, W. L. & Chisea, J. (1997), *Mandatory minimum drug sentences: Throwing away the key or the taxpayers money?* Rand Corporation Drug Policy Research Center. https://www.rand.org/pubs/monograph_reports/MR827.html.

Chatterjee, S. K. (1988). *A Guide to the International Drugs Conventions.* Commonwealth Secretariat, Legal Division.

Colander, D. & Kupers, R. (2014). *Complexity and the Art of Public Policy: Solving society's problems from the bottoms up.* [eBook edition]. Princeton University Press.

Coleman, J. (1990). *Foundations of Social Theory.* Harvard University Press.

Collins, J. (2015). *Regulations and prohibitions: Anglo-American relations and international drug control, 1939-1964* [doctoral dissertation]. London School of Economics and Political Science (LSE). http://etheses.lse.ac.uk/3107/

_____. (2016). Development First: Multilateralism in the Post-'War on Drugs' Era. In J. Collins (Ed.), *After the Drug Wars,* London School of Economics Expert Group on the Economics of Drug Policies. https://www.lse.ac.uk/ideas/Assets/Documents/reports/LSE-IDEAS-After-Drug-Wars.pdf

Comisión Peruana para el Estudio del Problema de la Coca. (1951). *Contrarréplica de la Comisión Peruana para el Estudio del Problema de la Coca a la Comisión de Encuesta de las Naciones Unidas sobre las Hojas de Coca.* Ministerio de Salud Pública y Asistencia Social.

CND. (2008). *Making drug control 'fit for purpose': Building on the UNGASS decade*. Document E/CN.7/2008/CRP.17

https://www.unodc.org/documents/commissions/CND/CND_Sessions/CND_51/1_CRPs/E-CN7-2008-CRP17_E.pdf

Constitute. (n.d.) *Constitution of the Plurinational State of Bolivia of 2009*. Oxford University Press, https://www.constituteproject.org/constitution/Bolivia_2009.pdf

Courtwright, D. T. (2002). *Forces of Habit. Drugs and the making of the modern world*. Harvard University Press.

Csete, J. & Wolfe, D. (2007). *Closed to Reason: The International Narcotics Control Board and HIV/AIDS*, Canadian HIV/AIDS Legal Network, and Open Society Institute.
https://www.opensocietyfoundations.org/uploads/c87ce9c2-eaf0-4fba-beee-03f732cc33b4/closed_20070226.pdf

De Kort, M. (1995) *Tussen patiënt en delinquent. Geschiedenis van het Nederlandse drugsbeleid* [Doctoral Dissertation, Erasmus University Rotterdam]. Hilversum: Verlore.

Del Olmo, R. (1992). *¿Prohibir o domesticar? Políticas de drogas en América Latina*. Rosa del Olmo y Editorial Nueva Sociedad.

De Rementería, I. (1995). *La elección de las drogas: Examen de las políticas de control*. Fundación Friedrich Ebert.

De Roux, R. R. (1990). *Dos Mundos Enfrentados*. CINEP.

Dhywood, J. (2011). *World War D. The case against prohibition. A roadmap to controlled legalization*. Columbia Communications Inc.

Dikötter, F., Laamann, L. & Zhou Xun. (2004). *Narcotic Culture: A History of Drugs in China*. The University of Chicago Press.

Escohotado, A. (1997). *Historia de las drogas*. (2th ed., Vol. 2). Alianza Editorial S. A.

____, (1999). *A Brief History of Drugs. From the Stone Age to the Stoned Age*. Park Street Press.

Falco, M. (1994). *The Making of a Drug Free America. Programs that Work*. Random House: Times Books

Faulkner, H. U., (1958). *Politics, Reform and Expansion, 1890-1900*. Harper and Row.

Fultz, M., Page, L., Pannu, A., & Quick. M. (2017). *Reconciling Canada's Legalization of Non-Medical Cannabis with the UN Drug Control Treaties*. Global Health Law Clinic Publication Series - Global Strategy Lab, University of Ottawa. www.globalstrategylab.org/clinic/reports/reconciling-legalization-of-cannabis-with-UN-treaties-2017.pdf

Gamarra, E. A. (1994). *Entre la droga y la democracia: la cooperación entre Estados Unidos-Bolivia y la lucha contra el narcotráfico*. ILDIS.

Gagliano, J. (1994). *Coca prohibition in Peru. The historical debates*. The University of Arizona Press.

Gallahue, P. (2012, March 28). Narcotics Watchdog Turns Blind Eye to Rights Abuses. *Inter Press Services – News Agency*. http://www.ipsnews.net/2012/03/op-ed-narcotics-watchdog-turns-blind-eye-to-rights-abuses/

Gesley, J. (2016). The Netherlands. In The Law Library of Congress (Ed.), Decriminalization of Narcotics (pp. 20-23). The Law Library of Congress
https://tile.loc.gov/storage-services/service/ll/llglrd/2016479004/2016479004.pdf

Ghodse, H. (Ed.). (2008). *International Drug Control Into the 21ˢᵗ Century*. Ashgate Publishing Limited.
https://doi.org/10.4324/9781315252063

González, F. E. (1997). *Poderes Enfrentados: Iglesia y Estado en Colombia*. CINEP.

Gootenberg, P. (1999). Reluctance or resistance? Constructing cocaine (prohibitions) in Peru, 1910-1950. In P. Gootenberg (Ed.), *Cocaine: Global Histories* (pp 46-82), Routledge. https://doi.org/10.4324/9780203026465

_____. (2008). *Andean Cocaine. The Making of a Global Drug*. University of North Caroline Press.

Grund, J-P. C. & Breeksema, J. J. (2017). Drug Policy in the Netherlands. In R. Colson & H. Bergeron (Eds.), *European Drug Policies: The Ways to Reform* (pp. 128-148). Routledge.
https://doi.org/10.4324/9781315690384

Guissarri, A. (1988). *La Argentina Informal: Realidad de la Vida Económica*. Emecé Editores.

Haasen, C., Verthein, U., Degkwitz, P., Berger, J., Krausz, M., & Naber, D. (2007). Heroin-assisted treatment for opioid dependence: randomised controlled trial. *British Journal of Psychiatry*, 191(July), 55-62.

https://doi.org/10.1192/bjp.bp.106.026112. PMID: 17602126.

Haidt, J. (2012). *The Righteous Mind. Why Good People Are Divided by Politics and Religion.* Pantheon Books. https://doi.org/10.1007/978-3-319-16999-6_3298-1

Hall, W. (2018). The future of the international drug control system and national drug prohibitions. *Addiction,* 113 (7), 1210-1223.

Hallam, C., Bewley-Taylor, D. & Jelsma, M. (2014). *Scheduling in the international drug control system.* Series on Legislative Reform of Drug Policies No. 25, TNI/IDPC.
https://www.tni.org/files/download/dlr25_0.pdf

Heath, D. B. (1992). US Drug Control Policy: A Cultural Perspective. *Daedalus,* 121(3), 269-291.

Heilbroner, R. L. (1953). *The Worldly Philosophers: The Lives, Times, and Ideas of the Great Economic Thinkers.* Touchstone.

Henman, A. (1992). *Mama Coca* (4th ed.). Hisbol

Hunt, P. (2008). *Human Rights, Health and Harm Reduction. States' amnesia and parallel universes* [eBook edition]. International Harm Reduction Association.
https://www.hrdp.org/files/2014/05/06/HumanRightsHealthAndHarmReduction_ParallelUniverses.pdf

Hurwicz, L. (2008). But who will guard the guardians? *American Economic Review,* 98(3), 577-585.
https://doi.org/10.1257/aer.98.3.577

Husch, J. A. (1992). Culture and US Drug Policy: Toward a New Conceptual Framework. *Daedalus,* 121(3), 293-304.

INCB. (1968). *First Report of the International Narcotics Control Board.*
https://www.incb.org/documents/Publications/AnnualReports/AR1968/AR_1968_E.pdf

_____. (1969). *Report to the Economic and Social Council on the Work of the Board in 1969.*
https://www.incb.org/documents/Publications/AnnualReports/AR1969/AR_1969_E.pdf

_____. (1970). *Report of the International Narcotics Control Board on its work in 1970.*
https://www.incb.org/documents/Publications/AnnualReports/AR1970/AR_1970_E.pdf

_____. (1971). *Report of the International Narcotics Control Board on its work in 1971.*
https://www.incb.org/documents/Publications/AnnualReports/AR1971/AR_1971_English.pdf

_____ (1974). *Report of the International Narcotics Control Board for 1974.*
https://www.incb.org/documents/Publications/AnnualReports/AR1974/AR_1974_English.pdf

_____. (1976). *Report of the International Narcotics Control Board for 1976.*
https://www.incb.org/documents/Publications/AnnualReports/AR1976/AR_1976_English.pdf

_____. (1977). *Report of the International Narcotics Control Board for 1977.*

https://www.incb.org/documents/Publications/AnnualReports/AR1977/AR_1977_English.pdf

_____. (1983). *Report of the International Narcotics Control Board for 1983.*
https://www.incb.org/documents/Publications/AnnualReports/AR1983/AR_1983_English.pdf

_____. (1990). *Report of the International Narcotics Control Board for 1990.*
https://www.incb.org/documents/Publications/AnnualReports/AR1990/AR_1990_E.pdf

_____. (1991). *Report of the International Narcotics Control Board for 1991.*
https://www.incb.org/documents/Publications/AnnualReports/AR1991/AR_1991_E.pdf

_____. (1992). *Report of the International Narcotics Control Board for 1992.*
https://www.incb.org/documents/Publications/AnnualReports/AR1992/1992_ANNUAL_report_eng.pdf

_____. (1993). *Report of the International Narcotics Control Board for 1993.*
https://www.incb.org/documents/Publications/AnnualReports/AR1993/AR_1993_E.pdf

_____. (1995a). *Report of the International Narcotics Control Board for 1994.*
https://www.incb.org/documents/Publications/AnnualReports/AR1994/AR_1994_E.pdf

_____. (1995b). *Effectiveness of the International Drug Control Treaties*, Supplement to the Report of the International Narcotics Control Board for 1994.
https://www.incb.org/documents/Publications/AnnualReports/AR1994/E-INCB-1994-1-Supp-1-e.pdf

_____. (1997). *Report of the International Narcotics Control Board for 1996.*
https://www.incb.org/documents/Publications/AnnualReports/AR1996/AR_1996_E.pdf

_____. (1998). *Report of the International Narcotics Control Board for 1997.*
https://www.incb.org/documents/Publications/AnnualReports/AR1997/AR_1997_E.pdf

_____. (2000). *Report of the International Narcotics Control Board for 1999.*
https://www.incb.org/documents/Publications/AnnualReports/AR1999/AR_1999_E.pdf

_____. (2001). *Report of the International Narcotics Control Board for 2000.*
https://www.incb.org/incb/en/publications/annual-reports/annual-report-2000.html

_____. (2003). *Report of the International Narcotics Control Board for 2002.*
https://www.incb.org/incb/en/publications/annual-reports/annual-report-2002.html

_____. (2004). *Report of the International Narcotics Control Board for 2003.*

https://www.incb.org/incb/en/publications/annual-reports/annual-report-2003.html

_____. (2005). *Report of the International Narcotics Control Board for 2004.*
https://www.incb.org/incb/en/publications/annual-reports/annual-report-2004.html

_____. (2007a). *Report of the International Narcotics Control Board for 2006.*
https://www.incb.org/incb/en/publications/annual-reports/annual-report-2006.html

_____. (2007b). *Guidelines for the import and export of drug and precursor reference standards for use by national drug testing laboratories and competent national authorities.*
https://www.incb.org/documents/NarcoticDrugs/Guidelines/reference_standards/NAR_Guidelines_reference-standards_en.pdf

_____. (2008a). *Report of the International Narcotics Control Board for 2007.*
https://www.incb.org/incb/en/publications/annual-reports/annual-report-2007.html

_____. (2008b). Introduction. In H. Ghodse (Ed.), *International Drug Control Into the 21st Century,* Ashgate Publishing Limited. https://doi.org/10.4324/9781315252063

_____. (2009). *Report of the International Narcotics Control Board for 2008.*
https://www.incb.org/incb/en/publications/annual-reports/annual-report-2008.html

_____. (2011). *Report of the International Narcotics Control Board for 2010.*
https://www.incb.org/incb/en/publications/annual-reports/annual-report-2010.html

_____. (2012a). *Report of the International Narcotics Control Board for 2011.*
https://www.incb.org/incb/en/publications/annual-reports/annual-report-2011.html

_____. (2012b). Youth have a right to be protected from drug abuse and dependence. *Annual Report Press Release*, 2.
https://www.incb.org/documents/Publications/PressRelease/PR2012/02_Youth_have_a_right_to_be_protected_from_Drug_Abuse_and_Dependence_PressKitE.pdf

_____. (2013). *Report of the International Narcotics Control Board for 2012.*
https://www.incb.org/incb/en/publications/annual-reports/annual-report-2012.html

_____. (2014). *Report of the International Narcotics Control Board for 2013.*
https://www.incb.org/incb/en/publications/annual-reports/annual-report-2013.html

_____. (2015). *Report of the International Narcotics Control Board for 2014.*
https://www.incb.org/incb/en/publications/annual-reports/annual-report-2014.html

_____. (2016a). *Report of the International Narcotics Control Board for 2015.*

https://www.incb.org/incb/en/publications/annual-reports/annual-report-2015.html

_____. (2016b). *Availability of Internationally Controlled Drugs: Ensuring Adequate Access for Medical and Scientific Purposes. Indispensable, adequately available and not unduly restricted.*
https://www.incb.org/documents/Publications/AnnualReports/AR2015/English/Supplement-AR15_availability_English.pdf

_____. (2017a). *Report of the International Narcotics Control Board for 2016.*
https://www.incb.org/incb/en/publications/annual-reports/annual-report-2016.html

_____. (2017b). *Application of the international drug control treaties in countries with federal structures.*
https://www.incb.org/documents/News/Alerts/Alert_on_Convention_Implementation_December_2017.pdf

_____. (2018). *Report of the International Narcotics Control Board for 2017.*
https://www.incb.org/incb/en/publications/annual-reports/annual-report-2017.html

____, n.d., *Guidelines for the Conduct of Members of the International Narcotics Control Board* [unpublished manuscript].

INCB, UNODC & WHO. (2018). *Joint Statement of INCB, UNODC and WHO in Implementation of the UNGASS 2016 Recommendations. Working together for the health and welfare of humankind.* 61st session of the Commission on Narcotic Drugs.
https://www.incb.org/incb/en/news/press-releases/2018/joint-statement-of-incb--unodc-and-who-on-implementation-of-the-ungass-2016-recommendations.html

Inglis, B. (1975). *The Forbidden Game: A Social History of Drugs.* Scribner

Institute for Health Metrics and Evaluation. (2013). *The Global Burden of Disease: Generating Evidence, Guiding Policy.* IHME. http://www.healthdata.org/sites/default/files/files/policy_report/2013/GBD_GeneratingEvidence/IHME_GBD_GeneratingEvidence_FullReport.pdf

ILC. (1966). *Draft Articles on the Law of Treaties with Commentaries,* Yearbook of the International Law Commission (Vol. ii).

International Opium Commission. (1909). *Report of the International Opium Commission Shanghai, China, February 1 to February 26, 1909. Report of the Proceedings.* (Vol. I). The North China Daily News and Herald Ltd. https://archive.org/details/cu31924032583225/page/n19

Jaramillo-Escobar, L. & Thoumi, F. E. (2012). Creative Drug Consumption and Production in Medellin, Colombia," *Substance Use & Misuse,* 47(5), 594-595. https://doi.org/10.3109/10826084.2012.650086

Jelsma, M. (2003). Drugs in the UN system: the unwritten history of the 1998 United Nations General Assembly Special Session on drugs, *International Journal of Drug Policy,* 14, 181-195.

_____. (2013). INCB vs. Uruguay: The Art of Diplomacy. Transnational Institute. Retrieved September 14, 2021, from https://www.tni.org/en/article/incb-vs-uruguay-art-diplomacy

_____. (2017). UNGASS 2016: Prospects for Treaty Reform and UN System-Wide Coherence on Drug Policy. Journal of Drug Policy Analysis, 10(1). pp. 20150021. https://doi.org/10.1515/jdpa-2015-0021

Jones-Brown, D. (2014). When the officer is unfriendly. In Vaughans, K.C., & Spielberg, W. (Eds.) (2014). The Psychology of Black Boys and Adolescents (Vol.2). Praeger https://doi.org/10.1080/15289168.2017.1341766

Klabbers, J. (2006). Treaties, Amendment and Revision. In *Max Planck Encyclopedia of Public International Law.* (pp. 1084-1089). Oxford Public International Law.

Kleiman, M. A. R. (2015). *Legal Commercial Cannabis Sales in Colorado and Washington.* Brookings Institution. https://www.brookings.edu/wp-content/uploads/2016/07/kleiman-wash-and-co-final.pdf

Kleiman, M. A. R., Caulkins, J.P. & Hawken, A. (2011). *Drugs and Drug Policy. What everybody needs to know.* Oxford University Press. https://doi.org/10.1002/wmh3.41

Kušević, V. (1977). Drug Abuse Control and International Treaties. *Journal of Drug Issues,* 7(1), 35–53. https://doi.org/10.1177/002204267700700104

Léons, M. B. & Sanabria, H. (1997). Coca and Cocaine in Bolivia: Reality and Policy Illusion. In Léons, M. B. y Sanabria, H. (Eds.), *Coca, Cocaine, and the Bolivian Reality* (pp 1-46). State University of New York Press.

Lerner, R. & Ferrando, D. (1989). El consumo de drogas en occidente y su impacto en el Perú. In García-Sayán, D. (Ed.), *Coca, Cocaína y*

Narcotráfico: Laberinto en los Andes. (pp. 51-85) Comisión Andina de Juristas.

Latin American Commission on Drugs and Democracy. (2009). *Drugs & Democracy: Toward a shift.* https://ycsg.yale.edu/sites/default/files/files/toward_paradigm_shift.pdf

Leroy, B., Bassiouni, M. C. & Thony, J-F. (2008), The International Drug Control System. In Bassiouni (Ed.), *International Criminal* Law (3rd ed, Vol. I) (pp. 855-905) [eBook edition]. Martinus Nijhoff Publishers. https://brill.com/view/title/14936

Lines, R. & Barrett, D. (2018). Cannabis Reform, 'Medical and Scientific Purposes' and the Vienna Convention on the Law of Treaties. *International Community Law Review,* 20(5), 436-455.

MacCoun, R., & Reuter, P. (2001). *Drug War Heresies: Learning from Other Vices, Times, and Places* (RAND Studies in Policy Analysis). Cambridge University Press. https://doi.org/10.1017/CBO9780511754272

Mars S. (2003). Heroin Addiction Care and Control: The British System 1916 to 1984. *Journal of the Royal Society of Medicine,* 96(2), 99–100.

https://www.ncbi.nlm.nih.gov/pmc/articles/PMC539406/pdf/0960099.pdf

March, J. C., Oviedo-Joekes, E., Perea-Milla, E., Carrasco, F. & the PEPSA Team. (2006). Controlled trial of prescribed heroin in the treatment of opioid addiction. *Journal of Substance Abuse*

Treatment, 31(2), pp. 203-211. https://doi.org/10.1016/j.jsat.2006.04.007

McAllister, W. (1991). Conflicts of Interest in the International Drug Control System. *Journal of Policy History,* 3(4), 143-166. https://doi.org/10.1017/S0898030600007466

_____. (2000). *Drug Diplomacy in the Twentieth Century. An international history.* Routledge.

Metzl, J. (2019). *Dying of Whiteness. How the Politics of Racial Resentment is Killing America's Heartland.* Basic Books.

Monge Medrano, C. (1950). *Apuntes para el informe de la Delegación Peruana al Ministro de Relaciones Exteriores del Perú, Conferencia de Narcóticos y Estupefacientes de las Naciones Unidas,* [Unpublished manuscript]. Carlos Monge Medrano Collection, Pontificia Universidad Católica del Perú.

Motta-Ochoa, R. (2018). Habit or addiction? Collaboration and misunderstandings in international debates about coca-leaf chewing. *Medicine Anthropology Theory.* 5 (2), 52-55. https://doi.org/10.17157/mat.5.2.534

Murphy, G. (2010). *Shadowing The White Man's Burden; Imperialism and the Problem of Color Line.* New York University Press.

Musto, D. (1999). *The American Disease. Origins of Narcotic Control.* (3rd ed.). Oxford University Press.

Newman, R. (1995). Opium Smoking in Late Imperial China: A Reconsideration. *Modern Asian Studies,* 29(4), 765-794. doi:10.1017/S0026749X00016176

North, D. C. (1990). *Institutions, Institutional Change and Economic Performance,* Cambridge University Press.
https://doi.org/10.1017/CBO9780511808678

Nolte, G. (Ed.). (2013). *Treaties and Subsequent Practice.* Oxford University Press.
https://doi.org/10.1093/law/9780199679195.001.0001

Oviedo-Joekes, E., Brissette, S., Marsh, D., et al. (2009). Diacetylmorphine versus methadone for the treatment of opiate addiction. *The New England Journal of Medicine* 361(8), pp. 777-786.
https://doi.org/10.1056/NEJMoa0810635

Painter, J. (1994). *Bolivia & Coca: A Study in Dependency.* Lynne Rienner Publishers.

Paoli, L., Greenfield, V.A. & Reuter, P. (2009). *The World Heroin Market. Can supply be cut?.* Oxford University Press.
https://doi.org/10.1093/acprof:oso/9780195322996.001.0001

Perneger, T. V., Giner, F., del Rio, M. & Mino, A. (1998). Randomised trial of heroin maintenance programme for addicts who fail in conventional drug treatments. *British Medical Journal,* 317 (7150), pp. 13-18. https://doi.org/10.1136/bmj.317.7150.13

Quiroga, J. (1990). *Coca/Cocaína: una Visión Boliviana.* AIPE-PROCOM-CEDLA-CID.

Redacción de la Colección de Libros sobre la Historia Moderna de China, 1980, *La Guerra del Opio,* Beijing: Ediciones en Lenguas Extranjeras

Richard Nixon Foundation. (2016, April 26). *President Nixon Declares Drug Abuse "Public Enemy Number One".* [video] YouTube. https://www.youtube.com/watch?v=y8TGLLQlD9M

Rydell, C. P. & Everingham, S. S. (1994). *Controlling Cocaine: Supply Versus Demand Programs.* RAND Corporation. https://doi.org/10.7249/MR331

Center for Substance Abuse Treatment. (2005). *Medication-Assisted Treatment for Opioid Addiction in Opioid Treatment Programs.* DHHS Publication No. (SMA) 05-4048.

Shanghai Opium Commission. (1909). *Report of the International Opium Commission Shanghai, China, February 1 to February 26, 1909.* Report of the Proceedings. Vol. I, The North China Daily News and Herald Ltd.
https://archive.org/details/cu31924032583225/page/n19

Siegel, R. K. (2005). *Intoxication. The Universal Drive for Mind-Altering Substances.* Park Street Press.

Sinha, J. (2001) *The History and Development of the Leading International, Drug Control Conventions.* Prepared for the Senate Special Committee on Illegal Drugs of the Parliament of Canada. Law and Government Division, Library of Parliament.

Sipp, W. (2016, April 19). *Statement by Mr. Werner Sipp, President, International Narcotics Control Board (INCB).* [United Nations, Special session of the General Assembly on the world drug problem]. New York, United States.
https://www.incb.org/documents/Speeches/Speeches2016/INCB_speech_UNGASS_plenary_opening.pdf

Small, D. & Drucker, E. (2007). Closed to reason: time for accountability for the International Narcotic Control Board. *Harm Reduction Journal,* 4(13) https://doi.org/10.1186/1477-7517-4-13

Snowden, D. J., & Boone, M.E. (2007), *A leader's framework for decision making.* Harvard Business Review, November. https://hbr.org/2007/11/a-leaders-framework-for-decision-making

Strang, J., Metrebian, N., Lintzeris, N., et al. (2010). Supervised injectable heroin or injectable methadone versus optimised oral methadone as treatment for chronic heroin addicts in England after persistent failure in orthodox treatment (RIOTT): a randomised trial. *The Lancet,* 375(9729), pp. 1885–1895.
https://doi.org/10.1016/S0140-6736(10)60349-2

Strang, J., Groshkova, T., & Metrebian, N. (2012). *New heroin-assisted treatment. Recent evidence and current practices of supervised injectable heroin treatment in Europe and beyond.* EMCDDA INSIGHTS # 11, Publications Office of the European Union.
https://www.emcdda.europa.eu/publications/insights/heroin-assisted-treatment_en

Szasz, T. (1992) *Our Rights to Drugs. The Case for a Free Market.* Praeger.

Taylor, A. H. (1969). *American diplomacy and the narcotics traffic, 1900-1939. A study in international humanitarian reform.* Duke University Press.

Thoumi, F. E. (1987). Some Implications of the Growth of the Underground Economy in Colombia. *Journal of Interamerican Studies and World Affairs,* 29(2), 35-54.
https://doi.org/10.2307/166072

_____. (2003). *Illegal Drugs, Economy and Society in the Andes.* Woodrow Wilson Center Press with Johns Hopkins University Press.

_____. (2005). Ventajas competitivas ilegales, el desarrollo de la industria de drogas ilegales y el fracaso de las políticas contra las drogas en Afganistán y Colombia. *Análisis Político,* 18(54), 30-48. https://revistas.unal.edu.co/index.php/anpol/article/view/46640/48021

_____. (2012). Vulnerable Societies: Why Antidrug Policies Fail, Why There Is a Need for Reforms and Why They Are Unlikely to Be Implemented. *Substance Use and Misuse,* 47(13-14), 1628-1632. https://doi.org/10.3109/10826084.2012.705718

_____. (2014). Marijuana in the United States and the international drug control regime: Why what is promoted abroad is not applied at home. *Crime, Law and Social Change,* 61(3), 273-285. https://doi.org/10.1007/s10611-013-9489-z

_____. (2015). *Debates y Paradigmas de las Políticas de Drogas en el Mundo y los Desafíos para Colombia.* Academia Colombiana de Ciencias Económicas.

_____. (2016). Re-examining the 'Medical and Scientific. Basis for Interpreting the Drug Treaties: Does the 'Regime' Have Any Clothes? In J. Collins (Ed.), *After the Drug Wars,* London School of Economics Expert Group on the Economics of Drug Policies. https://www.lse.ac.uk/ideas/Assets/Documents/reports/LSE-IDEAS-After-Drug-Wars.pdf

_____. (2017a). Medicina, ciencia e interpretación de las convenciones internacionales de drogas: ¿Será que el emperador está desnudo? *Colombia Internacional.* 89 (January-March) 133-158.

https://doi.org/10.7440/colombiaint89.2017.05

_____ (2017b). International Drug Conventions, Balanced Policy Recipes, and Latin American Cocaine Markets. In E. U. Savona, M.A.R. Kleiman, & F. Calderoni (Eds.), *Dual Markets - Comparative Approaches for Regulation,* Springer. (pp. 69-92). https://doi.org/10.1007/978-3-319-65361-7

Tobin, J. (2010). Seeking to Persuade: A Constructive Approach to Human Rights Treaty Interpretation. *Harvard Human Rights Journal,* 23, pp. 1-50.
https://harvardhrj.com/wp-content/uploads/sites/14/2010/10/1-50.pdf

Tuschman, A. (2013). *Our Political Nature. The evolutionary origins of what divides us.* Prometheus Books.

United Nations. (1950). *Report of the Commission of Enquiry on the Coca Leaf.* United Nations document E/1666 E/CN.7/AC.2/1, 28 April.
https://digitallibrary.un.org/record/637047?ln=en

_____. (1973). *Commentary on the Single Convention on Narcotic Drugs, 1961.* United Nations.
https://www.unodc.org/documents/commissions/CND/Int_Drug_Control_Conventions/Commentaries-OfficialRecords/1961Convention/1961_COMMENTARY_en.pdf

_____. (1998a). *Resolution Adopted by the General Assembly. Political Declaration,* document A/RES/S-20/2, 21 October.
https://www.unodc.org/documents/commissions/CND/Political_Declaration/Political_Declaration_1998/1998-Political-Declaration_A-RES-S-20-2.pdf

_____. (1998b). *Declaration on the Guiding Principles of Drug Demand Reduction,* document A/RES/S-20/3, 8 September
https://digitallibrary.un.org/record/261563?ln=en

_____. (2015). Transforming our World: The 2030 Agenda for Sustainable Development. Document A/RES/70/1
https://sustainabledevelopment.un.org/content/documents/21252030%20Agenda%20for%20Sustainable%20Development%20web.pdf

_____. (2016) *Outcome document of the 2016 United Nations General Assembly Special Session on the world drug problem,* April 19-21.
https://www.unodc.org/documents/postungass2016//outcome/V1603301-E.pdf

_____. (2019). *What we have learned over the last ten years: a summary of knowledge acquired and produced by the UN system on drug related matters,* UN system coordination Task Team on the implementation of the UN System Common Position on drug-related matters.
https://www.unodc.org/documents/commissions/CND/2019/Contributions/UN_Entities/What_we_have_learned_over_the_last_ten_years_-_14_March_2019_-_w_signature.pdf

United Nations Convention Against Corruption, October 31, 2003. https://www.unodc.org/documents/brussels/UN_Convention_Against_Corruption.pdf

UNDCP (1998). A drug-free world: we can do it. [UN General Assembly (20th special sess.: 1998)] UNDCP (02)/D794. United Nations. https://digitallibrary.un.org/record/258955?ln=en

UNODC. (1959) The Shanghai Opium Commission. Bulletin on Narcotics, 1, 45-46 http://www.unodc.org/unodc/en/data-and-analysis/bulletin/bulletin_1959-01-01_1_page006.html

_____. (2008). *World Drug Report 2008*. United Nations. https://www.unodc.org/unodc/en/data-and-analysis/WDR-2008.html

_____. (2009). Political Declaration and Plan of Action on International Cooperation towards an Integrated and Balanced Strategy to Counter the World Drug Problem. *High-level segment Commission on Narcotic Drugs,* Vienna, 11-12 March. https://www.unodc.org/documents/drug-prevention-and-treatment/High-level_segment_Commission_on_Narcotic_Drugs_11-12_March_2209.pdf

_____. (2013). *The International Drug Control Conventions* [Ebook edition). United Nations. https://www.unodc.org/documents/commissions/CND/Int_Drug_Control_Conventions/Ebook/The_International_Drug_Control_Conventions_E.pdf

van den Brink, W., Hendriks, V. M., Blanken, P., Koeter, M.W. J., van Zwieten, B. J., & van Ree, J. M. (2003). Medical prescription of heroin to treatment resistant heroin addicts: two randomised controlled trials. *BMJ,* August 9, 327, 310. https://doi.org/10.1136/bmj.327.7410.310.

van Kempen, P. H. & Fedorova, M. (2018). Regulated Legalization of Cannabis Through Positive Human Rights Obligations and *Inter se* Treaty Modification. *International Community Law Review,* 20(5), 493–526.
https://doi.org/10.1163/18719732-12341386

Vienna Convention on the Law of Treaties, May 23, 1969.

https://legal.un.org/ilc/texts/instruments/english/conventions/1_1_1969.pdf

Vidart, D. (1991). *Coca, cocales y coqueros en América Latina.* Editorial Nueva América.

Walker III, W. O. (1991). *Opium & Foreign Policy. The Anglo-American search for order in Asia, 1912-1954.* The University of North Carolina Press.

Warren, Adam, 2018, "Collaboration and discord in international debates about coca chewing, 1949-1950", *Medicine Anthropology Theory.*

http://www.medanthrotheory.org/read/10683/ international-debates-coca-chewing

WHO. (1950). *Expert Committee on Drugs Liable to Produce Addiction: report on the second session, Geneva, 9-14 January 1950.* Technical Report Series #21. World Health Organization. https://apps.who.int/iris/handle/10665/38943

_____. (1969). *WHO Expert Committee on Drug Dependence* [meeting held in Geneva from 1 to 7 October 1968] Sixteenth report, Technical Report Series #407. World Health Organization. https://apps.who.int/iris/handle/10665/40710

_____. (2013). *Research for universal health coverage: World health report 2013.* World Health Organization.
https://www.who.int/publications/i/item/9789240690837

Wilson, D. P., Braedon, D., Shattock, A. J., Wilson, D., & Fraser-Hurt, N. (2015). The cost effectiveness of harm reduction. *International Journal of Drug Policy,* 26 (supplement 1), pp. S5-S11.

https://doi.org/10.1016/j.drugpo.2014.11.007.

World Bank Group. (2017). *World Development Report 2017: Governance and the Law.* World Bank Publications. https://www.worldbank.org/en/publication/wdr2017

Wright, H. (1909). [The Opium Conference at Shanghai]. *Proceedings of the American Society of International Law at Its Annual Meeting (1907-1917)*, 3, 89-95.
http://www.jstor.org/stable/25656373

Yangwen, Z. (2005). *The Social Life of Opium in China.* Cambridge University Press.
https://doi.org/10.1017/CBO9780511819575

ANALYTICAL INDEX

Afghanistan, 31, 95, 159, 163, 281, 298
Alegría, Ciro, 74
Amphetamine Type Stimulants, 20
Anslinger, Harry J., 60, 63, 64, 71, 73, 75, 76, 82, 84, 85, 87, 90, 91, 92, 94, 95, 368
Antonio Maria Costa, 158, 163
Arlacchi, Pino, 113
Bignon, Alfredo, 69
Bolivia, 4, 11, 29, 43, 66, 69, 71, 72, 73, 76, 77, 79, 83, 89, 145, 189, 191, 241, 242, 243, 244, 245, 246, 247, 248, 249, 250, 251, 252, 255, 256, 257, 260, 261, 262, 264, 265, 318, 379, 380, 389
   Chapare region, 248
   coca, 241
   coca chewing, 241
   human rights, 250
   Law 1008, 249
   mate de coca, 257
   Pachamama, 255
   reservation to the 1961 Single Convention, 264
   reservation to the 1988 Convention, 251
   Single Convention on Narcotic Drugs of 1961, 262
   Sociedad de Propietarios de Yungas, 71
   traditional licit uses, 257
Brent, Charles Henry, 45, 46, 47, 48, 49, 112, 368
Bustamante, José L., 74
Calderón, Felipe, 12
Canada, 14
Cannabis Act, 14
Cannabis for recreational use, 14
Non-medical marijuana, 14
Cannabis, 14, 227, 237, 324, *See* Marijuana
Cannabidiol, 14
Cannabis for recreational use, 15
Carlos Monge, 75
Centre for International Crime Prevention, 110
China, 4, 19, 30, 35, 36, 37, 38, 39, 40, 41, 42, 43, 44, 47, 48, 56, 59, 60, 85, 88, 89, 90, 91, 94, 114, 124, 142, 177, 242, 312
   Boxer Rebellion, 37
   Chinese Communist Party, 36
   International opium monopoly, 89
   Manchu court, 38
   Opium wars, 36
   Qing dynasty, 36, 37
CND, 3, 22, 24, 54, 85, 86, 87, 88, 89, 90, 91, 94, 95, 97, 99, 104, 105, 109, 113, 122, 133, 135, 144, 146, 152, 153, 158, 161, 162, 163, 164, 177, 182, 186, 192, 194, 234, 239, 254, 255, 260, 309, 332, 341, 343, 351, 377, 390, 391
   Political Declaration and Plan of Action of the 2009, 164, 165, 167
Coca, 4, 6, 11, 17, 19, 21, 24, 29, 30, 31, 33, 35, 51, 52, 55, 66, 67, 68, 69, 70, 71, 72, 73, 74, 75, 76, 77, 78, 79, 80, 81, 82, 83, 84, 89, 94, 97, 98, 105,

119, 132, 142, 145, 147, 161,
165, 189, 190, 191, 241, 242,
243, 244, 245, 246, 247, 248,
249, 250,251, 252, 253, 254,
255, 256, 257, 258, 259, 260,
261, 262, 264, 265, 275, 298,
304, 307, 318, 330, 336, 361,
362, 379, 380, 382, 389
  coca chewing, 11, 35, 67, 68,
    69, 70, 71, 72, 73, 74, 77,
    78, 79, 80, 81, 82, 83, 89,
    132, 143, 147, 189, 241,
    242, 244, 245, 246, 248,
    249, 254, 257, 260, 261,
    262, 336, 379, 380
  coca leaves, 31, 33, 70, 71, 80,
    241, 244, 245, 256, 260
  Coca-Cola, 33, 71, 241, 243,
    256
  mate de coca, 256
  Maywood Chemical, 70
  Non-traditional uses, 4
  Traditional uses of coca leaf,
    11
Cocaine, 6, 11, 19, 30, 31, 33,
  41, 50, 59, 60, 68, 69, 70, 71,
  72, 73, 74, 75, 76, 78, 79, 80,
  81, 83, 84, 85, 89, 106, 107,
  115, 141, 146, 159, 165, 182,
  217, 225, 242, 243, 244, 245,
  246, 247, 252, 255, 257, 260,
  262, 273, 275, 280, 284, 285,
  293, 298, 305, 306, 307, 324,
  325, 336, 350, 352, 360, 361,
  363, 380, 382, 389
Coffee Shops, 222
  Closed Coffee Shop Chain
    Experiment, 15
  The Netherlands, 220
Colombia, 12, 21, 23, 29, 66, 69,
  106, 162, 163, 176, 177, 241,
246, 281, 295, 298, 307, 360,
361, 363, 382, 389
Commentary to the 1961 Single
  Convention, 96
Commission on Narcotic Drugs
  CND, 3, 54, 79, 188, 234
Complexity, 277
Cynefin, 276
Cynefin framework, 280, 281
Convention Against Corruption,
  169, 170, 171
Convention against Illicit Traffic
  in Narcotic Drugs and
  Psychotropic Substances of
  1988, 118
Convention against Illicit Traffic
  in Narcotic Drugs and
  Psychotropic Substances of
  1988, 3, 8, 20, 65, 107, 114,
  117, 118
Convention against Illicit Traffic
  in Narcotic Drugs and
  Psychotropic Substances of
  1988, 350
Convention on Psychotropic
  Substances of 1971, 3, 117
Costa, Antonio Maria, 159, 160,
  161
Delevingne, Malcolm, 60
Derrida, Jacques, 22
drug consumption, 24, 32, 99,
  114, 115, 144, 173, 188, 203,
  210, 295, 377, 378, 383
Drug consumption rooms
  (injection rooms), 207
Drug markets, 34, 182
Drug use, 35, 102
Drug-Free America Foundation,
  164
Du Bose, Hampden C., 44

ECOSOC, 3, 12, 85, 88, 108, 109, 111, 117, 131, 144, 262, 364, 380
Ekstrand, Eric Einar, 64
Emafo, Philip O., 203, 205, 305
European Monitoring Center on Drugs and Drug Addiction(EMCDDA), 216
Fonda, Howard B., 76
Germany, 19, 43, 50, 62, 63, 72, 85, 89, 119, 209, 216, 220, 264
Ghodse, Hamid, 133, 134, 170, 192, 193, 194, 262, 368, 369
Global Programme of Action, 133, 253
Graxier-Doyeaux, Marcel Alfred, 76, 242
Guterres, Antonio, 182
Gutiérrez-Noriega, Carlos, 73
Harm reduction, 11, 133, 142, 161, 162, 163, 188, 190, 202, 203, 204, 205, 206, 213, 295, 304, 325, 343
  harm reduction measures, 206
  harm reduction policies, 11, 142, 144, 188, 190, 202, 203
Hastings, Warren, 36
Hirschman, Albert O., 23
human rights, 11, 13, 24, 96, 109, 115, 143, 154, 157, 162, 164, 174, 175, 177, 178, 179, 180, 181, 183, 184, 185, 186, 188, 190, 191, 192, 193, 195, 196, 198, 250, 259, 262, 289, 302, 304, 306, 320, 321, 326, 328, 343, 378, 379, 381
INCB
  addiction maintenance programs, 211

administrative structure, 367, 374
Board members, 365
Bolivia, 241
Coca, 241, 243
coca chewing, 244
definition of *scientific purposes*, 138
drug consumption rooms, 210
drugs and corruption, 169
economic consequences of drug abuse, 172
Ghodse, Hamid, 164
Harm reduction, 144, 203, 206
heroin maintenance, 212
human rights, 157, 162, 191, 194, 195, 200
injection rooms, 207, 208, 210
Legalization, 139, 140
legalization of non-medical use of drugs, 139
Marijuana for medical uses, 226, 227, 231
medical and scientific purposes, 135, 139, 174
members, 131
Pre- Export Notification Online system (PEN), 350
Precursors Incident Communication System, 353
Precursors Incident Communication System (PICS), 351
Project ION (International Operations on NPS), 353
proportionality of drug-related offenses, 156
psychoactive drug uses, 143
quasi-judicial body, 131
Secretariat, 364

403

shared responsibility in international drug control, 171
social cohesion, 170
Standing Committee on Estimates, 349
The Netherlands, 221, 227, 228, 229, 230, 231
traditional licit use, 259
UNGASS, 145
Uruguay, 233, 234, 235, 236
WHO, 135
women and drugs, 180
India, 4, 36, 40, 41, 43, 59, 60, 92, 95, 124, 242
injection rooms, 11, 190, 208, 209
International Commission of Shanghai, 49
International Law Commission ILC, 135, 315
Kia King, 35
Kipling, Rudyard, 46
La Guardia, Fiorello, 63
Lande, Arthur, 104
Latin American Commission on Drugs and Democracy, 12, 163
League of Nations (The) Division of Narcotic Drugs, 85
Drug Supervisory Body, 62
League of Nations (The), 51, 54, 55, 59, 61
Legalization, 399, 418
Leguía, Augusto, 70
Marijuana. *See* Cannabis
Marijuana for medical uses, 6, 10, 13, 14, 17, 19, 20, 30, 58, 84, 116, 117, 118, 143, 146, 163, 219, 221, 223, 225, 226, 227, 228, 229, 231, 233, 234, 237, 239, 253, 280, 286, 307, 313, 314, 315, 319, 324, 336, 359, 379
Non-medical marijuana, 14, 21, 24, 120, 188, 219, 239, 309, 315, 359, 391
Non-medicinal marijuana legalization, 233
medical and scientific purposes, 4, 6, 7, 8, 10, 19, 23, 44, 47, 58, 61, 62, 87, 88, 95, 96, 97, 99, 100, 105, 116, 119, 121, 122, 128, 131, 153, 156, 175, 187, 192, 193, 199, 224, 239, 256, 264, 269, 280, 284, 287, 302, 303, 305, 308, 312, 313, 315, 316, 317, 318, 321, 332, 340, 342, 356, 375, 377, 391
Monge, Carlos, 73
Morales, Evo, 11, 255, 260, 380
Mujica, Jose, 234
New psychoactive substances NPS, 20, 187
Nixon, Richard, 103
Odría, Manuel Arturo, 74
Ogüz, Christina, 163
Opium, 4, 10, 35, 41, 43, 47, 48, 50, 51, 54, 55, 57, 61, 63, 64, 70, 72, 85, 89, 90, 91, 92, 93, 94, 95, 111, 119, 120, 142, 221, 222, 224, 226, 231, 372, 408
Agreement Concerning the Manufacture of, Internal Trade in, and Use of Prepared Opium, 56
British East India Company, 36
Internationalcontrol system for opium, 4
Opium Act Directive, 222

Opium Advisory Committee, 54
opium use, 4, 6, 19, 23, 30, 31, 35, 36, 37, 38, 39, 40, 41, 42, 43, 44, 45, 47, 48, 50, 55, 56, 57, 58, 59, 60, 63, 84, 86, 87, 88, 89, 90, 92, 93, 94, 95, 97, 98, 102, 115, 119, 123, 132, 142, 165, 191, 209, 212, 227, 242, 250, 258, 274, 280, 349
Permanent Central Opium Board (PCOB), 57
Protocol for Limiting and Regulating the Cultivation of the Poppy Plant, the Production of, International and Wholesale Trade in and Use of Opium, 92
The Hague International Opium Convention of 1912, 50
Paz-Soldán, Carlos, 69
PCOB, 57, 58, 59, 85, 86, 92, 94, 97, 111, 131, 366
Pérez Molina, Otto, 12
Peru, 4, 29, 43, 59, 66, 69, 70, 72, 73, 75, 76, 77, 79, 83, 89, 145, 177, 241, 242, 243, 244, 245, 246, 255, 256, 257, 379, 389
  Alianza Popular Revolucionaria Americana (APRA), 74
  Catholic Council in Lima of 1567, 67
  Comisión Peruana para el Estudio del Problema de la Coca, 81
  Estanco Nacional de la Coca (ENACO), 74

Plant-based psychoactive drugs, 6, 19, 31, 34, 50, 58, 115
Porter, Stephen G., 58, 60
Prevention programmes, 147
Psychoactive drugs
  domesticated drugs, 34
  domestication of psychoactive drugs, 32
  psychoactive drug uses, 17, 33, 34, 45, 46, 95, 103, 123, 175, 302, 387
  quasi-medical, 4, 48, 55, 58, 60, 66, 82, 87, 88, 92, 98, 123, 258, 389
Razet, Jean-Philippe, 76
Ricketts, Carlos, 70
Rolleston, Humphrey, 212
Sáenz, Luis, 73
Santos, Juan Manuel, ix, 12
Single Convention on Narcotic Drugs of 1961, 3, 4, 5, 6, 7, 8, 12, 88, 91, 93, 94, 95, 96, 97, 98, 99, 103, 104, 105, 111, 113, 114, 117, 119, 121, 122, 124, 128, 191, 200, 241, 261, 263, 295, 312, 318, 355, 364, 365, 366, 367
Soros, George, 305
Steinig, Leon, 89
Stimulant drugs, 31
Sustainable Development Goals SDG, 25, 178, 183, 185, 326, 328
Switzerland, 43, 49, 163, 213, 215, 216
  Swiss heroin programme, 215
Syringe and needle distribution, 205
Taft, William Howard, 46
The Hague International Opium Convention of 1912, 4, 10, 51,

54, 57, 63, 64, 72, 111, 119, 120, 372
The Netherlands, 10, 15, 163, 216, 219, 220, 221, 222, 223, 224, 225, 226, 227, 228, 229, 230, 231, 232, 233, 237, 238, 239, 253, 264, 379
    Coffee Shops, 15
coffee shops' experiment, 219
Treaty of Versailles, 51
Trump, Donald, 360
Tuang Fang, 47
Turkey, 43, 49, 50, 63, 86, 89, 92, 94, 95
UK Dangerous Drugs Act of 1967, 213
UNGASS, 23, 113, 122, 145, 146, 147, 152, 153, 162, 175, 176, 185, 193, 253, 255, 336, 341, 343, 391
    Declaration on the Guiding Principles of Drug Demand Reduction, 154
    UNGASS 1998, 153, 155, 158
    UNGASS 2016, 176, 179
United Nations Fund for Drug Abuse Control, 110
United States, 4, 13, 19, 21, 29, 30, 32, 41, 42, 43, 45, 46, 49, 50, 51, 53, 54, 55, 58, 59, 61, 62, 63, 64, 76, 84, 85, 87, 90, 91, 94, 96, 102, 107, 114, 116, 118, 119, 163, 177, 211, 228, 246, 248, 249, 264, 273, 281, 285, 306, 307, 308, 312, 316, 346, 347, 355, 358, 359, 360, 362, 365, 373, 385
    Alcohol prohibition, 32, 307, 362, 385
    Commerce Clause, 51

Harrison Narcotics Tax Act, 51
opiate addiction, 211
UNODC, 3, 5, 40, 47, 48, 54, 57, 58, 59, 61, 62, 85, 86, 87, 88, 93, 96, 99, 100, 102, 106, 107, 109, 110, 111, 114, 122, 125, 131, 158, 161, 162, 163, 164, 170, 177, 179, 183, 206, 257, 258, 262, 282, 284, 332, 336, 341, 353, 366, 367, 368, 369, 370, 371, 379, 386, 387
Uruguay, 14, 177, 189, 219, 233, 234, 235, 236, 237, 238, 239, 262, 313, 319, 379
    Cánepa, Diego, 234
    Mujica, Jose, 234
Valdizán, Hermilio, 69
Verzar, Frederic, 76
WHO, 25, 79, 95, 105, 123, 137, 138, 145, 146, 147, 164, 215, 216, 252, 254, 332, 334, 335, 337
    assessment of the 'usefulness' of a substance when it is considered for international control, 136
    Coca, 80, 252
    definition of health, 332
    Expert Committee on Drugs Liable to Produce Addiction, 79
    Harm reduction, 145
    medical prescription of heroin to addicts, 216
    principles, 334
    SDG goals, 344
    social determinants of health (SDH), 333
    WHO's Constitution, 332
William H. Taft, 49
Wilson, Woodrow, 55

World Federation Against Drugs, 163
World Forum Against Drugs, 163
Wright, Hamilton, 48, 49, 51
Yans, Raymond, 234
Young Cheng, 35
Zedillo, Ernesto, ix, 162

www.ingramcontent.com/pod-product-compliance
Lightning Source LLC
Chambersburg PA
CBHW052340220526
45465CB00003BA/888